Domesticating a Religious Import

Domesticating a Religious Import

The Jesuits and the Inculturation of the Catholic Church in Zimbabwe, 1879–1980

Nicholas M. Creary

Fordham University Press | New York 2011

Copyright © 2011 Fordham University Press

All rights reserved. No part of this publication may be reproduced, stored in a retrieval system, or transmitted in any form or by any means—electronic, mechanical, photocopy, recording, or any other—except for brief quotations in printed reviews, without the prior permission of the publisher.

Fordham University Press has no responsibility for the persistence or accuracy of URLs for external or third-party Internet websites referred to in this publication and does not guarantee that any content on such websites is, or will remain, accurate or appropriate.

Fordham University Press also publishes its books in a variety of electronic formats. Some content that appears in print may not be available in electronic books.

Library of Congress Cataloging-in-Publication Data

Creary, Nicholas M.
Domesticating a religious import : the Jesuits and the inculturation of the Catholic Church in Zimbabwe, 1879–1980 / Nicholas M. Creary.—1st ed.
   p. cm.
  Includes bibliographical references (p.) and index.
  ISBN 978-0-8232-3334-2 (cloth : alk. paper)—ISBN 978-0-8232-3336-6 (ebook)
  1. Catholic Church—Zimbabwe—History—19th century. 2. Christianity and culture—Zimbabwe—History—19th century. 3. Jesuits—Missions—Zimbabwe—History—19th century. 4. Zimbabwe—Church history—19th century. 5. Catholic Church—Zimbabwe—History—20th century. 6. Christianity and culture—Zimbabwe—History—20th century. 7. Jesuits—Missions—Zimbabwe—History—20th century. 8. Zimbabwe—Church history—20th century. I. Title.
  BX1682.ZC74 2011
  282'.6891—dc22

2010039511

Printed in the United States of America
13 12 11   5 4 3 2 1
First edition

Contents

List of Abbreviations vii
Preface ix
Acknowledgments xiii

Introduction   1

1. **A Failed Mission, Contesting Colonial Rule, and Ecclesiastical Developments**   22

2. **"The Struggle Approximated to the Heroic": African Catholic Women Becoming Nuns in Colonial Zimbabwe, 1922–1965**   39

3. **"The Most Important Work on the Mission": The Seminary of Saints John Fisher and Thomas More, 1919–1979**   79

4. **A "Do-Nothing" Organization? The Catholic Association, 1934–1974**   120

5. **Until Death Do Us Part? African Marriage Practices and the Catholic Church, 1890–1979**   170

6. **"Thou Shalt Not Take My Name in Vain": The Mwari Controversy, 1911–1961**   204

7. **Bread and Wine, Beer and Meat: The *Kurova Guva* Controversy**   222

Conclusion   243

Notes 255
Glossary 311
Bibliography 313
Index 329

Photographs follow page 78

Abbreviations

AAH	Archives of the Archdiocese of Harare
ABSI	Archivum Britannicum Societatis Iesu (British Archives of the Society of Jesus), London
ANTT	Arquivo Nacional de Torre de Tombo, Lisbon
CA	Catholic Association
CAA	Catholic African Association
DC	District Commissioner
JAZ	Jesuit Archives of Zimbabwe, Harare
LCBL	Little Children of Our Blessed Lady
NAZ	National Archives of Zimbabwe, Harare
NC	Native Commissioner

Preface

This project began with the crisis of trying to find a job. During my senior year at Georgetown University, I happened across a pamphlet advertising volunteer teaching positions with the Catholic Ancillary Teachers of Rural Zimbabwe (Catoruzi). The pamphlet noted that then–Prime Minister Robert Mugabe had asked the Catholic Church to provide teachers for schools in the rural areas. This struck me as odd: why would an alleged Marxist entrust the future of a newly liberated nation to the care of an ostensibly reactionary religious institution? At the time I had no idea that Mugabe had been raised as a Catholic at a Jesuit mission.

Four years later, after two years of teaching high school social studies and two years in the novitiate of the Jesuit New York province, I found myself in the M.A. program in American history at the Catholic University of America in Washington, D.C., studying the history of American Catholics of African descent. During a conversation with a fellow graduate student while on a research trip to the Archdiocese of Baltimore's archives, my colleague expressed surprise that I had completed my undergraduate degree with a concentration in African history rather than American history. In explaining to her the things about African history that I found most interesting, I found myself becoming excited about them anew—and longing to return to African history. Two years later, while working with Catholic Relief Services in Angola, after getting to know and working with missionary priests and the Spanish Hermanas Teresianas (Sisters of Saint Theresa), who dedicated their lives to working among the people at the mission of Mary the Mother of God on the outskirts of Cubal, the kernel of the idea for this project struck: the idea of testing inculturation, or the adaptation of Christianity to a local culture, as a process of social liberation that paralleled the struggle for political liberation.

As with many projects, field research changed the scope and structure of the inquiry. I had originally intended to trace the histories of three Jesuit missions in Zimbabwe and compare them with the histories of three Jesuit missions in Mozambique, using the Jesuits as a control to test the effects of differences in African and European cultures on the inculturation process. Comparing Jesuit missions in Zimbabwe and Mozambique would have provided a means to examine the practical effects of Jesuit spirituality and missiology, as well as differences in European cultures, colonial systems, and mentalities on the inculturation process. While Jesuits in Asia and the Americas were renowned for their efforts to inculturate the church prior to the nineteenth century, inculturation did not appear to be a priority or strategy within the African context prior to the middle of the twentieth century. Jesuit missions, accordingly, are excellent loci for case studies because Ignatian spirituality allows great flexibility and variety in its implementation, thereby ostensibly making it more amenable to inculturation processes within the Catholic Church. Furthermore, the church's centralized and uniform transnational structures, its emphasis on ritual, and its natural law philosophy and theology mitigated against schisms and the formation of African independent churches, as happened more often with many Protestant churches, thus making it well suited to study African initiatives within the global church and their efforts to transform it.[1]

I was unable to gain access to the records of the Jesuit missions in Mozambique, located in the Jesuit archives in Lisbon because the archivist, Padre Vital Perreira, a spry septuagenarian, was frequently away from the archives hearing the confessions of the nuns and youth of the city. Additionally, the overabundance of material on Chishawasha Mission, the oldest Catholic mission established in colonial Zimbabwe, versus the virtual nonexistence of material on St. Peter's Parish, Harare (the oldest urban parish for African Catholics in Harare) in the Jesuit Archives of Zimbabwe necessitated that I revise the structure of this project. Further, the political violence in Zimbabwe following the defeat of the constitutional referendum of February 2000 and the parliamentary elections of June 2000 resulted in this project's current format, for very few laypeople were willing to be interviewed about their experiences during the colonial and *chimurenga* periods, and even some priests and brothers were afraid to speak. Of the twenty-eight interviews I was able to conduct, only six were with laypeople (four men and two women). Consequently, the current study relies more heavily on written sources found primarily in the Jesuit Archives of Zimbabwe and the Archives of the Archdiocese of Harare than I would have preferred, and I have had to glean more African perspective through colonial sources to compensate for the relative lack of African voice obtained through direct oral research.[2]

I wanted to study Africans adapting and taking charge of the church, making it their own. I accept Basil Davidson's contention that African struggles against European colonialism were struggles for social liberation, and that the political form of the nation-state was accidental, not the goal of the liberation movements in and of itself.[3] And so inculturation seemed the best lens through which to test this question within the Catholic Church, as well as to test Jean and John Comaroff's theory that Western missionaries colonized Africans' consciousness and that the acceptance and external manifestation of Christianity was the manifestation of the results of the colonization process.[4] Their application of Western cultural experience generally to so-called non-Western societies saw interaction as predominantly one-way, with Western missionaries almost exclusively influencing Africans, and the implication of their premise of the colonization of consciousness is that African Christians could not think for themselves or know their own interests.

Inculturation was a way to show Africans as agents in their own right within the church, and within the drama of history. As I spent time living with the church in Zimbabwe, however, seeing what I can only call the relative lack of the inculturation of the church in Zimbabwe, I began to consider what appeared to be a significant gap between inculturation as written by Catholic theologians (both African and European), and the experience of the process on the ground in Zimbabwe, and to a lesser extent in Mozambique and Angola.

Acknowledgments

A ChiShona proverb says that success has many mothers, but failure is an orphan. To the extent that this study is in any way successful, I must express my gratitude to the many mothers (and fathers) who helped to give it life. At the same time, I alone take responsibility for any and all of its failings.

Thanks go first to David Robinson, Richard W. Thomas, Sam Thomas, Harry Reed, John T. Hinnant, and John Metzler of Michigan State University, and to Jeanne Marie Penvenne of Tufts University, for their constant patience, encouragement, and willingness to help me at several moments when all seemed bleak. I owe thanks as well to Elizabeth Eldredge.

Research for this study would not have been possible without generous financial support from the Social Science Research Council and the State of Michigan Department of Education's King-Chavez-Parks fellowship, for which I thank Dorothy Harper-Jones and Evette Chavez. I particularly thank Dean Karen Klomparens of the Graduate School, who provided supplemental funding when the surprises of academia and life in the field caught me unprepared, and Dean Patrick McConeghy of College of Arts and Letters for academic and financial support on a number of fronts.

I would like to thank the fellows of the Erasmus Institute at the University of Notre Dame for their comments on an earlier draft of Chapter 2, portions of which were published in "Jesuit Missionary Perspectives on the Formation of African Clergy and Religious Institutes in Zimbabwe, c. 1922–1959," *Le Fait Missionaire: Social Sciences & Missions* 14 (July 2004): 117–145. Portions of Chapter 3 were published in that article, as well as in "'Speaking the Language of Protest': African Student Rebellions at the Catholic Major Seminary in Colonial Zimbabwe, 1965–1979," in *1968 and the Third World*, edited by Samantha Christiansen and Zachary Scarlett (New York: Berghahn Books, 2009).

I thank my colleagues, who pushed me to be a better scholar: Manelisi Genge, Brett Cohen, Liz MacGonagle, Lindsay Frederick Braun, Getnet Bekele, Cheikh Babou, Ghislaine Lydon, Mark Graham, Dawne Curry, and Mary Mwiandi; and mentors and friends at the Catholic University of America in Washington, D.C.: Paul G. Robichaud, Gary Gerstle, Jon L. Wakelyn, Rose Marie Zagarri, Chris Kauffmann, and especially Maria Mazzenga for reawakening my interest in African history. I also thank Patrick Barr-Melej, Norm Goda, Lance Grahn, Keenan Grinnell, George Hartley, Heather Hathaway, Steve Howard, Herb Howe, Paul Kollman, Bryan Massingale, Mike McKinney, Meredith McKittrick, John McNeill, Gwen Mikell, Steve Miner, Joe Murphy, Phil Naylor, Ghirmai Negash, Terry O'Reilly, Patrick Provost-Smith, Sholeh Quinn, Julius Ruff, Kristin Schwain, Kathy Sobieralsky, Bob Sullivan, Jim Turner, and Madeline Wake for their kindness and inspiration.

For their assistance in helping me to find the invaluable data that became the content of this study, I thank Fr. Thomas M. McCoog, S.J., and Anna Edwards, of the Archivum Britannicum Societatis Iesu (British Archives of the Society of Jesus) in London; Maria Fernanda Marques Nabais Gomes of the Instituto dos Arquivos Nacionais/Torre de Tombo; and the staff of the Arquivo Histórico Útramarino (AHU) in Lisbon. I especially wish to thank Fr. Karl-Ferdinand Schmitt, S.J., Fr. Anthony Bex, S.J., and Fr. Joseph Arimoso, of the Jesuit Archives of Zimbabwe for their boundless patience and generosity, and Mrs. Mary Stonier and her able and patient assistant Mrs. Elizabeth Muchenje of the Archives of the Archdiocese of Harare. I also thank the Jesuit Community at Arrupe College, Harare, especially Frs. Val Shirima, Stephen Buckland, and Pat Madigan and Br. Felix Majichi.

Several people read early drafts of various parts of the study. I am grateful to Sam Thomas, Mary Ann Miller, Susan Kroeg, Deborah Gaitskell, Wendy Urban-Mead, Terence Ranger, Betsy Schmidt, Jean

Allman, Meredith McKittrick, Emily Osborn, Paulinus Odozor, Patrick Holt, and Jeff Marlett for their generosity and thoughtful comments.

I thank Tawanda Gumbo, Sipho Radebe Gumbo, Isabel Mukonyora, and Janice McLaughlin for invaluable assistance in translating early-twentieth-century Jesuit ChiShona, and for many delightful and thought-provoking conversations about religion, culture, colonialism, and the Catholic Church in Africa, as well as for their friendship. I also thank Leah Jaquith for helping to keep me sane during trying times in the preparation of this manuscript and Kelsey Eilers for helping me to believe in myself again. I also owe debts of gratitude to Raphael Nyaguze and Emily Miner for their assistance in preparing the glossary and index respectively.

I thank Fredric Nachbaur, Bob Oppedisano, Mary-Lou Elias Peña, Eric Newman, Gregory McNamee, and their colleagues at Fordham University Press for their patience, belief in this project, and willingness to publish it. Last, but by no means least of all, I dedicate this work to Audrey Leticia and Sophia Esperanza Creary–De La Cruz and thank them for sharing too much of their time with this project.

Domesticating a Religious Import

Introduction

Catholic theologians in the last fifty years have developed the term *inculturation* to discuss the old problem of adapting the church universal to specific local cultures. The theologians conceive of inculturation as a dialogue between Christianity (the church) and culture.[1] The concept of inculturation differs from the anthropological concepts of acculturation, which is the process of adapting to a culture that is not a person's native culture, and enculturation, the process of learning a culture as one's native culture. Europeans needed ten centuries to inculturate Christianity from its Judaic roots. The existence of the eastern churches in communion with the Roman Catholic church points to the time in history when there was greater development of local churches and, consequently, greater inculturation of the church (that is, prior to the schism of the eleventh century).[2] As such, African efforts to make the church their own are a manifestation of the same process, but in a much shorter period of time.

African Christians were aware that European missionaries transmitted aspects of their cultures with the Christian message during the evangelization of Africans in the nineteenth and twentieth centuries. This African Christian consciousness emerged in an effort neither to destroy or appropriate symbols of authority nor to reclaim appropriated cultural patrimony.[3] It was a deliberate attempt to introduce and incorporate elements of vernacular African religion into the Christian symbolic system. In Southern Africa, it appears that African Catholics, above all, sought to fashion for themselves a niche, a spiritual home within the church.

Theories of power, such as those of Jean and John Comaroff or James C. Scott,[4] that focus explicitly on contestation are of limited value in discussions of religious change, which must account for the religious ideals of unity between and communion among people. If the question had simply pitted African Christians against Western Christians in a contest for cultural patrimony, then African Christians more than likely would have left the Catholic Church in greater numbers and joined one of the many African independent/initiated Christian churches, where African Christians were free to formulate doctrines and practices with African symbols without interference from European missionaries. The articulators of African Christian consciousness, however, were deeply engaged in a "quest for belonging." They chose to pursue spiritual peace within the Catholic Church, where they began to transform the church from below by incorporating African symbols, music, and ways of being Christian into the universal church. They began to place their cultures on par with Western cultures in the church. Studies of religion and religious interactions within a colonial context, such as that of Henry Bredekamp and Robert Ross, expand discourses on power relations and render them more complex by arguing that because true Christians are Christians of their own free will, missionaries cannot impose Christianity on people unwilling to accept it. To argue that Africans' consciousness was colonized is "akin to saying that it was false. It can only be an insult . . . a demeaning of the real choice and the real dignity of those who came to accept, in part and in their own ways, the messages of the missionaries."[5]

Since the 1950s, scholars such as J. F. Ajayi and Roland Oliver have associated Christianity with the European imperial conquest and colonization of Africa.[6] Other scholars, such as Greg Cuthbertson and Paul Landau, have seen Christianity from a materialist perspective and contend that Africans were motivated to become Christians for reasons of material gain.[7] These are problematic views of Christianity because they see Christianity only as part of a hegemonic civil society that Europeans used to make Africans docile subjects of colonial states and do not take seriously either the possibility that Africans may have been sincere in their acceptance of Christian ideology or African Christians' ability to influence Christian beliefs and practices. Christianity is reduced to a function of European culture. Though many European and African converts and missionaries did collaborate with the imperial powers, the subtlety and variety of African responses to the Christian message make the problem more complex.

In 1952, Roland Oliver posited that Christianity was a European import to Africa, and that missionaries were part of the vanguard of the colonial enterprise in *The Missionary Factor in East Africa*. Since then, scholars studying the history of Christianity in Africa have had to contend with Oliver's assertion. Given the variety of approaches and the phases through which the historiography of African Christianity has passed,[8] the current scholarship has become far more subtle and nuanced in its approach to Oliver's legacy: it no longer questions whether mission Christianity was complicit with colonialism, but rather the degree and manner in which Christians—both African and European—participated in shaping Christianity as a force for the oppression and/or liberation of Africans.[9]

A different conceptualization of the problem, one that moves beyond Oliver's approach, is to consider the history of African Christianity within the broader context of religion in Africa. Lamin Sanneh's work placed African Christianity within the wider context of the history of Christianity. He showed the African presence within Christendom from its earliest days in the first century and Africans actively shaping and spreading the faith, and not merely as the passive recipients of European ministrations. Sanneh, however, also established a history of Christianity within an African context. Focusing on the beliefs and practices of Christians and Muslims in West Africa, he argued that when first-century Christians translated their sacred texts into Greek, they began a process by which the Christian message continually took on the language and cultural forms of the communities that accepted it. According to Sanneh, this "translatability" is Christianity's hallmark, despite the intentions and actions of ministers who believed in a fixed version thereof. European missionaries in Africa, therefore, set in motion a process that produced Christian churches with indigenous African leaders, beliefs, and practices. Once the Bible was translated into the vernacular, missionaries could not control its spread and adaptation to local forms and practices. Translation, then, was a necessary first step in the inculturation of the church, or a privileging of the local culture.[10]

If, as Sanneh argues, any vernacular language can be a vehicle for Christian ideology and any culture can be a vehicle for its expression, then it is possible to apply this concept (literally, to translate means to carry over) to religious expression in general, and speak of *vernacular African religion*, or the religious beliefs and practices that a given African group shares in common in a specific place and time. As with a vernacular language, vernacular religion is subject to change over time based on how people within the group use it.

In "African Conversion," Robin Horton presumed that when people are confronted with new situations they adapt them in terms of their existing ideas and attitudes, and that when people assimilate new ideas they do so because the ideas make sense to them in terms of notions they already have. He then proposed a "traditional [African religious] world view" in which "lesser spirits underpin events and processes in the microcosm of the local community and environment, whilst the supreme being underpins events and processes in the macrocosm of which the local community is ultimately a part."[11]

Horton then elaborated several implications that stemmed from his model: given appropriate social changes, certain religious innovations normally associated with the influence of Islam and Christianity (for example, development of the concept and cult of an active, morally centered supreme being) are likely to occur even in the absence of these world religions; even where Islam and/or Christianity are present, the ideational changes normally associated with them are likely to occur only in the presence of the appropriate social changes; given the appropriate social changes and the presence of Islam and/or Christianity, acceptance of ideas from the world religions will be highly selective, with that which is accepted or rejected being determined largely by the basic vernacular cosmological structure and by the limits that this structure sets to the cosmology's potential for adaptive change. Given these three points, it follows that African responses to Islam and Christianity will be responses that, under the appropriate social and economic conditions, might well have occurred in some recognizable form even in the absence of these world religions.[12]

Although Horton presumed a functionalist anthropologist understanding of African religion,[13] his work is significant because it validated vernacular African religion as not inferior to Christianity or Islam while making a strong argument for the adaptability of Christianity to African culture, as well as for the capacity of Africans to adapt Christianity to their cultures selectively. In other words, Africans did not necessarily have to surrender their indigenous cultures and become more European when they converted to Christianity.

Humphrey Fisher disagreed strongly with Horton's position, criticizing him for having taken most of his evidence from "Christian African experience" and generalizing from it for both Islam and Christianity. Examining the phenomenon of conversion to Islam, and using Uthman dan Fodio and the rise of the Sokoto caliphate as his primary example, Fisher posited a three-phased process through which Islam established itself and spread through West Africa. The first process was quarantine, or the period in which Muslims entered a given area and maintained a "relatively secure" orthodoxy "because there are no converts, and thus no one to bring into the Muslim community heterodox beliefs and observances drawn from his or her non-Muslim past." The second process was mixing, where "as local people converted in increasing numbers . . . people combined the profession of Islam, and as it might be the quite sincere observance of many Islamic tenets, with many pagan survivals." After a period of time ("often after the lapse of centuries"), mixing is replaced by the third process, a period of reform in which "clerics . . . succeed in maintaining an element of quarantine against the mixing all round them" and return to a more orthodox practice. He then proposed two senses of the meaning of conversion: "exchange of one faith (or none) for another, and exchanging indifference and dilution for fervency within the same faith." Because Horton's paradigm relied on the former definition, "the essential, underlying movement of religious growth, through the first conversion towards the second, is lost." According to Fisher, European Christian missionaries tried to maintain the quarantine phase, and the rise of independent African Christian churches represented the mixing stage in Christianity.[14]

Horton's theory that African religious responses to Islam and Christianity could have happened independently of the presence of the world religions opens new possibilities for studying Christianity in Africa, particularly when combined with Fisher's models of the spread of Islam and the conversion process. Christianity no longer remains an external imposition but becomes one of many elements that contribute to the development of distinctively African worldviews. Such a method also centers Africans and their perspectives in studies of Christian presence on the continent.

Historians of Southern Africa have also studied the interactions between vernacular African religions and Western Christianity and showed the value of studying Christianity within the context of African religious development. David Beach studied the cultural history of the region associated with the modern state of Zimbabwe, including religious developments, dating to the ninth century.[15] Ngwabi Bhebe, who studied the development of AmaNdebele religion in western Zimbabwe, showed that it was the "amalgamation" of several African religious traditions, including those of AmaNdebele, BaTswana, and VaShona. According to Bhebe, this process began before European missionaries arrived, and it significantly contributed to their early failures. Gabriel Setiloane examined the persistent resistance of vernacular BaSotho and BaTswana religions in Botswana and South Africa to European missionaries' teachings, arguing that African acceptance of Christianity was due less to individual convictions than to the significant social changes wrought by episodes of European aggression during the nineteenth century.[16]

Paul Landau's study of the indigenization of Christianity among the BaNgwato of Botswana contended that Christianity was a "polymorphous construction built from the practice of actual people."[17] He argued that the Ngwato chiefdom under Khama wrested control of "ecclesiastical statehood" from the words and actions of European missionaries and created a state that thrived within the context of British colonialism. African Christians succeeded in creating a political "realm of the word" through an alliance between Ngwato royalty, British clergy, and Tswana women, as well as the support of the British colonial administration. Landau did not take for granted the a priori acceptance of faith on the part of African Christians. It is this starting point that made his work controversial, and that laid the basis for his critique of the Comaroffs and Lamin Sanneh.

Landau argued that religion is a specifically Western concept that Europeans used to categorize non-Europeans whom they did not understand. He rejected the notion of transcendent religious symbols as "unreal [in] nature" and, employing Wittgenstein's referential theory of meaning, highlighted the "colonizing" nature of translation as a model for understanding missionary discourse. He then argued that meaning must come from linguistic usage or practice, and not from transliteration of concepts, since to do so is to impose the translator's concepts onto the other's worldview. This is a direct affront to Sanneh, who argued that the historic ability to transcend culture is the hallmark of the Christian message. While the Comaroffs would agree with Landau on this point, he took issue with them, however, because they postulated that Tswana Christians identify with the language and symbolic order that "European hegemonists" appropriate. This privileges Christianity (and by extension Western culture) and sees it as being imposed and Tswana culture as lived, when, according to Landau, the opposite was more likely to be true. He posited that Christianity diffused through Tswana society as did Tswana cosmology, and that Ba-Tswana generated their own conflicts, and thus, their own history. Thus, Landau revolutionized the conventional understanding of African religion, as well as struck a major victory for African agency within the colonial discourse.

Similarly, English historian Richard Gray demonstrated the extent of the successful evangelization of the kingdom of Soyo, showing that the people's acceptance of Catholic Christianity was more than superficial. The mission, however, failed primarily due to the complicity of secular clergy with Portuguese slave traders, in spite of the Vatican's 1686 condemnation of the slave trade. He further refuted the idea that Christianity in Africa was coeval with the missionaries' understanding of it. Evangelization depended heavily on African catechists, teachers, and migrant laborers, and thus they had a significant influence on the shape that Christianity took by means of their interpretations and understanding of concepts and categories, such as those of good and evil. Gray posited religious pluralism instead of religious syncretism, arguing that literacy and other means of mass communication aided Africans in the spread of their varieties of Christianity, rather than privileging European missionary perspective.[18]

Although scholars have examined the role of both vernacular African religions and Christianity prior to and during Zimbabwe's liberation war,[19] discussions of the Catholic Church during the second *chimurenga*, or rebellion against European colonial rule, deal almost exclusively with its politicization in the face of an increasingly belligerent Rhodesian settler state. There have been several studies of the development of the institutional church,[20] but no single study examines the pastoral mission of the church or the efforts of African Christians to shed European influences and create an African religious expression, that is, to inculturate the church.

Ian Linden, Terence Ranger, and more recently Janice McLaughlin, Barbara Moss, and David Maxwell showed that in Zimbabwe African Christians played significant roles in directing and leading the struggle for independence.[21] They show, however, that it was not a uniform process and that not all parts of the church acted in a united front. The realities on the ground resulted in a much more fractious involvement in and influence upon Christianity's expressions during and after the time of the second *chimurenga*. So too, then, the process of inculturation within the Catholic Church: it was a very uneven, un-universal process that took root in some parts of the church in some parts of Zimbabwe more readily than others.

The study that follows will show that the areas under the care of the fathers and brothers of the Society of Jesus (the Jesuits) were some of the least inculturated in Zimbabwe, and not for want of desire on the part of the African Christians in their charge. There were significant struggles within the church between Africans and Europeans, but also among Africans and Europeans, respectively. It reveals two simultaneous and intersecting processes: the Africanization of the Catholic Church by African Christians and the church hierarchy's discourse of inculturation, specifically that of the Jesuits. David Newbury contrasted

African acknowledgment of European power over them with their lack of recognition of European authority during the colonial period.[22] This study will show that in this case, VaShona Catholics frequently ignored the authority of the Catholic hierarchy and continued to marry according to "customary" law, to pray to Mwari, and to honor the spirits of their ancestors.

If the Jesuits were most resistant to inculturation, and other orders such as the Bethlehem Mission Society (Bethlehem Fathers) and Spanish Missionary Institute were more open to the idea of inculturation, why study the Jesuits' relative failure to inculturate the church? Because their failures, particularly in the early decades while they had exclusive control of the Zambezi Mission, set the stage for the uphill battles against which these other missionary orders had to work; because the repercussions of the choices and decisions that they made are still playing themselves out today. The issues addressed in this study are still very much live issues, and to some degree will always be so. But issues such as *kurova guva* (rites to honor the spirits of the dead) and marriage are still playing themselves out, and so I hope to contribute in a small way to the current debates that still confront the Catholic church in Zimbabwe and the African continent more broadly.

This study examines inculturation processes in Zimbabwe primarily during the colonial period from 1890 to 1980. It presumes that for "the dialogue between the church and culture" to occur, there must be people with the requisite insider knowledge of the culture in place; thus, I begin with three chapters on the formation of African religious women, clergy, and laity. The focus then shifts to the specific issues of marriage, God's name, and honoring ancestor spirits as sites of inculturation. These chapters begin with the historical development of African cultural beliefs and practices prior to the colonial dispensation, and they show Africans adapting Christianity within the context of their own history. That is, they show Africans making their own history. As will be seen, Europeans had to adapt to African cultures at least as much as Africans had to adapt to European cultures.

This study will contend that European missionaries' preaching "the word" merely implanted Christianity in Southern Africa. The process of *inculturating* the church, by which African Christians shed the European cultural influences from Christianity and transformed it into an African religious expression, was ultimately more important for the spread of Christianity across the African continent.

I write with the intent of placing the history of African Christianity within the broader context of the history of religion in Africa. By so doing, Christianity will no longer be seen as an external imposition, but as one of many elements that contributed to the development of distinctively African world senses.[23] This methodology will also effectively center Africans and their perspectives by showing that Africans discerned the differences between Christian ideology and elements of European cultures that European missionaries transmitted with the Christian message and adapted Christianity to their own respective cultural contexts. It will also speak to the history of religion in general, providing concrete examples of complex processes of interactions between different cultural groups at the levels of religious belief and practice. It also addresses and fits within the corpus of literature concerning Western missionary/African Christian "dialogues."

Following David Maxwell, my argument moves beyond the material level and examines the interactions between Africans and Western missionaries in colonial Zimbabwe at an intellectual level over an extended time frame, focusing on ideas such as the existence of a supreme being, what that being should be called, and how that being ought to be recognized (as opposed to the recognition due potentially lesser spiritual beings), and the implementation or practice of those ideas. Where Maxwell concerns himself with "the social significance of religion,"[24] I attempt to address similar issues at the spiritual, or theological, level as well. For example, in discussing VaShona Catholic marriage practices, it will be seen that by the 1960s approximately 80 percent of African Catholics were not marrying according to church law. A materialist explanation of this fact would claim that African Catholics opted not to marry according to canon law because there was no concrete, tangible material benefit to doing so. A social historical analysis would argue that the development of African "customary law" by means of a series of marriage ordinances intersected with African marriage practices and the strictures of Catholic canon law to preclude the vast majority from forming canonically regular unions. A theological explanation seeks to identify the reasons why and how African Catholic couples chose to marry according to canonical form, and what the implications of that choice were for them, as well as the implications for those who did not.

Restoring a Positive View of Theological Analysis to Religious Studies

In his analysis of the literature concerning "primitive religions," E. E. Evans-Pritchard raised the issue of the religious background (or lack thereof) of scholars of religion—specifically functionalist anthropologists—its significance for their studies, and the implications for broader understandings of religion. He wrote:

We have to bear in mind, in estimating theories of primitive religion, what the words used in them meant to the scholars who used them. If one is to understand the interpretations of primitive mentality they put forward, one has to know their own mentality, broadly where they stood; to enter into their way of looking at things, a way of their class, sex, and period. As far as religion goes, they all had . . . a religious background in one form or another. . . . But with one or two exceptions, whatever the background may have been, the persons whose writings have been most influential have been at the time they wrote agnostics or atheists.[25]

Evans-Pritchard argued that anthropologists generally viewed religion as "an illusion," and that their "impassioned rationalism" had "coloured their assessment of primitive religions and has given their writings, as we read them today [1965], a flavour of smugness which one may find either irritating or risible."[26] This, he argued, led them to consider all religion as ultimately irrational and "absurd," and to explain religion's "absurdity" in "psychological or sociological terms."[27] He further noted his belief that an anthropologist need not subscribe to a religious faith because "there is no possibility of [the anthropologist] *knowing* whether the spiritual beings of primitive religions or of any others have any existence or not, and since that is the case he [sic] cannot take the question into consideration."[28] Religion, thus becomes a sociological phenomenon:

> The beliefs for [the anthropologist] are sociological facts, not theological facts, and his [sic] sole concern is with their relation to each other and to other social facts. His problems are scientific, not metaphysical or ontological. The method ... [is often called] the phenomenological one—a comparative study of beliefs and rites, such as god, sacrament, and sacrifice to determine their meaning and social significance. The validity of the belief lies in the domain of what may broadly be designated the philosophy of religion.[29]

Evans-Pritchard believed the rationalist functionalist anthropologists had taken a theological position, "albeit a negative and implicit one," and their efforts to explain religious phenomena causally went "beyond the legitimate bounds of the subject."[30] Sociological and psychological studies of religion are still popular among contemporary scholars of religion.[31]

The negative theological positions about which Evans-Pritchard complained, however, seem to have become explicit. One scholar has argued that since religion's relation to the sacred was what made it distinctive, it was necessary to sever that link in order to arrive at a purely sociological study of religion.[32] This highlights the problematic nature of phenomenological studies of religion, that is, studying religion as merely a sociological and/or psychological phenomenon, while discounting theological aspects.

In *Nuer Religion*, Evans-Pritchard also raised the issue of the religious background of anthropologists of religion:

> It may be said that in describing and interpreting a primitive religion it should make no difference whether the writer is an agnostic or a Christian, Jew, Muslim, Hindu, or whatever he may be, but in fact it makes a great deal of difference, for even in a descriptive study judgment can in no way be avoided. Those who give assent to the religious beliefs of their own people feel and think, and therefore also write, differently about the beliefs of other peoples from those who do not give assent to them.[33]

Although many scholars would take issue with him, Evans-Pritchard raised the issue of the kinds of judgments, and hence conclusions, scholars make concerning religion in general, and "African religion" (the quintessential "primitive" religion) specifically.[34] Whether scholars of religion who hold religious beliefs write differently from those who do not is certainly a matter for debate. The kinds of questions that these scholars ask in terms of framing their studies and the kinds of information they seek, however, do differ, and consequently have significant implications for the study of religion, as a brief examination of the history of African Christianity would demonstrate.

With regard to what historians can know about the past, Philip Gleason has identified three levels of historical inquiry: the factual level (what happened?), the explanatory level (why did it happen?), and the evaluative level (was what happened good or bad?). What a historian can know with certainty decreases with each level of inquiry. There is a high degree of certitude at the factual level that is limited by the nature of the events in question and the sources of information available. At the explanatory level, certitude is limited by the historian's inferences about the relationship between events and the influences on them. The evaluative level contains the least certainty because the historian's value system and beliefs influence any judgments that the historian makes.[35]

Gleason noted that while separating the three levels of inquiry was useful for analyzing the historian's craft, in the practice of writing about history they are inextricably intertwined. The historian sees facts in relation to one another, and thus historical interpretations combine explanations and evaluations of those facts either implicitly or explicitly.[36] And like historical knowledge itself, historiographical interpretations are limited by the incompleteness and subjectivity of their perspectives. Gleason characterized the evaluative level of historical epistemology as being influenced by the historian's values and beliefs; thus, the application and operation of religious beliefs and values will affect a study of religion in ways that their absence will not.

Thomas Spear, a historian of East Africa, in examining the historiography of Christianity in Africa, argued that few studies "have taken up the critical sociological and theological issues involved if we are to define precisely how Africans interpreted the Christian message and appropriated it in terms of their own historical and cultural experiences."[37] Noting that while studies of African independent Christian churches made by church historians came closest to this objective, Spear posited that "academic studies of the historical or mainstream churches have tended to assume rather mechanical models of conversion that focus on socio-political and economic factors rather than religious belief and practice."

Questions of religious belief pose problems for academic social scientists, many of whom are made uncomfortable, for example by Sanneh's conclusion that, while the missionaries themselves failed, God's mission (*missio dei*) in Africa succeeded. We need to cross the boundaries between academic and religious scholarly discourses if we are to understand those converts who say that while they were initially attracted by the schools and jobs, they were captured by "the poetry of the religion." How else, after all, can we understand the sacrifice of the Buganda martyrs, the motivations of catechists who labored for the church with little material rewards, the philosophic basis of Nyerere's concept of *ujamaa*, the abundant religious symbolism contained in Ngugi wa Thiong'o's *Matigari*, the principled political opposition of Kenya's churches, or the resurgent dynamism of the faith today?

The study of African Christianity has drawn variously on Church History as well as academic history, anthropology, and religious studies, but the differences between them have not been as dramatic as might be imagined. Nor have there necessarily been great differences between scholars writing from within and outside the churches. Thus, while it was largely academic historians . . . together with some church historians . . . who pioneered revisionist studies of missions, it was primarily church historians who rejected mission condemnations of the independent churches to stress their fundamental Christianity. Conversely, academic scholars . . . have been forthright in developing African religious history, but church historians . . . have probed religious ideas in great depth. The most significant fault lines in the literature have thus not been religious, but political, functions of the changing political climate over the past century as concerns have shifted from metropolitan and ecclesiastical to nationalist and African religious history.[38]

Thus, there appears to be a great need to study "African religion" in its own right, not merely as a function or reflection of sociopolitical processes.

I am not here calling for the religious conversion (in either of Fisher's senses of the word) of scholars of religion, nor am I saying that only those with religious beliefs can study religion well, or better than those without them. Scholars of religion in Africa must address and take seriously in their own right—not merely as functions or reflections of social processes—the theologies at work in a given community's religious beliefs and practices, or to put it simply, they must include some form of theological analysis at some level. I do not take the narrow Catholic meaning that Pope John Paul suggested in *Ex Corde Ecclesiae*; rather, I take "theological analysis" to mean a perspective that addresses and incorporates a given community's relationship with the sacred as well as—not merely—their perceptions of that relationship, especially if we follow Landau's position that "African religion" is a Western intellectual fiction that does not exist.

Landau's argument that "African religion" is an imposition of Western intellectual categories on African societies rather than an indigenous African phenomenon effectively renders the concept as *bricolage*, or as French philosopher Jacques Derrida would have said, places it "under erasure."[39] Effectively, being *bricolage*, or under erasure, means that the term "African religion" can no longer be used because of its inaccuracy and inadequacy. Scholars, however, like a *bricoleur*, continue to use that term because there is not yet an appropriate concept to describe or analyze the reality of "African religious" beliefs and practices.

Whether or not the concept "African religion" exists remains a matter for debate and discussion. In some respects it is a secondary consideration that ultimately and unnecessarily detracts from the more important sociological fact that across the African continent—regardless of what Western scholars have called it—people have seen and continue to see a relationship between and among the realm of humanity, the realm of the "spirits," and the "divine" (that is, god/supreme being). If it is no longer possible to apply customary Western religious concepts to African realities, then scholars of "African religion"—in this case, of ChiShona-speakers in colonial Zimbabwe—must find a way to address and speak about the relationships between and among *munhu* (human), *mudzimu* (ancestor spirit), and *Mwari* (god/supreme being). And unlike the early anthropologists whom Evans-Prichard criticized, we must do so with better and more accurate knowledge and understanding of the concepts as found in respective African cultural groups, bearing in mind that concepts—like cultures themselves—are dynamic, changing over time.

Inculturation Theory

Historian John Thornton discussed the nature of religious knowledge and its foundation upon revelation of the divine/supernatural world.[40] Within this theoretical framework, I establish theological understandings for both vernacular VaShona and Western Christian religious beliefs and practices by comparing rites of passage among ChiShona-speakers in Zimbabwe and those in the Catholic Church concerning marriage and death, and trace the adaptation of Christian forms of worship to African vernacular cultural norms through the colonial period.

Religion often plays a central role in the cultural life of a human society by attempting to provide explanations of the world's origins and humanity's place therein, concepts of morality and codes of acceptable social behavior. Indigenous African peoples developed a great variety of religious systems with complex cosmologies, rituals, and traditions.[41]

During the late nineteenth and early twentieth centuries, European imperialists and evangelists tried to impose alien religious beliefs and practices—Western forms of Christianity—on many African peoples.[42] This raises the issues of the extent to which Africans were able to adapt external religious institutions, such as the Catholic Church, to their own circumstances and to transform them into African forms of religious expression, that is, to inculturate Christianity; and to what extent they used these religious expressions in their struggles for liberation from European domination. Though there is literature about the politicization of the Catholic Church during the liberation war in Zimbabwe,[43] there appears to be no monograph that deals exclusively with the pastoral mission of the Catholic Church, or more importantly, with the efforts of African Christians to shed the European influences of an imported Christianity and transform it into an African religious experience.

As such, inculturation ought to become a process of social liberation *within* the church, as well as a social liberation *of* the church. The extent to which inculturation took place on the symbolic level would have significant implications for this process of ecclesiastical decolonization in Zimbabwe, because its absence would result merely in a religious colonization of African peoples by European Christians at best, or what Jean and John Comaroff describe as a colonization of African consciousness at worst.[44]

The term *inculturation* is now used to discuss the old problem of adapting the church universal (that is, the beliefs, actions, and structures of the church that are applicable to humanity throughout the world ostensibly irrespective of culture) to specific local cultures. The term was first used by a French Jesuit, Joseph Masson (*"un Catholicisme inculturé"*[45]), in preparations for the opening of the Second Vatican Council (1962–1965), and it was popularized by the Jesuits—the largest religious order of men in the Catholic Church, and with the most extensive training—and particularly by Pedro Arrupe, the superior general of the order from 1965 to 1983.[46] The Jesuit neologism clearly had established itself in the Catholic theological lexicon by the late 1970s, when it appeared in a speech by Pope John Paul II in 1979.[47]

Arrupe defined inculturation as:

The incarnation of Christian life and of the Christian message in a particular cultural context, in such a way that this experience not only finds expression through elements proper to the culture in question (this alone would be no more than a superficial adaptation) but becomes a principle that animates, directs, and unifies the culture, transforming it and remaking it so as to bring about a "new creation."[48]

British theologian Aylward Shorter went on to define inculturation as "the on-going dialogue between [Christian] faith and culture or cultures. More fully, it is the creative and dynamic relationship between the Christian message and a culture or cultures."[49]

Inculturation has largely supplanted other terms dealing with the adaptation of the church to local culture, such as "indigenization," or "contextualization." The term, particularly as defined by Arrupe and Shorter, is useful in this study because it refers to the process of how a transnational and multicultural entity adapts itself (or is adapted) to local cultures and contexts. Thus, while inculturation is a relatively new term, the process of adaptation dates to the beginning of Christianity over two thousand years ago, and encompasses cross-cultural practices. Inculturation as a concept is valuable to measure the relative success (or failure) of African Christians and Western Jesuits in receiving and/or responding to broader church initiatives and objectives. The concept also speaks directly to the broader issue of Western missionary/African Christian dialogue and encounter, particularly as found in the works of the Comaroffs and Paul Landau. As such, inculturation is a useful concept to test a specifically Catholic ideology in a specifically African cultural context.

One of the underlying assumptions of inculturation is to distinguish the gospel from the cultural assumptions often embedded in the language and practice of evangelization/preaching. One missionary, Vincent Donovan, decried the fact that despite over one hundred years of missionary activity in the African "missions," the church in Africa was still largely dependent on the Western world for financial support and for personnel. The church's failure to bring Christ's message of salvation to the Maasai in Tanzania (Donovan's specific missionary experience), and to Africa in general, is the result of its failure to "peel away from the gospel the accretions of the centuries, and of Western, white, European, American culture," and incarnate[50] it in the culture of the people whom it evangelizes.[51] The idea of inculturating the faith, or transforming it into a form of religious expression for a given people is very much rooted in the theology of the mystery of the incarnation.[52]

According to Donovan, so long as the church fails to inculturate itself, it denies its very existence: "The church exists only insofar as it carries Christ to the world. The church is only part of the mission, the mission of God sending his son to the world. Without this mission, there would be no church. The idea of church without mission is an absurdity."[53] Thus, he suggested a return to the missionary methods of Saint Paul, as found in the New Testament, in implementing the work of evangelization.

A concrete example of Donovan's method was his presentation of the liturgy of the Eucharist. Rather than impose the traditional Latin Rite Mass in its entirety, with all its structures, and symbols rooted in Roman culture (for instance, priestly vestments and incense) on the Maasai, he merely presented them with bread and wine and Christ's words of institution from the Last Supper and allowed the people to develop the liturgy as they saw fit.[54] While doing so resulted in a great variety in the liturgical celebrations from group to group of Maasai, it also allowed each community the freedom to incorporate local symbols that had greater meaning for them than those found in the traditional Western Catholic Mass.[55]

Donovan's critique was insightful and challenging to "traditional" notions of missiology, theories of mission. He provided a new ecclesiastical model and method rooted in practical experience that would augur well for the church in Africa: such a model would effectively obviate the separation of religious expression from daily experience (as done in the West). This would allow Africans greater freedom to reclaim and reinvest with greater meaning symbols that the church may have co-opted in its failed efforts to inculturate itself on the continent. This would ultimately result in more explicitly African expressions of Christianity.[56]

Eugene Hillman's *Toward an African Christianity* was an applied theological study of inculturation in an African context. Hillman spent many years working among the Maasai in Kenya and Tanzania. Beginning with the mystery of the incarnation, "the idea that the divine Word [Jesus Christ] became a human being like the rest of us in everything except sin,"[57] Hillman argued that the church, despite statements and pronouncements to the contrary, mired itself in European "monoculture," and that "what passed for evangelism during the past hundred years was in reality a dissemination of the western experiences and expressions of Christian faith. These foreign religious interpretations of the faith . . . were translated literally into African cultural words," such translations being more often than not merely "linguistic and literalistic."[58]

The Second Vatican Council represented a major rhetorical and theological departure from the past by "retrieving and reaffirming the incarnational principle, [and] promis[ing] to put the Church back on its original course of authentic involvement with the whole inhabited earth."[59] According to Hillman, the church has not lived up to its newfound "duty" to inculturate, since it has to free itself from "a congenital and chronic ethnocentrism at the higher levels of ecclesiastical management . . . [and] a fear of innovation at the grassroots level."[60]

Revelation and Religious Knowledge

In *Africa and Africans in the Making of the Atlantic World, 1400–1800*, John Thornton provided a useful model with which to consider the coalescence of different religious beliefs. Thornton was writing about religious practices that occurred during the fifteenth through eighteenth centuries of the common era, that is, prior to the European conquest and occupation of the African continent of the late nineteenth and twentieth centuries, when there was a relative parity between African Christians and European missionaries and a theological openness that had not yet been closed by the European colonial dispensation. He posited that in order to appreciate the adaptations of African religious beliefs and practices with European forms of Christianity in the early transatlantic world, it was first necessary to "understand the underlying dynamics of religious knowledge . . . and from this the mechanisms for religious change, conversion, and transformation in the presence of other systems of religious knowledge." According to Thornton, "[the] merging of religions requires something more than simply mixing forms and ideas from one religion with those of another. It requires a reevaluation of the basic concepts and sources of knowledge of both religions in order to find common ground." Thus, religion "was not simply an intellectual conception, made up by people and subject to reconsideration or debate. Rather, the ideas and the images were 'received' or revealed from nonworldly beings in one or another form, and humans' only role was to interpret these revelations and act accordingly." Religious philosophy, therefore, "was not the creator of religion; revelations were. Religious philosophy simply interpreted them." The most immediate implication of this model is that "strictly speaking, humans were not free to change religions or to question the revelations, and in the end virtually all religious change required at least reinterpretation of existing revelations, at most a new set of stronger revelations."[61]

Thornton's model is useful because it allows an examination of inculturation processes at several levels, including the symbolic, the personal (or the level of individuals or groups of people), the institutional or structural, and the ideological. The model of revelation as the basis of religious knowledge is more useful and accurate than syncretism because it allows for an equality of dialogue partners and a possibility for mutual influence—that is, "non-Western" religious beliefs, practices, and perspectives can influence their Western counterparts at least as much as Western ones influence them.

There is sufficient symbolic common ground between African religious belief and practice, and Catholic teaching and ritual not only to warrant but also to require an effective inculturation of the church in Zimbabwe and throughout the rest of the world. The single greatest variable and obstacle to this end is the willingness on the part of the ministers of the church to do so. This willingness has been present to a greater degree since the advent of the Second Vatican Council. Such was not the case in 1890, when the English first occupied the territory of what is now Zimbabwe.[62]

1   A Failed Mission, Contesting Colonial Rule, and Ecclesiastical Developments

Two Bantu language–speaking groups, the VaShona people (ChiShona speakers), who entered the southern African region as early as the ninth century CE and established the state known as Great Zimbabwe by the thirteenth century, and the AmaNdebele people (IsiNdebele speakers), who came to what is now western Zimbabwe during the first half of the nineteenth century in the wake of the disturbances caused by the state consolidation associated with the rise of the Zulu state, primarily populated the territory of modern Zimbabwe.[1] Europeans first arrived in 1560, when Gonçalo da Silveira led an expedition of Jesuit missionaries from Mozambique to the court of the Munhumutapa empire in present Zimbabwe. Although Silveira baptized the ruler, the cleric was killed in 1561 as a result of court intrigues involving Muslim traders opposed to Portuguese encroachment on the lucrative trans–Indian Ocean trade.[2] The Great Zimbabwe state was succeeded by the Changamire and Rozvi states on the plateau between the Zambezi and Limpopo rivers.[3]

Zimbabwean historian Ngwabi Bhebe posited that AmaNdebele religion was an amalgam of AmaNdebele, VaShona, BaSotho, BaTswana, and BaVenda religious traditions, which predated European Christian missionaries' arrival, and African religious leaders frequently incorporated elements of Christianity as a way to prevent conversions to Christianity. These developing religious traditions also apparently met the spiritual needs of their adherents.[4]

The rise of the Zulu state and the collapse of the Shona Rozvi state brought people of different religious beliefs and practices together in western Zimbabwe. In 1828, Mzilikazi broke away from the Zulu state and settled in the Transvaal region among BaSotho, BaTswana, and BaVenda polities. In 1837, following several military encounters with Boer trekkers from the Cape, Mzilikazi and his followers withdrew north of the Limpopo River and settled in what is now western Zimbabwe.[5] At roughly the same time, the Rozvi state fell. The religious structures of the Mwari cult, the Rozvi religion associated with the king, remained largely intact and integrated into the AmaNdebele religious amalgam, identified with issues of national concern (notably, rain).[6] These structures seem to have fit the political structures and needs of the newly arrived centralized AmaNdebele state. As king, Mzilikazi also functioned as chief priest. Following his death, during the succession crisis of 1868 to 1870, religious leaders supported his son, Lobengula, forming the basis of his power and prestige. Any success on the part of European missionaries, who came as early as 1859, would have threatened the authority of the religious leaders; thus, they combined with Lobengula "to exert their influence against the new faith."[7] Despite significant debate about the nature and extent of the Mwari cult's influence, particularly during the 1896–97 rebellion, it appears that the cult's oracular shrine adepts influenced the AmaNdebele kings' activities, as well as contributed to the significant opposition to the early spread of Christianity.[8] Although perspectives differ on the nature of relations between AmaNdebele and VaShona, it is clear that the former incorporated significant numbers of the latter into the lower echelons of AmaNdebele society.[9]

David Livingstone's death in 1873 sparked great interest in missionary work in Africa across Europe.[10] Consequently, in 1874, Bishop James Ricards, the vicar apostolic of the Eastern District of the Cape Colony, began corresponding with Alfred Weld, the general assistant to the Jesuit superior general for English affairs, about the possibility of establishing a Catholic mission north of the Cape colony. In 1875, several Jesuits arrived to establish a secondary school in Grahmstown, South Africa.[11] Four years later, the first Jesuit missionaries went to evangelize the AmaNdebele. This first encounter between Jesuit missionaries and Africans in late-nineteenth-century precolonial Zimbabwe, like Silveira's, was brief and had little lasting impact on Africans.

The first group of Jesuits, an international group of seven priests and four brothers from Belgium, Britain, Germany, and Italy, left Grahmstown in April 1879 and arrived in Lobengula's territory in September. On September 4, mission superior Fr. Henri Depelchin, Fr. Augustus Law, and Br. de Sadeleer met with Lobengula and received permission to remain in his kingdom temporarily. The other Jesuits remained at Tati, a mining station on the edge of AmaNdebele territory, where they set up an "intermediate station." In February 1880, Fr. Charles Fuchs died of fever at Tati, which "distressed" Depelchin. In May, seven more Jesuits arrived from the Cape, including Austrian Fr. Charles Wehl and six Dutchmen.[12]

Thus reinforced, Depelchin, who was from Belgium, split his forces: Law, de Sadeleer, and Br. Joseph Hedley accompanied an embassy from Lobengula to the kraal of Umzila, a Gaza chief in what is now southern Mozambique. Depelchin, Fr. Anthony Teroerde, Br. Nigg, and three of the Dutch Jesuits headed for Pandamatenga, a trading station on the edge of BuLozi territory, about fifty miles southwest of Mosi wa Tunya, or Victoria Falls. Frederick Courtney Selous advised them not to deal with the BuLozi, and so they decided to make inquiries with Mwemba, a BaTonga chief, who lived about a hundred miles downstream from Mosi wa Tunya.[13]

In August, Law and his party—minus Wehl, who got lost—arrived at Umzila's kraal. Law died of malaria in November 1880, while De Sadeleer and Hedley returned to Bulawayo. Wehl eventually arrived at Sofala on the Indian Ocean coast in May 1881 and died shortly thereafter. In Depelchin's party, Teroerde died in September 1880, and Br. Vervenne almost died as well. Br. Nigg was sent to retrieve Depelchin and Vervenne from Pandamatenga.[14]

At the beginning of 1881, the superior general assigned fifty-nine men to the Zambezi Mission. In June, Depelchin decided to try to enter BuLozi territory and spoke with Lewanika. Shortly thereafter, the Belgian returned to Mwemba. In February 1882, the superior at Tati was thrown from a horse and killed. Depelchin replaced him with Englishman Peter Prestage. One of the newly assigned men drowned en route from the Cape. The remaining men were distributed between Bulawayo, Pandamatenga, and Tati.[15]

In March 1883, Fr. Francis Berhegge, one of the Dutch Jesuits who arrived in 1880, and two brothers left Pandamatenga to begin the mission among the BuLozi. Again one brother drowned en route, and the other two members of the party, after being held captive for several weeks by Lewanika, returned in August. In April of the same year, Depelchin sent two priests along with Nigg and Vervenne to Mwemba's kraal, but they had to retreat due to malarial fevers. On December 3, 1883, Alfred Weld stepped down as general assistant and had himself appointed mission superior, replacing Depelchin.[16]

In September 1884, Prestage transferred from Tati to Bulawayo. By December, Lobengula gave him permission to open a school at Empandeni, which was quite distant from Bulawayo, on the fringes of the Kalahari Desert. In 1885, two more priests died, one at Pandamatenga and the other at Bulawayo. Weld recalled the Jesuits in AmaNdebele territory back to South Africa in March 1886, allegedly as the mission "was to be given up."[17]

In October, Weld allowed Prestage to return to Empandeni, and in 1887, Weld sent Frs. Henry Booms and Andrew Hartmann. Prestage opened a school in December 1887. Although forty-three children attended the first day, attendance varied widely, ranging from four to 161. By October 1888, however, Booms wrote of the "discouraging situation" in which attendance was low and very erratic.[18] In November 1889, Prestage withdrew from Empandeni and returned to the Cape due the escalating tensions surrounding the controversial Rudd concession, a mining treaty negotiated with Lobengula by Charles Rudd on behalf of Cecil Rhodes, who used it as a pretext to invade and occupy VaShona territory in 1890.[19]

By 1889, when the mission was temporarily abandoned, the Jesuits had only received four converts to Christianity, none of whom were AmaNdebele. While scholars agree that the mission was a failure, they disagree over the reasons why the Jesuits failed. Bhebe argued that "Ndebeleland [sic] was ruled by a government that was permeated through and through by a powerful traditional religion which set its face against the evangelisation of its adherents."[20] Similarly, Dachs and Rea argued that "traditional religion" was the primary obstacle to the Jesuits' success.[21] Medical doctor and anthropologist Michael Gelfand, however, believed that malaria "more than anything else contributed to the downfall of [the Jesuits'] mission."[22] Although Gelfand noted competition between Catholic and Protestant missionaries as a contributing factor and refers to the Jesuits' "mistakes in judgment,"[23] none of these scholars account for Lobengula's political acumen or address the issue of the Jesuits' incompetence as the ultimate causes of their failure. Gelfand noted the Jesuits' inadequate medical preparations for their work: eight of twenty-two died between 1879 and 1883. Despite extreme illness, however, the Jesuits continued searching fertile mission fields. They tried to cover too large a territory. The Mission of the Upper Zambezi included territory in the present states of Zimbabwe, Zambia, the Democratic Republic of Congo, Mozambique, and Malawi. Thus, as first mission superior, Henri Depelchin spread his men too thinly with little apparent strategy.

Lobengula used his experience with Protestant missionaries and European traders to develop an effective strategy that severely limited the efficacy of the Jesuits' efforts. First, he kept the Jesuits guessing about whether or not he would allow them to remain in his territory. There are frequent references in the Jesuits' correspondence that Lobengula would only allow them to stay temporarily, or that they could stay in his territory but would not be allowed to preach or teach. He frequently told the Jesuits that he "had had Protestant missionaries for several years and they had not converted one. His people didn't want to learn."[24] It was not until 1886 that Peter Prestage obtained permission to establish a "permanent" settlement and open a school at Empandeni.

Second, Lobengula kept the Jesuits at significant physical distances from the important centers of his territory. The Jesuits established mission stations at Tati, Pandematenga, and Empandeni. Tati was a trading station some three hundred miles from Bulawayo. Pandamatenga was just below Victoria Falls and about two hundred and fifty miles from Bulawayo. Empandeni was on the fringes of the Kalahari Desert, suffering from chronic drought and sandy soil, and fifty miles away from Bulawayo. Although they had a station near Bulawayo, the Jesuits were allowed to settle only in an area about a half-mile away from Lobengula's capital. It appears that Lobengula allowed them to remain so close because he was more interested in obtaining services from the Jesuits, and thus he kept them close at hand. Jesuit correspondence indicates that the missionaries at Bulawayo painted and maintained Lobengula's wagons, repaired several guns for him, painted several ritual dances over which Lobengula presided, and provided medical treatments for him and his people.

Most effectively, AmaNdebele religious leaders frequently accused potential converts to Christianity of being witches, which was a capital offense. This, in turn, placed pressure on families to discourage conversion to Christianity. Consequently, early converts were generally social outcasts and either lived at the missions with the Europeans or went to South Africa.[25] One Jesuit missionary reported that Lobengula's subjects feared "and not without reason, that if they are instructed with the *abafundisi*, as the missioners are called, they will come under suspicion with their inkos (chief, king), and sooner or later be accused and convicted of witchcraft and put to death. In their opinion the chief is their visible god, he can make rain, cause draught, and do many things beyond the power of ordinary mortals."[26] Accordingly, the Jesuits only gained two converts: "a Hottentot" with leprosy, who lived in the Jesuits' kraal, and a "coloured man of the Cape Colony." In other words, they were aliens in Lobengula's state.

The Jesuits' responses to this opposition indicate incompetence on the part of the mission's leadership. There were also questions about the general quality of the men assigned to the mission. Henri Depelchin spread his men too thinly and wore himself down vainly searching for alternative locations for mission stations beyond Lobengula's territory. Alfred Weld, unlike Depelchin, had a vision for the mission but almost destroyed it with financial mismanagement.

Weld, the general assistant for English affairs, frequently complained of Depelchin's management of the mission, saying that he frequently left men alone at distant mission stations in areas where malaria was endemic, failed to send accurate information to Weld (but rather to his former provincial superior), and spent most of his time traveling extensively without results.

An example of Depelchin's poor leadership occurred on the 1880 expedition to Mwemba's kraal: the African guide he hired, who did not speak the Tonga language, was crushed under a wagon, two of the Jesuits died from malaria, and Depelchin himself came down with so severe a case of malaria that the brother who was sent to bring him back to Pandematenga did not recognize him. Yet Depelchin said that he had "proof of the Providence that watches over us" because the African guide had converted and that they had been well received by "Moemba, king of the Batonga." The positive reception included receiving a land grant, even though the land was "too close to the river . . . [and] abounds in serpents."[27] In this one incident, Depelchin chose personnel that were unqualified for the work at hand, lost two missionaries, and accepted land that was unsuitable for the work of the mission, showing that Lobengula was not alone in keeping missionaries at great distances from centers of power.

Weld's assessment of Depelchin further indicates that he was ill qualified to head the Zambezi Mission:

I think [Depelchin] ought to be told to make no more explorations till he has got the houses he has already into a proper state for health and religious life—never again to leave one man alone, and if that place is too unhealthy for the rainy season as seems evident, at once to prepare a house in a healthier situation.

I am certain we must try no more experiments in new places till we have got our three places Gubulawayo Tati and Panda ma Tenga [sic] in proper order. It takes something very clear to make F. Depelchin take in an idea. He is full of zeal and go, and has several excellent qualities for a missionary leader, but has not a practical judgment (at least so I think) and thinks he has. His letters have grand projects for the future, but a great want of practical plans for the present.[28]

Weld, for his part, stepped down as general assistant in 1883, and on December 3 of the same year he was appointed to replace Depelchin as superior of the Zambezi Mission. Weld had a specific plan for the mission that involved establishing Jesuit houses of formation for the Zambezi Mission that were separate from those of other Jesuit provinces. Within Jesuit administrative structures, the world is divided into several geographic provinces, and each province recruits and trains personnel, as well as having responsibility for apostolic work within a given region. Mission territories, or areas that did not have enough human or financial resources to support a province, were either given to a specific province or came under the direct authority of the Jesuit superior general. The Zambezi Mission fell into the latter category and received personnel from other Jesuit provinces. Missionaries in Southern Africa came from England, Belgium, Germany, Italy, Austria, Ireland, France, Quebec, Portugal, Poland, and the Netherlands. Weld was concerned that the men that various provinces sent were not the best available for the mission. He was also concerned that the men in the mission see themselves as belonging to the Zambezi Mission, not as having been loaned by the provinces that sent them. Accordingly, Weld acquired the Dunbrody estate from Trappist monks in the Eastern Cape and established several houses in the Cape colony and the Transvaal. While still general assistant, Weld explained his rationale in several letters. The following is one salient example:

Unless we are allowed to enroll Scholastics, the mission cannot work. On the one hand, Provincials will not give Priests after having supported them all through their studies: but they are much more willing to give Scholastics.

On the other hand, we shall never have unity in the Mission if the men are picked out and sent off after their Priesthood without any previous connection with the Mission. We have now in the higher Zambezi four Dutch men who can speak & write little or nothing but Dutch. They write to their Province but *never* to us, and we know nothing of what they are or what they are doing, and if it were a question of naming a successor to F[r]. Depelchin, I have no idea as to the fitness of one of them. All this is obviated by receiving Scholastics.[29]

Although Weld had a well-intended plan to reorganize and consolidate the mission, his execution of the plan failed miserably. In addition to acquiring Dunbrody Weld opened several houses in the eastern Cape and the Transvaal, including a novitiate in Graaf-Reinet. In addition to incurring the expenses of transporting and supplying as many as ninety-three men, the Mission had to pay extensively to renovate the physical infrastructure at Dunbrody.

Weld intended for Dunbrody to be the heart of the mission, and as such its farm had to be self-sufficient, as well as generate enough income to support the other stations in the Mission. Unfortunately Weld invested significant financial resources in a scheme to raise ostriches and sell their feathers to the designers of women's fashions. Within eighteen months of Weld's having been appointed superior, the Zambezi Mission incurred net debts in excess of £2,600. Consequently, Weld was removed as mission superior in 1887 and reassigned as novice master until his death in 1890.

While it is possible to question the causes of Weld's financial ineptitude, the source of his plan seems fairly certain. From 1607 to 1768, Jesuits established *reducciones*, or independent agricultural cooperatives, among Guarani Indians in Paraguay using methods of evangelization that were sensitive to Guarani culture.[30] Weld apparently had a romanticized notion of the *reducciones* in mind when he established the Zambezi Mission in 1879 and had dreams of recreating a version of them when he became mission superior in 1883. In several letters he specifically referred to the examples of the *reducciones* and the work of Jesuits in North America as models to be imitated. Additionally, in several letters, he referred to establishing "reductions" for Africans in the houses that he opened in South Africa. Unfortunately, his grandiose vision and financial incompetence almost destroyed the mission.

Historians A. J. Dachs and W. F. Rea regarded the failure of the mission to Lewanika and the BuLozi in 1883 as "the end of the hopeful plans of 1878 and 1879" and Weld's appointment as mission superior as the beginning of "quite a new policy" involving "giving up the Zambezi Mission in all but name and concentrating on the Eastern District of the Cape Colony, where conditions were much more promising."[31] While Weld did devote considerable financial and human resources to developing Jesuit apostolic works in the Cape, Dachs and Rea's assessment was shortsighted. Weld kept men in the field while trying to consolidate the mission and improve the quality of relations between mission personnel. He wanted the Mission's own novitiate and scholasticate to develop men who were devoted to the Mission, who were of good quality, whom he knew and whose talents and capacities he could assess, and thus place them where they would best be suited. In short, he exhibited the classical characteristics of a Jesuit superior.

Dachs and Rea further argued that the missionaries were predestined to fail because

> traditional religion so ran through the whole of African life . . . [that] the teaching of a few missionaries could effect [little] change. . . . The whole martial Ndebele way of life led them to reject Christianity, but that in a sense was accidental. Other African peoples were no less resistant. No change was possible until some event broke the solidarity of African society, and that only came about when it came into large-scale contact with the West. With the loss of old certainties, the lessening of tribal and family solidarity, and the greater movement of population, individual choice became possible and missionary effort had some prospect of success. But in Zimbabwe this did not happen before 1890.[32]

While in hindsight this may have been the case, their analysis is problematic because it unquestioningly accepted nineteenth-century rhetoric and ideology concerning the degenerate nature of African societies. They did not retrospectively consider the evangelical model of the Paraguayan *reducciones* or the efforts of Jesuits Francis Xavier and Matteo Ricci, in Japan and China respectively, to adapt the Catholic Church to local cultures. They further dismissed Depelchin's scattering his men, arguing, "It would not have profited him to have concentrated his men in any one of these places."[33] Why not? If he had concentrated his men in one or two places, they could have eventually developed enough of a relationship with local leaders and people to begin evangelizing as Peter Prestage had done at Empandeni from 1887 to 1889. Had this been the case, it would be easier for historians to assess Bhebe's assertions about the relative strength of African religion in the face of encroaching European Christianity.

Establishing and Contesting Colonial Rule

Jesuit priests served as chaplains in 1890 and 1893 when British settlers, sponsored and financed by Cecil Rhodes's British South Africa

Company (BSAC), invaded and conquered both Mashonaland and Matabeleland respectively. The colonizers seized the land and cattle of the local inhabitants and, with permission from the imperial government, established the company-controlled colony of Rhodesia in 1890. Jesuit superiors in South Africa received extensive land grants to establish permanent mission stations in and around Salisbury and Bulawayo.[34]

Hoping to find a "second rand" akin to the large diamond and gold deposits in the former Boer republics in South Africa, BSAC and British settlers set about establishing large-scale mining and commercial farming operations on the lands that they confiscated from the African inhabitants. As in South Africa, the financial success of both systems depended on the exploitation of cheap African migrant labor. Charles van Onselen studied the rise and consolidation of the Rhodesian mining industry and its reliance on forced African labor, and contended that the industry did not grow from expanded production, but rather on the constant diminution of African wages. David Johnson showed that coerced African labor was a constant feature in the Southern Rhodesian economy beyond the 1920s and the Rhodesia Native Labour Bureau (1903–33), continued into the 1940s with the passage of the Compulsory Native Labour Act of 1942, which garnered some 11,400 forced African laborers per year through August 1946, and which was succeeded in the same year by the Rhodesian Native Labour Supply Commission which functioned into 1970s. Robin Palmer analyzed the processes by which European settlers also dispossessed Africans from their lands during the early part of the colonial period. According to Palmer, the 1931 Land Apportionment Act was the culmination of the Rhodesian settlers' efforts to enforce racially segregated land tenure, to deny African agriculturalists the right to purchase land beyond the African reserves, and to prevent competition to settler farmers from African agriculture. Palmer's description of the act as the white Rhodesians' "Magna Carta" was apt, for the patterns it established remained in effect with no significant change—save for Africans losing more territory following the 1965 Rhodesian Unilateral Declaration of Independence, specifically with the passage of the 1968 Land Tenure Act—for the remainder of the colonial period, and they continued to be the dominant patterns of land tenure for two decades until the farm invasions following the March 2000 constitutional referendum. Taken together, these studies highlight processes by which European settlers established and maintained social control over Africans during the colonial period.[35]

In 1896, both the VaShona and the AmaNdebele rebelled against British rule. Indigenous African religious leaders played a significant role in planning, organizing, and coordinating armed resistance against BSAC and its settlers. Before the rebellion, called *chimurenga* in ChiShona, was suppressed in 1897, it drastically impeded or destroyed the missionary efforts of the Christian churches in colonial Zimbabwe. As soon as the AmaNdebele had negotiated a settlement with the company, BSAC in turn forcibly subdued the VaShona, whereupon European and American missionaries began aggressive evangelization campaigns. By the 1970s there were approximately 1.4 million Christians in Zimbabwe, including Catholics, Protestants, and adherents of African independent churches.[36]

The Anglo-Boer war of 1899–1902 reconfigured Southern Africa politically and geographically with the formation of the Union of South Africa in 1910. European settlers in Zimbabwe declined to join the Union of South Africa, opting instead to become the British crown colony of Southern Rhodesia in 1923. Northern Rhodesia (today Zambia), which had a much smaller European population, in contrast was transferred to the British colonial office as a protectorate in 1924. Settlers in Southern Rhodesia convinced the British colonial office to establish the Federation of Rhodesia and Nyasaland (today Malawi) in 1953, which included the colonies of Northern and Southern Rhodesia and Nyasaland. But increasing African demands for participation in government led the colonial office to dissolve the Federation in 1963, and Zambia and Malawi became independent in 1964.[37]

Amid growing African nationalism and increasing pressure from London to allow Africans to participate in the colonial government, Rhodesian settlers, led by Prime Minister Ian Smith's Rhodesian Front Party, sought to maintain white supremacy and unilaterally declared independence in 1965. But Rhodesia became a pariah state denied official recognition by other nations and subject to international economic sanctions. The following year, the Zimbabwe African National Union (ZANU) began the second *chimurenga* against the Rhodesian state at Sinoia (Chinhoyi), northwest of Salisbury (now Harare). War raged until 1979, and on April 18, 1980, Rhodesia became the Republic of Zimbabwe and the African majority chose its government.[38]

Development of the Catholic Church in Southern Rhodesia: Fissures and Fault Lines

The Jesuit superior general removed the Zambezi Mission from his direct oversight as a result of Weld's failed financial ventures and the settling of the border between Portuguese Mozambique and British Southern Rhodesia in 1891. Missions in Portuguese Mozambique became the Mission of the Lower Zambezi and were assigned to the Jesuit Portuguese province. The Jesuit British province received the remaining territory from the Eastern Cape in South Africa to Northern Rhodesia. The British province apparently assumed the debts that Weld incurred, for financial records in Lisbon indicate positive accounting balances with no payments for debt reduction from 1893 until the Portuguese republic expelled the Jesuits in 1911.[39]

Whereas the Zambezi Mission had a culturally heterogeneous, international staff while it was directly under the superior general, German and British Jesuits primarily staffed the mission stations in colonial Zimbabwe.[40] According to Dachs and Rea's model of the "dual mission,"[41] the Germans generally worked among the Africans (predominantly rural) and the British worked among the white settler population, particularly in the towns. Competing nationalist sentiments more than likely created tensions between British and German Jesuits.[42] Further, even in the first decade of the twenty first century, all German Jesuits in Zimbabwe have volunteered to do so, whereas most of the British Jesuits were assigned to the Zambezi Mission.[43]

As early as 1894, the English prefect of the mission complained that the German brothers ought to spend more time speaking English. Successive mission prefects made similar complaints into the 1930s, and they exhorted the German brothers to learn English so as to be able to "give simple orders in English" to the Africans whose industrial training they supervised. There were concerns that Africans were not properly trained in English and were having difficulty finding jobs. Correspondence from Chishawasha indicates that several German Jesuits had recommended staffing the mission station entirely with their countrymen, and that several German Jesuit brothers were "all unhappy" while English Jesuit Charles Bert was superior. The situation evidently continued for several years from 1905 to 1908, and Prefect Apostolic Ignatius Gartlan eventually removed Bert and replaced him with German Francis Richartz, despite serious concerns about the effects the job would have on Richartz's health.[44]

In 1958, Archbishop of Salisbury Francis Markall, S.J., entrusted the northern missions of the archdiocese to the Jesuit East German province.[45] In 1974, the Congregation for the Evangelization of Peoples (formerly Propaganda Fide) erected this territory into the Prefecture Apostolic of Sinoia, with Fr. Helmut Reckter, S.J., as the first prefect.[46] In the early 1970s, Pedro Arrupe, the Jesuit superior general, announced his intention to establish Southern Rhodesia as a separate independent province within the order, so that the north would no longer be dependent on the East German province and the Jesuits in the southern parts of the archdiocese would no longer be dependent on the British province. Arrupe asked the members of both missions how much time they would need to integrate into a single province. The overwhelming response on all sides was to request at least five years. Arrupe gave them eighteen months.[47] The first German provincial was appointed only in 1996. Tensions between German and British Jesuits continued into the twenty-first century.[48]

In 1879, the first Jesuit missionaries left the Eastern Cape to begin the mission to the AmaNdebele. In the same year, German Trappist monks arrived in the Eastern Cape at the request of Bishop Richards to work among the primarily IsiXhosa-speaking African population. In 1896, the Trappists' abbot, Franz Pfanner, requested and received permission from the Jesuit prefect of the Zambezi Mission, Henry Schomberg Kerr, to establish a mission station in Southern Rhodesia. The four monks, one priest and three brothers, who arrived to establish St. Triashill Mission near Old Umtali in the eastern highlands left several weeks later owing to a rebellion of the ChiManyika-speaking VaShona population in the area.[49]

The Trappists returned to Southern Rhodesia in 1902, founding Monte Cassino Mission at Macheke, about sixty miles southeast of Salisbury. In 1908, they reoccupied Triashill. These monks established the first Catholic outschools as evangelization centers, a method that the Jesuits would later adopt while Francis Richartz was superior at Chishawasha. In 1909, as a result of conflicts with their monastic superiors in Rome, the Trappists in South Africa and Southern Rhodesia voted to separate and form a new religious order dedicated to the apostolate of evangelizing Africans. The new religious institute was called the Congregation of Mariannhill Missionaries, named for their headquarters in Natal, South Africa. In 1910, the Sisters of the Precious Blood, whom Pfanner also founded, arrived at Mariannhill missions in Southern Rhodesia to work particularly with African women, and as schoolteachers.[50]

Even Dachs and Rea admitted that Monte Cassino and Triashill were the most successful Catholic mission stations in the colony: by 1917, when the German missionaries were interned in South Africa during World War I, Monte Cassino registered more than one hundred and fifty baptisms at the central station, and had established twelve outschools with more than nine hundred children enrolled, most of whom had received baptism into the church. Triashill, from 1908 to 1914, registered sixteen hundred baptisms and more than a hundred Christian marriages. Of the twelve outstations its missionaries and lay African catechists established, two—St. Barbara and St. Benedict—had become stations in their own right.[51]

The expulsion of the fathers and brothers in 1917 was a major setback to Mariannhill's mission work. They were allowed to return in 1920. Within a year, Fr. Adalbero Fleischer had received permission to open a boarding school at Monte Cassino that enrolled more than two hundred students, and evangelization work resumed at all twelve outstations. Similar progress was made at Triashill: by 1922, it had twelve outstations and more than twenty-seven hundred baptized Catholics.[52]

The Mariannhillers came into conflict with the Jesuits, who supervised the Zambezi Mission, over the translation of the name of God in various publications, the establishment of religious orders for African women, and teaching African boys Latin with a view to preparing them for seminary education. As early as 1924, Fleischer apparently requested that the mission stations in the east be separated from the Zambezi Mission and entrusted to Mariannhill. Robert Brown, the Jesuit prefect, suggested that because the four Mariannhill missions were relatively easily accessible from Salisbury they be given to the Jesuits, and in exchange the Mariannhillers would receive the Jesuit missions among the AmaNdebele at Empandeni, Embakwe, and Bulawayo. Ultimately, Rome sided with the Jesuits, who in 1929 took possession of the Mariannhill mission stations at Monte Cassino, Triashill, St. Barbara, and St. Benedict. The Mariannhillers, for their part, withdrew entirely from Southern Rhodesia and took possession of the former Jesuit missions at Empandeni, Embakwe, and Bulawayo only in 1930. In 1931, Propaganda Fide erected Salisbury as a vicariate apostolic, with Aston Chichester, S.J., as titular bishop. At the same time Matabeleland was established as a separate mission entrusted to Mariannhill. In 1932, Bulawayo became the see for a new prefecture apostolic.[53]

In 1937, Chichester invited members of the Swiss Foreign Mission Society of Bethlehem to staff the mission stations in the southern part of the Salisbury vicariate. By 1939, there were eight Bethlehem priests and four brothers working in Southern Rhodesia. In 1947, Propaganda Fide appointed Fr. Aloysius Haene, SMB, as prefect apostolic of Fort Victoria (Masvingo), which had been entrusted to the Bethlehem missionaries. In 1950, it became a vicariate apostolic, and in 1955, when the hierarchy was established, Haene became the first bishop of Gwelo. Similar developments occurred in the eastern part of the Salisbury vicariate, beginning in 1946 when Irish Carmelites accepted Chichester's invitation. In 1950, Propaganda Fide appointed Fr. Donal Lamont prefect apostolic of Umtali (Mutare), and he became its first bishop in 1957.[54]

In this brief sketch of the establishment of the institutional foundations of the Catholic Church in Southern Rhodesia, it is possible to see the outline of many fault lines come into relief: tensions among Africans: VaShona and AmaNdebele, Christian and "pagan"; tensions among Europeans—British, German, Swiss, and Irish—and between Jesuit and Mariannhill; tensions between Africans and Europeans: converts and missionaries, women and men, settlers and chiefs. Negotiating these fault lines would prove no mean feat, particularly for those

Africans who sought admission into positions of authority and influence within the Catholic Church. As will be seen in the following chapters, small groups of soft-spoken yet resolute groups of African women seeking to become nuns, and boldly vocal young men seeking to become priests, and laypeople seeking better lives for themselves and their fellows within and outside the church would radically realign the fault lines throughout the course of the twentieth century.

2 "The Struggle Approximated to the Heroic": African Catholic Women Becoming Nuns in Colonial Zimbabwe, 1922–1965

> *The Magistrate remarked that if she wished to become a Sister she had a great deal to learn. My own thought just now after the talk I have had with her is that the Chief Native Commissioner might also marvel at the stuff out of which a Sister may be made!*
>
> Francis Markall, S.J.

In August 1965, the community of the Little Children of our Blessed Lady (or LCBL Sisters) at Hwedza asked Sister Rocha Mushonga to accompany Sister Ancilla, their delegate to the congregation's first general chapter, as a secretary. "That's how I got trapped," Mushonga recalled. During the vote for the first mother general, she was asked to count the ballots with Sister Consolata. She recalled,

To my surprise I saw that they were writing my name! I complained to [Archbishop Markall], and he told me that "the Sisters are free to vote for whom they want." I was very upset. We had a [run-off] with another sister, and [on the second ballot] twice the number had my name! "I am not a delegate," I told them. They said, "We know that." The Dominican Mother General said, "We just stay away and listen to the votes."

As the youngest person at the chapter, Mother Rocha thought to herself, "I can't argue with these people." It was then that Archbishop Markall told her, "We cannot fight with the will of God. You can refuse, but I would not advise it." "There was no way out!" she recalled thinking.

Thus began the indigenization of the LCBL Sisters' leadership. Founded in 1932 as the first diocesan congregation of African women in Southern Rhodesia, the LCBLs were the third order of African nuns that European missionaries established, and placed under the supervision of German Dominican Sisters. Recapturing the history of the founding of religious communities for African women in the Catholic Church in colonial Zimbabwe is a useful way to analyze the changing relationships between Africans—both men and women— and Europeans, including colonial administrators and Catholic missionaries, during the early decades of the twentieth century. It is also a powerful means to examine the limitations that both African and Western cultures placed upon African women, and their options for social mobility.

In an unpublished essay, Terence Ranger stated that women in colonial Zimbabwe were more the subject of political processes rather than participants in them, and that as subjects they had only "informal means of 'political' action" available to them, one of which was "by seeking new patrons" and becoming Catholic nuns.[1] Unfortunately, with regard to the issue of African women becoming nuns, Ranger's essay focused entirely on events at Triashill Mission predominantly in the 1920s, and only treated the founding of one of two congregations begun by Mariannhill missionaries in the Makoni District of Southern Rhodesia.

Elizabeth Schmidt and Diana Jeater have briefly addressed the issue of African women defying early-twentieth-century VaShona cultural norms to become nuns and showed that both African and Western cultures significantly circumscribed African women's social roles.[2] Neither, however, addressed the broader implications of that particular choice for African women, VaShona culture, or the relations between the Rhodesian colonial administration and the Catholic Church. Although women choosing to become nuns may have continued as subjects of patriarchy, first African and then Western, their actions in declaring and then acting on their desire to become nuns led to protracted debates between African men, the colonial administration, and the Catholic Church on the status and rights of women in colonial VaShona and Rhodesian societies. Women became sites of struggle over who could control them, but more importantly, their actions began contests to determine whether they themselves had a right to choose the form of patronage to which they were subjected, and culminated in the colonial administration ruling that African women twenty-one years or older had that right. Further, experiences of African women becoming nuns paralleled those of women in Europe, North America, and Latin America, showing their struggles as more common than exceptional in the Catholic Church.

Beginning in 1922, Mariannhill missionaries from South Africa established two religious institutes for African women in colonial Zimbabwe. Although the Jesuit superiors of the Zambezi Mission strongly disliked these institutes, several superiors of local mission stations sent women as candidates. Conflicts developed between the church and the practitioners of VaShona culture over the question of whether African women had the right to enter convents. African men of the time, with the support of British colonial authorities, held that women were perpetually dependent on their fathers or guardians until they were married, and they further claimed that the church interfered with African culture by denying the men their right to receive *lobola*, or bride price. The issue of African nuns also caused significant tensions in the otherwise cordial relationship between the Catholic Church and the Southern Rhodesian colonial administration. The Catholic Church under Aston Chichester's leadership as the first vicar apostolic and archbishop of Salisbury provided African women in colonial Zimbabwe with another option to marriage, yet in doing so it explicitly and intentionally subverted a significant facet of the African culture of the early and mid–twentieth century.

African Women at Mariannhill Missions

As early as 1912, Mariannhill missionaries planned to start a religious congregation for African women when five women had asked to become nuns. The First World War, however, delayed the plans because the German Mariannhillers were interned in South Africa and were not allowed to return to Southern Rhodesia until 1920.[3] In 1922 Mariannhillers and Sisters of the Precious Blood began receiving African women as candidates for religious life into a congregation called the

Daughters of St. Francis of Assisi at Monte Cassino Mission in Southern Rhodesia and at Mariannhill in Natal, South Africa.[4] In an apparent effort to protect the candidates from the early-twentieth-century African belief and practice that an African woman was perpetually dependent on her father, guardian, or husband, as well as to protect the church from having to pay the father or guardian *lobola*, mission superiors had the fathers and guardians of female religious candidates sign declarations before colonial district commissioners that renounced all rights and claims to *lobola* payments for their daughters from the church.[5] At this time, the Precious Blood Sisters apparently asked for consent from both a woman's father and brothers, indicating awareness of contemporary African cultural practice.[6]

By this time, however, the Native Department of the Southern Rhodesian colonial administration had come to support strongly African men in their efforts to maintain women as perpetual dependents. Previously, the colonial government had been at odds with African men, trying to free African women from being "pledged" in marriage to older men while they were still children.[7] Accordingly, in 1922, the Native Commissioner of Rusape apparently told the fathers of two candidates who gave their consent for their daughters to become nuns that the women "have to marry and with that were both told to leave the office." According to Ranger, "the determination of some girls to become nuns opened up the whole question of the legal status of women."[8] This caused Francis Johanny, the Jesuit Pro-Prefect Apostolic of the Zambezi Mission, to seek the legal opinion of Charles Coghlan whether an African woman had the right "to lead a single life" and become a nun.[9]

Coghlan opined that a parent or guardian (either European or African) "cannot abrogate his functions as a guardian and no agreement ... can affect his rights of guardianship over his minor wards."[10] Thus, the declarations that missionaries obtained had no "value in law" and could not "be used against the father or guardian, if afterwards he changes his mind and claims compensation in cattle or money." According to Coghlan, the legal precedent established first in the Cape Colony and later in Rhodesia held that in civil cases between natives "the Courts of this Territory are to be guided by native law so far as that law is not repugnant to natural justice or morality . . . [and] that in the case of both Europeans and native minors a Court has a discretion . . . of refusing to allow an unfit guardian to obtain possession of the person of his ward . . . but this discretion would not be exercised merely because the guardian happened to be a pagan, and the ward was a Christian even if there had been a prior agreement entered into by the guardian."[11]

Coghlan wrote, however, that once a woman reached the age of twenty-one (that is, the age of majority in English common law) "she becomes *sui generis* and is a free agent released in law from parental control or guardianship, natural or otherwise, and that in this respect the status of a native girl differs in no way from a European girl." Although he believed it "advisable" to obtain parental consent for the woman to enter the convent, such consent was not "necessary."

Citing a 1915 legal case from the Transvaal in South Africa, Coghlan argued that the perpetual minority of African women was "repugnant to natural justice and morality" because it was "contrary to civilization," and that the principle applied equally "to a widow [and] to a spinster as well." Coghlan concluded, "an unmarried native woman of twentyone [sic] years of age is free to do as she pleases and is not subject to the control of parents, guardians, Native Commissioners, or any one else and that she is as much at liberty to choose her own vocation as is a European woman, who has arrived at the age of majority."[12]

Despite Coghlan's opinion that parental and guardian declarations held no legal value, church superiors continued to collect them for sister candidates, and frequently did not include the woman's age or date of birth.[13] They did, however, note the significance of women's attaining legal majority at twenty-one and frequently required that women be at least twenty-one before admitting them as candidates.[14]

In 1923, Bishop Adalbero Fleischer of Mariannhill established a second religious community, the Children of the Most Holy Trinity, for African women at Triashill Mission in the eastern highlands of Southern Rhodesia.[15] According to A. J. Dachs and W. F. Rea, "the Trinity Sisters" were "above all . . . mission helpers, not members of a canonical congregation, although they nonetheless gave valuable service to the [Triashill] mission."[16] They based this claim on the fact that the sisters "for three years worked as candidates, for another three years as postulants and then annually took private vows to the Church." The congregation's constitutions, however, provided that upon the completion of the second three-year probation the sisters received "definite admission [to the community] and the full habit." These constitutions received formal ecclesiastical approbation from Robert E. Brown, Prefect Apostolic of the Zambezi Mission, on September 14, 1926.[17] Dachs and Rea ignored religious congregations for European women—such as the Daughters of Charity of St. Vincent de Paul—whose members profess silent, private vows of religion (that is, poverty, chastity, and obedience) annually. Vincent de Paul and Louise de Marillac founded the Daughters of Charity of St. Vincent de Paul in France in 1633. Because they were one of the first noncloistered women's congregations, they were not permitted to profess perpetual vows and were required to profess annual vows, yet they are still considered a canonical religious institute of women.[18]

Rea, a Rhodesian Jesuit of English descent, brought his appreciation of Rhodesian and Jesuit perspectives to *The Catholic Church and Zimbabwe*, but in some cases did so to the neglect of important contending perspectives. This is certainly the case with the analysis of the formation of African religious women. Dachs and Rea focused on the foundation and development of the LCBL Sisters by Aston Chichester, who was also a Jesuit, but in doing so paid too little attention to the Daughters of St. Francis and the Children of the Holy Trinity, both of which were established by German Mariannhill and Precious Blood missionaries.

The Jesuits with few exceptions were unenthusiastic about the Mariannhillers' work with the Daughters of St. Francis and the Children of the Holy Trinity. Priests at Chishawasha disparaged the possibilities and potential of African women to become nuns: "The education of our girls here is a signal failure. Very few of the girls of our school go to the Sacraments."[19] Although Robert Brown gave official ecclesiastical approbation to the Children of the Holy Trinity, he expressed personal dislike for the name of the Daughters of St. Francis of Assisi, "for what do they know about him or what had he to do with Africa? If it were

St. Francis Xavier or St. Peter Claver [both Jesuits] it would be another thing."[20]

In 1926, Jesuit missionaries at Chishawasha Mission, with the approval of the recently appointed apostolic delegate to South Africa, tried to avoid sending African candidates to either of the orders that the Mariannhillers established by seeking permission from Rome to establish a novitiate for what appears to have been an order of their own for African women: "[The Apostolic Delegate] told the [Dominican] Sisters that these girls should not go to *Macheke* [Monte Cassino Mission], but stay here, and . . . it will be something new, independent of the Mariannhill Congregation."[21] Emil Schmitz, S.J., wrote further, "In order to attract more girls the Delegate told the [Dominican] Sisters to give those girls a special dress in August, but this is quite a private business, they are not yet postulants in any official way."[22] Although five women received dresses on August 4, 1926, and they were called "postulants" there are no records extant in the Jesuit archives explaining what happened to these women, for example, whether they eventually entered one of the Mariannhill orders or the LCBL Sisters when Aston Chichester organized them in 1932.[23] Dachs and Rea discussed these women within the context of existing religious orders (namely, the Dominicans and Precious Blood Sisters) accepting African candidates, some of whom were then not admitted to vows "for as long as ten years."[24] Given Schmitz's description of their reception of habits, one cannot help but wonder how serious the Jesuits at Chishawasha were about establishing "a canonical congregation" for African women in Southern Rhodesia. What is clear, however, is that the Jesuits reacted to the efforts of the Mariannhillers and Precious Blood Sisters to erect women's religious institutes, which themselves were a response to African women expressing the desire for such communities.

Despite the existence of Chishawasha's private, unofficial religious community for African women, superiors at Jesuit mission stations continued sending candidates to the congregations at the Mariannhill mission stations. Less than a year after Chishawasha's "postulants" received their habits, the Daughters of St. Francis at Monte Cassino Mission received three women from the Jesuit mission at Kutama (about fifty-five miles west of Salisbury). At the time, Francis Johanny noted that receiving sealed declarations from NC Sinoia declaring the women "free from lobola, etc." was "an official breach into native custom worth noting." As late as February 1932, an African woman from St. Benedict's Mission in the eastern highlands—by then a Jesuit mission—chose to enter the Daughters of St. Francis.[25]

The Founding of the LCBLs

The question of whether an African woman could legally enter the convent continually vexed church leaders in Southern Rhodesia. Around the time Aston Chichester was appointed Vicar Apostolic of Salisbury, the Jesuits referred the matter to the office of the Chief Native Commissioner (CNC) for a ruling. Because "an important question of policy" was involved, the CNC "did not feel justified in deciding on [his] own initiative . . . [and] referred the matter to the [Southern Rhodesian] cabinet.[26] The ministers apparently found the question "a knotty problem," since they never gave the CNC a reply. He did, however, suggest that the recently appointed Chichester "take up the matter direct with the Minister of Native Affairs."[27]

Although there is no evidence that Chichester took the matter to the Minister of Native Affairs, there is evidence that he continued to correspond with the Chief Native Commissioner in Salisbury. In a letter dated November 12, 1931, the CNC stated that the matter of parental opposition to women entering the convent had received "the serious consideration of the government for some time," and that, contrary to the opinion of Charles Coghlan,

the Government is advised that the status of Native women is governed by Native Law and Custom, and that, therefore, unmarried Native women remain under the guardianship of their guardian by Native Law. It follows that the entry of Native women into a sisterhood must be a purely voluntary act, undertaken with the consent of the woman's guardian. . . . [The church] should go slowly in this matter, and look to the future for expansion, when it may be anticipated that complete Native families will have embraced the Roman Catholic Faith, and will be prepared to freely surrender [sic] their daughters to the service of the Church. Any other course will merely cause dissention [sic] in the families concerned, which is bound to be reflected in tribal irritation and unrest.[28]

Chichester expressed concern at the CNC's "very wide and general ruling," and somewhat defiantly stated that "if the effect of that ruling is that it is practicable under the laws of this Colony for a native parent or guardian to insist that a native women [sic] who has attained her majority and who has been brought up as a Christian in a Christian Institution can be compelled against her wish to leave such an institution and return to a pagan kraal under such guardianship, it must not be assumed that I acquiesce in regarding such legislation as in conformity with Christian morals or natural equity."[29]

He showed a willingness, however, not "to raise any general question" if he could "be assured of the support of the Government and of the good offices of your Department in the actual cases which arise." Although there were "a certain number" of African women who were at least twenty-one years old, "who [had] been trained for adequate periods, and . . . after mature consideration [were] desirous of entering Sisterhoods," Chichester was "not prepared to administer vows, even for limited periods, until I am assured that these individual women cannot, under the laws of the Colony, be compelled to leave the Sisterhood and revert to native life under their parent or guardian."[30]

Chichester's letter illustrates two significant facets of his tenure as vicar apostolic and archbishop. First, it shows his willingness to cooperate with Rhodesian colonial authorities regarding its policies for Africans. More important, it shows the ambiguity in his willingness to support and protect African women who wanted to become nuns.

Chichester's zeal to establish a religious institute for African women directly affronted contemporary VaShona cultural practice that held women as legally perpetual minors, which the colonial administration supported. Although the bishop apparently held African cultures in the same low esteem that his contemporary Europeans regarded it, he felt "admiration" for these women considering that "acquaintance" with VaShona culture [reveals] the ordinary accepted status of the Mashona girl [sic] and that whole, vast, and complex custom and superstition which militates against anything indicative of individual choice and acts as a most powerful deterrent against any personal initiative away from the accepted and recognised. Yet into this uncongenial atmosphere has come not only Christianity, but, as its logical development too, the desire of some for a higher life. . . . [Although] the giving up "of all" by the [MuShona woman] may not appear great when assessed by this world's evaluation but it is much, very much when it is realised how opposed the call to the religious life is to every tradition, social and religious of the people. . . . Few of [the women who became nuns] have entered the noviceship without a hard struggle and, in many a case, the struggle approximated to the heroic.[31]

Because Chichester, like Coghlan, equated "natural justice" and British "civilization," he was willing to fight for an African woman's individual right to become a nun against the wishes of her parents, but consequently also believed it necessary to make their "probation a long one for the noviceship is preceded by three years as a candidate and one year as postulants. Only then does the noviceship commence when at its completion at the end of two years, [the women] are admitted to vows. Vows are taken for one year and on its termination each sister has to apply for permission to renew them. After several years of yearly renewals they are admitted to triennial vows."[32]

Chichester further believed it unwise to try to "Europeanize" the sisters, as "the religious life is built on all that is best in their own lives," and that "[the] simplicity of their lives, in externals, will always keep them as one of their own."[33] Chichester's claim seems highly suspect, given that the novitiate was conducted in English and Latin, and all that was "best in their own lives" apparently entailed domestic work.[34]

Shortly after his appointment as vicar apostolic, Chichester consulted Adalbero Fleischer, the vicar apostolic of Mariannhill in South Africa and founder of the Daughters of St. Francis and the Children of the Holy Trinity, about establishing a novitiate for the Daughters of St. Francis in the Salisbury vicariate, and later sent the request to the Sacred Congregation for Propagating the Faith (or Propaganda Fide) in

Rome.[35] Cardinal van Rossum, the Prefect of Propaganda Fide, replied, however, that rather than opening a novitiate Chichester should found a diocesan congregation for African women for the Salisbury vicariate, using Fleischer's constitutions as models.[36] Chichester, accordingly, sent the appropriate request and received approval to begin a formal postulancy.[37] Wasting no time, he then admitted four women at Chishawasha who had "been there for ages—one, I believe, 13 years," as postulants on June 3, 1932, even though a congregation as such did not yet exist.[38]

On December 8, 1932, nineteen women began their novitiate at Makumbi Mission, approximately twenty-five miles north of Salisbury, of whom eighteen professed first vows on December 8, 1934.[39] Of those nineteen novices, nine were from the areas around Mutare in the eastern highlands of colonial Zimbabwe. At least one of them—Sister Bernadette Garatsa—was in part inspired to become a nun by the sister of her paternal grandmother who was a Daughter of St. Francis, Sister Julia.[40] Sister Bernadette recalled meeting a *bonga*[41] who was also an Anglican and asking her whether she would "have to leave if she made a mistake," to which the bonga replied in the affirmative. Later the same day, she met Sr. Julia and asked the same question, to which she responded in the negative. Bernadette "saw the link between the two and the possibility." She "confirmed in her heart not to be like the bonga but like Sister [Julia]."

Bernadette had attended the school at St. Barbara's Mission in Inyanga, and when her father objected to her becoming a nun, she ran away to the mission. When her father came for her she told the priest to tell him to "take his daughter," though she knew in her heart she wanted to be a sister. So the priest said, "Take your daughter," but she refused to go. Eventually, she went home to be reconciled with her father, and was then received as a candidate for the Daughters of St. Francis. She was prepared to enter their novitiate in South Africa when Bishops Chichester and Fleischer "decided to send her [and the other candidates from Manyika] to the LCBLs."

When the nine women arrived at the train station in Salisbury, Chichester himself was there to meet them, and he took them to the Dominican convent by the Cathedral of the Sacred Heart in town. He also accompanied them to Makumbi Mission, where the novitiate was to be located. When they arrived there was no house, so the African novices and the German Dominicans not only had to build their own houses but also had to make the bricks with which to build. Additionally, the novices had to clear their fields for planting and tend the crops, grind their own corn meal, tend their cattle and other animals, milk the cows, and do their own and the Jesuits' laundry (the Dominicans did their own). "All that was done at home [by women], they continued to do in the convent."[42]

Fr. John Apel, the superior of Makumbi Mission, and other Jesuits gave spiritual and doctrinal instructions to the novices. They prayed the small office from breviaries in Latin. Although some of the novices did not read, they learned the Latin prayers and songs.[43] Sr. Bernadette recalled liking the office because of the "strange language." Their spiritual formation also included Bible reading, litanies, and the rosary.

When asked whether other women had encountered similar family resistance, Sister Bernadette replied that they did not talk about it or whether they also had to run away. She also noted that due to family opposition, the government—in an effort to support the families—made a "ruling" forbidding them to receive veils, "but the missionaries gave them veils" anyway.[44]

The vows that the first LCBL sisters professed were temporary vows of religion that they had to renew annually. Beginning in 1940, Chichester allowed some of the sisters to renew their vows once every three years. It was not until after the final approbation of the congregation's constitutions in 1959 that sisters began to be admitted to final vows.[45]

After the novitiate, the sisters continued to perform domestic duties at the missions to which they were assigned. But they also served as catechists and teachers,[46] and it was in these capacities that the LCBL Sisters began to have a significant influence on the development of the Catholic Church in colonial Zimbabwe, most notably on the early education of many of the first Africans who would enter the seminary and become the first African priests.

Chichester entrusted the fledgling congregation's governance to the Dominicans. According to Chichester, the LCBLs' organization was "a muddle," being "neither independent nor amalgamated—yet is governed by the European Sisterhood."[47] The Dominican mother general served as the superior of the LCBLs, the novice mistress was also a Dominican, as was the person in charge of the African women's spiritual formation at respective mission stations.[48] Chichester noted that Propaganda Fide advised him that he "must change this and have the government under natives. They added, however, that I could then ask for a dispensation—stating that the natives were incapable of governing themselves and go on as at present."[49] Although the dispensation was to be temporary, it could "on application be renewed till long after [Chichester] was dead and had no further responsibility."[50] Not surprisingly, Chichester retired as Archbishop of Salisbury in 1956 and died in 1962. The LCBL Sisters were not allowed to elect their own superior until 1965. The constitutions of the congregation, which Chichester wrote, received praise for the "exactness" with which they followed the requirements of the 1917 Code of Canon Law; however, one commentator noted that they were "all code without any peculiar indication of a special spirit to indicate the sisterhood . . . a framework for any religious body without any of the individualizing notes that a special order should display."[51] With relatively few changes, the LCBLs constitutions received formal and definitive approbation from Propaganda Fide in 1959.[52]

Shortly after the first eighteen women professed their first vows, they apparently sent a letter to Pope Pius XI, as they received a letter from Cardinal Eugenio Pacelli, the future Pope Pius XII, conveying Pius XI's "constant prayer" that they "may grow up to be good and worthy Catholics and that you may by your teaching and example bring all the people of your country into the great Christian family of which he is the common Father."[53] It is unclear whether they took the initiative to write to Pius XI or if Chichester prompted them.

It is clear, however, that the first LCBL sisters were not afraid to bring Chichester their concerns about what they perceived to be shortcomings in their on-going formation, their basic needs, and their status. Around the year 1937, they wrote a letter to Chichester asking for permission to wear a scapular dedicated to Mary, to cook their own meals for themselves, to have "a *small garden* at each mission of vegetables," and to have "a European sister as a mother who cares for Native Sisters only."[54] The "most important" questions, however, without answers to which they felt themselves to be "good for nothing" were: "May we ask if we may be taught all the work properly and to work independently without somebody looking after us? What [initials] may we write behind our names?"[55] Shortly thereafter, the sisters began writing the initials "LCBL" in their correspondence.

Chichester was very much a man of his time, and he believed in the incapacity of African religious women to govern themselves. Yet he also fought with the colonial administration for their right to enter the convent, and he was very solicitous for their general welfare once they began the formation process as candidates. Although specific cases in which Chichester supported African women in becoming nuns against the wishes of their parents and the colonial administration follow below, it is significant to note here that he apparently appealed to individuals in the League of Nations and the Vatican in an effort to pressure the Rhodesian colonial government to change its policies regarding women's right to become nuns.[56] Such entreaties, however, met with no success.

Chichester, however, was generally much more successful at providing for the women once they were able to enter candidacy and as they gradually incorporated into the congregation. While he and the Dominican mother general frequently paid for clothing and blankets for the sisters, he imposed a levy which came to be known as the Makumbi tax on all the missions in the Salisbury vicariate to raise sufficient funds to support the sisters. Additionally, superiors of mission stations had to pay for the transport of sisters assigned to their missions or reassigned elsewhere, as well as provide "the ordinary necessaries and comforts for the native sisters," including a standard ration of food that consisted of fourteen pounds of cornmeal, one pound of fresh meat or half a pound of biltong (dried cured and spiced meat), one to two pints of sour milk, and three pounds of ground nuts per person per week and green vegetables daily.[57] Chichester was adamant that the sisters "should have sufficient time for their spiritual life."[58] The LCBL sisters who knew Chichester remember him as visiting them regularly and frequently asking if they were receiving enough food.[59]

Evidently there were instances when the sisters did not. Sister Catherine Mazorodze recalled that one of the "tough" things about the novitiate was that the novices "sometimes didn't have enough food or soap."[60] It is unclear whether or what kind of action Chichester took to rectify the situation in such instances.

The establishment of the LCBL Sisters was a product of its time: the external government in the hands of the predominantly German Dominicans recommended by the Vatican was clearly a reflection of the general European colonial belief in the incapacity of Africans to govern themselves or know their own interests. The Dominican and Precious Blood Sisters stopped receiving African candidates for their congregations once the LCBL Sisters began receiving candidates. Although there is no documentary evidence, there is an oral tradition among the Dominicans in Harare that Chichester asked them to stop receiving African candidates,[61] and it is unclear why he would have made this request. Two possibilities immediately present themselves. First, as the bishop of a mission territory, Chichester would have seen the need for the people of his vicariate to develop indigenous vocations to the clergy and religious life in order for the church in Rhodesia to progress to the point of establishing the regular hierarchy. Establishing a diocesan congregation of African religious, as recommended by Pope Pius XI in his 1926 encyclical letter *Rerum Ecclesiae*, would encourage local vocations and reduce the need for religious to come to Southern Rhodesia as missionaries from Europe, Canada, or the United States. Or, Chichester, being aware of—and possibly sharing—the racial attitudes of British Rhodesian settlers, chose to establish a diocesan congregation for Africans in order to maintain a significant degree of racial segregation within the church in Southern Rhodesia.[62]

Curiously, the LCBLs broke with the contemporary Rhodesian racial policy and accepted "Coloured," or mixed-race, women as well. By 1941, the community had grown to fifty-four sisters who had professed annual vows and twenty-one novices,[63] and by 1943 there were at least two Coloured sisters among the professed members of the congregation, one of whom wrote to Chichester that they could not help feeling that "we two Coloured Sisters are not among our own," and suggested that Chichester start an order for Coloured women.⁶⁴ Apparently, Chichester did not take any action on the Coloured sister's plea.

Lobola and Family Opposition to Women Becoming Nuns

It is impossible to know Chichester's motives for establishing the LCBL Sisters as a diocesan congregation, but he was clearly ambivalent in supporting individual African women in their active choices to become nuns amidst heavy opposition—in some cases emotionally manipulative, in others physically violent, and in still others, both—from their families.

The question of *lobola* lay at the heart of the disputes over these women between the church and African parents. In late-nineteenth- and early-twentieth-century VaShona culture, marriage was the joining of two families, not merely the union of two individuals. During this period there was no single wedding ritual that signaled the beginning of a marriage. Rather, marriage was a process of negotiation between the families, and a man and woman were considered married once the first part of the bride price was paid to the woman's family.⁶⁵ VaShona families of this period would have been loath to lose the *lobola* that they received in their daughter's marriage as they frequently used it to pay for the wives of their sons.⁶⁶

During the 1920s, some Catholic missionaries apparently paid *lobola* for the candidates whose parents or guardians objected to their entering a religious congregation.⁶⁷ A 1929 guardian's declaration reads:

I, Mashumba Chigara, RN 12074 Mtoko, hereby swear and agree that my sister [Katarina] Masodzi can be sworn as a candidate to become a "Sister." I have been given £16–0-0. In the event that Masodzi withdraws or gets expelled, I promise to return all the money received.⁶⁸

Alternatively, women had to work to earn the money to pay *lobola* to their fathers or guardians.⁶⁹ Jerome O'Hea, the Jesuit superior of Kutama Mission during the 1930s, knew of three cases in which that had happened.⁷⁰ Chichester, however, seems to have taken a position in line with Coghlan's 1923 opinion, which said that once an African woman reached the age of majority at twenty-one she had the right to choose not to marry and to enter a convent, and choosing not to marry implied no obligation to pay *lobola*.

On becoming a candidate, a woman had to conform to the strict regimen of pre–Vatican II religious life, and she was free to leave at any time. Accordingly, Chichester seems to have used this freedom of choice as a means to test a woman's vocation when her parents complained and sought to withdraw her. This frequently left the women exposed to emotional violence.

The Cases of Theresa Marumbeni and Maria Mukoma

In July 1935, Theresa Marumbeni was admitted as an LCBL candidate at Makumbi Mission. John Apel, the mission superior, reported that Theresa's family made "violent protests" and that her father, Chaitezwi, "made representations" to the Native Commissioner's office in Bindura. Apel further stated that Theresa was twenty-two years old and that she "has resisted all entreaties of her parents and brothers, and she is likely to remain firm."⁷¹ When Assistant NC Bindura asked Chichester to "issue instructions" that Theresa's father "be granted facilities to request that Marumbeni may return to him,"⁷² Chichester replied,

> There never has been a difficulty about Chaitezwi seeing Marumbeni. However I am not prepared to force her to leave or even advise it. You know as well, in fact better than I, that the parents and guardians of these girls sometimes treat these girls cruelly and the police are in practice often quite powerless in the matter. Marumbeni must herself settle her affairs with her parent who is free to discuss matters with her at any time or place. The father has always had perfect freedom to see his daughter whenever he desires and make whatever request he chooses of her. She is free to do what she likes.⁷³

In a similar case, Maria, the daughter of Jacobo Mukoma and Kunzeno from Rusape, was admitted as a candidate at Chishawasha Mission in June 1940. D. C. H. Parkhurst, the Native Commissioner in

Salisbury, wrote to Charles Ferguson, the superior at Chishawasha, that Maria's parents "are distressed at the thought of losing her and they wish her to return home with them. Mukoma wishes to retain parental control over his daughter and he states he is opposed to her joining the Sisterhood."[74] Ferguson, however, complained to Parkhurst that Kunzeno, Maria's mother, "has been hanging around the mission ever since Sunday morning and is causing a great deal of annoyance to all concerned. She refuses to leave under any consideration." He further noted that because she was in the later stages of a pregnancy he was "unable to use [the] necessary force" to remove her and requested that Parkhurst send some African messengers "with the necessary powers to have her removed."[75]

Parkhurst sent messengers "to *persuade*" Kunzeno to leave Chishawasha, and said that he had explained to Mukoma that he "believe[d]" that Theresa had "attained her majority" and that she "declines to acknowledge parental and paternal control [which] has considerably upset her parents."[76] He further stated that Mukoma was aware of his right to appeal to the Secretary for Native Affairs. In the next round of correspondence Parkhurst informed Ferguson that Kunzeno intended to kill herself "unless Maria goes home with her," and "urge[d]" him "to compromise and let Maria take her mother home to Rusapi [sic] and to remain with her until after the confinement by which time they will very probably become reconciled. I understand Maria wishes to do this."[77] Ferguson replied that Maria "is very insistent that she should see you personally, so I am sending her to your office. She does not want to go back home." Additionally, he noted that Mukoma "was talking of wanting '*lobola*' for her," and referred Parkhurst to consult with Chichester.[78]

Parkhurst met with Maria and reported that he was "sorry" that

> all my powers of persuasion have been ineffective. She simply will not listen to reason and flatly refuses to go home with her parents for a limited time; nor does she seem concerned regarding the possibility (I would even say probability) of her mother Kunzeno doing away with her self. . . . Maria's selfishness and lack of finer feelings are to be deplored, and I have told her that if Kunzeno does take her own life she will always bear an uneasy, unhappy

conscience. Despite this remark Maria remains as hard and immobile as a sphinx. I beg you to exercise your influence over Maria and to compel her to accompany her parents to Rusapi. . . . I feel sure she would experience no insurmountable difficulties in returning to Chishawasha later.[79]

Following Ferguson's suggestion, Parkhurst wrote to Alfred Burbridge, Chichester's secretary, explaining the case. Parkhurst noted that Maria had attended school at St. Benedict's Mission with her parents' consent, but that when she told her parents that she wanted to become a nun, they refused and lodged a complaint with the Native Commissioner in Salisbury, claiming "that they did not want to lose parental control," and that subsequently she left her home in 1938, "when a minor," against her parents' wishes and went to Chishawasha. Following the interview with Maria, he related to Burbridge that Mukoma and Kunzeno

positively refuse to leave without some satisfaction. . . . The question of dowry has been raised by Mukoma. He argues that if his daughter is to be wedded to the Church he has some claim under Native law before renouncing parental control. I believe he will acquiesce if His Lordship [Chichester] accedes to his claim.[80]

The debate over Maria's fate must have continued over the next two months, although there is no documentary evidence. In August 1940, Parkhurst held another interview with Maria and her parents, which resulted in "no change in the girl's conduct." The NC in Salisbury believed that Mukoma's rights "had to be acknowledged," and more importantly reported that "it has now been decided that Maria should leave the mission and return with her parents to Rusapi and appear before her Native Commissioner who will attempt to bring about a satisfactory relationship between the girl and her parents."[81] He then asked Ferguson to allow Maria to accompany his messenger back to Salisbury.

Ferguson accordingly sent Maria to Parkhurst with his messenger, even though she was "most unwilling to go to Salisbury," on the condition that she see Burbridge first.[82] He also sent two other girls to accompany her and made arrangements for them to stay at the Dominican convent in town, trusting that "if the Authorities force [Maria] to go to Rusapi proper precautions will be taken for the girl's safety."[83]

Following the meeting between Maria, her parents, and the Native Commissioner, Parkhurst, "with a view to persuading [Maria] to return with them to Rusapi," wrote to Chichester that Maria again refused to return home and that he feared Kunzeno would commit suicide.[84] Accordingly, he thought it "advisable to refer the matter to higher quarters," and requested that Maria remain in Salisbury "pending further developments."[85] Parkhurst's appeal resulted in the decision that "it remains with the girl Maria to decide her own future and she is free to return to Chishawasha Mission. This has been explained to her and her parents."[86] Maria returned to Chishawasha the following day. It is unclear whether or not her mother committed suicide.

Maria's case illustrates the degree to which Chichester's *lobola* policy exposed African women candidates for the convent to emotional and psychological manipulation, as well as the degree to which the colonial administration supported African men in the controversies. More importantly, it illustrates the strength of will and character of many of the women who chose to become nuns. The cases of Theresa Marumbeni and Maria Mukoma together demonstrate the significant shift in the church's *lobola* policy: from 1922 to about 1930, by paying *lobola* or having women work to pay it, the church's superiors recognized and respected the VaShona cultural practice to some degree. Chichester's policy, however, was directly and intentionally hostile to VaShona culture, and caused significant tensions between the church and African elders on the one hand and the Southern Rhodesian colonial authorities on the other.

The Case of Catherine Mazorodze

Chichester's *lobola* policy also exposed African women who wanted to become nuns to physical violence. Chichester knew the Native Department's policy of supporting parental control over African women until they were married and became their husbands' wards. His comments to the administrator handling the Theresa Marumbeni case certainly imply that he was aware of the harsh treatment these women received. Although his *lobola* policy may not have caused the violence, it was a contributing factor, as the case of Sister Catherine Mazorodze demonstrates.

According to her baptismal certificate, a document required for admission to a religious institute in the Catholic Church, Catherine Mazorodze was born on April 6, 1935.[87] Sister Catherine, however, stated that she was born in 1938.[88] That the controversy surrounding her entrance occurred in 1955 and 1956, combined with Chichester's policy that once a woman had reached the age of twenty-one she was free of parental control, indicate the probability that on more than one occasion church officials changed birth dates on official documents to facilitate the possibility of an African woman becoming a candidate for religious life.

Both of Catherine's parents were Methodists, and Catherine was baptized as a Methodist at the Wesleyan mission school at Sandringham, near the town of Norton, when she was about six years old. When she completed her lower primary education she asked her parents to send her to the school at St. Paul's Mission in Musami—the mission was run by the Jesuits and the school by the LCBL Sisters—where her mother's younger brother studied. At St. Paul's, Catherine completed her primary education as well as the first two years of secondary school.[89]

In 1954, an influenza epidemic affected many of the students at St. Paul's school. Catherine was baptized as a Catholic *in periculo mortis*.[90] While in the hospital after her baptism, she told one of the Jesuit priests that she "wanted to be like the sisters." He advised her to "get better first." After she left the hospital and returned to school she continued "praying about it." When she went home for school holidays, she told her father. Thinking she wanted to be a nursing sister, he gave his consent. When she was to become a candidate and returned home to ask for his permission, however, he refused and "as a punishment said that he wanted [the] school money back." Catherine spoke with the superior at Musami, who advised her that it would be better for her to teach in order to earn the money to repay her father for the school fees. He arranged a teaching position for her at St. Michael's

Mission school in Mhondoro, where she taught for a year. In December 1955, she took £15 to her father and again asked for permission to become a nun. In the presence of her mother, and elder and younger brothers, Catherine recalled, "My father beat me, and told me never to pronounce anything like that to him again."

After staying at home for several weeks, she asked her father for permission to return to Mhondoro to "collect [her] last wages." Catherine arrived in time to join the other candidates for a three-day retreat and was received as a candidate with the other women, and returned to St. Michael's. When her father came looking for her, Catherine "tried to hide." But the superior of the mission, Fr. Otto, told her that she must talk with him. Upon seeing her in the candidate's habit, Catherine's father "took off the veil and threw it into the dining room, and pulled me away." Fr. Otto told her to go with him, as a way of "trying to see how committed I was."

When they returned home, Catherine was "beaten and beaten." Her father tore her "dresses," although she was able hide her veil among her clothes. She began to look for a chance to run away, but her father or mother was always with her. They forbade her to sing Catholic hymns or to make the sign of the cross. Catherine was "crying in her heart" because she knew she "had to leave." One day, Catherine put on her veil and began to sing Catholic hymns. Her father asked her to stop, "but I didn't stop that day," she said. He beat her again and asked the Methodist minister to pray over her because he thought she was possessed. For the next month, people in her family and neighborhood told her "to forget being Catholic and being a sister." Her father stayed outside her door when she slept. If he thought she "was thinking of being Catholic, he asked me, and if I said 'yes' I was beaten."

While attending a football match, Catherine ran away, "traveling in the dark." She received succor from a white farmer, who took her to the railroad the next day, where she took a train to Salisbury, and eventually made her way to Makumbi, where her aunt, a Catholic, had married a Catholic man and settled. Catherine's aunt took her to the hospital "for treatment for a week," and then took her to the mission and introduced her to Fr. Bevis Collings, the mission superior, and Sr. Mary de Mercedes, O.P., the LCBL's novice mistress. Catherine's uncle spoke with Fr. Collings, who was "very concerned about the situation: my parents didn't know where I was." Collings thus went to the NC Hartley, who reported her location at Makumbi.[91]

It was at this point that Chichester got involved. Writing to S. E. Morris, the Chief Native Commissioner in Salisbury, Chichester explained the case and argued, "The girl is a Catholic and therefore I think it is my duty to claim that now she is over twenty one, she has a right to become a nun without her father's consent. It is, after all, one of the fundamental rights of a British subject, that after the age of twenty one, he or she is at liberty to choose any mode of life they may think themselves fitted for."[92] Chichester "put the case before" Morris, asking for his "advice on the matter." He concluded that Catherine was staying with her uncle, and that "his story is that she went to him for protection."[93] Morris replied that at twenty-one Catherine had "no problem joining the African sisterhood," and that she did not require her father's permission, "however, that view has never been determined in a Court of Law, and I may be wrong." He further opined that it was "not right" for the Native Department to advise Catherine

> one way or the other. If she joins the Sisterhood against her father's wishes, the father has the right to bring an action in the Courts. He may complain to his Native Commissioner in the first instance, in which case the correct reply to him would be that under *our* law, Catherine would be entitled to become a nun without his consent, but that if he wished to do so, and had the necessary funds, he could make an application to the Court, probably ending up in the High Court, to restrain her from carrying out her intention and the Church from contracting with her. We [wouldn't] *advise* him to adopt this course, but it would be our duty to inform him of his rights, and also to warn him that he might lose his case, and, therefore, his money as well.[94]

Morris decided to send the case to the provincial native commissioner "to see if all parties can settle amicably." He added:

> It seems a pity that parents should become estranged from their children through a conflict of laws. . . . I am sure you will agree that it is our duty to look after, not only those who have taken over our Western Civilisation and

its laws, but also those who rely on Native Law and Custom to guide them in their everyday lives.[95]

Morris closed by inviting Chichester to attend the meeting with the provincial native commissioner. Chichester declined to attend the meeting.[96] Accordingly, Morris sent him extracts from the minutes taken by the PNC, which reported that he was

> unable to make any impression on either the parents or the daughter; she intends to go ahead with her plans, and they, in consequence, renounced her although the mother was distressed over the prospect of not being allowed by her husband to see her daughter. . . . The difficulty is over adjustment of marriage considerations paid in respect of Catherine's elder sister who has died and which the father hoped to do when he married the second daughter off. He wanted to know why the Roman Catholic Church should not be called upon to give consideration in marriage for his daughter.[97]

Chichester replied that such a result was "in a kind of way to be expected."[98] He further predicted that "the father will relent fairly soon and things will get better. In other cases this is what happened."

Ultimately, Chichester's prescience was borne out: Catherine was admitted as a postulant upon completing her candidacy and was asked to reconcile with her family. Accompanied by a man from Makumbi, Catherine returned home. Her father refused to receive her in the home, but others in the homestead prevailed upon him and she stayed for three weeks. The relationship between them "wasn't good," but he confessed to her his reason for not wanting her to become a nun. He said "It wasn't the money he wanted. He told me, 'You are my beloved daughter and I didn't want to be separated from you.'" He explained that the family was not familiar with the Catholic Church and its ways but had heard that nuns were not allowed to go home, and that "he didn't want that" with Catherine. Consequently, he and Catherine were able "to work out an understanding."

If members of Sister Bernadette Garatsa's cohort in 1932 were unwilling to talk about parental opposition, by the mid-1950s the situation had changed dramatically. Sister Catherine recalled that other members of her novice class also had "big problems" with their families and were beaten. She described one sister's father as "very violent," and referred to several instances of "parents coming to missions to take [the women] home." Whether a woman withstood family pressure and stayed or not "depended on how you fought for yourself. You were left free to decide. Nobody would make a final decision for you." Sister Catherine, assistant director of postulants at the time of research, further noted that "even now a parent's permission is needed [for a women] to enter, although she is free do so at eighteen or twenty-one. But culturally we want to respect parents and maintain positive family relationships."[99]

The Case of Clara Margwisa

Regardless of whether Chichester may have been able to do more to protect women who wanted to become nuns from parental violence, his willingness to do so was evident in his fight for Clara Margwisa against her father and the Rhodesian government. In this case, Chichester unambiguously subverted the efforts of the Native Department to implement its pro-parental policy by helping a nineteen-year-old girl flee from her father, and then denied any knowledge of her whereabouts until she turned twenty-one.

On October 3, 1949 the provincial native commissioner for Northern Mashonaland wrote to Chichester that Francis Morosi had complained that his daughter Clara, a student at St. Paul's Mission school in Musami, wanted to be a nun and that she had been sent to Monte Cassino Mission. He asked that the bishop allow Clara to return home with her father. Chichester, in writing to the chief native commissioner in Salisbury, explained that Clara was only nineteen years old, and that although her father refused to allow her to become a nun and had induced the native commissioner of Goromonzi district to issue "orders" for her to return home, she was "not being kept by us from fulfilling those orders, but seems quite determined that she will not go back to her father."[100] Additionally, Clara "[wished] now to appeal to

His Excellency the Governor," accordingly Chichester asked the CNC to "kindly give a note forbidding the father to remove her forcibly."[101]

This put the Native Department in "a difficult position," because there was "no evidence that Morosi has ill-treated Clara or in any material way failed in his duty as a parent towards her."[102] The position was not so difficult, however, as to prevent A. G. Yardley, the assistant chief native commissioner from "confirming" that

Morosi has the right to forbid his daughter Clara to remain at a mission station for the purpose of becoming a nun. Clara appears to be nineteen years of age and is definitely a minor. Further, although nothing is being done to retain Clara, and she is free to leave the mission and return to her father if she wishes, I feel this is not enough, and that so long as she is allowed to remain at the mission while her father wishes to take her away, she is being assisted in her disobedience to parental authority.[103]

Yardley further stated that while he understood that Clara wanted to appeal to the governor of Southern Rhodesia, in the meantime the bishop should have told her "to go back to her father."[104]

The same day, Chichester went to Monte Cassino to explain to Clara that he "had bad news for her." Her appeal to the governor of the colony required her native commissioner to make a ruling that was subsequently investigated by the chief native commissioner, whose decision Yardley had communicated. Chichester believed that "there was no chance that the Governor would reverse that decision," and that he "could not keep her at Monte Cassino nor could [he] keep her as a candidate for the Sisters."[105] Clara said that she understood, but asked about the possibility of remaining at Monte Cassino to "deal with her father herself." When Chichester and Francis Markall, a Jesuit priest on the mission staff who would succeed Chichester as archbishop of Salisbury in 1956, explained to Clara that "the Bishop was not free to hold even a white girl under the age of twenty one whose father objected," she said that she "understood that she could not remain a candidate and was very upset."[106] Chichester wrote to Yardley that when she asked "whether she could remain at Monte Cassino as an ordinary girl and fight her own battles . . . I assented [because] I rather had the impression . . . that she had some hope her father would allow her to finish her teacher training course as an ordinary girl."[107]

Shortly thereafter, around February 13, 1950, Clara went missing.[108] Markall, in responding to a letter from Chichester described "the rumour about Clara's whereabouts" as "news" to him, and further stated that he "was not really interested to know" where she was "until she is 21."[109] Apparently Clara had told Markall that she would not go home because "her father would force her to marry." Markall counseled her that "she could protect herself against that in any way she thought fit," and gave her a letter authorizing her to travel as well as "a new blanket and some pocket money [because] I remembered that when [Jesuit] novices leave [the novitiate] in Europe it is usual to provide pocket money. I had left the station before she booked her ticket and do not know where she went."[110]

In addition to abetting Clara's flight, Chichester apparently gave serious consideration to bringing Clara's case before the courts in order to resolve the questions of whether African women were free to remain single, and whether they could become nuns against their parents' wishes. He gave attorney L. M. N. Hodson a copy of Coghlan's 1923 opinion and apparently asked Hodson for a reading of the legal climate. Regarding the question of whether an African woman could "remain single," Hodson cited the 1927 Native Marriages Act, which required "native marriage officers" to inquire "into [a woman's] freedom of consent, and determined that "If a girl may refuse to marry one man, obviously she can go on refusing all offers of marriage."[111] Thus, an African woman had the right to remain single.

Concerning the issue of whether an African woman could become a nun without her parent or guardian's consent, Hodson opined that it was doubtful that an African woman under twenty-one would be allowed to enter a religious community without the consent of her guardian; that, with all due respect to Coghlan, an African guardian "may validly contract" not to receive *lobola* for his daughter or ward if she married, "whether she be under or over the age of 21"; and that an African woman over twenty-one may become a nun without the permission of her "guardian-in-native-customary law."[112] Citing anthropologist Charles Bullock's *The Mashona and the Matabele*, Hodson argued that VaShona marriage customs were experiencing changes:

Lobolo [sic] is no longer a bond between family groups; but it is almost in the nature of the purchase price of sexual rights to a quite willing girl. . . . Decorum between son-in-law and father-in-law in such a relationship is no longer observed; for more often than not most of the lobolo [sic] agreed on is owing—not paid.[113]

He believed that the culture had become "so unsettled" that there was "little but a decaying tissue of custom" to prevent an African woman from deciding to become a nun, and that "there must be some age at which an African female ceases to be a child." Hodson based his opinion on this point on three cases that collectively made "inroads upon strict native custom," which stated that African women were free from the authority of their guardians upon marriage and that they did not revert to that guardianship on the dissolution of a marriage; that "in certain circumstances, a woman may hold property as a *femme sole*"; and that a divorced African woman may be awarded custody of her children in her own right.[114]

In discussing the "the inaccuracy of using a term of art of one legal system to describe a relationship . . . of another system," and given the apparent changes in VaShona culture, Hodson argued that an African parent or guardian could make a valid agreement to forego receipt of *lobola*, and "such an agreement, then, would be one way of releasing a girl [sic] under the age of 21 who wished to become a nun."[115] Although this position was not established in law, Hodson believed that the Southern Rhodesian courts were approaching it in principle, and cited a legal case that established that "a claim for return of lobolo [sic] . . . must not be used as a lever to enforce marriage, notwithstanding that the marriage which the unwilling party would be prepared to contract is one recognised by a religion without any basis in native custom." He then further proposed "a broader principle" that the future possibility of receiving *lobola* for a woman who does not wish to marry anyone "must not be allowed to stand in the way of her entering a religious state, of which there is no counterpart in native custom," and that the negation of this principle would be "repugnant to natural justice an morality."[116]

Regardless of whether Hodson's (and Bullock's) perspective of change in VaShona marriage practices was accurate, the perception of change in the minds of British colonial official and academic circles is significant for its effects on the indigenous African culture. By 1950, Rhodesian colonialists apparently believed that the introduction and imposition of Roman-Dutch law from the Cape Colony upon African culture had significantly altered the marriage process to the point that they could craft and implement policies based on perceived—not necessarily actual—cultural change. Additionally, Hodson and Bullock seem to have been either unaware of or chose not to recognize the role of the Bonga in early twentieth century VaShona culture.

Chichester seems to have adopted a strategy of trying to discredit Francis Morosi as a fit father, thereby releasing Clara from his parental authority. As early as February 1950, Chichester had advised the Native Department that the native commissioner of Goromonzi district had "already had some passage of arms with the father, Morosi. He will therefore probably know him as a wrong-headed fellow."[117] Chichester received a report from the mission superior at Makumbi Mission that in October 1951, Morosi's wife had come to the mission with her children because "he had refused to give them food or clothing . . . because Mary [Morosi's wife] had not obeyed his order that neither she nor the children were to come to Sunday service. . . . Her husband beat the children when they came back from Sunday service but he did not beat his wife Mary because he considered that conduct unworthy of a former teacher."[118] Chichester brought this information to the attention of CNC Powys-Jones, though he was quick to point out that "Clara's wish to become a nun has nothing to do with ill-treatment from her father," but that he seemed to have been abusing his parental authority.[119]

According to unverified information that Chichester apparently had collected, Francis Morosi had been living and teaching at Kutama Mission in 1945 and left when he had to pay damages for allegedly burning the roof at an outschool. "He considered this unjust and has never forgotten it. His state of mind was further influenced" when Chichester admitted Clara as a candidate without having consulted him. Morosi said "that apart from not having been consulted he was not against his daughter trying her vocation as a Sister. [Clara], on the other hand, says before her departure from Monte Cassino [February 13, 1950] that her father wished to force her to marry."[120]

Francis Morosi, for his part, stated that after having received no direct answers or any satisfaction from the church or Native Department dating back to 1948, when Clara first declared her desire to become a nun, he withdrew his school-aged children from Catholic mission schools and enrolled them in Salvation Army schools because "there could be one father only in a house, and in the circumstances I could not allow my children to continue their education at a Catholic school."[121] Fr. Maurice Rea, a Jesuit at Makumbi Mission, allegedly told Morosi, "Francis, your Priest is the big Father in a family; what he says is the wisest thing."[122] In a subsequent meeting Rea threatened Morosi with physical violence for having withdrawn the children from the Catholic school, and when Morosi went to look for his wife at the mission, Rea, despite the intervention of two African teachers, "landed a light kick" on Morosi and told him "you will not receive your wife until you come here and submit to punishment for six months."[123] By January 1952, Morosi reported to the PNC that Clara "seemed quite lost, and I had neither news or trace of her."[124]

In the meantime, Chichester continued to hold the Native Department staff at bay concerning Clara's whereabouts and to negotiate with them about resolving the case. The secretary for native affairs deemed the problem "a complex one," and hesitated about issuing a ruling so as to avoid "repercussions." He informed Chichester that he would refer the entire question of women becoming nuns against their parents' wishes to the Native Affairs Board.[125] Chichester asserted that the issue was "a question of fundamental human rights," and that if the Native Affairs Board's decision was negative, he would "have no choice but to explain my position to the Minister [of Native Affairs] and have a test case.... But as the matter has been discussed now for a long time and the girl in this particular instance is still waiting for an answer, I hope the decision will not be delayed."[126] On January 31, 1952, however, the secretary for native affairs advised Chichester that the Native Affairs Board had met and decided that according to African law, women were considered to be perpetual minors under either their fathers or husbands. If another African interfered with the guardian's rights, the matter would be settled in a native court, that is, before a native commissioner. If a European were involved in the case, however, it would go before a magistrate's court and English common law would apply, not "native custom." Thus, an African woman twenty-one years or older was free to do whatever she wanted, against her parents' wishes. Referring to Clara Margwisa's case, the secretary for native affairs concluded that "a native girl, upon reaching the age of 21, may defy her guardian and become a nun," though he was not sure if that precluded the guardian from bringing a lawsuit for loss of *lobola* "should he be in a position to show that the girl has been enticed from his custody."[127]

Chichester expressed his pleasure and gratitude "that the matter has at last been decided and that the decision is in accordance with ecclesiastical law and practice."[128] Claiming that cases such as Clara Margwisa's were infrequent, Chichester assured the secretary that "in any individual case [that did arise], the Ecclesiastical Authorities will always act as circumspectly as possible."[129] Thus, after thirty years, the Rhodesian colonial administration issued a ruling ostensibly to settle the question of an African woman's right to become a nun, ruling in favor of the church's position, one that was in line with Coghlan's and Hodson's opinions.

The ruling, however, did not end Clara Margwisa's case. Chichester informed the Native Department that although Francis Morosi was "now treating his family properly," he was not "at liberty to use my influence to persuade [Clara] to return home," not only because he believed that she would be unwilling to go, but also because

if I were to exert any pressure on her, not only she, but also most of the Sisterhood (who will of course hear all about it if they don't know already) will certainly think I have sacrificed Clara for the sake of smoothing over a difficulty. If however you can give an assurance to Clara that no harm will happen to her and that she will be fit and able to join the Sisterhood on September 5 of this year [Clara's twenty first birthday], then I would be prepared to have the proposition put to her that she return home until that date.

[NC Gormonzi] asked me to tell her, if this should come about, that her father is now allowing the family to practice their religion without molestation.[130]

Chichester also went on at length to deny any responsibility for sending Clara anywhere or knowing where she was during the greater part of her disappearance:

Perhaps I should add that the apparent supposition of the father that I am responsible for her present whereabouts, is quite wrong. You will see from my letter to your office dated February 11, 1950 that I told her she could no longer stay at Monte Cassino nor could I continue to harbour her. When exactly she left Monte Cassino after that I do not know; nor did I for nine months [know] where she had gone to. I certainly did not send her anywhere; nor did the priest in charge at Monte Cassino. Where she went was entirely her own choice.

Chichester further recalled that Clara had wanted to appeal to the governor of Southern Rhodesia in January 1950, but that she did not, and that she "blamed" him for denying the appeal.

Although Francis Morosi and the officials of the Native Department did not know Clara's location, contrary to Chichester and Markall's claims of ignorance, correspondence between Clara and the two Jesuits clearly place her at the convent of the Sisters of the Precious Blood at Empandeni Mission southwest of Bulawayo between August 1950 and the end of July 1952.[131] According to Chichester, he only learned of Clara's whereabouts nine months after she fled, or in November 1950. There are, however, three letters from Chichester and one from Markall to Clara between August and October 1950.

Apparently, Clara's desire to be received as a candidate did not diminish during her exile in Matabeleland. Clara's letters also show the extreme irony of the situation into which the exchange of African patriarchy for European paternalism put these women, who had to be strong enough to stand up to African men and European bureaucrats, yet humble and servile in their dealings with Chichester and other church authorities:

O father please, I have no other hither father than you. You are really my Godfather. Please have mercy on me. Let this be unto me for the name of Jesus. When it is better let me come [to Salisbury]. If only you could allow me to enter, nothing else I would wish of you. In fact I hope that he [Morosi] will give leave. You will see that he will not do as he did before. I have never written to him since I came here. I think it is better that he does not know where I am. Did he come to trouble you because of me? But don't tell him anything about me. Perhaps when you think that its possible for me to do so, then count this time as my candidate years and let me learn my Teacher Training here at Empandeni mission.[132]

Chichester's letters constantly told Clara that she would either have to get Morosi's written consent to enter the LCBL candidacy or wait until she was twenty-one years old. His insistence that she be patient seemed to have little effect, as she continued to ask to be received as a candidate.[133] He did, however, allow her to complete her teacher training at Empandeni.[134]

By the end of May 1952, with her twenty-first birthday approaching, Clara informed Chichester she had decided to go home to speak with her father.[135] Prior to going home, however, Clara asked the bishop "to note clearly" the date she was to be received, where she was to go, and whether she would be received as a candidate or a postulant.[136] Additionally, she inquired as to how she should dispose of £10 that she had saved while teaching at Empandeni. Chichester replied that she would be received as a candidate at Monte Cassino on September 5, 1952, and that any money she had left after having paid for her expenses was to be left in trust with Markall.[137]

Clara returned home in August 1952.[138] Although this pleased Chichester and the Native Department staff involved with the case, the effort at reconciliation was a failure. According to Morosi, Clara "shut herself up in a hut," refused to speak with him, and was "disrespectful to and about" him.[139] Morosi, accordingly, went to NC Goromonzi's office to report her "disobedient" manner, and "to have my case written down as my daughter says she is nearly 21 years of age, and will then be free to do as she wishes." Additionally, he made the accusation that "all the time the Priests and the Bishop have known where Clara was, and as she had no money they must have known where she was and how she got to Bulawayo."[140]

After four years of disputes, Clara again became a candidate for the LCBL Sisters on September 5, 1952, at Monte Cassino Mission. About a month later, she wrote to Chichester asking for permission to take the Southern Rhodesia Junior Certificate course (completion of primary school) and the advanced teacher-training course before becoming a postulant.[141] The bishop replied that it was a bad suggestion, since she was to become a postulant in December 1952, and that she would then do the advanced teacher training over the following year before entering the novitiate. He further noted that "all good religious orders are particular about keeping their rules . . . so it will be better to do the postulum."[142]

Not long thereafter, Clara received a summons to appear before the native court in Goromonzi because Francis Morosi had filed charges that she

[did] wrongfully and unlawfully and maliciously burn a quantity of exercise books and textbooks, the property of Morosi [and that she had] admitted to the Police Officer that she had burnt those books [saying] "I burnt those books, because I was searching for my letters. I first looked through the books, but did not find them. My father has no right to take my letters. If he wants to read them he can ask me, and if I like I give him permission. If I don't like, I tell him."[143]

Clara appeared in court, testified, and was fined £5 for the destruction of property, even though she believed that they were not even worth £1, being mostly school exercise books, "periodicals, and newspapers."[144]

Morosi had apparently taken Clara's letters and submitted them as evidence of Chichester's and Markall's knowledge of her whereabouts when he made his statement to NC Goromonzi. Clara believed that her father had violated her rights according to VaShona marriage practices that allowed a woman to possess gifts from a suitor—which by the 1950s apparently had come to include letters—without a parent's knowledge or consent.[145] She argued that "her father has no right to keep [her letters] anymore than he had a right to take them. In Native

Custom he cannot touch her property, especially her clothes and letters: she has absolute right to receive letters from anyone, just as any girl has who may wish to be courted by a boy."[146]

What is most interesting is Clara's understanding and awareness of her rights in both African and European legal traditions. On one hand, she clearly expressed a firm knowledge of the property rights accorded to her as a MuShona woman considering marriage. On the other hand, she expressed those rights as applicable to her situation in a decidedly Western context, evidently using the church's long standing metaphor of a woman becoming a "bride of Christ" when she becomes a nun.

Not only did Morosi take Clara to court for destruction of property, but he also retained legal counsel to "see that . . . Clara be returned to him as he alleges she has been put into a convent without his consent at Monte Cassino." Apparently Morosi's younger daughter Matilda also expressed a desire to become a nun. Morosi complained that "the mission authorities" had "encouraged" the daughters "to be underhanded in the method by which they have entered their vocations," and was "most disturbed at the treatment he has received" from church authorities. If, however, "his daughters return to him and properly ask his permission, as they should, and if they convince him that they do, in fact, want to put aside the things of this world, he will forthwith give his permission for them to commence the novitiate."[147]

Chichester denied any knowledge of Clara's sister Matilda or her possible interest in becoming a nun.[148] He also notified his lawyers, and gave Markall instructions "to refuse [any] request or demand . . . [to return Clara] if it is possible" because she was over twenty-one.[149] There is no record of the case either having gone to court or any settlement having been reached.

Morosi's legal actions devastated Clara. Although Chichester had apparently counted her exile in Matabeleland as part of her candidacy—she was received as a postulant three months after becoming a candidate at Monte Cassino—Markall reported that Clara was

not happy about the judgment of the Court, and her heart is very black: she has not so far given way to temptations of revenge against her father, but now she feels very strongly towards it.... Far from being penitent about what she did, Clara still thinks she had a perfect right to try to destroy her property in the hands of her father, therefore, she is very unhappy, cannot forgive her father, and is tempted to revenge. She wishes to take revenge, I gather, by speaking out about her father to the Chief Native Commissioner, and then both her father and the Chief Native Commissioner will see what she can do in the way of revenge.[150]

By May 1953, the director of postulants at Monte Cassino reported to Chichester that Clara's attitude "would seem to indicate that her character is not suited for community life."[151] Apparently Clara refused to become head postulant and take on its responsibilities, necessitating the rotation of the office among the postulants monthly. She "obeyed unwillingly for one month and then disobeyed again, refusing to perform all the little duties" associated with the job by, for example, being late for meals and other occasions "in order to avoid leading the prayers." She caused "a lot of annoyance and inconvenience among the Postulants and Candidates" by never taking "the place appointed to her in the Church and in the dining room."[152]

Chichester apparently asked Markall to speak with Clara, but aside from conveying "her wish to become a nun" to the bishop, she "said that she did not want to discuss the matter any further with me."[153] Accordingly, Chichester "decided to send [Clara] to Musami, and arranged work for you to do there."[154] Clara eventually left the community, although it is not clear whether she left of her own accord or was dismissed by Chichester.[155]

Mother Rocha Mushonga: Indigenizing Leadership

The experiences of women such as Clara Margwisa and Catherine Mazorodze must have had an impact on how the LCBL Sisters dealt with African families once they began to assume the leadership of their congregation, and inherited the legacy of Chichester's *lobola* policy. The Africanization of the leadership came in August 1965 with the election of Sister Rocha Mushonga as the first mother general.[156]

Born in 1928 near Triashill Mission in the eastern highlands, she attended the mission school for her primary education. She was inspired by the "dedication," "sacrifice," and "love" of the Jesuits and the Precious Blood Sisters at Triashill. Although her mother did not complain when Rocha was baptized Catholic as a student, she objected strongly when Rocha told her she wanted to become a nun. She followed Rocha to Monte Cassino and "argued" with Chichester, who surprisingly told Rocha to "go home." Rocha was "lucky" to have had the support of the Jesuit community at Monte Cassino, who prevailed upon Chichester to admit her as a candidate and let her stay at Monte Cassino in 1946.

Sister Rocha completed a teacher-training course at Monte Cassino during her candidacy and taught for a year as a postulant. Although she told Chichester she wanted to be a nurse, he told her that she would be a teacher. In 1948, she entered the novitiate at Makumbi, and after professing vows, she taught at Monte Cassino for several years before being sent to complete secondary studies at the Jesuit school at Gokomere, after which she continued to teach, ultimately being sent to the school at Mount Saint Mary's Mission in Hwedza.

As the first African general of the LCBL Sisters, Mother Rocha began improving the spiritual and educational formation of the sisters by sending them to colleges to complete their advanced (or A-level) exams, as well as several to school in Britain and others for studies at the University College of Rhodesia. Although she never served as a nurse, she sent several sisters for nurse's training, and others to be trained as formators.[157] Sister Catherine Mazarodze, for example, studied courses in bookkeeping, accounting, and hospital administration.[158]

During the liberation war in the 1970s, Mother Rocha continued to visit all the communities of LCBL Sisters who stayed at the missions with the people, even when the priests had fled for their safety, or had been deported by the Rhodesian authorities.[159] She frequently met the freedom fighters en route to the communities, and they "always had details on me." When asked why she was traveling, she replied, "I can't leave the Sisters alone, so I go." On several occasions she had to advocate for sisters who had been arrested by Rhodesian forces for "helping guerrillas." According to Mother Rocha, these sisters were giving material aid to the guerrillas, specifically medicines and clothing, and she protected them when the police harassed them, even though the police frequently followed her.

During Mother Rocha's administration, parental opposition to their daughters becoming nuns gradually lessened through culturally sensitive education,[160] although "some still object even today [and] girls have to struggle." When asked what she remembered most about Mother Rocha's years as general of the order, Sister Bernadette Garatsa simply said, "She loved us."

Conclusion

The experiences of African women who chose to enter Catholic religious congregations in colonial Zimbabwe generally support Elizabeth Schmidt's argument that African women who eschewed patriarchy in the African cultures of the late nineteenth and early twentieth centuries merely exchanged it for a western form of masculine domination. VaShona women's actions in becoming nuns, however, transformed their culture by causing a change in the practice of keeping women as minors in perpetuity; Southern Rhodesian society by moving the Native Department from unwavering support of African men in maintaining control over African women to allowing the women the right of choice at age twenty-one; and the Catholic Church by introducing African elements into the entirely missionary elite of the church's hierarchical structure.

Terence Ranger, Elizabeth Schmidt, Diana Jeater, and A.J. Dachs and W. F. Rea all either implied or explicitly stated that many of the women who became nuns did so to run away from marriages arranged by their families in exchange for *lobola*.[161] Oral and archival evidence, however, clearly shows that a significant number of the sisters spent time as students at Catholic mission schools and, during or after the course of their studies expressed a belief that they were responding to a divine vocation to live a life of service in a religious community, a motive more readily ascribed to Westerners.[162] Similarly, that these women had to overcome familial opposition points to the fact that this was a phenomenon that also occurred in the church in other places at other times.[163]

Colonial domination within the church was certainly a factor in the founding of religious congregations for African women. The constitutions of the Daughters of Saint Francis, the Children of the Holy Trinity, and the Little Children of our Blessed Lady all initially denied the African women who constituted the congregations any voice in their governance, and they left the regular administration either to a European bishop (Fleischer or Chichester) or to European nuns (Precious Blood Sisters or Dominicans). Even Chichester was surprised to see that "the white Sisters are determined to keep the native Sisters downtrodden."[164] That these government structures not only had approval from Rome, but that the Vatican more than likely suggested them, indicates the degree to which European colonial domination had affected the Catholic Church and its leadership. Not surprisingly, the LCBL Sisters remain a diocesan congregation under the direct authority of the Archbishop of Harare, even though they have been living and working beyond the diocesan and national boundaries since 1955. In the church in the rest of the world, most orders that work in more than one diocese or nation usually apply for and receive pontifical status and come under the supervision of the Vatican Congregation for Religious.

Although exchanging African patriarchy for Western paternalism affected the kinds of activities available to African women who wanted to become nuns, it did not stop them from acting in what they perceived to be in their best interests. The Children of the Holy Trinity initially only admitted widows, but the requests of younger unmarried women to enter this and the other orders forced the issue upon the Native Department. Although Rocha Mushonga wanted to be a nurse and Chichester told her that she would have to be content as a teacher, when she became mother general she sent sisters for nurse's training. Clara Margwisa's case certainly shows the limits that religious life circumscribed: while she had no problems confronting her father, even burning his books, she was always plaintive and suppliant in her correspondence with Chichester, even when defiant of the Precious Blood Sisters' authority.

The stories and experiences of these African nuns clearly shows them as agents taking some measure of control over their lives, and their actions had significant effects on African culture as well as on the relations between European administrators and missionaries. These were not merely passive, docile women who did what they were told to do by parents, priests, or politicians. Rather, they defied their parents and their culture. Maria Mukoma specifically requested an audience with Native Commissioner Parkhurst. Catherine Mazorodze and Theresa Marumbeni endured years of physical and emotional violence in order to pursue their vocations. Clara Margwisa's attempt to appeal to the Southern Rhodesian governor, as well as her defiance and flight, not only influenced Chichester to seek a second legal opinion and to consider bringing a test case to court to settle the question of the legal status of African women and their right to become nuns but also resulted in the ruling of the Native Affairs Board that ostensibly gave African women the rights of legal majority under English common law when they turned twenty-one. The letter of the early LCBL Sisters to Chichester requesting fulfillment of their basic needs, sound religious formation, the right to work freely from the supervision of European nuns, and initials for their religious congregation like those of all religious institutes in the church showed their cognizance of the church's traditions as well as a demand for some degree of status recognition.

African men's actions also contributed to the forging of a new Southern Rhodesian colonial social practice. Francis Morosi knew his rights in both VaShona and English laws. His lawsuits against his daughter for destruction of property and against the church for improperly influencing his daughters demonstrated his fluency in the contemporary British legal practice. His requests that his daughters ask his permission properly before entering the convent were demands for recognition as a man and head of family in VaShona cultural practice, as were Chaitezwi's, Jacobo Mukoma's, and Joseph Mazorodze's actions. The practices of Africans and Europeans, men and women alike, created new relationships between persons and institutions in Southern Rhodesian society. The actions of the African men concerned, of the Native Department staff, and of the church elders, however, were reactions and responses to the initiatives of African women in not only expressing but also acting on their desires to become nuns.

Father Alfred Weld

Father Peter Prestage

Father Andrew Hartmann

Father Henri Depelchin

Father Francis Richartz *(third from left)*

Sisters of the Little Children of Our Blessed Lady

Robert E. Brown, Prefect Apostolic of the Zambezi Mission

Father John Berrell

Father John Diamond

Vicar Apostolic Aston Chichester

Father Isidore Chikore

Seminarians

Father Francis McKeown

Chishiwasha Seminary

Brother Herman Toma

Father Simon Tsuro

Joseph Dambaza Chikerema

Mrs. Simon Taoneyi

Father Alfred Burbridge

Father Lachlan Hughes

Father John Apel

Father Francis Richartz

Father Jean-Baptiste Loubière

Father Jerome O'Hea

3 "The Most Important Work on the Mission": The Seminary of Saints John Fisher and Thomas More, 1919–1979

There is one final, and very important, point for anyone who has charge of a mission. He must make it his special concern to secure and train local candidates for the sacred ministry. In this policy lies the greatest hope of the new churches. For the local priest, one with his people by birth, by nature, by his sympathies and his aspirations, is remarkably effective in appealing to their mentality and thus attracting them to the Faith. Far better than anyone else he knows the kind of argument they will listen to, and as a result, he often has easy access to places where a foreign priest would not be tolerated.
     Pope Benedict XV, *Maximum Illud*

Their Lordships the Bishops regret that due to the recent events they are obliged to order the temporary closure of the Regional Major Seminary. [This] marked the end of a process which commenced on Monday, 30th September 1974, when the entire student body with the exception of four students boycotted lectures and retired to the football pitch. . . . The reason given why the students had not attended lectures was the withdrawal of one student. This particular student whose ordination had been deferred had been accepted back on the understanding that he would behave himself. It was, however, found necessary to ask him to leave on Saturday, 28th September 1974.
     Secretary General of the Rhodesian Catholic Bishops' Conference

On September 30, 1974, the students of the Regional Major Seminary at Chishawasha went on strike. The Rhodesian Catholic Bishops Conference's Secretary General specified the dismissal of Deacon Ernest Mukuwapasi as the cause of the strike, but several seminary staff members and the commission that investigated the causes of the students' actions opined that Mukuwapasi's expulsion ignited "a strong feeling of dissatisfaction amongst the seminarians [that had caused] much tension between the [Jesuit] staff and [African] students."[1]

The 1974 strike was the third significant disturbance at the seminary since 1965 in which there were calls for independent investigations of the Jesuit administration, and the second time in seven years that the seminary closed as a result of student protests. In 1965 and 1967, the Jesuits succeeded in preventing investigations. In 1974, however, they failed to prevent an external investigation and the Rhodesian bishops relieved them of their responsibility for running the seminary. These events represent a significant disjuncture between a discourse on the part of the Vatican and Jesuit missionary superiors claiming the seminary education of local priests as the most important part of the church's mission work and a practice on the part of the same Jesuit superiors and seminary staff that was diametrically opposed to the Vatican's rhetoric.

Increasing manifestations of African nationalism in the seminary culminated in the 1974 strike, which was contemporaneous with the rise of African political parties and African nationalism in Southern Rhodesia during the 1950s and 1960s and the liberation war in the 1970s. African seminarians were aware of the turbulent political situation and pushed the constraints of the strict seminary order. The Jesuits became increasingly isolated as they grew out of touch with the seminarians' concerns, interests, and aspirations, effectively inculturating themselves into the dominant white Rhodesian culture. Thus, the failed effort to integrate the seminary racially in 1965 catalyzed the nationalist impulse, and did not cause African discontent, as the seminary rector alleged.

The disturbances at the seminary were more than merely demands for the symbols of privilege, such as morning and afternoon tea. They were manifestations of increasing African self-consciousness and expressions of African nationalism within a Christian context. Basil Davidson asserted that African nationalism "had less to do with any national cause than with demands of a social nature and context," and that "the promise that the coming of the nation-state would strike away the chains of foreign rule and all that these had meant in social and moral deprivation" inspired African nationalists to action.[2] Thus, the seminarians' actions at Chishawasha during the 1960s and 1970s were an effort to effect the social liberation of the Catholic Church from Rhodesian racism in general and Jesuit paternalism in particular.

There has been no scholarly examination of expressions of African nationalism at the Catholic seminary in colonial Zimbabwe, although developments in Zimbabwe seem to have followed a pattern similar to that in Catholic seminaries in South Africa.[3] The only reference to such events in the literature is in A. J. Dach's and W. F. Rea's *The Catholic Church and Zimbabwe*, in which they referred only to the 1974 strike, and wrongly asserted that "[in] August 1974 the seminary students refused further studies unless more African priests were immediately appointed to the seminary staff. The Catholic hierarchy was already willing to do this and in 1976 Fr. Tobias Chiginya was appointed Rector, Fr. Alexio Muchabaiwa was appointed Spiritual Director, and Fr. Isidore Chikore became his Assistant."[4] Dachs and Rea greatly misrepresented the African students' concerns and also significantly overstated the Rhodesian bishops' eagerness to Africanize the seminary staff as they stood squarely behind the Jesuit administration until the 1974 strike.

The previous chapter showed African women, in expressing and acting upon their desires to become Catholic nuns, affecting the relationships and interactions between themselves and African and European men, as well as the relationship between the church's hierarchy and the colonial administration, and that between the church and African men. This chapter will examine the changing relations between European Jesuit missionaries and African seminarians from the early 1930s to 1975. The influence of African nationalism on the seminarians and the reactionary isolation of the Jesuits culminated in the student rebellions that resulted in the indigenization of the seminary staff that began in 1975.

Vatican and Jesuit Perspectives on the Formation of a "Native Clergy"

The deportation and internment of missionary priests and nuns during the First World War motivated the Catholic Church to reassert its long-standing desire for the development of indigenous clergies in its mission territories. In 1919, Pope Benedict XV issued an apostolic letter, *Maximum Illud*, to the bishops and mission superiors concerning the spread of the Catholic faith throughout the world. The letter encouraged evangelization in mission territories and suggested methods to improve evangelization efforts. Benedict encouraged each mission superior to "expand and fully develop his mission" by establishing more mission stations "as soon as it is practicable to do so."[5] He commended vicars apostolic and bishops who invited members of Catholic religious institutes different from their own to work in their territories when their own orders were not supplying enough people to staff the mission's needs. Similarly, he condemned those vicars and bishops who treated their territories "as a piece of private property, a domain not to be touched by the hands of an outsider," and refused to work with other orders.

Pope Benedict particularly emphasized the need to encourage local vocations and develop an indigenous clergy, and that these men should receive "the same kind of education for the priesthood that a European would receive. For the local clergy is not to be trained merely to perform the humbler duties of the ministry, acting as the assistants of foreign priests. On the contrary, they must take up God's work as equals, so that some day they will be able to enter upon the spiritual leadership of their people."[6] The pontiff also "deplored" the inferior training and quality of local clergies in several parts of the world despite papal insistence to the contrary, and described the system of training "future missionaries" as "feeble and faulty." Consequently, he "ordered" Propaganda Fide "to apply remedies adapted to the various regions of the world, and to see to the founding of seminaries for both individual regions and groups of dioceses," and charged the congregation with "particular care" for "the supervision of the growth and development of the local clergy" in the missions. Further, the pope considered it "tragic" for missionaries "to busy themselves with the interests of their terrestrial homelands" instead of their spiritual duties. Such nationalistic expressions, in Benedict's opinion, would be obvious to the local populations to whom they were sent.[7]

In the following year, contrary to the pope's recommendations, Richard Sykes's successor as the prefect apostolic, Edward Parry, and the Jesuits at Chishawasha Mission forbade German Mariannhill missionaries at Triashill Mission from teaching Latin to African boys in their schools so that "they could later on become priests."[8] Although the Mariannhillers did not intend "to bring them so far that they could start at once Philosophy and Theology," Jesuit John Apel thought it "premature to teach even a few of them Latin, in view of eventual training for the priesthood," because the Africans at Chishawasha were "steeped in superstition . . . immorality and drunkenness."[9] He believed that "to teach Latin and to give hopes of the priesthood would be to put the cart before the horse," and that they "should first aim at having good, well behaved teachers. Perhaps their children may be fit for something higher."[10] Similarly, Jesuit James O'Neill opined that "first generation Christians in South Africa hardly ever, if ever, have the backbone for the priesthood."[11] In an apparent criticism of the Mariannhillers' work at Triashill, O'Neill wrote that the Jesuit in charge of Saint Peter's parish in the Mbare township of Salisbury had told him "the Triashill gang men who come to Salisbury for work are very unsatisfactory." Furthermore, O'Neill thought that because "there is a real desire for learning among the Manicaland natives [sic]," it was questionable whether they wanted to learn Latin for the sake of learning it or were really interested in the priesthood.[12]

In 1926, Pope Pius XI, Benedict's successor, issued his encyclical letter *Rerum Ecclesiae*, which reiterated the call of *Maximum Illud* for the establishment of indigenous clergy in mission territories within the church throughout the world:

Before everything else, We call your attention to the importance of building up a native clergy. If you do not work with all your might to attain this purpose, We assert that not only will your apostolate be crippled, but it will become an obstacle and an impediment to the establishment and organization of the Church in those countries. . . . How can the Church among the heathens be developed today unless it be built of those very elements out of which our own churches were built; that is to say, unless it be made up of people, clergy, and religious orders of men and women recruited from the native populations of the several regions? Why should the native clergy be forbidden to cultivate their own portion of the Lord's vineyard, be forbidden to govern their own people? . . . [Would] it not be of great assistance if you would entrust to the native clergy the people already converted so that they could minister to them and preserve their faith?[13]

Pope Pius demanded a seminary formation for priests from mission territories equal to that given to Europeans, not only because these were priests "who will be destined one day to govern parishes and dioceses," but because there was a fundamental equality between the races:

Anyone who looks upon these natives as members of an inferior race or as men of low mentality makes a grievous mistake. Experience over a long period of time has proven that the inhabitants of those remote regions of the East and South frequently are not inferior to us at all, and are capable of holding their own with us, even in mental ability. . . . Certainly you should not allow the native clergy to be looked upon as if they were a lower grade of priests, to be employed only in the most humble offices of the ministry. These priests have been admitted to the same priesthood that the missionaries possess, they are members of the selfsame apostolate. On the contrary, you should prefer the native priests to all others, for it is they who will one day govern the churches and Catholic communities founded by your sweat and labor. Therefore, there should exist no discrimination of any kind between priests. . . . There must be no line of demarcation marking one off from the other.[14]

In response to the encyclical, Zambezi Mission superior Robert Brown surveyed his missionaries, asking for their thoughts on the possibility of establishing an African clergy in Southern Rhodesia, specifically, whether African Christians were intellectually and morally "fit" for the priesthood; whether any Africans had expressed interest in the priesthood, and if not, why not; how long before there would be "appreciable numbers" of "suitable candidates for the priesthood"; whether the missionaries had presented the priesthood as a possibility for African men to parents and children, and if not, why not; and what would be the best means to establish "a thoroughly Christian home atmosphere" in which to develop vocations to the priesthood.[15]

Of the seventeen extant replies, the overwhelming majority was "broadly pessimistic."[16] Only two Jesuits, Emil Schmitz and Henry Quin, unreservedly thought that there were Africans with the requisite intellectual and moral capacity to become priests.[17] Most of the Jesuits and Mariannhillers believed that Africans lacked the necessary intellectual and moral "fitness" to become priests. Of these, five indicated a belief in the innate intellectual and moral incapacity of Africans for the priesthood,[18] while five of the seven who believed that there were Africans capable of becoming priests attributed their lack of fitness to poor education.[19]

Ten respondents had heard at least seventeen African men or boys express an interest in the priesthood.[20] Apel "[came] across one boy at Gwelo who expressed the desire to study for the priesthood," and even went so far as to "[apply] for him at Mariannhill" but was told that "the boy" at twenty-eight years of age was "too old."[21] Andrew Hartmann, a Jesuit at Empandeni Mission among AmaNdebele, encountered two men who were interested and met with them "sympathetically." He explained the required studies, but they eventually became teachers in outschools and married. Francis Richartz, the superior of Chishawasha Mission, referred to "one northern boy, Dominico Raposo," who had received instruction and baptism at Chishawasha. According to Richartz, Raposo entered the White Fathers' seminary in Nyasaland in 1920 and was "studying Latin to become a priest," and that as of June 1923 there were forty-one seminarians.[22]

Three respondents said they had seen signs of impending priestly vocations. Thomas Gardiner noted, "the question of celibacy is being discussed among [African Christians]."[23] Henry Quin and Emil Schmitz noticed more typically Catholic spiritual qualities such as "a personal devotion to our Lord, a spirit of prayer, humility and self sacrifice, a desire to imitate the saints and to instruct their fellow natives in the faith."[24] Jean-Baptiste Loubière and Francis Richartz suggested possible signs but had not seen them in the Christians under their care.[25]

While most respondents agreed that the "pagan atmosphere" in which African Christians lived was the primary cause for the dearth of "signs" of vocations, they disagreed significantly about the nature of the atmosphere: eight stated or implied that it was inherent in Africans. Four believed that it was a question of changing the culture in which they lived. Significantly, five believed that African boys and men were not expressing interest in the priesthood because the European missionaries had "purposely withheld [the possibility] from our Christians."[26]

There was sharp division over when there would be an "appreciable number" of "suitable candidates." Although the majority (nine) believed that it would be "many years" or "several generations," they disagreed over the reasons. Edward Biehler stated that only twenty years before, "all these natives were barbarians of the lowest type, mere animals intellectually and morally. A change can only be orchestrated by many generations." Jean-Baptiste Loubière thought it necessary to establish a "truly Christian atmosphere" in order to foster vocations. John Apel believed that Christian girls should be raised by "sensible nuns." Andrew Hartmann and Francis Richartz both believed that there would be no progress in vocations until the contemporary generation of adults, the guardians of the indigenous culture, died. Hartmann stated, "at least the present generation will have to pass away before any candidates for the priesthood will come forward in any appreciable number, if even then." Richartz wrote, "as long as the grandparents and parents of our Christians are alive with their old superstitions and heathen customs and the latter remain more or less dependent [on] and connected with their people, it will be difficult for would-be candidates to follow their vocations."[27]

There was a variety of minority views on this question that ascribed responsibility for the absence of African vocations to the failure of the European missionaries to present the priesthood as an option for Africans, or to the inferior education that the church and the Rhodesian colonial administration offered Africans. Emil Schmitz believed that "as there are good signs for vocations, suitable candidates will come forward if we start awakening and encouraging vocations." One Jesuit responded that an increase in vocations "entirely [depended] on the means of education and character of education which will be available for native christians [sic], and when it will be available."[28] Another thought an increase in vocations depended on divine grace and "a good deal on our treatment of the native Christians." Henry Quin suggested starting a minor seminary immediately: "I think that if we had a little seminary for small boys from 10 to 14 years old, we would begin to find vocations now, especially amongst the children of Christian parents. But as long as we follow our custom and leave our Christians and their children to live and grow up amongst heathen surroundings in heathen kraals no vocations are likely to be developed."[29] Similarly, Jesuit Thomas Gardiner presciently believed that "the boys of 12, 13, and 14 are the boys that, from today, will bring the movement forward. Their sisters will be the vanguard. [The] next decade ought to see many native nuns amongst us. These boys will have to be trained during many years. The Holy Father has just spoken and his words will be listened to as *Vox Dei*."[30] While Jesuit Zambezi Mission superiors did not take the pope's words as *vox dei*, Gardiner correctly predicted the growth of women's vocations to religious communities.

Eleven respondents had presented the idea of the priesthood to African Christian parents, yet only ten had done so with African "boys." Missionaries who did not discuss the priesthood thought the children of Christian parents were too young, or that African Christians were too immature to consider it a realistic possibility.[31]

When asked how best to establish "a thoroughly Christian home atmosphere"[32] in which to develop priestly vocations, ten of the seventeen respondents recommended establishing Christian villages similar to the one Jean-Baptiste Loubière had set up at Kutama Mission, or some isolation from African culture, such as a boarding school. Some Jesuits suggested that such villages should be exclusively for the "best" Christians.[33] Thomas Gardiner suggested isolating African Christians because women were the key to establishing Christian family life.[34] Although they did not provide such detailed plans, three other respondents expressed similar beliefs in the importance of women in developing a Christian home environment.[35]

Not all of the respondents favored Christian villages, however. Edward Biehler stated, "we have many Christian villages; but there is little difference between their children and children of pagans."[36] Jesuit Henry Seed thought Christian villages the best means to prevent African Christian men from going to search for work in mines and towns, though in his view it was "impossible until the missions are able to give them employment and pay them well."³⁷

Emil Schmitz gave a singular response that was forty years ahead of its time by the standards of Catholic mission theology, yet in keeping with the dictates of *Rerum Ecclesiae*:

Candidates for the priesthood should be boarders and for the first years under the supervision of a good *Native* teacher; the less European influence the better for the young candidates. Housing, food should be as at their home—books strictly forbidden—*all* the studies, also Philosophy and Theology, should be made in Rhodesia. In general: let us teach those boys as little as possible of our European views and customs, then there is all probability that they become good priests for their people.³⁸

Terence Ranger identified similar perspectives about the possibilities of an African clergy in the Anglican and Methodist churches. Thus, such attitudes were not exclusive to Jesuits or the Catholic Church. Ranger showed "how the providence of God had established a vigorous Zimbabwean Christianity" despite the missionaries."³⁹ Schmitz's recommendations seem all the more striking given the general belief in Africans' lack of preparedness for the priesthood. Dachs and Rea's analysis of the survey posited a split between older and younger Jesuits:

Importantly it was the older Fathers who were the more pessimistic, men like Hartmann, Richartz and Biehler, who had worked on the mission before any Christian influence had been sowed and who had seen the African Risings of 1896. They remained cautious and they saw progress as only very slow. But those who had come up to Rhodesia [from South Africa] under the more settled conditions of the twentieth century, were more optimistic. They saw successes already achieved and looked for more and greater accomplishments in the near future.⁴⁰

Their view, however, is overly simplistic. The seventeen replies to the survey show a sharply divided clergy: many believed in the inherent degeneracy of Africans, dismissing their religions as "superstition" and their cultures as "heathenism." Others believed that they themselves, as European missionaries, bore responsibility for not providing African Christians the necessary opportunities to develop vocations, that is, the adequate and effective education for and preaching of the possibility of becoming priests. The divisions do not break cleanly along lines of age, national origin (British or German), religious order (Jesuit or Mariannhill), or groups of African people with whom they worked (VaShona or AmaNdebele). Emil Schmitz and Thomas Gardiner, two ostensibly younger Jesuits, held radically different views on the prospects for African vocations. Similarly, Francis Richartz and Andrew Hartmann, both older German Jesuits, differed in their perspectives concerning the intellectual and moral capacity of Africans to become priests: Richartz saw intellectual capacity, difficulty, yet possibility, in maintaining celibacy, whereas Hartmann saw hope on neither front.[41] The divisions over the Mwari controversy further undermine Dachs and Rea's assertion.[42]

The 1926 clergy survey's net result was that Robert Brown and the Jesuit leadership of the Zambezi Mission founded Kutama Teacher Training School to train African male catechists.[43] While Brown and his confreres did not ignore a papal encyclical's exhortations as Richard Sykes had, they did not implement them. The Mariannhillers—who sought and were denied permission to teach African boys Latin in the year following the proclamation of *Maximum Illud*—in the wake of *Rerum Ecclesiae* admitted three Manyika men from their missions in the eastern highlands of Southern Rhodesia to their seminary in Mariannhill, South Africa, one of whom, Kilian Samakande, was ordained as a member of the order in 1939.[44]

Seminary Beginnings, 1931–1958

"Against the warnings and forebodings of the experienced missionaries,"[45] Aston Chichester began preparations to establish a seminary shortly after his installation as vicar apostolic in 1931. Apparently Jesuit Jerome O'Hea, who succeeded Jean-Baptiste Loubière as superior of Kutama Mission, suggested that Chichester accept candidates for minor seminary training and send them to the teacher-training school at Kutama mission.[46] Three candidates arrived and began their formation. A fourth student joined them in 1932. Because they had completed Standard VII, they spent that year teaching at Kutama Mission.[47]

Seminary training in the Catholic Church across Africa was still in its relative infancy in the 1930s. The Holy Ghost Fathers ordained their first African priests, trained at a seminary in Senegal, in 1864, and the White Fathers (Missionaries of Africa) began seminaries in Uganda in 1893 and Malawi in 1912.[48] In South Africa, a minor seminary for African candidates from the Union, Lesotho, and Botswana was established at Mariannhill in 1924, at the urging of the recently appointed apostolic delegate. A major seminary was added in 1929, and the first priest was ordained in 1936. Despite the apostolic delegate's desire to have one central seminary for the region, the vicar apostolic of Maseru also opened a seminary for African candidates at Roma and received his first ordinand in 1931.[49]

About a year before Chichester's installation as vicar, a Zambezi Mission Jesuit inquired about missionaries' experiences training African seminarians in the Belgian Congo and Uganda, as well as the experiences of the African priests.[50] Chichester apparently visited seminaries in Uganda and Tanganyika before opening the seminary and seems to have based his formation program on models he witnessed in East Africa.[51]

Chichester opened a preparatory seminary at Chishawasha in January 1934 and transferred the original candidates from Kutama, who were joined by seven others.[52] Candidates who had not completed Standard V were to go to Chishawasha to complete their primary education and then to Kutama to study for their teaching certificates, after which they returned to Chishawasha to enter the minor seminary program, which included the study of Latin. Thus, he believed that "the training will take twenty or more years." Both "aspirants" to the priesthood as well as mission "helpers" (that is, brother candidates) had "to join a confraternity which will be erected exclusively for them."[53] Early drafts of the rules of the Confraternity of the Sacred Heart declared its purpose was "to train religiously-inclined boys in the apostolic spirit," with "mission helpers" to receive vocational training "as carpenters, gardeners, printers, bricklayers, etc."[54] Candidates for the priesthood had to be "sufficiently young to reach Standard VI by the age of 18," and brother candidates had to be "under 30 years of age." Confraternity members were to have separate dormitory, lavatory, and refectory facilities, and were required to speak English "for the first five minutes of dinner every day" and "to have a shower or its equivalent daily."[55]

Chishawasha superior Francis Ketterer expressed concerns about the costs to Chishawasha of supporting the candidates. Though he thought "it an honour that [Chichester] had chosen Chishawasha for a start on the road to the priesthood," it cost £3/4/10 per year to feed and clothe each candidate. The Native Development Department did not provide any assistance, whereas it gave Kutama a £5/10 per student subsidy for candidates to obtain teacher-training certificates. While Ketterer was "only too glad to help on the good work," he wished "to point out to Your Lordship that we are not making money on it, but rather the contrary."[56]

In 1935, ten students "bound themselves by promise to study for the priesthood, provided they found they had a vocation."[57] Additionally, Emil Schmitz oversaw the seminary physical plant's construction for a cost of £1000.[58] The Seminary of Saints John Fisher and Thomas More officially opened at Chishawasha Mission on January 1, 1936, with eight candidates for the priesthood and four candidates for the diocesan brotherhood of Saint Peter Claver. Conditions were "primitive."[59] The first buildings were made of thatch and mud, and permanent structures were built between 1942 and 1945, largely with the labor of Italian prisoners of war. According to Bernard Ndlovu, who entered the seminary in 1949, conditions at the seminary were "awful."[60] Seminarians had to sleep on the floors.

Lice was everywhere. [When students had to collect firewood in a scotch cart,] we were the donkeys. We did all the work [around the seminary] ourselves. We served the priests in white uniforms. We were trained to wait on them. Some were sent to clean their bedrooms. Others [were sent] to classrooms and the chapel. . . . [Collecting firewood] was feared by everyone. There was no borehole. We [drew] water from the stream and carried it back in a wheelbarrow.[61]

There were constant complaints about the food. For meals, the students received *sadza* and *usavi*[62] three times per day, but the sadza for breakfast "was cooked the night before," and the usavi was frequently made from the outer leaves of cabbage. For lunch on Sundays only, the seminarians received meat. "If you got three pieces you were lucky," recalled Fr. Ndlovu.[63] The situation with poor food apparently continued into the 1960s:

Relish [usavi] is often spinach, which very many do not like to eat. Variety is essential. . . . The mealie meal [cornmeal] at present is bad, smells, and has weavils' [sic] corpses in it. I'm thanking God that there are potatoes at present . . . . It would be good if the choice of relish could be left to an African."[64]

Fr. Christopher Gardiner, who entered the seminary at Chishawasha in 1965, recalled that "the quantities of food were so small—that was the first time ever I was hungry," and that "breakfast was the killer: slimy *sadza*, a little bit of milk, some bread which was pretty stale and you could see right through it, [and] butter the size of your thumbnail."[65]

Given the state of education available to Africans at the time, it is notable that the four candidates sent from Kutama to Chishawasha in 1934 had completed Standard VII (the highest level available to Africans at the time) and were certified teachers. The students who joined them, however, had not completed Standards III and IV; thus the seminary staff, including Bishop Chichester, had to begin training at the primary level.[66] According to Chichester, in 1936 six of eleven candidates had passed Standard II, three had passed Standard III, and two had passed Standard IV. By 1955, no one was admitted without having completed Standard VI, and upon entrance into the minor seminary candidates began studying for the University College of Rhodesia junior certificate (JC). In 1956, seminarians began studying for the Cambridge exams. Chichester noted that generally "boys at the top of their classes in the missions do not come to the seminary," with most coming from "the top middle." The bishop refused anyone from the bottom third of his class. Chichester's evaluation of the seminarians' academic performance was that they were "poor" at arithmetic, "fair" at algebra, and "hopeless" at geometry.[67] Their studies of Latin declensions and verb conjugations were "excellent" and of English "quite fair." The students were "rather poor" at Roman history.

By 1940, the first seminarians began their studies in Philosophy, and the seminary officially became a major seminary and then a theologate in 1944.[68] Despite the gradual increase in academic standards, the Jesuit staff geared the course of studies to what they perceived as the students' low educational level and focused on preparing the seminarians to be mission or parish priests. As was customary in the pre–Vatican II church, philosophy and theology courses were taught in Latin, even though English was the second (and in some cases the third) language of the seminarians. Courses for the major seminarians focused mainly on "theoretical scholastic (Thomistic) philosophy and theology . . . defending theses with three examiners. Looking back, one is astonished by one's own stupidity," recalled Jesuit Father Patrick Moloney.[69]

In 1949, Chichester applied to the director of the Native Education Department (NED) to have the Rhodesian administration recognize the seminary's academic formation as equivalent to the standards established for its schools.[70] The NED recognized philosophy students who completed the Kutama teacher-training course "as holding the equivalent of the University Junior Certificate," (JC) and theology students who completed the four-year course "as holding the equivalent of the Matriculation Certificate."[71] Curiously, Chichester claimed that the three-year philosophy course was "a course embracing the same subjects as at the seminaries in England, but not entered into so deeply."[72] He seems to have forgotten the dictates of the papal encyclicals, *Maximum Illud* and *Rerum Ecclesiae*, that called for equal education for Western and mission seminarians.

By 1953, the formation program at the seminary had taken shape:

Boys are accepted after passing Standard V, generally at one of the Mission Central Schools, so that the first year at the Seminary is spent in working for the Native Education Department Standard VI exam. . . . After Std. VI, there follows a three year course for the Union of South Africa Junior Certificate exam but with the opening of a University in Salisbury, there will probably be a change in the near future, and Seminarians will sit for the exam offered by Salisbury. After the Junior Certificate comes a two year course, either Elementary Teacher Training or National Primary Higher [PTH], and for this our Seminarians go either to Gokomere (Bethlehem Fathers), or to Kutama (Marist Brothers) or to Chikuni, Northern Rhodesia (S.J.). Then follows one year of Probation Teaching. All this time, the Seminarians are classed as minors. On their return to the Seminary for three years [of] Philosophy, they become Majors. Philosophy is followed by the four-year course of Theology and Ordination, and then the newly-ordained Priest has still one further year at the Seminary—that is, the Seminary is still his "home," but he [is] often away in the Mission fields doing supply-work, giving retreats, catechism classes etc.[73]

The NED, however, rescinded the seminary's junior certificate equivalency in 1958 and required the more advanced PTH certificate in order to teach the upper primary standards.[74]

Discipline was typically strict for that period as well, including the use of corporal punishment: "They [the seminarians] understood they would be smacked if disobedient. In the first two years about ten were smacked each year; now [1955] about two or three."[75] Chichester also imposed a regimen that strictly regulated the seminarians' daily lives. Typically, the students would be awakened at 5:45 in the morning (6:15 on Sundays and during holidays):

All must rise quickly when the calling bell is rung, and must wash before entering the church. All must take a shower bath or wash all the body every day except in very cold weather. At mass all should answer the priest with the servers and join in the prayers which are recited. The Minor seminarians cook the food. When young boys (under 15) are cooking, two will be appointed. No one may take hot water from the Fathers' kitchen without leave. The Philosophers may take hot water to wash their dishes. . . . Seminarians must not talk to the [St. Peter Claver] novices. English must always be spoken at meals and at works on school days. . . . On Thursday afternoons, those who do not want to play football must work.[76]

Similar rules required the students to remain at the seminary during vacations, mandated silence for extensive periods each day—particularly "from the end of night prayer until after mass the next morning," regulated their clothing, and where (and how many) seminarians could go on the seminary grounds.[77] Seminarians had "general leave" to send two letters per month. "The letters must be handed in to Fr. Superior. [The seminarians] are not expected to write many letters. Four a month is considered sufficient."[78] Lights out came at 9:00,[79] although the superior could permit students to study privately after night prayers until 9:30.[80] Seminarians could be dismissed if they failed Kutama's entrance exam or failed to earn their teaching certificate.

Spiritual duties, including prayers in Latin, English, and ChiZezuru, included

a quarter hour's meditation daily, before mass [for Major seminarians]. Morning prayers are to be said in common before mass. All must hear Mass daily, unless they be sick. They should answer the prayers with the server, and join in all prayers which are recited. When prayers are not recited publicly they ought to use a prayer-book. Servers at Mass are to observe the directions contained in the leaflets issued on this subject for the Vicariate. Five minutes examination of conscience is to be made in Chapel before the mid-day meal. Rosary is to be said in common in Chapel every day. Night prayers are said together before retiring.[81]

As with LCBL Sister candidates, Chichester was ambivalent about the quality of the seminarians and their education. In an essay apparently written to mission donors, Chichester sounded optimistic and confident about the formation of the African clergy:

They have been given quite a comprehensive education, more liberal than that of many millionaires, in fact, they have surpassed them as the reading of Caesar and Livy in the original is quite above many millionaires' accomplishments. As the venture is new and as the native population has first to be educated up to the idea of the priesthood, it is natural that some should not stay the long course; but in spite of defections, the number remains constant, about twenty five. . . . [The students receive instruction in Latin] which is obviously essential for a future priest [but they also receive training in other subjects including] other useful subjects like First Aid and for the proper maintenance of their small wardrobe, sewing and laundry work. They are good at languages, weaker in algebra and geometry than in other subjects, and they positively hate sewing as being the work of girls. . . . They dress in shirts and shorts and their diet is ordinary native fare, but cleanliness is always insisted on, shower-baths and a liberal ration of soap being provided.[82]

Yet, when communicating with other bishops, Chichester's view of African seminarians was far more patronizing and paternalistic:

As one would expect, they enter without any real idea of a vocation—willing to give it a try. Various defects of the African are manifested in their children's lack of background, no knowledge or appreciation of love or the meaning of love, little sense of gratitude, a great economy of the whole truth. . . . When they leave, I fancy they seldom give the true reason—that they find the life hard and do not fit in or find it too humiliating to be unsuccessful at their studies.[83]

Regardless of the quality of education, the seminary had a high attrition rate. According to Chichester, from 1936 when the seminary opened to the establishment of the hierarchy in 1955, almost 260 students began studies for the priesthood, about half of whom had been from the Bulawayo vicariate or Northern Rhodesia. By 1955, twelve priests had been ordained, four men were studying theology, thirteen were studying philosophy, forty-seven were in the minor seminary, and one hundred and eighty-four had left the seminary. Of those who had departed, two were dismissed "for something nasty," five for "gross disobedience," one for "general slackness," and two for lack of brain power." Thus, during the seminary's first two decades two thirds (67 per cent) of the candidates apparently left of their own accord.

Jesuit W. F. Rea wrote that from 1934 to 1974 "300 [students] passed through the minor seminary and survived at least one term. Of these 91 entered the Major seminary and of these 39 were ordained priests."[84] Thus, according to Rea's numbers, only 13 percent of those students who entered the minor seminary successfully completed the full course of studies and were ordained priests. The lists of ordinands appended to Fr. Constantine Mashonganyika's brief history of the seminary, however, show that from 1947 to 1974 there were seventy men ordained to the priesthood.[85] While Fr. Mashonganyika did not include the number of minor seminarians who were eventually ordained, he reported 413 men who entered the major seminary between 1940 and 1983, of whom 113 became priests, or 27 percent.[86] While not possible to account for Rea's significant underreporting of the number of ordinands, if Mashonganyika had included the number of students who had entered a minor seminary and completed their studies through ordination, his attrition rate would have been significantly higher.

Although reasons for leaving seminary formation are varied and very personal, some members of Chichester's staff apparently had concerns that many students were leaving during the period of study for the teacher-training certificate at Kutama between the minor and major seminary courses. After two years on the seminary staff at Chishawasha, Jesuit Francis Barr, upon hearing that "an outstanding" candidate at Kutama had left, wrote to Chichester that "something is radically wrong at Kutama. . . . Apparently the Seminarians there are not merely tested but broken."[87] He complained that the Jesuit chaplain had been grossly lax in his spiritual care of the seminary candidates, and that the other students frequently assaulted the seminarians with a "mass of mis-representations" that, without some measure of support from the chaplain, "discourages them so that they cannot bear it any longer and give up." The misrepresentations that "are said several times a week to each one" included

a) Candidates are unable to pay school fees, so they pretend that they wish to be priests, get their education free and then leave the Seminary.

b) They want to get free clothes.

c) Candidates have been castrated. They want to be priests because they cannot have children.

d) Some of the candidates are courting girls at Kutama, so it is clear that they do not really mean to be priests.

e) Why do the candidates say, after the Consecration, "Jesus, Mary, Joseph, give us priests from our own nation"? They ought to say, "Jesus, Mary, Joseph, *make us* priests of our own nation." It proves that they don't want to be priests themselves.

f) *All* candidates will go to hell for they are robbing His Lordship.[88]

Further, Barr reported that the seminarians felt that the Marist brothers who ran the school were also discouraging of their vocations:

Some of the Brothers say the following things to the Candidates:

a) Those boys who do not pay fees are the ones who complain the most and give most trouble.

b) The Candidates must be caned from time to time.

c) Once candidates get their E.T.C. [Teacher's Certificate] their heads begin to swell and they think themselves "somebody," and give up. That is stealing. It would be better for them not to receive any certificate when they finish the course.[89]

Barr concluded that two years of such treatment so early in their formation was "asking too much from the Seminarians," and that "few European boys would carry on in the face of such opposition." This situation casts serious doubt on Dachs and Rea's assertion that "indeed Kutama proved a seed bed for vocations."[90] Although not with the same frequency or virulence as sister candidates, several priests mentioned familial opposition to their entering the seminary and foregoing the cultural norm of having children.[91]

Simon Tsuro and Isidore Chikore were the first seminarians from Chishawasha to be ordained priests in 1947. They had to spend an additional pastoral year at the seminary. Five others had joined them by 1955.[92] The bishop housed and fed them "as any other priest and [they] live with them on the missions," and paid a stipend of £6 per month. The new priests could keep any "stipends and honoraria for sermons and retreats." They had to submit any government teaching salaries to the bishop, which Chichester saved in respective accounts for them. The new priests could not buy cattle, houses, or land and had to request permission from the mission superior where they resided to spend over £5.[93] Chichester also required the *ordinandi* to refrain from drinking alcohol for a year after ordination, and "after a year I tell them they are no longer bound by any promise but it I think it would be wise for them to keep it up." The priests were assigned to St. Peter's parish in Mbare and other missions, and according to Chichester, "they all give 'missions' and retreats and are in fairly constant demand. They seem to be much respected by their own people and do much good."[94] The number of younger priests who said that the examples of these pioneer African priests inspired them to enter the seminary bears out Chichester's positive estimation.[95]

The Brothers of St. Peter Claver

Of the four "helpers" who entered the seminary in 1936, only Boniface Gondo professed and renewed annual promises to serve the Zambezi Mission. In 1939, the "helpers" built and moved into their own house on the seminary grounds, and in 1940 four entered their novitiate. On February 2, 1942, Boniface Gondo, Stephen Chiwanza, and Andrew Pashane professed vows as the first Brothers of St. Peter Claver.[96] Like the LCBL Sisters, the Brothers of St. Peter Claver were a diocesan congregation with Chichester as their superior and a German Jesuit as their novice master, and whose members had to renew their vows annually until 1954 when they were allowed to renew them every three years. Unlike the LCBLs, however, the Brothers of St. Peter Claver apparently never received a constitution, only a set of common rules governing their daily lives.[97] Furthermore, "it was decided that there was no future for them," so the congregation was disbanded in the 1960s, and its members were incorporated into the Jesuits.[98] The seminary house diarist noted Boniface Gondo's death but neglected to record the deaths, departures, or transfers of Stephen Chiwanza, and Andrew Pashane.[99] All three were remembered as "holy," "prayerful," and "spiritual" men.[100]

The brief history of the Brothers of St. Peter Claver again raises questions about Chichester's motivations regarding his choices for the formation of African religious. One possible explanation is that as with the LCBLs and the diocesan clergy Chichester was trying to implement Pius XI's directives from *Rerum Ecclesiae*. Thus, men's orders such as the Jesuits would not have received African candidates as brothers until 1959 or priests until 1962. Chichester's pre-1942 description of the nascent brotherhood supports this view: "The Seminary also houses the noviceship for the Brothers. There are already Native Sisters in the Vicariate, but as yet none of the Brothers have vowed to follow the life of the counsels [i.e., poverty chastity, and obedience]. But a beginning has been made and soon we hope to have men, living under vows and working on the mission stations."[101] Furthermore, there is an oral tradition among the Jesuits in Harare similar to that among the Dominican sisters that the new bishop asked his confreres not to admit African candidates, but rather send them to the fledgling diocesan seminary.[102]

The agreement between Chichester and the Marist brothers whom he invited to supervise Kutama Teacher Training School in 1939, however, complicates the possibility of this option. The agreement stipulated that

the brothers shall contribute 2% [of] the money received from the government. This contribution is common to all the schools in the Vicariate, but it will cease for Kutama if ever the Brothers undertake the training of native subjects for brotherhood. . . . Though negotiations are already on foot to begin a congregation for natives, the Vicar Apostolic will put no difficulties [in] the way of any native wishing to join the Institute of the Marist Brothers.[103]

The agreement clearly violated the spirit of *Maximum Illud* and *Rerum Ecclesiae*, if not their letter.

Another possible motive is that given the 1926 survey respondents' views about African candidates' lack of intellectual and moral "fitness" for the clergy, the Jesuits were loath to admit Africans. It is a commonly held view of the members of the Jesuits' Zimbabwe province that the first African candidates they admitted were brother candidates who could not follow the course of studies for ordination. The first two Zimbabwean African Jesuit priests, Gilbert Modikayi and Raymond Kapito, were ordained as priests for the Archdiocese of Salisbury in

1956, and of the other two ordained before independence, Patrick Makaka had completed philosophy studies at Chishawasha seminary.[104] In other words, in the Jesuits' first century in Zimbabwe they only admitted one African candidate, Ignatius Zvarevashe, to the full course of studies for ordination to the priesthood.

The Regional Major Seminary and Student Protests, 1958–1979

In 1955, the Vatican established the hierarchy in Southern Rhodesia, raising Salisbury to a metropolitan see and erecting suffragan sees in Bulawayo, Gwelo (Gweru), Umtali (Mutare), and Wankie (Hwange). Chichester became archbishop in April 1955, and in 1956, Francis Markall was appointed *coadjutor cum iure successionis* and succeeded Chichester.[105]

The hierarchy's establishment significantly affected the seminary. In 1958, Jesuit Francis McKeown succeeded Donald Johnson as seminary rector.[106] Also in 1958, Propaganda Fide decreed Chishawasha a regional seminary.[107] Previously, the superior of the Jesuit community was de facto superior of the seminary, reporting to Chichester and later to Markall as the bishop and de jure superior of a diocesan seminary. As such, the bishop had a canonical right and responsibility to visit the seminary under his jurisdiction, even if he entrusted its administration to a religious institute, such as the Jesuits in this case. As a regional seminary, however, Chishawasha served candidates from all of the dioceses in Southern Rhodesia. As such, the seminary became the property of the Holy See and came under Propaganda Fide's responsibility, which entrusted the administration to the Jesuits. The bishops were free to interact with and direct their respective candidates, but did not have the canonical right or responsibility to visit the seminary. Rather, they were required "to meet each year to receive and discuss the report of the Rector on the moral and economic state of the Seminary," and "any observations they may wish to make to the Rector will generally be communicated to him by the local ordinary" of the diocese where the seminary is located.[108]

The change in the seminary's status resulted in confusion concerning the role and authority of the bishops in the seminary's governance and an ambiguous relationship between the seminary rector and the newly established seminary board of bishops.[109] This ambiguity was one of the significant factors that contributed to the rise and expression of student protests at the seminary in the 1960s and 1970s.

The drive to make Chishawasha an exclusively major seminary contributed significantly to the rise of student radicalism. Before 1958, there were never more than seven staff members teaching at the seminary at any time and, after 1940, they had to teach both minor and major seminarians.[110] By the 1950s, the number of seminarians had increased to the point that Chichester had to solicit funds to expand the physical plant and seek additional money for their support.[111] In 1953, there were two fifth year priests, seventeen major seminarians, and thirty-eight minor seminarians reported at Chishawasha.[112] In 1955, the number of major seminarians remained the same, but minor seminarians increased to forty-seven.[113] In 1956, there were four theologians, three major seminarians teaching during their probationary year, and three others studying advanced teacher training at Kutama; seventeen philosophers and thirty-one minor seminarians at Chishawasha; and an additional eighteen in the regular teacher-training course at Kutama, for a total of seventy-six students.[114] Given the number of prospective applicants for 1957, the number of seminarians would "soar up and it is a matter of some anxiety where to house all those who wish to come. The twelve new rooms provided by the recently finished extensions are not going to be sufficient and, as a temporary measure, will have to be shared: not at all a satisfactory arrangement as they are scarcely large enough for two. To sleep, yes; to study, no. But unless we pitch tents, there would seem to be no other immediate solution."[115]

As early as 1956 there was a "rumour . . . that the minors are to go to [the secondary school at St. Paul's Mission,] Musami to leave this establishment for Majors only."[116] On becoming rector in 1958, Francis McKeown pursued the separation of the minor seminarians vigorously, hoping to ease an increasingly acute staffing problem resulting from the shortage of Jesuits in the Zambezi Mission, the growing number of minor seminarians, and the disparity in ages between incoming minor seminarians and older major seminarians.[117] Beginning with the 1963 academic year, the Seminary of Saints John Fisher and Thomas More at Chishawasha became a regional major seminary. Candidates for the priesthood were then sent to minor seminaries at Chikwingwizha near Gwelo or Melsetter (Chimanimani) in the Umtali diocese.[118]

As a result of this decision, African candidates for the priesthood received exposure to perspectives on the church and African culture different from those of the Jesuits, and the effects of that exposure cannot be underestimated. The Swiss Bethlehem Mission Fathers, whom Chichester invited to take charge of the southern part of the Salisbury vicariate in 1938, ran the minor seminary at Chikwingwizha. In 1947, the Vatican erected the prefecture apostolic of Fort Victoria (Masvingo) under their direction, and in 1948 Bishop Aloysius Haene, SMB founded a minor seminary, which he expanded and moved to Chikwingwizha in 1962.[119] Unlike the Jesuits, the Bethlehem missionaries took a very positive view of African culture, and greatly encouraged the incorporation of African cultural symbols and vocabulary into the corpus of the church's practice.[120] By and throughout the 1970s, "there were more students from the Gwelo Diocese at Chishawasha Major Seminary than from any other diocese, and in 1977 more than from the two old dioceses of Salisbury and Bulawayo together. Between 1973 and 1976, 9 African priests were ordained for the Gwelo Diocese, compared with 6 for Bulawayo, 4 for Umtali, and 2 each for Wankie and Salisbury." The relatively intellectually open environment in the minor seminaries under the Bethlehem missionaries and the Carmelites,[121] combined with increasing African nationalism on the part of the seminarians, and an increasingly aging and reactionary Jesuit community set the stage for the rebellions that would shake the seminary in the 1960s and 1970s.

By the 1950s, African nationalism in Southern Rhodesia was on the rise with the renaissance of the Industrial and Commercial Workers' Union (ICU), and the founding of the National Democratic Party in 1959, and African nationalism began to manifest itself in the seminary during this period as well.[122] Jesuit documents make frequent references to "less visible respect for authority," "challenges to authority," and "lack of respect," including a seminarian proclaiming to a staff member that Rhodesia needed a "Mau Mau," and another incident in which an African deacon struck a Jesuit priest on staff.[123] Rector Francis McKeown reported that "the seminarians seem to be far too conscious of their own status and dignity, and too ready to feel slighted and offended."[124] There are frequent references to the seminarians' awareness of the political situation—adding that this was causing the problems. African priests who spent their fifth year at Chishawasha were not only becoming less willing to be treated in the same manner as seminarians, but also "apparently did not consider themselves as seminarians, as was shown by the fact that they tended to ignore notices addressed to seminarians," and that the seminarians were "slack" in "raising their hats to priests" and on "a number of similar points."[125] McKeown noted that "the fifth year has difficulties of its own, the chief being the mental or psychological adjustment necessary to live as a priest and yet one in statu pupillari." He suggested that bishops should withhold fifth-year priests' faculties and delay their attendance at annual diocesan clergy conferences "to help remind them that they are still student priests."[126] Another Jesuit on staff voiced concern that a fifth-year priest reported that the African workmen at the seminary "were complaining of their wages"; he considered it "dangerous if the Seminarians went around enquiring into such matters and sympathising with the workmen."[127] This attitude is indicative of the Jesuits' paternalism and their growing isolation from the seminarians' concerns.

It was only in 1959, and partially responding to student demands, that seminary staff began inviting speakers from outside the seminary to present guest lectures on topics such as African culture and urban life, Rhodesian and South African racial policies, and Shona history and religion.[128] It is "indicative" of the "closedness" of the majority of the staff that the staff member who invited Dr. Michael Gelfand to give a lecture on Shona ancestral spirits and religious practitioners had "to bribe" the rector by taking on several different assignments.[129]

During his annual visitation to the seminary in 1961, Salisbury Mission superior T. E. Corrigan thought it "incredible" that seminarians would "talk politics" and found it necessary to suggest means "of controlling this."[130] In 1962, Corrigan noted that the staff was "worried" about "the general discipline," "the contact and knowledge of the staff with regard to the seminarians," and "the corresponding personal confidence [that] individual seminarians have in the staff." Urging the staff to make "a very positive effort . . . to know and be at the disposal of the students," Corrigan observed that it seemed "that the [Jesuit] community is dangerously isolated from the seminarians, and consequently confidence and discipline are endangered. There is also a very great danger that accurate knowledge of individual seminarians is lacking." By 1963, although Corrigan commended the staff for having decided to take two meals per day with the students, he scolded them for not having done anything to improve the lines of communication with the seminarians. The staff revised the seminary constitutions and custom book "to [impose] a stricter regime." Corrigan urged the cooperation of all "to make it reasonable."[131] According to Jesuit Patrick Moloney, the staff had established "a little Jesuit enclave at the seminary."[132] As late as 1974, Jesuit professors told African seminarians who asked in-depth philosophical questions in class not to "bother with it" as they were being trained to be "simple parish priests."[133]

The idyllic enclave came to an abrupt end. In 1964, Francis McKeown proposed to and received approval from the bishops to enroll two white students at the seminary for the 1965 academic year.[134] Apparently he did so without either having consulted the other members of the staff, or having notified them that he would be stepping down as rector and leaving for sabbatical in 1965.[135] Four students arrived from the segregated seminary of St. John Vianney in Pretoria. Less than a week after the term began, John Diamond, McKeown's successor, noted that the whites had expressed "great dissatisfaction" with the food, accommodations, timetable, and general living conditions. "They have allied themselves quickly with the professional malcontents." They adamantly opposed manual labor, especially laundry. Although two of them, Geoffrey Goodwin and Peter Saunders, left the seminary less than three weeks after the term began, alleging "that they were grossly misled by Fr. McKeown as to conditions here,"[136] their grievances resonated with the African seminarians, who sent an anonymous letter of complaint to the Southern Rhodesian bishops from "the Seminary Group," despite the institution of daily afternoon tea for all the seminarians at the end of February.[137] Additionally, one of the two remaining whites, Anthony Turner, sent a lengthy memorandum on how the seminary should be run to Francis Markall, the Archbishop of Salisbury and Chairman of the Seminary Board of Bishops, after he (Turner) left the seminary in April.[138]

According to Christopher Gardiner, the fourth of the seminarians from St. John Vianney and the only one to stay past the first term of the 1965 academic year, Saunders, Turner, and Goodwin had approached Markall, their bishop, about transferring to Chishawasha from Pretoria, and shortly before Christmas 1964 asked Gardiner, who was from Bulawayo, "What are you gonna do?" Gardiner, the only one of the four born in Rhodesia, decided that he had to "give an honest evaluation," and spoke with Adolph Schmitt, the bishop of Bulawayo. Whereas Markall had some reservations about admitting the whites to Chishawasha, Schmitt was "opposed because the seminary was not ready [for integration]. It would cause problems for the staff and students." One of the Jesuits on staff at Chishawasha gave them a tour of the grounds and physical plant. "The old philosophers' wing was dilapidated," but the new theologians' wing "gave the impression they were looking forward to our coming." Against the opposition of his family and the displeasure of his bishop, Gardiner decided to go to Chishawasha for his theology studies: "The good Lord touched my heart. This is what I have to do."[139]

Conditions in January 1965 were "primitive": "There was no light in the rooms: there were high ceilings in a brick building with maybe a 40 watt bulb." When the four met their African confreres, Gardiner recalled, "They were very welcoming. They were just terrific." Despite the warm welcome, "problems arose very quickly" regarding the schedule ("Lights out was at nine o'clock"), food ("Lunch and supper were okay because the faculty ate with us but the quantities of food were so small—that was the first time ever I was hungry . . . and that breakfast was the killer: slimy *sadza*, a little bit of milk, some bread which was pretty stale and you could see right through it, [and] butter the size of your thumbnail"), classes ("Studies were really poor. Except for one or two lecturers they were ex–high school teachers from St. George's: they were shipped out when they were worn out there. . . . Texts were in Latin. The standard was pathetic compared to St. John's. There was no time for study"), and manual labor ("As students we were used as servants for the complex. Most of it was really unnecessary. . . . We had to wash our own clothes [by hand] and use coal irons").[140]

The students were treated "as second class citizens compared to the Jesuits," recalled Father Gardiner. "We began talking with the other students about St. John's, and their eyes opened up: The Jesuits told them this is how it was at other seminaries. We told them that [the Jesuits] were using and abusing you." Father Constantine Mashonganyika confirmed this, noting

some Africans reacted when they [the four whites] criticised things. The [seminary] authorities reacted. The Jesuits were not happy to have them at that point. We were worried that [the Jesuits] were sending them away because they were showing us things we had a right to. A number of students worked every day. They said they can't work every day. The food was very different for them: *sadza* and *miriwo*, and the *sadza* was not properly cooked. . . . Lectures [left] something to be desired. Studies were in Latin. [They asked] Why not use English books? [The four] objected to these things.[141]

The four "decided to rebel" by not going to manual labor. "We stayed in our rooms and read," said Fr. Gardiner, "There was conflict from the beginning." When they were not punished for their disobedience, many of the African students questioned what they perceived to be differential treatment by the Jesuits, a charge John Diamond would deny vehemently in the ensuing imbroglio with the bishops.[142] According to Gardiner, the African students were "disappointed" when Saunders, Goodwin, and Turner left.

The letter from the Seminary Group written at the end of February and received by the bishops in mid March[143] alleged that the students had been complaining to the seminary authorities for years, yet "nobody hears us." They complained that the library books were at least twenty-five years old, all written by Jesuits, and contained no modern philosophy. The timetable was too rigid, not allowing enough time for study, and that they were "merely studying for examinations." As they wanted more time "to read widely," they proposed a new timetable. They were adamant against having to do manual labor, especially laundry. They also wanted more vacation time and to spend vacations away from the seminary. With the money saved by not being at the seminary during vacations, they requested that it be used to provide morning and afternoon tea. The Seminary Group also asked that ordinations be moved from December to August–September due to the rains limiting access to the event, and that their relatives be allowed to visit, as they "are becoming secular priests and not an order or the like."[144]

Turner also criticized every aspect of life at the seminary and accused the Jesuits of being "too paternal" and looking "down on the African clergy and students as second-rate." Thus, Turner believed, there was an anti-Jesuit feeling among the Africans of Southern Rhodesia. Though Turner critiqued the Jesuits' alleged racism, he expressed equally problematic views.[145]

Despite the tensions that the whites' presence caused, Christopher Gardiner believed that the Jesuits wanted the experiment to work:

[On Sundays] Breakfast was prepared around five o'clock in the morning, and those of us who served the mass at Chishawasha [Mission] didn't eat until after ten o'clock. [One Sunday in 1966] there were weevils in the porridge [which] had a hard crust on top. I complained to the refectorian, who said he couldn't do anything about it and to complain to Fr. Moloney. I was in my second year, so I picked up the porridge and went to show it to Diamond. The other students were afraid of what was going to happen. There was a staff meeting in the rector's office, and I put it on Diamond's desk and said, "Would you eat this?!" Moloney grabbed me, and yelled, "Down to my office!" He read me the riot act. He told me I was "taking advantage of [my] white skin." He told me to tell everyone to be in the refectory in a half an hour. We went back in a half an hour, and at Moloney's order there were eggs and bacon, toast and tea. Diamond then called a meeting and said there would be changes: better food and afternoon tea. And there were. Things radically changed.[146]

The minutes of the numerous seminary consultors' meetings dealing with the issue of how to keep Christopher Gardiner at Chishawasha confirmed these changes.[147]

The Jesuits often complained of the African seminarians' poor educational abilities:[148]

Equipped on entry with only three or four years of secondary education (little more than grade-school education) of mediocre quality, our average Seminarian finds the ideas and language of his studies and of the liturgy unfamiliar, subtle and hard to make his own. He must besides learn through the medium of English, which he understands only imperfectly, because his own native tongue is too local and too inadequate for philosophy and theology. As for Latin, he seems to find its accuracy and conciseness peculiarly frustrating and unmanageable. It is only to be expected that he finds the going steep, industrious though he is.[149]

Yet by the 1960s, they were becoming aware of the poor quality of the men teaching at the seminary.[150] McKeown iterated the "need for men of the highest calibre":

It is a fatal mistake for people in England to think that we are dealing with simple "savages" and simple problems and that therefore anybody at all is good enough for Mission work. We want first-rate men, spiritually, intellectually, and with imaginative sympathy to get outside a Western skin and inside a Bantu one. . . . There is mental staleness and spiritual staleness also to be taken into account. Missionaries are so overworked that they do little or no reading or thinking. They get into a rut. . . . Old and broken Missionaries, middle aged and stale missionaries back on leave after 17 or 20 years are not the best advert. Many who are wavering would be influenced by the knowledge that there is regular leave. Everyone else seems to practise it except ourselves.[151]

Both African and European students wanted more time to study for O-level exams by correspondence. Despite Jesuit opposition to the seminarians' taking external courses, older seminarians frequently encouraged incoming students to study for their O-levels.[152]

Diamond did not take the Seminary Group or Anthony Turner seriously. He thought Turner's memorandum was "really only a heavy joke," and he characterized the anonymous letter as "a typical example of a certain type of African opportunism and meanness."[153] Diamond's response may have been due to the bishops' apparent inaction as well as his view of African culture.

Because Turner apparently sent a revised copy of his memorandum to Francis Markall after he left the seminary on April 12, 1965, on May 5, the board of bishops met and decided to ask Propaganda Fide to approve an external investigation of the seminary by "someone experienced in Seminary administration in countries similar to Rhodesia in background," and commissioned Markall as chairman to draft and send the letter of request to Rome.[154] The bishops' action sparked an immediate and furious response from Diamond and Edward Ennis, the Salisbury Mission superior. In a flurry of correspondence between Diamond, Markall, and Jesuit superiors in London and Rome, Ennis pressed hard to prevent Markall from sending the letter to Propaganda Fide, and by June succeeded in making the bishops back down. Ennis and Diamond argued that when Chishawasha became a regional seminary in 1958 it came under Propaganda Fide's control, which entrusted its administration to the Jesuits. Before the Rhodesian bishops' May 1965 decision neither the bishops nor Propaganda Fide ever criticized the Jesuits' administration. Thus, calling for an external investigation without previously notifying either Diamond or Ennis was a gross discourtesy and an unwarranted drastic measure that would be a vote of no confidence by the bishops in the seminary administration, and the rector in particular; would undermine the seminary administration's authority and compromise discipline among the students; and would signal to the seminarians that such behavior could achieve results and reward malcontents for inappropriate behavior. This latter reason was particularly unpalatable to the Jesuits because they believed that the failed effort at integration that had caused such difficulties was not their fault, but because the four whites from Pretoria were not the right students with whom to try such an experiment. Evidently Diamond kept all information of the conflict between the bishops and himself and Ennis from the students and staff.[155]

Although Diamond had not taken the seminarians' letters seriously and had intended to let matters at the seminary cool off by themselves, the events of May 1965 were not lost on him. On June 22, he held a staff meeting and asked his fellow Jesuits to "consider whether any modifications of existing rules and arrangements are desirable."[156] He added, "This is an opportune time. Suggestions and criticisms have been made, and we should, I think, look at the substance of them, prescinding from the accidental circumstances which surround the making of them. It is possible that some changes of arrangements or emphasis would be wise."[157] Resulting from this failed integration experiment, Christopher Gardiner and the African seminarians were allowed to go home for the vacation between the second and third terms, the daily order changed to include more time for study and less time at manual labor, ordinations were held in August, and washing machines were installed.[158]

Although the seminary was peaceful in 1966, Christopher Gardiner left Chishawasha to return to St. John Vianney Seminary in Pretoria.[159] The students and staff were "very supportive," and "surprised" that he stayed as long as he did. The decision to leave "was a very hard decision" on Gardiner's part, but he felt he had to do so because "the academics [at Chishawasha] were so poor I wouldn't be academically prepared [for the priesthood] if I stayed." Of his time at Chishawasha seminary, Fr. Gardiner recalled that "they were good years. There was lots of frustration. . . . There was lots of injustice in the place. It was a place of servitude. They were unprepared, but wanted it [integration] to work. The Jesuits knew about the injustice and the servitude, and they got away with it."[160]

The 1967 Crisis

The 1967 academic year brought another crisis to the seminary. According to Diamond, discipline declined throughout the year, including "representations to RPR for increased study time and abolition of manual works, culminating in an ultimatum delivered by the beadle, Constantine [Mashonganyika]." Although Diamond noted that study time had been almost doubled to four hours per day since 1965, he decided to close the seminary on October 10, 1967, and send the students home "for further reflection." On November 1, when all the seminarians except Mashonganyika were allowed to return, they were required to sign an "understanding to abide by seminary rules, manual work, etc."[161]

Given that, unlike the integration episode of 1965, the seminary was closed in 1967, there is relatively little documentation of the incident. On October 12, Diamond sent a letter to the bishops and to Edward Ennis explaining his rationale for closing the seminary: the whites in 1965 "had succeeded in conveying to our seminarians the impression that they were receiving treatment inferior to that of seminarians elsewhere just because they were Africans." Mashonganyika had been away from the seminary on pastoral probation in 1966, and upon returning brought demands for more study time and morning tea, and an end to manual works, culminating in the petition signed by fifteen seminarians. According to Diamond, subsequent investigation revealed that Mashonganyika coerced younger seminarians to sign the petition, and the decision to close the seminary was an effort to prevent irreparable damage to the vocations of the younger seminarians as well as to "facilitate getting rid of the unhealthy elements who were at the root of the troubles." Mashonganyika, however, claimed that he was merely bringing the concerns of the majority to the seminary administration in his capacity as prefect, and that "there wasn't any defiance of authority." The petition came from the "majority of students," and there were four or five who "didn't want anything to do with it," of whom three were asked to remain behind to answer staff questions, alleging coercion.[162]

As in 1965, the bishops apparently wanted "to call in an external commission to make a visitation of [the] seminary."[163] As in 1965, Diamond responded with virtually the same argument against an external investigation. Unlike 1965, however, there is only one letter from Diamond extant, which appears to be the only evidence of Jesuit resistance to episcopal interference in the running of the seminary. Unlike 1965 as well, there was no process of self-reflection on the part of the seminary staff or any effort to consider student demands.

There was, however, a confidential two-page summary of comments on seminary training by five recently ordained African priests, which indicated a perception of a condescending, paternalistic attitude on the part of the Jesuits; a narrow focus on scholastic philosophy and "no knowledge of African life" on the part of the staff; an overemphasis on the seminary constitution and custom book, "too much manual work," and priests having to observe the same rules as seminarians ("[the Jesuits] did not regard you as a priest"). The young priests concluded that

there was no contact, let alone dialogue, between staff and students. It was a master-servant attitude. . . . The trouble in October was not a matter which came suddenly, nor was it instigated by one seminarian, it could and should have come 3 years earlier. It was brewing all the time. Fr. Diamond tried to improve things but was too hesitant and did not have the cooperation of the other staff members.[164]

A letter from the Jesuit General Assistant for Africa to Bishop Haene of Gwelo stated that he and Ennis had discussed removing Diamond as rector by the middle of 1968.[165] Diamond, however, remained as rector through 1969, and Constantine Mashonganyika was readmitted to the seminary in 1970 and ordained in 1973.

During the 1960s, although the seminary staffing crisis became more acute, Diamond and his confreres at the seminary flatly refused a suggestion that the Carmelites and Bethlehem missionaries be invited to assist in staffing the seminary.[166] The seminary rector was either unfamiliar with or had forgotten Benedict XV's exhortation to invite other religious institutes to share the work of a mission when the institute given charge of the mission was not providing an adequate supply of workers. In 1970, Edward Ennis advised the bishops that staffing at the seminary was "minimal" and that the majority of the staff was "of an advanced age." He believed it was "a matter of great urgency" that an African priest be appointed to the staff, and that "thought should be given to preparing selected seminarians for future teaching in the Seminary." Although the bishops "agreed" with Ennis's points and sent two African priests for higher studies, they made no effort to appoint an African priest or a priest of a different religious order to the seminary staff until 1975.[167]

The 1974 Strike

By 1974, African seminarians were no longer willing to settle for "being trained to be second class priests." Private studies for O- and A-levels were rampant, and lectures, according to Fr. Walter Nyatsanza, "challenged us to want to be liberated not just politically but intellectually, socially, and spiritually . . . we wanted to have the totality of liberation."[168]

The 1974 strike began on Saturday, September 28, when Seminary Rector John Berrell dismissed Deacon Ernest Mukuwapasi for extended improper conduct.[169] The next day, the theologians met on the football pitch to determine a course of action and drafted a letter to Berrell supporting Mukuwapasi signed by six recent ordinands.[170] The student priests requested an explanation for the deacon's dismissal and his return to the seminary. If their demands were not met they rescinded responsibility "for what might follow." They acknowledged that "all [Mukuwapasi] had done was to challenge [Berrell's] disturbing actions at the Table of the Lord," and that while "it did disturb the whole community at worship," it was "not without reason," and "in itself is not sufficient reason to terminate a man's long response to God's call." The students were "very disturbed" by the manner in which Berrell tried to remove Mukuwapasi "secretly."[171] They feared that "what has happened to Ernest may be going to happen to many more and, therefore we feel in conscience that things be put right for the good of the Church of God," and asked to meet with the rector following night prayers.[172] The two sides met after afternoon tea, and Berrell refused to discuss the reasons for Mukuwapasi's dismissal. The priests informed their fellow students that "the meeting had been a complete failure": "One can say that it was here on Sunday evening that the students decided to speak a language that was going to make Fr. Rector see that he was badly understanding the students and that he was underestimating their deep feelings. This language, sorry to say, took the form of a protest."[173]

On Monday, September 30, the strike began in earnest with a boycott of classes until Mukuwapasi returned to the seminary. All but four students, including two priests, withdrew to the football pitch, except for meals and spiritual duties. During meals the strikers maintained "a rigid silence." Berrell notified the bishops' secretary general who in turn notified Archbishop Markall. The rector and the seminary consultors decided that they could not meet the students' demands.[174] The next day, the priest-organizers tried to meet with Patrick McNamara, the Jesuit superior, and with Archbishop Markall and Bishop Patrick Chakaipa, all to no avail.

Tensions escalated on Wednesday, October 2.[175] At mass that morning, one of the priests who had not gone on strike was the principal celebrant. All the strikers "declined to make the sign of the cross at the beginning of Mass, declined to answer the responses (except those to the Reader) and when [the celebrant] and a deacon were distributing Communion only twelve or 15 [sic] came to receive the Sacrament." At meals, those students who were working in the kitchen "were outrageously rude to the Sisters in the kitchen." Berrell and some of the consultors met with the student-priests, strikers and nonstrikers, in an effort "to save the seminary from moral and physical ruin and destruction . . . if a way could be found." The priests claimed that Mukuwapasi's dismissal was the only issue when Berrell asked if there were "deeper issues," and they asked for "a Kissinger [to] be brought in as a facilitator to take the heat out of the situation: His Grace [Markall] or Bishop Chakaipa was suggested."[176] Neither was available to mediate. Later that night, anonymous threatening letters were placed under the doors of several staff members. At benediction, the strikers chose the hymn "Whatsoever you do to the least of my brethren, that you do unto me," and sang *Ishe Komborera Afrika* (God Save Africa) "with gusto."[177] On Thursday, October 3, efforts to secure a mediator failed again, and incidents of "rude" and "insulting" behavior by the strikers toward nonstrikers and staff increased.

On Friday, October 4, the students' efforts to contact Bishop Chakaipa failed again. The bishops' secretary general, Fr. Kevin Kinnane, informed the other bishops of the strike, and efforts at negotiation between the seminary staff and the strike leaders also failed. In the afternoon, a reporter from the *Rhodesia Herald* came to the seminary, and Markall finally arrived to meet with Berrell and the seminary consultors. Markall told the staff that the seminary would have to be closed, and left the details to Berrell.[178]

On the morning of Saturday, October 5, Berrell gave Fr. Ignatius Mhonda, one of the strike leaders, a letter announcing the closure of the seminary. Mhonda read the letter to his fellow strikers, and they all withdrew again to the football pitch. Mhonda and two other priests

returned from the football pitch with the notice of closure saying the Rector's signature was not sufficient. They needed a document from Fr. Kinnane to prove that the Bishops really did endorse the closure of the seminary. . . . Fr. Kinnane kindly consented to come at once and brought the necessary documents from the Archbishop and the Secretariat, going with these to the football pitch and eventually convincing the strikers that they must pack and go.[179]

The strikers also asked if they could stay until the morning of Monday, October 7, since transportation to their home dioceses would be easier than on Saturday or Sunday. Berrell agreed on the condition that the strikers behave themselves.[180] According to Berrell, "silence and surliness and worse rudeness to the Staff continued. . . . Some spent Saturday night annoying and attempting to terrorise members of Staff on the internal telephone system, which had to be disconnected. The same rudeness and surliness continued through Sunday."[181]

On the morning of Monday, October 7, the seminarians attended mass at 5:30, ate breakfast at 6:00, and then loaded the bus that would take them to Salisbury. "The Seminarians then ascended the terrace steps, formed a group and sang *Ishe komborera Afrika* and a folk hymn about going home after all these wasted years, whilst the Rector and Staff members stood by. The whole group of Seminarians were then solemnly blessed by Fr. Mhonda, entered the bus in silence and departed."

In the wake of the 1974 strike, against Jesuit objections, the bishops appointed an external commission to investigate the causes of the strike and to make recommendations for long-term restructuring of the seminary. The commission concluded that the situation in the seminary had been tense for some time and Ernest Mukuwapasi's dismissal was the necessary spark to set it off, and recommended that: the seminarians not be punished collectively, rather that each bishop deal with each seminarian individually; the seminary be reopened for the first term of February 1975 with Berrell as rector through the end of the year and an African priest as vice rector with right of succession in 1976.[182] Thus, after forty years the seminary's administration passed from the Jesuits to African priests. About forty of the one hundred and seven seminarians returned in 1975. Several of those who did not return joined the guerrillas fighting against the Smith regime.[183]

The seminary's atmosphere under Fr. Tobias Chiginya improved significantly. Chiginya was "quite adept and defused many of the students' concerns," including granting an elected student representative council.[184] He removed many of the petty rules that had been in force under the Jesuits and "treated us as adults," which was a great "relief" to the students: "It was what we were waiting for all along," reflected Fr. Walter Nyatsanza.

Yet, there were tensions between students that followed the divisions between ZANU and ZAPU. "Hell broke loose" shortly before the February 1980 elections when ZAPU supporters tore down a ZANU poster.[185] According to Fr. Nyatsanza, Francis Mugadzi, Chiginya's successor as rector, "had very little choice" but to close the seminary as there was "almost war between the students." The seminary reopened only after independence in April 1980.

Conclusion

In a commentary assessing the causes of the 1974 strike, W. F. Rea opined that many Africans became Catholics and entered the seminary for "unworthy motives, and mixed ones," alleging they did so for the only higher educational opportunities available at the time. "But when they see their contemporaries in secondary schools and the Universities making more progress than they," he continued, "they cannot face up to the fact that this is due to their own lack of capacity and blame everyone and everything except themselves." He similarly alleged that Africans chose to become priests for the social status that advanced education in seminary training would bring them, and absolved the seminary administration of any responsibility for the strike, which in his view was the product of African frustration at the lack of status recognition combined with the political situation and the bishops' bad treatment of the seminary.[186]

Rea blamed everyone for the strike except his brother Jesuits. The seminary staff repeatedly refused to change in the face of rising student expectations and demands: they did not heed T. E. Corrigan's reproaches from 1961 to 1963; John Diamond thought the seminarians' complaints to the bishops in 1965 were a joke; nor did the staff act on the young African priests' comments following the seminary closure in 1967. While escalating political tensions in colonial Zimbabwe certainly contributed to the seminarians' increasing consciousness of themselves as African Christians, the primary cause of the students' activism in the 1960s and 1970s was the Jesuits' failure to break with the dominant white Rhodesian culture and its paternalistic mindset. This failure on the Jesuits' part is indicative of their larger failure to inculturate the Catholic Church at their missions in colonial Zimbabwe, which resulted from a variety of factors including racism, the colonial framework of Rhodesia, and rising African nationalism. As such, African seminarians' expressions of nationalism were part of a broader struggle to indigenize the leadership, theology, and practices of the Catholic Church in Zimbabwe.

In reflecting on his time as rector, Francis McKeown remarked that "it never crossed my mind that we would have bishops" training at the seminary.[187] One can only wonder how different life at Chishawasha seminary would have been had McKeown, his contemporaries, and his successors borne in mind Pope Benedict XV's admonition that "the local clergy is not to be trained merely to perform the humbler duties of the ministry, acting as the assistants of foreign priests. On the contrary, they must take up God's work as equals, so that some day they will be able to enter upon the spiritual leadership of their people,"[188] or Pius XI's prescient belief that locally trained seminarians would be the priests "who will be destined one day to govern parishes and dioceses . . . it is they who will one day govern the churches and Catholic communities founded by your sweat and labor,"[189] as Chichester had done to some degree when he was superior of Chishawasha when it was a diocesan seminary.

4 A "Do-Nothing" Organization? The Catholic Association, 1934–1974

The Catholic Association (called variously the Catholic African Congress, the African Catholic Congress, and the Catholic African Association) was the first organized lay movement in the Catholic Church in colonial Zimbabwe. While African laymen founded the organization, Jesuit and clerical understandings of Catholic Action significantly constrained it. Consequently, such attitudes about Catholic Action can be construed as manifestations of European colonialism within the church. In that light, the Catholic Association's (CA) efforts were the African laity's moderate attempt to liberate the church. In addition to the constraints of missionary colonialism, CA leaders had to contend with intimidation and violent opposition from African nationalist movements.

The Catholic African Congress: 1934–1950

Ambrose Majongwe founded the organization that would become the Catholic Association in 1934. Born of Catholic parents in 1912 in Manicaland, from 1927 to 1933, Majongwe served in the British South Africa Police in Salisbury, rising to the rank of sergeant and senior interpreter at police headquarters.[1] In 1933, Aston Chichester, the vicar apostolic of Salisbury, asked Majongwe to participate in a Jeanes teacher-training course at Domboshawa, about fifteen miles outside of Harare. Majongwe trained for a position that combined the duties of "school manager, agricultural advisor, and community development officer." He was at first reluctant, but his father, "under pressure from Bishop Chichester, talked [him] into accepting the offered training."[2]

Dachs and Rea claimed that "the first annual conference [of the CA] was held in 1934."[3] Hugh O'Donnell, on whose account Dachs and Rea based their summary, however, noted that Majongwe "organised a meeting at Chishawasha" in 1934 for the members of the teacher-training course. The meeting apparently included a spiritual retreat in which fourteen people participated, including two Methodists.[4] Bernard Huss, a German Mariannhill priest who founded the South African Catholic African Union in 1927 "to preserve the spiritual, moral, social and economic welfare of the Bantu" against the spread of the Industrial and Commercial Workers' Union (ICU) and its alleged communist threat, was one of the speakers at this meeting.[5] Huss believed it "useless to affirm the dignity and the vocation of the human person without working to transform the conditions which oppress the person," and his writings on topics such as improving agricultural methods and education for Africans, and self-help schemes for African farmers had a great influence on Majongwe, who completed the teacher-training course with honors and subsequently inspected schools in the Makoni District in the eastern part of the colony.[6] Majongwe developed the idea of incorporating monthly local meetings to implement the suggestions and resolutions of what would become the larger annual congresses during meetings to give agricultural demonstrations to adults.[7]

Joseph Dambaza Chikerema from Kutama Mission also completed the training course at Domboshawa and participated in the 1934 meeting. As early as 1932, Dambaza expressed interest in agricultural cooperative schemes. According to Kutama superior Jerome O'Hea, Dambaza had

> outlined a plan for a native farmers co-operative which should be run by him [Dambaza] amongst the Christians here and he has taken up the whole thing with enthusiasm. He has a hard job to convince the slow-witted Native; but he is sure, from his own experience of co-operation with Dominico and Emmanuel that it will be a good thing. If he will do the work of Secretary, I have promised to be President and to advise where called upon to do so. To-night he was again on the plans and I believe it might be made a very fine thing. I

certainly think he will be happy if it can be got going as he is naturally a leader and an organiser above the average native."[8]

The meeting was successful, and there was a formal teachers' congress at Chishawasha in 1935, which seventy teachers attended. There were presentations on a variety of topics such as Gregorian chant, "cooperation in Society" (which O'Hea gave and the Chishawasha diarist deemed "rather too deep for the natives present"), "Catholic Action and Public Opinion," the formation of a Catholic Teachers' Union (Joseph Dambaza), and women's work in Africa (given by an African nun). The congress organizers began thinking in terms of institutionalizing the meetings and improving the quality of the presentations: "N.B. Future Congresses better get papers [and] pass [them] on to two or three critics, who will first be called upon for their judgment and opinion, followed by general discussion."[9] While African teachers were enthusiastic about forming a Catholic teachers' union, apparently the Jesuits were not. O'Hea noted that Joseph Dambaza did not want to give a presentation about "the model krall [sic] school teacher," but preferred to speak "about the formation of a teacher's union—a thing we shall have to do sooner or later."[10]

While Jesuits may not have liked the idea of forming a teacher's union, Bishop Chichester wanted to institutionalize annual congresses. On September 10, 1935, he appointed a permanent committee "to arrange all about the annual congresses" that included Jesuits Francis Ketterer and Henry Seed; African teachers Majongwe, Dambaza, Britto Membere of Triashill Mission; and Simon Taoneyi of Chishawasha.[11] Chichester wanted to make arrangements for the 1936 congress "as soon as possible" because he was "very keen that [they] should carry on the good work begun this year at the Chishawasha congress." Thus, Ketterer polled committee members for convenient meeting times and locations and for suggestions for the next congress program.

Ambrose Majongwe's reply is the longest and most detailed extant. It is useful to see how the movement's founder's concerns and interests helped to determine the shape the movement would eventually take. Majongwe suggested that the congress be held at either Chishawasha "because it is more like the centre" or at Kutama "because it is a training school and therefore those young teachers in training ought to know more of what is going on. Secondly, members of the congress will also learn a great deal from what they see at the place." Lecture topics that Majongwe suggested included teachers' standard of living, "missionaries attitudes towards the general improvement of living conditions among the Christians, or people in the mission farms of all our missions" with particular emphases on "hygiene, better houses, better methods of ploughing, [and] afforestation," daily attendance at kraal schools, what teachers should do "to keep abreast with the moving world," refresher courses for teachers, a suggestion that attendance at the congresses be mandatory for "nearly all the teachers," and a request that if the committee considered making Chishawasha the permanent location of the congress that it consider "what the Teachers of that mission should do to help others since they shall year after year have no travelling expenses of any kind."[12]

Majongwe's vision was not as radical as that of his contemporaries in the ICU or those who would found the political parties that led the nationalist struggles in 1960s and 1970s.[13] His suggestions, however, show a very keen awareness of the problematic living conditions of crushing rural poverty that the majority of Africans living in overcrowded reserves during the Great Depression in the wake of massive land expropriations following passage of the 1931 Land Apportionment Act, and a desire to improve those conditions, particularly for teachers as they were the ones who would most practically be able to help African agriculturalists help themselves.[14] He was evidently concerned about what he perceived as disinterest on the part of the missionaries with the temporal conditions of their flocks, particularly on the missionaries' own farms. Majongwe also seems to have had a great interest in the ongoing formation and professionalization of African teachers, as well as a belief in the equality among people and a need for parity in bearing the costs of the congress' schema. Despite the many changes that the congress movement would undergo in ensuing years, these themes would remain constant in the concerns and statements of its African leadership.

The congress planning committee met on December 9, 1935, with Chichester and all members present except Majongwe.[15] Among the matters discussed were resolutions to be presented during the business meeting of the congress, including whether the congress should be held annually or biennially; the location and time of the next congress, to be held in 1937; and whether "the time [was] ripe to widen the doors of the Catholic Teachers' Federation to include others, e.g., artizans [sic], policemen, etc., and form a Catholic Rhodesian Federation?" The program that the committee planned for the congress began with religious instructions by Membere on the Bible, on "Our Blessed Lady" by Dambaza, and on the sacraments by Taoneyi, followed by a three-day silent retreat given by Jesuit Charles Daignault.[16] The congress resumed with presentations by Chief Native Commissioner Charles Bullock on living conditions in "native areas"; the chief medical director, who "compared the trickery and witchcraft of the native medicine-men with the knowledge of the white doctor" and informed the participants of the Southern Rhodesian government's efforts to set up dispensaries; Sr. Bronoslava, C.P.S., on visiting the sick in kraals; Majongwe on cooperative purchasing; the director of native education exhorting the teachers to cooperate "with all the Government schemes for the progress of the natives, and thus become leaders of their people"; and Sister Cora, O.P., speaking on "the influence that a truly educated native girl might wield in her family and kraal: not so much by her being able to read and write, but by the good example of a model home, that she was able to run as the result of her training in sewing, cooking, and domestic science."[17] The only significant differences in the presentations from what the committee planned and what occurred at the congress were that Jerome O'Hea did not give a presentation on "practical cooperation among the natives" and that Director of Native Education George Stark was supposed to discuss "How education helps village life."

One hundred and eighteen African teachers attended the congress. They voted for annual congresses and decided to hold the 1937 congress at Driefontein Mission. The delegates either chose not to address the issue of expanding the membership of the congress or were not allowed to do so, as "Bishop [Chichester] promised a draft of the rules for the

Catholic Teachers' Federation for the next general meeting." Evidently, however, they were allowed to do so the following year at Driefontein, for the Chishawasha diarist noted, "Fr. Ketterer and Br. Blackledge went with five teachers to the Congress at Driefontein. Congress a success. New Federation includes all Catholic Natives. President: Emilio Muzira (Gokomere), Secretary: Joseph Dambaza (Kutama), Treasurer: Simon Taoneyi (Chishawasha); Executive Committee: Ambrose Majongwe and Britto Membere (Triashill), Geronimo Tarasinja (Gokomere)." Thus, in four years what had begun as a meeting and retreat for fourteen teachers became a movement open to all African Catholics.[18]

Despite the resolution at the 1936 congress in favor of annual meetings, between 1937 and 1945 the congresses were apparently held less frequently; indeed, there is no information in the Chishawasha papers as to whether congresses were held at all—and if so how frequently— from 1938 to 1945. In a letter to mission superiors following the congress held at Chishawasha in May 1946, Chichester noted that the delegates "expressed a wish that there should be annual congresses [and that they] propose to hold one in 1947."[19] The 1946 congress was also the first event in which the African leadership manifested significant difference of opinion and disappointment with the European hierarchy and clergy.

According to the Chishawasha house diarist, congress planners expected about one hundred African delegates to attend, but "about 150 turned up and then 100 or so locals rolled up to see what was going on." Consequently, all sessions after the first were held outside. The sessions included presentations by Director of Native Agriculture E. D. Alvord on "the development of the African in the reserves;" "Catholic Action and the Participation of Catholics in the Public Life of their Nation," by Jesuit Michael Hannan; Jesuit W. Donovan on "Retreats and Missions in the Reserves"; a session on education by Jesuit Ernest Kotski and Native Education Director Starke; and sessions on "Native Councils" and "Homecraft Work in Connection with Culture and Home Life among African Women" by Chief Native Commissioner E. Hudson Beck and Miss E. Blomefield respectively. The only Africans on the program were Ambrose Majongwe, who led a session on cooperative movements among Africans on the first day, and Mariannhill

Father Kilian Samakande, who sang a High Mass at the beginning of the second day.[20]

The resolutions passed during the business session reflect a rift between the African laity's interests and desires and the apparent state of affairs at the missions under the European missionaries. The delegates resolved "that it would be good to have annual congresses" and "that the cooperation of the laity in the apostolate of the hierarchy would be greatly facilitated" by forming Catholic action committees in every Catholic community to "report to and receive advice from a central Catholic Action Committee of the Catholic African Congress." They also requested that "missions be preached to strengthen our own faith and to bring back to the Church those who have given up the faith," and that "each mission station provide retreats for men and women." Further, the delegates asked that they be permitted to read the gospel in the ChiManyika dialect in churches and schools in Manicaland, and that a reprinting of "the big Bible History in this same dialect be speeded up." Lastly, they asked that missions encourage "co-operative buying and selling so as to encourage people to form cooperative societies in years to come."[21]

Following the congress, Chichester reported to his fellow missionaries that "the Africans were disappointed with us, the missioners. They considered that we had not done enough to ensure that the people [presenters] were practical Catholics & that we had not shown sufficient interest in their economic development. My belief is they think we let them down."[22]

According to the bishop, the "aim" of the 1946 congress was "to put before the Catholic Africans of the Vicariate THE PARTICIPATION OF CATHOLICS IN THE DEVELOPMENT OF THE AFRICAN. This participation is not satisfactory, how can we make it more satisfactory."[23] He also expressed his "regrets that the original proposal (C.A.U.) [Catholic African Union] cannot be carried out. Apparently the African leadership of the congress movement was dissatisfied with the institutional church's lack of support for African social and economic development, particularly in the rural areas, and sought to form a union to redress the situation. Although Chichester believed it possible that "a Catholic African Union will eventually emerge from these congresses," he was not enthusiastic about the idea because of "The danger of communism in these unions." Yet, having "recognised" the communist threat, the bishop thought it "ought to be faced if the African Catholic is to take his place in the development of the African nation. At present African Catholics are doing little, which does not seem to be in conformity with the wishes of the Popes."[24] Although Chichester thought cooperative purchasing and selling "a wise measure," he was not "prepared to allow priests to be responsible financially or to hold the money for any length of time in the [mission] house." The bishop flatly refused to allow the gospel to be read in ChiManyika, and he referred anyone interested in obtaining the ChiManyika Bible history to contact the superior of Triashill Mission.[25]

African Catholics felt a lack of concern for their well-being on the missionaries' part. They also apparently felt that the missionaries were not providing them enough spiritual nourishment; hence the requests for more preached missions and retreats. Chichester seemed to think that African Catholics were not doing enough to help in their own development. He also, however, apparently listened to the delegates' complaints about the missionaries' lack of support. In January 1947, in preparation for the congress to be held in May at Monte Cassino Mission, Chichester appointed Jesuit George Binns to gather reports from each mission superior "as to how far the resolutions of the 1946 Congress have been implemented at your station."[26] The congress organizers scheduled a session to discuss "Reports from Mission Stations [on] Implementing Last Years' Resolutions."[27]

The eleven extant responses can be grouped into three categories: missions at which there was no activity to implement the resolutions, missions that provided retreats only, and missions at which there were several activities to implement the 1946 congress resolutions. The superior at Loreto Mission in Que Que [Kwekwe] reported "nothing has been done as there is nobody to do it and no proper Station either to implement it at [sic]."[28] Jesuit Francis Barr, the superior at Makumbi Mission, had nothing to report except unspecified "increased activity amongst the Women's Sodalities."[29] The superior of the Catholic church in Gwelo had nothing to report "due to [his] not having much of an idea what the resolutions were."[30]

The superior at All Souls Mission in Mtoko gave "a 'sort' of retreat before annual baptisms," and started a "Catholic Men's Society" which had nine members and met one Sunday every month. According to the superior, the group was "not inactive, but time must elapse to judge of its usefulness."[31] Jesuit James Cogger reported that he gave respective two-day retreats to eleven men, six women, and seventy-five schoolchildren in standards IV through VI at St. Michael's Mission in Mhondoro. According to Cogger, the "majority of local men [within a three mile radius of the station] were not interested and did not come."[32] At St. Paul's Mission in Musami, twenty-three men and seventy women participated in respective retreats "on different days" in August 1946. Nothing was done regarding cooperative action because the men at the central station "refused to hold monthly meetings to discuss ways and means of cooperation." Because the men at Musami's outstations were waiting to follow the lead of the men at the central station they did nothing either, though "one delegate to [the 1946] Congress returned to stir up trouble against the teacher at the local Catholic school and since the Congress has not attended Mass." Although "many more Catholics of the district [were] stumping their fields and adding manure to the soil," the mission superior at St. Paul's could not necessarily attribute these development activities to the Congress. Similarly, although there were several Catholic headman on the newly formed native council for Mrewa District, "none had reported . . . as to how or whether he is making a stand for Catholic principles at the council meetings."[33]

At St. Barbara's Mission in Manicaland, in addition to giving two retreats to women and one to men at the central station, the priest not only gave instructions to practicing Catholics on "the importance of family life [and] the benefits ensuing from the sacrament of matrimony" but also provided assistance "in many ways" to the proprietors of two stores on the mission farm and helped a congregant returning from Bulawayo "to obtain a Native Purchase Area farm." According to the report, there were forty-two marriages in 1946, the number of girls staying in school for standards I and II was "on the increase," and the assistance to the shopkeepers "[had] been reciprocated." Regarding agricultural development, the residents were working with the local native commissioner "to arrest the serious deterioration of the land on the mission farm" by not plowing their fields for a year and building contour ridges. The residents of St. Barbara's began efforts at cooperative purchasing and selling as early as 1943, but "the whole scheme was vetoed by the Native Commissioner." By the time of the report, the "leaders amongst our people [were] not raising a voice concerning the matter [because] some of the prime movers of the scheme have moved elsewhere." Similarly, although there had been a Catholic Action Committee meeting among the elders (*vakuru*) at the central station "for many years," the mission superior could not "report great results from its activities because of what he perceived as "the mutual fear which the members have for one another." At the missions' outschools there were similar committees of *vakuru* established for the "more effective management of the school in question" which, in the superior's opinion, were more effective in providing material support than spiritual assistance.[34]

Jesuit Ernest Kotski, the superior at Kutama Mission, reported that the four retreats given at "the mission proper" and the two given at outschools "proved to be a success." He also noted that the residents at Kutama had submitted a petition to the native commissioner at Sinoia (Chinoyi) to form a native council. The Kutama Catholics also held several meetings to discuss a variety of agricultural improvements, as well as hear their pastor explain "the principles and methods of Catholic action in two successive talks," from which resulted "a new small body or congregation of married women with the purpose of sanctifying family life and practicing family virtues."[35]

The Swiss Bethlehem Mission priest in charge of St. Joseph's Mission in Gwelo reported "six groups of Catholic Action-people": about forty men who catechized and led prayers including "Processions for rain in the kraals"; about fifty women "who do little in public, but their influence in their homes can't be overseen"; "boys from the kraals [who] number few, as they go most for work. Some of them teach Catechism"; more than one hundred "girls from the kraals [who] teach catechism to children in the kraals, [and] come every Sunday to Mass and promise never to go outside the Reserve without leave from the priest, which is hardly ever given"; and boarder boys and boarder girls who "are buzy [sic] on Sundays in calling all the Mass-Attendance-Registers for Men, Women, boys and girls, Adult-pagans, who are learning Catechism [about three hundred]. All the 1000 outschool children are called up every Sunday. All the registers together amount to 20. People would not like any more to be without this [sic] Attendance-Registers. It is not ideal, but it is a help for new christians [sic]."[36]

In a departure from the Jesuit way of proceeding, Father Reich gave the men and women a two-day retreat together, for which they brought their own food: "the women will cook for their husbands. They keep silence except for dinner and supper." In all, there were about 350 "Catholic Action-People" working with Reich who were also members of the Apostleship of Prayer, and who frequently reported "cases" to the priest. He did not allow them to do more, such as joining the Legion of Mary, Pathfinders, and Wayfarers (the latter two groups were Catholic scouting groups for boys and girls), because they did "good work, and I think some are even very good."[37]

In addition to providing an outline of the contours of life at the respective missions, these reports show the difficulties that African Catholic lay leaders had to face, specifically frequent lack of support and encouragement on the part of the clergy and sometimes general lack of interest on the part of their fellow Catholics, particularly for schemes involving agricultural improvements and cooperative ventures. They also show an extreme desire on the part of the people for activities aimed at their spiritual renewal, such as retreats. It is also possible to glimpse African lay efforts to take a measure of control over their surroundings and organizing their lives at the missions. If Father Reich is to be believed at face value, his report shows African Christians looking after their own spiritual well-being in a very concretely structured way: taking and keeping track of attendance at Sunday mass. These early efforts at grassroots organization, while seemingly lackluster in their results, would prove significant for laying the groundwork for later more effective efforts.

The theme of Catholic Action was prominent in the 1947 reports as well as in the congresses throughout the 1940s and 1950s. Much of this was due to the influence of English Jesuit Michael Hannan after his arrival in Southern Rhodesia in 1941 and his understanding of that theme. According to D. J. Geaney, Catholic Action was "both a concept and an organization of the laity."[38] First used by Pope Pius X, his successor Pius XI developed the concept, defining it as "the participation of the laity in the apostolate of the Church's hierarchy."[39] There seems to have been a spectrum of understandings of Catholic Action: on one extreme theorists like Pius XI saw Catholic Action as "a tightly structured organization that serves as an arm of the hierarchy in lay life," restricted to action or work of the laity which was organized, apostolic, and done under a mandate of the local bishop. On the other end of the spectrum were priests such as Belgian Cardinal Saliège and laypeople who saw Catholic Action less rigidly, and as a means to effect the institutional change of "conditions of life that many found unworthy of human beings." According to Saliège, the goal of Catholic Action was "to modify social pressure, to direct it, to make it favorable to the spread of Christian life, to let the Christian life create a climate, an atmosphere in which men [sic] can develop their human qualities, can lead a really human life, an atmosphere in which the Christian can breathe easily and stay a Christian."[40]

American Catholic historian William Portier describes Catholic Action as follows:

"To restore all things in Christ." This was Pius X's motto and the standard for Catholic Action. Combat metaphors recur. . . . Restoration and integration or integralism imply damage and disintegration. Combat and conquest imply an adversary . . . . Under Pius IX and Pius X, two prominent Catholic Action popes, the Vatican was locked in combat with anti-clerical governments in Europe. In this context, Catholic Action appears as a papal call to the laity, the Catholic people, to join them, and literally to participate with them in winning back European culture from a very concrete and legally entrenched political enemy [i.e., the modern liberal state]. Since lay people were all citizens of the modern states against which the Vatican was struggling, the popes really were calling them to be "double agents."[41]

With regard to the combat imagery and the more conventional Christian images of church leaders as shepherds and the laity as sheep,

Portier observed that the combat inscribed in writing on Catholic Action was "relatively recent . . . [accompanying] the emergence of modern states in Europe and becomes acute after the French Revolution. As a result . . . Catholic Action popes [did not] really have a clear idea of what they want[ed] Catholic citizens to do in the "world." Boundaries are contested. Unexpected developments occur. Sheep even graze with shepherds." According to Portier, regionalism was also a significant factor in the implementation of Catholic Action. Referring to the situation in the United States, Portier claimed, "As Catholic Action's move from Europe to North America, or from Chicago to Philadelphia to Boston, illustrates, Catholic Action works out differently in different places."[42]

Michael Hannan frequently discussed the Congress movement and the Catholic African Association in terms of Catholic Action. Pius XI's model of laity in Catholic Action was as an extension of the hierarchy and clergy, not of the laity sharing in priesthood of Christ. Although the Catholic African Association would face many problems, none was more serious than those stemming from Hannan and his Jesuit confreres—with the support of Chichester and Markall—trying to maintain rigid episcopal and clerical control of the organization. They apparently made no effort to try to adapt the theory of Catholic Action to the local circumstances in Southern Rhodesia. Thus, the Jesuits' hierarchical understanding of Catholic Action placed significant constraints on its organization and activities.

Organization and Constitution of the CAA

The lay movement's organizational structure became increasingly complex as it transformed from a relatively informal meeting and retreat for Catholic teachers to a diocesan organization, and eventually into a national body. From humble beginnings among fourteen teachers, the Catholic African Association at its zenith in 1958 claimed 5,300 paid members in all five of the dioceses in Southern Rhodesia. As the Catholic Association from 1961, membership declined significantly during the early years of the 1960s due to violent political intimidation of association members by members of the African nationalist parties. Catholic Association membership, however, began to increase again around 1967, and by 1974 association leaders reported more than eight thousand members.

The initial meetings of Catholic teachers in 1934 and 1935 seem to have been fairly informal affairs. Given that there was no organizational structure to speak of, and that at the former there were only fourteen men attending and seventy teachers at the latter, it is probable that Majongwe and his colleagues simply made all the necessary arrangements with the staff at Chishawasha Mission and informed Bishop Chichester of their activities.

In September 1935 Chichester appointed a permanent committee for the Catholic African congress consisting of two Jesuits and four African teachers. There are no records of the permanent committee's activities beyond their preparations for the 1936 congress held at Chishawasha, but given its modus operandi and those of the institutional structures that followed it, it seems plausible that the members met a few times a year to decide where the annual congress would be held, what topics would be addressed and by whom, and to determine what issues would be addressed during the business sessions, as well as to debrief following the congress. There are no records of congresses having occurred between 1938 and 1945, though it would seem fairly safe to say that there must have been some meetings during this period, since Majongwe and his colleagues would not have suffered such a setback in silence. The question of whether to stage congresses annually came up in 1946 and 1948 as well. Apparently, the missionaries preferred to hold the congresses less frequently, but every time the issue arose, the African laity opted for the annual meetings.[43]

In 1937, the delegates to the Driefontein congress decided to open membership to all African Catholics. In 1946, about 250 people were present for the congress at Chishawasha. There are no statistics for the 1947 congress, but about a hundred people attended the congress the following year at Kutama Mission.[44] The smaller numbers were due to difficulties resulting from late rains and the high costs of travel to Kutama: some delegates paid ten shillings or more for transport.[45]

At the 1949 congress at St. Peter's Church in Harare, the congress secretary noted that "the general impression" from delegates' reports of local activities was that "much progress had been made during the past year."[46] Apparently the congress organizers did not allot enough time for all the delegates to read their reports. Approximately 1,250 delegates received communion at the Sunday masses offered during the congress, and some 13,800 delegates participated in the procession of the Blessed Sacrament.[47]

There are no records of there having been a congress in 1950, but the minutes for the 1951 congress at Monte Cassino note that Ambrose Majongwe proclaimed that "the Congresses have grown from year to year in number and therefore now is the time for a Reorganization. There should be Local Congresses of the various Mission Centres and a Central Congress." He proposed establishing a structure in which local congresses

should be established to meet the needs of the various mission centres in the country, and work out schemes for the work of the station. . . . All that concerns the single Missions [sic] or rather Parishes should be discussed at the Mission Congress. The Mission Congresses should be the Cells for a greater Organization, the Central Congress. There should be a standing Committee of the Central Congress collecting and sieving all that concerns all people and deciding what is necessary.[48]

The fifty-one delegates representing the missions of the Salisbury vicariate approved resolutions to establish local congresses and a congress central committee consisting of six officers and two delegates from each mission. Majongwe was elected chairman of the central committee. The delegates also voted to adopt temporarily the constitutions of the Monte Cassino local congress.[49]

The Monte Cassino constitution, written in about 1948, provided four very general aims for the local congress:

a. To safeguard, promote, and foster the Catholic Faith among the African people in the area under the Monte Cassino parish and the country in general.

b. To work for the establishment of Catholic African Charitable organisations and any other Catholic societies.

c. To promote the spiritual, economic, social, intellectual, and industrial education of Catholics, their hygienic welfare and general well-being in this area and in the country as a whole according to Catholic principles.

d. To work for a better understanding between Africans, Europeans, and other races.[50]

The constitution required of its constituents very broad and basic spiritual and social means to achieve its aims, including: mutual assistance to "live up to the Faith," frequenting mass and the sacraments, assisting priests to bring back lapsed Catholics and convert non-Catholics, visiting the sick and dying, providing "the example of good Catholic lives in everyday life, in family and community" particularly in "good Catholic marriages," raising children according to "Catholic ways," working against influences "contrary to the Faith" especially those "tending towards the breaking up of families," attending meetings sponsored by government officials or customary chiefs with the intent of presenting "ideas as applicable to Catholic principles in social life and [opposing] those adverse and harmful to society," and working "through the community to counteract plays, dances, etc. which are a danger to the moral welfare of the people." Congress members also had to "follow proper agricultural methods, crop rotation, compost making, manuring, and all that pertains to good farming as advised by demonstrators and Govt. officials." Political, intellectual, industrial, and hygienic duties respectively included attending local council meetings, "[buying] good books and [reading] them," "[working] hard" and providing for one's family, and building and maintaining "better houses" and improving sanitation and water supplies.

Membership in the congress was open to all Catholics at all schools and religious centers affiliated with Monte Cassino Mission, and members had to pay an annual fee of two shillings and six pence. The congress had an executive committee with six officers and one or two representatives from each center, to which "only practicing persons" should have been elected. Each center was to have a standing committee whose members were to be elected annually. The executive committee was required meet quarterly in order to make all arrangements for the local annual congress, collect and keep records and dues, decide how to spend the money it collected, "bring about a true spirit of Catholic Action among members, permeate the community with Catholic influence," and to "help the priest in all that relates to the above by urging improvement of schools and spiritual life in general." The priest in charge of Monte Cassino schools was designated as the executive committee's spiritual director. With regard to the annual congress his decision "in all matters was final." Similarly, he alone had the "power to approve, amend, [or] alter plans etc." of the congress in general.[51]

The emphasis on agricultural improvements, particularly stressing that congress members heed the counsel of agricultural demonstrators, as well as the broad powers given to the spiritual adviser, makes it likely that Ambrose Majongwe was the principal author of the Monte Cassino constitution. The narrow understanding of Catholic action found throughout the constitution, however, indicates that Francis Markall, who was on the staff at Monte Cassino during this period, more than likely influenced Majongwe's thinking.

The Monte Cassino constitution is notable for its utter generality in terms of its aims and the means to achieve them. It essentially called on its members to pay two shillings and six pence per year to do those things that the church's hierarchy enjoined upon all Catholic adults; that is, there was no particular action or spirituality to distinguish congress members from Catholic laypeople who chose not to join it. Further, the constitution firmly placed the congress and its activities under the control of the hierarchy in the person of the executive committee spiritual adviser. While congress members of the time would have argued that they were helping the clerical hierarchy in fulfilling its mission, the practical result was that one European missionary had the capacity to veto arbitrarily the decisions or actions of committed African laypeople. These problems of vague mission and clerical control would plague the organization throughout its existence. It is also significant to note the inclusion of a clause providing for the encouragement of interracial cooperation in the constitution. Congress leaders would find their bishops hesitant about encouraging this value, and African nationalists literally violently opposed to such an ideal.

The newly established congress central committee voted to adopt the Monte Cassino constitution for all the mission centers in the Salisbury vicariate and Umtali prefecture apostolic, amending it only to allow each mission executive to set the annual subscription fee respectively, and to require that executive committee officers be elected annually.[52] In 1953, the central committee received and accepted an invitation from the spiritual adviser of the Bulawayo vicariate's Catholic African Union to join a federation-wide union of African Catholic organizations. Michael Hannan noted that joining such an organization would require changing the congress constitutions as the Bulawayo vicariate followed the South African Catholic African Union's 1946 constitution.[53]

Thus, in August 1953, Hannan met with six other priests involved with Catholic African lay organizations and Bishop Aloysius Haene in Gwelo to draft a constitution for a national organization.[54] Significantly, there were no African laypeople or priests present to contribute to the enterprise. Despite making some concessions and compromises to the priests representing Bulawayo, Hannan was largely successful in having the structures found in the Monte Cassino constitution imposed on the newly formed Catholic African Association (CAA).[55] Membership in the CAA was open to all Catholics who belonged to specific branches. Each branch had a local executive committee with six officers—the chairman, vice chairman, secretary, vice secretary, treasurer, and vice treasurer—that met monthly and sent two representatives to the mission council, which met at least twice a year and consisted of the branch delegates, a six member executive, and a spiritual director appointed by the ordinary. The mission council sent two delegates to the regional council, which met at least once every eighteen months and comprised representatives from all the missions of a given diocese, a six-member executive committee, and a spiritual director appointed by the diocesan bishop. The regional council sent two delegates to the territorial council, which was supposed to meet at least once every three years and was composed of the delegates, six elected officers, and a spiritual adviser appointed by the apostolic delegate. In practice, the Salisbury regional council generally met twice a year to plan and debrief the annual regional congress and deal with issues arising from the missions. The territorial council met annually from its inception in 1955, and its spiritual adviser was appointed by the bishops' conference.

According to the constitution that the European priests wrote, "the spiritual adviser of any Council" had "the right to veto any action or decision of the Council or its Executive, subject to the right of the Council or Executive to appeal" to the spiritual adviser of the next higher council. Spiritual advisers could also remove any officer from a council for "gravely [neglecting] the duties of his office or [leading] a scandalous life," with the same proviso concerning appeals. Presumably the right of appeal should have allowed the territorial council to appeal to either the apostolic delegate or the bishops' conference; however, there was no such provision in the CAA constitution. Thus, for the Catholic African Association's existence from 1953 to 1961, Michael Hannan, as the spiritual adviser of the territorial council, had the constitutional power to veto the decisions and actions of the African laity, though there is no evidence that he actually did so.

The aims of the CAA were just as vague as those of the Monte Cassino constitution:

generally to promote unity in Catholic Action under the guidance of ecclesiastical authority; to make known and act on Catholic teaching so that Catholics may realize their responsibility as citizens, particularly as regards social justice and race relations; to promote the general improvement of the African community. "Better homes, better hearts, better harvests"; to encourage its members to take an active part in all forms of co-operation and self-help; to hold Catholic Congresses periodically; to speak for Catholics.[56]

In 1961, the territorial committee debated and passed a resolution asking the bishops to change the CAA's name to the Catholic Association (CA) and establish it as the "territorial administrative body for all Catholic Action within [Southern] Rhodesia." CAA leaders at all levels "always show[ed] good will, a readiness to cooperate and to accept guidance. But many feel frustrated by the lack of interest shown by some priests."[57] Additionally, members of the CAA thought the change would allow non-African Catholics to form branches and join the organization.[58] The bishops approved the name change with the proviso that it not "be implied that [the CA] is to be the parent body of all Catholic Action."[59] The bishops included the condition, which directly contradicted the will of the African lay leadership, because of

> the problems which might be encountered vis-à-vis the European organisations. If the C.A. was to be the parent-body of all Catholic Action, then the European Organisations would have be to affiliated to it. The Bishops saw some problems in this—and for other reasons—decided that with the new name, viz. Catholic Association, it was not implied that the C.A. was to be the parent-body of all Catholic Action.[60]

The confusion this contradiction caused resulted in the bishops calling a commission of inquiry to investigate the relationship of the CA to other Catholic organizations. Although the commission recommended amending the CA constitution so that its principle aims were to unite Catholics and "to impress on its members the full living of the Catholic life, loyalty to the Church, attendance at Sunday mass, and frequent reception of the Sacraments," there is no evidence that the territorial council ever adopted the proposed amendment.[61] Clearly, African Catholics were far more advanced in their thinking with regard to interracial cooperation than the bishops.

Two significant developments marked the decade of the 1960s for the CA: the rise of parish councils and political intimidation of its members by supporters of African nationalist parties. The theological shift from Catholic Action to the lay apostolate associated with the beginning of the reign of Pope John XXIII, brought with it the parish council, or a group of lay leaders elected by the members of a given community who worked with the parish priest in meeting the pastoral needs of the community. As the primary organizational unit within the church, people belonging to or working with the parish council did not have to pay any membership fee. Not surprisingly, this led to conflicts with the CA, which still thought of itself as the primary mechanism for organizing the laity. At the inquiry committee meeting in 1962, Bishop Haene of Gwelo allegedly reported that he planned to "urge the parish committee" at a meeting of CA spiritual advisers, and Francis Barr, the CA spiritual adviser for Salisbury, noted that Archbishop Markall planned to introduce parish councils in the metropolitan see as well.[62] Tensions between the CA and parish councils apparently mounted steadily. CA leaders evidently believed that parish priests opposed to the organization actively worked to subvert it. In April 1974, concerned by "the energy with which certain priests—particularly expatriate ones—have been setting up [parish] councils (an energy which often by-passes existing organizing structures, particularly the CA)," the CA territorial council passed a resolution asking the bishops to "express to us your feelings on the continued existence of the C.A. Because we feel that the C.A. contributes to the growth of the Church activities that do not appear to be part of the scope of these councils, particularly—the contact C.A. provides between different parishes, the work the C.A. does in economic development, the combined funding the C.A. has for projects beyond the scope of individual parishes."[63] Although Markall stated that he believed that the CA "should continue to exist according to its Constitution," the organization's continued existence depended on its fidelity to its constitution. The archbishop was adamant that "the C.A. must not try to usurp the functions of such structures of the Church as the Parish Council. Where the C.A. has undertaken such a function because a Parish Council did not exist it must cease completely to act in place of a Parish Council *as soon as* a Parish Council is formed at any particular place. Failure to do so has been the cause of great misunderstanding in some places."[64]

Edward Muchenje, the territorial council secretary, admitted that groups at various levels in the CA committed "breaches of the constitution," but also reminded Markall that "the C.A. was started before any other structures in parishes, and parishioners almost 'grew' up with the C.A. as 'the' structure in the parish." He suggested "an evolutionary rather than revolutionary" means to introduce the parish council would minimize confusion on the people's part and tensions with the clergy.[65]

Mabvuku, a periurban area on the outskirts of Salisbury, was one local community that evidently had tensions between the CA and the parish priest. According to Muchenje, writing to Salisbury regional council spiritual adviser Fr. Emmanuel Mavudzi, Jesuit Fr. G. Finnieston, the parish priest at Mabvuku, apparently "banned" the CA parish board and instructed the local CA council chairman to give "all the money collected by the C.A. to the Executive Committee of the Parish Council there."[66] Muchenje stated that in attempting to take such action the parish priest was in violation of no less than three articles of the CA constitution, and he asked for Mavudzi's help to resolve the situation "for the benefit of the C.A. and good relations in that Parish." Muchenje copied the letter to Patrick Chakaipa, auxiliary bishop since 1973 and in charge of all pastoral work for the archdiocese. Mavudzi, while glad that Muchenje had sent a copy of the letter to the bishop, stated that he could take no action as spiritual director because he had no "direct authority over a fellow parish priest," and he suggested that Muchenje invite Chakaipa to meet with Finnieston, the local CA board, the parish council, and himself.[67] The documentary evidence shows that by April 1975, the conflict still had not been settled.[68]

CA members also had to contend with political violence from African nationalists during the late 1950s and early 1960s. Nationalists frequently associated Christianity with European culture and hegemony, and accordingly sought to dissuade African Christians from practicing their faith.

In 1958, the British Criminal Investigation Department advised the Salisbury CAA regional council to change the name of the annual congress so as not to be confused with the Southern Rhodesia African National Congress, the first African nationalist party established in 1957.[69] Accordingly, the minutes thereafter refer to the "annual general meeting," though by 1964, they had switched back to using the term "congress." Also in 1958, Archbishop Markall forbade CA officers from holding political office[70] and frequently urged that speakers at the congresses avoid political subjects:

More particularly in view of the present day circumstances it will be important to be certain that nothing resembling any political allusions should find place in the speeches or be allowed to be proposed for discussion [at the 1962 annual general meeting at Makumbi Mission].[71]

While on a visit to Kutama Mission to inspect schools in 1960, Francis Barr, the secretary for education for the Archdiocese and spiritual adviser for the Salisbury regional council, thought it "absolutely essential" that "a European [be] present at each and every Meeting of the Parents, whether at Kutama or anywhere else in the Archdiocese" because the "older people are in serious need of help from such person at the present time if younger men with political leanings are not to overwhelm them by words and actions."[72] Similarly, in 1962, Joseph Dambaza, the long-time catechist and teacher at Kutama, in asking the Jesuit provincial superior to send more priests to the teacher-training school noted that "the state is and looks more alert about peace being threatened in Towns and in the Reserves that it sends Security Police to TROUBLE PLACES. Kutama area is one of these places."[73]

The superior at Chishawasha reported that for the period from 1962 to 1964 the mission had made "moderate progress," and that "the uncertain status of political affairs and of the future civil government of this territory [terrae]" was "the principle impediment" militating against "greater perfection." According to the Jesuit,

This uncertain status perturbs the minds and hearts of the masses and several times instigates an adverse perception of the church's doctrine and teachers. Some leaders of the indigenous, political methods have strongly kept a jealous watch over [incubuerunt] their disciples against the church, encouraging them, that they not worship God. For they claim that [Christianity] is an alien thing in this land and it is flourishing only among our people in Europe, if you will, [among those] born from the European stem. Other preachers about political matters, [which are] ruinous to indigenous Catholics, are the ones who threaten those who show themselves faithful to the church. [This is] why any Catholics, committed to our care, in view of the fear they show do not want to [be] sincere and strong friends of the church.[74]

By 1964, Jesuit Fr. John Dove, the newly appointed CA Salisbury regional council spiritual adviser, reported that CA members throughout archdiocese were becoming targets of increasing political intimidation and physical violence by African nationalists:

In the past month Fr. Dove and Mr. [Samson] Chibi have attended three local congresses of the CA at Mhondoro, Muda (Chishawasha district), and Parirewa (Makumbi district). They have also visited members of local CA Executives at Kutama, Mtoko, Wedza, Musami, and Marandellas. The general impression is that there has been a fall off of membership due to the prevailing political situation and intimidation. Mr. Chibi spoke at all the congresses and the questions raised were mostly concerned with intimidation. From this it has been seen to be necessary to build up a strong [CA] and other groups to resist local intimidation. People are still being beaten up for going to mass and in some cases mothers have been severely threatened if they have their children baptised. Mr. Chibi has done much to encourage those who live under these conditions.[75]

A ten-page report on events at Chishawasha in July and August 1964 in the Jesuit archives provides insight into the dynamics between African Christians, African nationalists, and Jesuit missionaries. The priest-reporter, presumably Cedric Myerscough, noted that he had received reports that there was to be a "political youth meeting" and other "illegal meetings" at the various schools and other locations on the mission property.[76] Myerscough duly notified the police and reported that subsequently the hut of one of his African informant's brother was burned down, and that a woman who refused to attend one of the meetings was told to attend the next meeting or her hut would be burned.[77] In late July 1964, "a respectable resident" and long-time employee of the mission had a conversation with one of the Jesuit brothers. When asked what he knew about the meetings and the possibility of organizing Christians to fight against the nationalists, the African Christian responded "that would not be a good thing" because

The trouble is that they would only come along and burn our huts. . . . The people have been living here happily: why should they have troubles now? We don't want it but we are afraid: there is no happiness now: we are all afraid. If you call a meeting then there will be rumours and these people will call in those in Highfield [an African township of Salisbury] people and we will be burnt. If they can come at night and burn your slaughter house would you know who had done it? What if they burn our homes? . . . Some two weeks ago some of them came to my son and said he should join. They said also that they had been told that I had given the names of the people to you and that he had better join otherwise his father's house would be burnt.

"And did he go?"

"Yes, I think he did."

"But why did you let him?"

"What can I do?"

"And now what can we do about it? We are determined to stop it. What is the best way?"

"Call the Police and put them in gaol!"

"We have already told the Police."

"Yes, but something must be done. Done quickly otherwise there will be a very bad spirit all over Chishawasha. There is going to be trouble tomorrow and at the C.A. Meeting."

"Now what about having our meeting and fighting against them?"

"Ah well: it would be better if you did something but I will think about it."[78]

The following day, the police came to prevent an "illegal meeting," and detained five people. The next day the wife of one of the mission kraal heads

came to complain that her brother-in-law [name deleted] had been beaten up (her husband not being at home). She herself had been threatened and accused of giving information concerning the meeting and was responsible for them having to move their cattle kraals. They said her husband was an informer and that they were going to take revenge. Before she finished her story, [name deleted] came with his son who had been beaten and said that they were threatening to wreck the whole village. The wife of [name deleted] (he was not home) came up and said that she had been attacked while cooking and that her house was being wrecked. The Police were sent for. Six huts belonging to [name deleted] and [name deleted] were smashed up inside and doors broken—ransacked. The more active perpetrators of this were [names deleted]. The Police took away [names deleted].[79]

The remainder of the report details similar intrigues and accusations concerning "illegal meetings," similar types of physical violence, and threats thereof. The report's author noted that he provided a copy to a police sergeant at the Goromonzi District police office.[80] These incidents clearly show why African nationalists thought the Jesuits were complicit with the Rhodesian authorities: their frequent recourse to the police to thwart the spread of support for African independence, and by extension "faithful" African Catholics. They also demonstrate the violent nature of the nationalists' strategy: they had few qualms about beating or burning the houses of people they perceived (without necessarily having any concrete proof) not only to be opposed to them, but also those who simply may not have been active supporters. These brief episodes also highlight the extremely difficult circumstances in which Catholic Association leaders had to work, and the relations they had to negotiate in order to keep the organization alive. Thus, it is not surprising that paid membership plummeted during this period (see Table 4.1).

Despite such difficulties, however, by 1966 the number of people joining the CA began to increase. In 1974 (the last year for which there are numbers reported), the CA reported more than 8,100 dues-paying members—the most in its history—and three regional congresses in which more than 6,500 people participated. After forty years, and despite chronic lack of support and even hostility from the clergy, fierce competition from parish councils, and physical violence from African nationalists, the Catholic Association had learned to survive and adapt to the prevailing conditions. The documentary evidence shows that as late as 1976—at the height of the liberation war—the Salisbury regional council was preparing to stage another annual congress.

While the actual structure of the CA was effective, the organization suffered from a distinct lack of direction and confusion in its purpose. This confusion gave rise to considerable debate as to what the CA's purpose was beyond holding meetings. Even its spiritual advisers were unsure what its members actually did.[81] It also provided the CA's critics—mostly European missionaries—with ample fodder with which to criticize it and to advocate its demise. And yet, despite this inherent flaw in its mission, the CA continued to function into the 1970s.

Table 4.1. The Catholic Association, 1934–1974

Year	Diocese	Members	Congress Venue	Congress Participants[a]
1934	Sby	—	Chishawasha	14
1935	Sby	—	Chishawasha	70
1936	Sby	—	Chishawasha	118
1937	Sby	—	Driefontein	NA
1946	Sby	—	Chishawasha	c. 250
1947	Sby	—	Monte Cassino	> 100
1948	Sby	—	Kutama	c. 100
1949	Sby	—	St. Peter's Harare	1,250
1951	Sby	—	Monte Cassino	1,000
1952	Sby	788[b]	Chishawasha	1,400
1953	Sby	NA	Triashill	NA
1954	Sby	1,106[c]	Musami	NA
1955	Sby	634[d]	No Congress due to poor harvests	
	Byo	589	NA	NA
Total:		1,223[e]		
1956	Sby	1,615	Mhondoro	784 / > 2,000[f]
	Gwo	1,804		
	Umt	< 956		
	Wan	< 113		
	Byo	NA		
Total:		c. 4,450		
1957	Sby	2,616	All Souls, Mtoko	NA ("Well attended")
	Gwo	864		
	Umt	956		
	Wan	113		
	Byo	NA		
Total:		4,488		
1958	Sby	2,616	Chishawasha	1,420
	Gwo	1,453[g]		
	Umt	793	NA	1,800
	Wan	180[h]		
	Byo	259		
Total:		5,301		
1959	Sby	2,774	Musami	1,304
	Gwo	1,377	Gokomere	NA

Table 4.1. (Continued)

Year	Diocese	Members	Congress Venue	Congress Participants[a]
	Umt	613	Triashill	"Poorly attended"
	Wan	NA		
	Byo	NA		
Total:		4,764		
1960	Sby	2,626	Wedza	2,000
	Gwo	1,108		
	Umt	921	St. Kilian's	2,200
	Wan	109		
	Byo	NA		
Total:		4,764		
1961	Sby	1,150	NA	NA (No report/ delegate at TC)
	Gwo	1,003		
	Umt	365[i]		
	Wan	NA		
	Byo	NA		
Total:		2,518		
1962	Sby	799	Makumbi	NA (No report/ delegate at TC)
	Gwo	817[j]	Gokomere/ Zimutu	2,500[k]
	Umt	357[l]	St. Therese	NA
	Wan	NA (Inquired if Regional Council still functioning)		
	Byo	NA (Byo seeks to combine CA w/other groups; CA as "head organization")		
Total:		1,973		
1963	Sby	1,197	Chishawasha	No congress, leadership retreat
	Umt	187[m]	NA	300
Total:		1,384		

Table 4.1. (Continued)

Year	Diocese	Members	Congress Venue	Congress Participants[a]
1964	Sby	1,057[n]	Kutama	NA
	Gwo	735		
	Umt	347	St. Joseph's Umtali	1,200
	Wan	NA		
	Byo	528[o]		
Total:		2667		
1965	Sby	986	Mhon doro No Congress due to finances, leadership retreat	
1966	Sby	1,008	No congress due to petrol rationing, political situation, and finances; local congresses instead	
1967	Sby	2,022	Mt. St. Mary's Wedza	NA
1968	Sby	1,781	St. Peter's Harare	>1000
1969	Sby	3,008	Musami	NA; 16 local congresses
1970	Sby	3,495	Enkeldoorn	c. 2,000; 18 local congresses
1971	Sby	3,028	Chishawasha	> 4,000; 16 local congresses
	Gwo	51		
	Umt	278		
Total:		3,357		
1972	Sby	2,500	Kutama	2,000; 11 local congresses
	Byo	declared "dead"		
1973	Sby	1,405	Chishawasha Sem.	> 3,000
	Gwo	52 declared "dead"		
	Umt	278		
Total:		1,735		
1974	Sby	2,800	Makumbi	> 3,000
	Umt	366	Triashill	1,500
	Mar	5,000	Marandellas	2,000

Table 4.1. (Continued)

Year	Diocese	Members	Congress Venue	Congress Participants[a]
	Sin	NA	Sinoia	NA
Total:		8,166		

[a] All data were taken from minutes and reports of the various councils and meetings of the Catholic African Congress (1934–1949), African Catholic Congress (1951–1953), Catholic African Association (1953–1961), and Catholic Association (1961–1974) in the Archives of the Archdiocese of Harare and the Jesuit Archives of Zimbabwe. Byo = Bulawayo; Gwo = Gwelo; Mar = Marandellas (Marondera); Sby = Salisbury (Harare); Sin = Sinoia (Chinoyi); Wan = Wankie (Hwange); Umt = Umtali (Mutare).
[b] Does not include Monte Cassino, "perhaps the most advanced of the local congresses."
[c] Six of ten mission councils reported numbers.
[d] Members paid through September 1955.
[e] 1955 statistics for Catholic population: Sby: 36,000; Byo: 14,000; Gwo: 41,000; Umt: 16,000; Wan: 1,000; Total Catholic population: 108,000. Thus, even allowing for twice the number reported, CAA membership comprised only 1–2 percent of African Catholics in Southern Rhodesia.
[f] 784 = number of meal tickets sold; > 2,000 = number of meals Simon Taoneyi served.
[g] "Many more people attend the meetings but don't pay their membership."
[h] 180 members; only 120 paid membership fees.
[i] Three of seven mission councils reported numbers.
[j] "Very many more attended without paying."
[k] Total from two congresses. "Generally more women than men at meetings."
[l] Four of seven mission councils reported numbers, one mission council presumed defunct.
[m] Only two active mission councils in diocese.
[n] Numbers decline due to "intimidation of the faithful."
[o] Six of seven mission councils reported numbers.

Women in the CA

Regarding the CA's structure, Hugh O'Donnell stated, "After the annual congress . . . the *monthly meetings* were the means of communicating ideas and implementing the resolutions and suggestions of the congress [which were] based on the traditional [sic] idea of the *dare*, but with a new element, the inclusion of women."[82] While Majongwe and other African lay leaders may have wanted to include women in the activities and deliberations of the movement, they are conspicuous by their virtual absence from the CA's leadership, and the double patriarchy of midcentury African culture and the Catholic Church clearly constrained their actions.

Marriage and Catholic family life were frequent themes at the annual congresses during the 1940s and 1950s, and these addresses reveal dominating patriarchal discourses from both European and African sources. Jesuit Ernest Kotski addressed the 1948 congress at Kutama on Catholic Action. He suggested that "each mission should have its Catholic Action Committee of men." Then, "turning to the women, he exhorted them also to overcome their fear, and to train their children from earliest youth in genuine Catholic practices. They should also visit and try to convert the lapsed. He exhorted all to show forth visibly and concretely that unity which we have as members of God's family and to show more trust towards the local head of God's family, the priest."[83]

Later the same day, Joseph Dambaza spoke about the Catholic family. He first "invited the delegates to visit Nazareth and to learn from the Holy Family what a Catholic family should try to imitate."[84] According to Dambaza, the Catholic husband should "like St. Joseph, try to please his wife, work for her and do all he can to make her happy." Similarly, the Catholic wife should "as Our Lady did, respect her husband and regard him as the head of the family. Though hers was the greater dignity, yet she always put St. Joseph before her." Although noting that Catholic parents had an obligation to educate their "children of both sexes," he

> grew very emphatic in the course of his remarks on the way in which young men choose their future wives. Nowadays they seem to make their choice merely on the grounds that the girl has a good figure or wears attractive headgear. In the old days a bachelor on the look-out for a future wife used to notice the huts from which much water was thrown. If there were much water thrown from a house, this was a sign that the girl who lived there was a hard worker, and the ability to work hard was taken as the first requisite for a good wife.[85]

Similarly, at the 1949 congress at St. Peter's church in the Harare section of Salisbury, the director of native affairs highlighted the "difficulties [caused] by girls who come to town without their fathers' permission," and teacher Raphael Ruzive, in his presentation on marriage "reported satisfactory progress at the Homecraft school of Miss Bloomfield, who welcomed those girls who were already married or who would be married shortly."[86]

Thus, according to the foregoing discourses, Catholic African women, though ostensibly possessing greater dignity than men, were expected: to be submissive to male authority in the home and church; to remain in their rural homes subject to parental authority and not to go to the towns; to be "hard workers" if they ever hoped to leave their homes and marry; to bear children; to receive an education "in genuine Catholic practices" and impart these practices to their children; and to try to bring back people who had grown slack in their practice of "the Faith" or who had abandoned it altogether. Where African religious women exchanged one form of patriarchy for another, African Catholic laywomen experienced the double oppression of both African and European patriarchies.

Despite this double oppression, however, African women did attend the congresses, though it is not possible to know how many did so in either absolute numbers or as a relative proportion of attendees. Few, if any, seem to have been invited to give major addresses. At a meeting of the congress central committee in 1952, Peter Magwaza "mentioned that women were given less chance of speaking at the Congress than men: he thought it better to allot some more time or to increase the days of the Congress to three instead of two, so as to allow women to speak. This will be dealt with when we are going to draw up the time-table for the next Congress."[87]

Congress planners evidently chose not to extend the conference because at the central committee's next meeting in April 1953, a member noted that "women who attend the Congress do not get enough time or opportunity to express their views," and proposed that "at least one woman should give a talk at [the 1953 congress held at Triashill Mission]." Of course, congress planners also "expected that the five African priests will be the ones giving the talks: these Speakers will each take a different aspect of the general theme of the Congress, 'The Liturgical Movement.'"[88]

Though women were not major speakers at the congresses, neither were they silent at the sessions they attended, though these and the congress liturgies were frequently segregated by gender.[89] At the 1949 congress, after Raphael Ruzive's speech on marriage, Francis Barr asked what steps could be taken to ensure Christian marriages among our young people: too often, he said, a girl would know everything about her intended husband except his religion. This question was not really answered in the ensuing discussion. A Catholic father should know his duty, and as he is the one who receives lobola [bride price], he is to blame if his daughter is pledged to one who is not Catholic. But what if the father is not a Catholic? Various views were expressed, especially by the women, about the difficulties of marriage and the obstinacy of their children, and the discussion wandered from the point at issue.[90]

In the business session, during discussion of a proposal for the 1950 congress to be held at Makumbi Mission, the 1949 congress minutes note, "Further, the women asked that at this congress they should have a meeting of their own."[91] There is no evidence, however, that a congress was held in 1950. In a discussion of the leadership training courses in December 1953, a delegate to the Salisbury Regional Council from Chishawasha "said that women should attend their own Leadership Course, otherwise they feel much neglected." Peter Magwaza also expressed the opinion that "some capable women ought to be attending Central Committee Meetings," and Ambrose Majongwe noted "Monte Cassino had once held a Leadership Course for women."[92]

Although it is extremely unlikely that congress organizers would have cancelled the annual meeting to forego allowing women to have a session of their own, it is clear that African Catholic women who attended the congress knew their own interests and were not afraid to express their views, even to the annoyance of Jesuit scribes. Significantly, there is no record that any woman ever represented a mission council at a congress, thus, all the women who attended congresses did so voluntarily and paid for their own transportation to and from the congress venue, as well as for food while there—although there are complaints in the Salisbury Regional Council's minutes of women cooking their own food and not paying the two shilling and six pence meal fee required of all those attending the congresses.[93]

In 1956, the training team that presented the leadership courses reported that the mission council at Marandellas elected "for the first time in the history of Salisbury Archdiocese," a woman to the executive committee.[94] Where women received the most frequent mention, however, was in the reports from the mission councils on the activities of the CA local branches. In addition to raising "good" Catholic children and visiting the lapsed, women did almost all of the cooking to feed the delegates at the congresses; after the 1956 congress at St. Michael's Mission in Mhondoro, one delegate "spoke feelingly of the effects of the bad food and asked that women and not men be appointed to cook."[95] The women also visited the sick, participated in explicitly prayer-centered groups such as the Legion of Mary and sodalities dedicated to Mary the Queen of Heaven and the Sacred Heart of Jesus, contributed their money to the support of the church in general and to funds to support scholarships, as well as to build churches, schools, and hospitals, attended retreats, taught catechism, and shared in the work of evangelization, among other activities. In fact, the mission councils that reported the most success frequently had more than one local women's group. Thus, to the extent that the CA garnered any success in its activities women held a stake at least equal to if not greater than that of the men.

Clericalism and Lack of Clerical Support

Although the congress movement began as a meeting for laypeople and subsequent meetings sought to develop African Catholic lay leadership, the Jesuits' emphasis on clerical and hierarchical control of Catholic Action perpetually hamstrung the CA, most particularly Michael Hannan, the founder of the CA territorial council and its first spiritual adviser, and Francis Markall, the first spiritual adviser that Chichester appointed and second archbishop of Salisbury.

At the 1948 congress held at Kutama, Hannan addressed the delegates concerning "what is meant by the growth of the Church in a mission country." This speech illustrates his understanding of Catholic Action and the laity's role therein. According to Hannan, the church's growth was "conditioned by the degree in which the people of the country help the Church to progress . . . [and that] without generous cooperation, beyond the bounds of mere obligation, the Church could not make the progress that is wanted by God. The growth of the Church means the multiplication of places where the ordinary means of salvation are permanently available."[96]

Hannan equated hierarchy or clergy with "Church" in this context: he referred to "the people of the country," who are distinct and apart from "the Church" and are required to help "the Church" progress with their "generous cooperation," but not their initiative or own action. According to Hannan, the growth of "the Church" that God wants is an increase in the places where "the ordinary means of salvation," that is, the sacraments, "are permanently available," namely churches, chapels, and schools under "the Church's" control. According to pre–Vatican II Catholic theology, the priest was the minister of the sacraments and stood as the bishop's representative in a given territory within the bishop's jurisdiction. The bishop, chosen by the pope, Jesus Christ's vicar on earth, shares in the mission of the apostles chosen by Jesus Christ and is their successor. Thus, the priest shares in the apostles' pastoral and teaching mission. Hannan, accordingly, exhorted "the people of the country" to do more than observe the sacraments and help "the Church" (priests and bishops) in its mission to spread the sacraments to various locations on a permanent basis. To do so, would require active people to help bring converts into "the Church's" fold, and to build the churches and schools necessary to accommodate them. If the church were to have a resident pastor, he would require a residence, and the school—often staffed by religious women—required a separate residence. Catholic Action in this narrow context, then, meant the laity sharing in the mission of the hierarchy, not having a mission of its own.

Hannan then "reminded" the delegates "of certain obligations" that they found difficult to carry out:

to give good example, to support the Church with their offerings, to send their children to Catholic schools, to refuse to accept lobola from a non-Catholic suitor for their daughter's hand. These obligations are burdensome, but there are other hard things that must be done, even though no individual is bound to them under pain of sin. Examples of such difficult, though necessary, things were given: to teach in Catholic schools instead of government schools, to teach in village schools instead of central schools, to live in the reserves and act as catechist and leader instead of working in town or buying one's own farm, to stay at home after passing Standard VI instead of going to work in the towns.[97]

Here Hannan again showed a clerical understanding Catholic Action. If the scribe's rendering of Hannan's speech is correct, then he implied that not giving a good example or supporting the church with offerings of money or labor, or sending one's children to Catholic schools, or preventing one's daughter from marrying a non-Catholic (that is, by refusing his *lobola*) were all sinful actions that could only be atoned for by confessing one's sins and performing a penance assigned by the confessor. As the minister of the sacraments, the priest served as the confessor who mediated the penance upon the penitent. Furthermore, according to preconciliar theology, any person who was not in a "state of grace" (that is, who had committed a sin and not received absolution from a confessor) was not allowed to receive the eucharist during the liturgy of the mass, and therefore was denied full participation in the quintessential action that signified and distinguished one as a Catholic. Again, according to pre–Vatican II theology, the priest as minister of the sacraments could withhold communion from a person if he knew that that person was in a state of sin.

Thus, Hannan clearly placed the priest ominously in the delegates' lives, and by extension in the lives of lay African Catholics, as well as gave a clearly clerical tone to Catholic Action: the Catholic faith's obligations required the clergy's approbation. The demands of Catholic Action beyond the obligations of the faith required concrete and substantial sacrifice of one's self, one's family, and one's community ostensibly for the greater good of the church: teaching in Catholic schools instead of government schools, or in an outschool instead of a central mission school meant that a teacher would receive less money for more as well as more difficult work, which resulted in the teacher's earning less money with which to support his/her family and spending less time with them even though the children in a given area were benefitting from that sacrifice. Similarly, remaining in a reserve farming on communal land to work as a catechist or be a leader of a local church community (usually at an outstation remote from the central station where the priest was based) meant significant economic hardship compared to the potential benefits from owning one's own farm or (ostensibly for men only) migrating to an urban area to earn cash wages, especially if one had completed primary school (Standard VI)—the highest educational level available to Africans in the 1940s and 1950s.

Nevertheless, the congress scribe noted that during the discussion following Hannan's speech "time was wasted . . . by those who felt irked by the Church's law forbidding children's education in non-Catholic schools, and by teachers who wished to be appointed African principals of boarding schools."[98] Evidently, the lay African delegates attending the congress had priorities different from those Hannan espoused.

Hannan's actions manifested concretely his beliefs concerning the status of the clergy vis-à-vis the laity. During the 1949 congress at St. Peter's Church in Harare, Hannan chaired all sessions. At the 1951 congress at Monte Cassino Mission regarding reports from missions and centers, the congress scribe noted, "There seems to have been some misunderstanding somewhere as only 3 reports altogether were submitted. The teachers said that they have not been informed, but this cannot be understood as this is a standing item on all Congresses."[99] Several months prior to the congress, however, Hannan wrote to Bishop Chichester asking him to send a circular letter to the superiors of mission stations, "of which more than one copy should go to each mission," advising "the Fathers-in-charge . . . that they should warn their people that unless a report is sent in from a centre, a verbal report will not be accepted from a representative from a centre. Indeed, only those centres which report something worth hearing will be asked to make a verbal report at the Congress."[100] Evidently Hannan either neglected to inform the lay organizers of the congress of this new rule or determined that only three missions had "something worth hearing" to report, and/or "the Fathers-in-charge" failed warn the local CAA leaders. Either way, the poor communication speaks to African claims of clerical disregard for the lay organization.

More significantly, Hannan played a significant role in the formation of the CAA in 1953, as the territorial council's spiritual adviser until 1961, and simultaneously as the Salisbury regional council's adviser from 1956 to 1958 following Francis Markall's appointment as the archbishop of Salisbury. At the August 1953 meeting of seven European missionaries with Bishop Haene of Gwelo, Hannan was elected as chair of the meeting, and with relatively few concessions to Mariannhill representatives from Bulawayo and Wankie, Swiss Bethlehem missionaries from Gwelo, and Irish Carmelites from Umtali, he pushed through the structures of the Monte Cassino constitution in their entirety, including broad powers for the spiritual advisers. In addition to the spiritual adviser's aforementioned powers to veto any decisions or actions of the council he advised and to remove an officer for dereliction of duty or scandalous behavior, the priest was required to sit at the immediate right of the chairman (a position of honor), could censor press releases, and was "absolved" of any financial responsibilities.[101]

Hannan also wrote explanatory notes that were printed with the constitution in 1955. The notes discussed in exacting detail how to run a meeting according to parliamentary procedure, as well as suggested points for discussion of Catholic teaching and perspective on spiritual, educational, social, economic, and liturgical progress and action. Here again Hannan betrayed his mind regarding African laity and Catholic Action. According to Hannan, educational progress not only entailed the education of the children of Catholic parents at Catholic schools "by only Catholic teachers," but also the recognition "that if, through no fault of ours, there are not places for our children, it is better for them to stop going to school than to go to higher standards at a non-Catholic school."[102]

The section on social progress and action stressed the preservation of Catholic marriage and home life, the rejection of "drunkenness and beer parties" and "immoral dances and immodest songs," and obedience to clerical and secular authorities. Economic progress involved promoting "the best agricultural methods," saving money, conserving timber, working with cooperative schemes, practicing "home industries" such as "mat making, basketry, carving, sewing, pottery," and working "hard to gain what is necessary to feed their children well, clothe them well (not in a flashy way) and to pay for their education. Let others buy motor cars and put asbestos or zinc on their roofs. Catholics want to make a show in heaven, by their care for their children."[103]

During workshops that the CAA Salisbury training team gave to branch and mission officers, Hannan's lectures focused on how to run CAA meetings, emphasizing issues such as preparing meeting agenda and how to "make [the meeting] work."[104] Similarly, at a meeting of regional spiritual advisers in preparation for the first meeting of the territorial council, Hannan claimed that he prepared the explanatory notes to obviate the problem of "useless discussion of finances" at local council meetings.[105] At the territorial council meeting, Hannan tried and failed to prevent the council's adoption of the Gwelo diocese's version of the translation of the CAA constitution into ChiShona—which was overseen by the Bethlehem missionaries, but succeeded in having a three pence per capita tax to raise funds for the territorial council over the objections of the Mariannhill spiritual adviser from Bulawayo.[106] At the next Salisbury regional council meeting, Hannan asked the secretary to submit the minutes to him so that he could censor them before they were distributed to the council members and the mission councils.[107]

Michael Hannan was not alone in his efforts to exert clerical control over the CAA, however. Francis Markall, as the spiritual adviser of the Salisbury congress executive committee and of the CAA regional council, and from 1956 as archbishop of Salisbury significantly influenced the actions of the African laymen who led the organization.

Markall's thinking with regard to Catholic Action was very similar to Hannan's. Following the establishment of the CAA in August 1953, the Salisbury regional council received a letter from an African layman in Northern Rhodesia (colonial Zambia) requesting a copy of the CAA constitution because he wanted to start a similar organization in that colony. Markall responded that the layman should first ask his local priest, and if the priest approved Markall would send the layman a copy of the constitution when it was printed because "it is important to remember that no form of Catholic Action may be started or carried out without the approval of the parish priest."[108]

As early as 1952, Markall recommended that the congress executive committee should appoint a priest as "organising commissioner."[109] Evidently, he did not realize (or care about) the irony of suggesting a priest to be the organizing secretary of a lay movement, but he did so again five years later when the territorial council appointed a Bethlehem priest from the Gwelo diocese to represent the CAA at a lay congress in Rome.[110] In 1956, after having become archbishop, Markall forbade CAA council members and officers from getting involved in politics, though this did not prevent the Salisbury regional council from asking Tom Zawaira from staying on as regional chairman after having been elected to parliament in 1972.[111]

Given Aston Chichester's ambivalence concerning African candidates for the priesthood and women's religious institutes, it is not surprising that he had a similar attitude regarding the African Catholic laity. Despite his professed support for the lay movement, he was not always willing to take actions that CAA leaders thought necessary to strengthen its position, particularly with other missionaries. In his letter to the first meeting of the congress central committee in 1951, Chichester noted the lack of support on the part of his priests, but also expressed ambivalence concerning the African laity's ability to organize the annual congresses and simultaneously exerted episcopal control over the movement:

He [Chichester] went on to give the various opinions of different Fathers with regard to the African Congress. Some, owing to the pressure of work, may not seem to be giving much help. Others, because of our peoples' lack of interest and initiative during the year, may think it too early to place the complete organisation of the Congress in the hands of an African Committee. But there are those who, while admitting that not everyone is born an organiser, think it time to try an African Committee, just as African Associations have been formed for secular affairs. His Lordship has adopted this point of view, and you have from today to show whether you can carry on the Congress or not, because all is in your hands. As elected men you have the power to vote. But all resolutions passed have to receive the Bishop's approval. Anything disapproved will be sent back to the Committee for a review.[112]

Thus, in 1955, when the Salisbury regional council asked Chichester to appoint spiritual advisers to mission councils per article 18 of the constitution, he replied that he would not appoint spiritual advisers at every mission because Hannan was the spiritual adviser for the CAA, "and that will suffice for the present."[113] Hannan, in an effort to calm the angered prelate, remarked that he understood the respective mission superiors to be the CAA mission council spiritual advisers, and that

The CAA is meant to be a way of organising those lay people who wish to share in the apostolate of the hierarchy. Of the essence of the hierarchy is that the sacred authority gives orders. If the laity just do what seems good to them without formal union and submission to authority, that is not Catholic Action. The only person who can represent the Ordinary is one who has been appointed to do so by the Ordinary.[114]

CA leaders frequently complained of the chronic lack of support for the organization from European missionaries, including the spiritual advisers. In 1955, the CAA Salisbury regional council sent letters to Archbishop Chichester and Bishop Donal Lamont of Umtali asking the bishops to ask their priests to stop throwing out CAA correspondence and reports.[115] In 1958, at Hannan's urging, the Salisbury regional council passed a resolution allowing only the mission spiritual adviser (the mission superior according to Hannan's explanation to Chichester) to invite the training team to conduct its workshops.[116] By December, Peter Magwaza, the chair of the regional council, noted that as a result of the resolution only one mission had invited the training team, and that "This was a very disturbing development as the work and influence of the Training Team was very important for the progress of the C.A.A. [sic]."[117]

A resolution that the Salisbury regional council passed in 1953 best demonstrates the practical results of the combined clerical understanding of Catholic Action and lack of support from the clergy for the CAA:

Mr. John Cizarura, Makumbe [sic], brought up a point of paramount importance. He said that in the outschools during the holidays teachers go out holidaying and then there is nobody to lead Sunday Prayers when Christians group together. Cannot something be done to train some good Christian leaders at each outschool to conduct Sunday Prayers during the absence of the teachers. A *resolution* was drawn up that the Bishop [Chichester] be asked whether some good natured Christians could be trained to lead Sunday Prayers during the absence of the teachers in the outschools.[118]

Although the resolution passed, and although it is not clear whether it was implemented, that laypeople felt incapable of leading themselves in prayer in the absence of a priest or appointed teacher is very telling of the attitudes with which African laypeople had to work on the part of the clergy.

In 1958, Michael Hannan resigned as spiritual adviser for the CAA Salisbury regional council, and three years later he stepped down as the spiritual adviser to the territorial council, although he occasionally advised the Salisbury regional council when the regularly appointed spiritual adviser could not be present. Hannan's departure combined with the theological shift to focusing on the lay apostolate as opposed to Catholic Action that came with papal reign of John XXIII and the Second Vatican council gave the CA leadership greater opportunity to direct the affairs of their Catholic lay organization. Salisbury regional council spiritual advisers Francis Barr and John Dove (both Jesuits) acted in a much more advisory capacity than Markall or Hannan, making far fewer interventions during council and executive committee meetings. Although Markall appointed Alois Nyanhete as the CAA spiritual adviser for St. Peter's in Harare as early as 1957, and Patrick Chakaipa for Makumbi Mission in 1968, it was not until 1974 that an African priest, Fr. Emmanuel Mavudzi, became the spiritual adviser for the Salisbury regional council.[119]

African Voice and Perspective

Despite clerical constraints, the African laypeople that comprised the CA negotiated space for themselves to express their own perspective to the bishops and leaders within the Catholic Church, but also to broader Rhodesian society as well. Although CA members were politically more moderate than members of the African nationalist parties, they expressed a critical awareness of their position within the church and wider society, particularly through *Moto* magazine.[120]

Beginning with the 1948 congress at Kutama the African laity asked specifically for African priests to give retreats and missions, whereas before they had asked only that there be missions preached and retreats given.[121] Evidently they had not only a desire for spiritual fulfillment, but also hoped to receive that spirituality from church leaders who would be more sympathetic to their cultural perspectives, or minimally who shared the same language and who could preach intelligibly. In 1951, at the congress at Monte Cassino Mission (and again in 1955 at the regional council meeting), the congress delegates passed a resolution asking that an African priest be appointed assistant spiritual adviser.[122] Apparently, they also wanted a priest who understood their language and/or perspective to have a voice in the governance of their organization. It was not until November 1957 that Archbishop Markall appointed Fr. Alois Nyanhete as assistant spiritual adviser, but only for St. Peter's Parish in Harare.[123]

Although the Jesuit scribes of the 1948 Kutama congress believed that the discussions following the presentations by Frs. Kotzki and Hannan and Joseph Dambaza on marriage and the mandatory Catholic education of Catholic children at Catholic schools were "wasted time," the African Catholics' complaints are significant because they represent African perspectives on these issues that did not accord with positions that the missionaries espoused. The complaint about nuns limiting African men's access to young African women in boarding schools, while perhaps a nuisance to a celibate European scribe, reflects a concern on the part of African men that the church was interfering with VaShona marriage practices. The issue of marriage was so important to the African laity that they raised the question of solemn betrothal as a means toward the canonical regularization of African marriages, frequently raised the issue of high *lobola*, and in 1968 they decided that the theme for the congress at St. Peter's should focus on marriage.[124]

Despite the determination of missionaries such as Michael Hannan to ensure that Catholic Africans send their children exclusively to Catholic schools, even to the point of encouraging parents to keep their children home rather than send them to a non-Catholic school, many African Catholics apparently did not value Catholic education to the same degree as they valued educational opportunity in itself. In this respect, African Catholics mirrored the attitudes of many of their coreligionists in the United States and elsewhere.[125] Nevertheless, delegates to the Congress central committee (and later regional council) from Lourdes Mission proposed a resolution asking that Catholic parents be allowed to send children from Standard IV and beyond to any Catholic school in the Salisbury vicariate, and they expressed a concern that their school be granted a Standard IV, since their children, upon completing Standard III at the Catholic school, had to go to a Dutch Reformed Church school to continue their education.[126] Similarly, in 1954, the Salisbury regional council wanted to double subscription fees for each mission from £5 to £10 per year in order to raise money for scholarships so that Catholic students could pursue higher education.[127]

Following the establishment of the African Catholic Congress central committee, the complaints from the lay leaders about the lack of support from the clergy were almost as frequent as the latter's claim of the former's incapacity to function as an organization. As early as 1952, during reports from local branches, the committee secretary noted "the stupendous difficulties" that local committees met.[128] In 1953, the delegates passed resolutions asking the bishops to allow priests to give more missions and retreats at outschools, not just at the central mission stations, and that the bishops encourage priests to allow laypeople to form local branches.[129] In 1955, the regional council sent letters to Archbishop Chichester and Bishop Lamont of Umtali requesting that they ask their priests to stop throwing out CAA correspondence.[130] During the same year, the regional council petitioned Chichester to appoint spiritual advisers to the respective mission councils per the CAA constitution, which he refused to do.[131] In 1958, the territorial council complained that the bishops still were not appointing spiritual advisers to the mission councils, and that if they had done so, the CAA would have received more respect.[132] In 1959, the territorial council again asked the bishops to "promulgate" mission council spiritual advisers, apparently to no avail.[133] Various council minutes register the same complaints throughout the 1960s.[134]

More significantly, in 1961, the territorial council decided to send an African layperson to London for training in Catholic teaching on social justice and grassroots organizing and committed £200 to support the venture. The council subsequently chose Tom Zawaira, who would later serve as chairman of the Salisbury regional council, to attend the seminar at Claver House.[135] At the same meeting, the territorial delegates passed a resolution asking the bishops to establish study groups and a territorial conference "on African life and custom and [their] possible adaptation to Christian life."[136] This action pushed the bishops to take up the question of adapting "African life and custom" to Christian life in their committee on vernacular liturgy.[137] This began a process of debate about what could be admitted to approved Catholic practice in the church in colonial Zimbabwe, particularly the practice of honoring the spirits of deceased ancestors in the *kurova guva* rite (see Chapter 7). In 1970, the territorial council passed a resolution asking the bishops "to make better use of the C.A. in investigating African opinion in such matters as KUROVE GUVA [sic] ceremony, liturgical questions, Diaconate, political problems, etc., and that the findings of such committees be reported to C.A. through the Territorial Council."[138]

As the political crisis became more acute following the Rhodesian Front's unilateral declaration of independence (UDI) in November 1965, the CA leadership weighed in on several issues, supporting the stand taken by the Catholic bishops on the "Principle of Justice concerning the Land Tenure Act and School Issue," and in favor of racial integration in their pastoral letter "A Crisis of Conscience."[139] In 1971, the CA territorial council and the Salisbury regional council established committees to study the Pearce commission proposals and both recommended that the bishops reject any internal settlement.[140] Similarly, the territorial council asked the bishops "to inform the people in simple terms of any approaches made by them [the bishops] to the Government on matters which affect the people as a whole. This is to avoid the impression by the people that the Church is silent at a critical period." They also asked the bishops "to produce a summary of the relevant Vatican Council decrees in the vernacular."[141]

The foregoing brief survey of the activities of the Catholic Association's leadership councils clearly shows that as laypeople they were well informed on the political and theological issues of the day, that they had a clear vision of and interests in the society and church in which they lived, and that they worked to implement that vision. Determining their success in implementing the vision, and the degree to which that vision was shared the grassroots level will require more extensive research. Nevertheless, the Catholic Association leadership had a fairly broad base of support for its program, and filled African Catholic laypeople's need, be it social, spiritual, or a desire for unity in Catholic Action. The numbers of participants who voluntarily paid to attend the annual congresses attest to this. Lest one think that the councils which conducted the business of the association were a small handful of the same people, by 1970, the Salisbury regional council consisted of 151 delegates from twenty-two mission councils,[142] and four years later there were more paid members from the Marandellas region (which had been split from Salisbury with an eye to making it a separate vicariate apostolic) than from the metropolitan see (see Table 4.1).

Conclusion

A. J. Dachs and W. F. Rea, after reading Hugh O'Donnell's paper on the Catholic Association, argued,

The very success of the Association in many ways contributed to its decline. The keen involvement and leadership of the laity meant in many areas corresponding neglect of the Association by priests, whose skills and energies were in heavy demand elsewhere. The size of the membership provoked attacks from nationalist politicians and assault upon the Association members. Moreover within the church large territorial associations were yielding to local community groups, annual national conferences were giving way to regular and frequent parish council meetings; and from 1962 both membership and organization began to fade, especially in the regions away from Salisbury.[143]

This brief study of the Catholic Association's documentation, however, clearly shows that the missionaries' neglect of the organization did not correspond to those areas in which the laity was active. Rather, it would appear that the CA tried to fill many of the gaps that the clergy left unattended: the constant demand for spiritual renewal in retreats and missions, frequent efforts to provide for the education (Catholic or otherwise) of African Catholic youth, evangelization and engaging in the corporal works of mercy, advocacy for the integration of African culture into the church's liturgical and theological lives, support for the bishops on highly charged political issues—without which the bishops would not have been nearly as successful in their advocacy.

Similarly, African nationalists did not attack CA members merely because of the organization's size. Rather, the African Catholic laity received threatening intimidation and physical violence because nationalists saw them as willingly subordinate to foreign Whites who associated with and participated in a morally bankrupt regime that oppressed the majority of the people in the colony along racial lines. Whether that was actually the case or not, that was certainly the perception.

Lastly, the "large territorial association" did not yield to local community groups—in fact, it was composed of small community groups at its base, and the annual national conferences did not give way "to regular and frequent parish council meetings." Rather, it appears that the bishops intentionally introduced the structure of the parish council at the same time that their investigative committee tried to gut what little sense of direction and organizational purpose from the constitution that Michael Hannan and the other European missionaries imposed on the CAA in 1953. The African leadership of the CAA knew fully well what it was doing when it asked to drop the "African" from its title and become the "parent body of all Catholic Action." The bishops balked at this clear and relatively early opportunity for interracial cooperation and equality on a national level. While they may not have intended the CA's demise, their actions had a deleterious effect on the organization, which continued to coexist ambiguously with the parish councils, without receiving any clear guidance as to what distinguished one from the other. In fact, Edward Muchenje's assertion that the parish councils in colonial Zimbabwe grew out of the CA's structure is correct.

O'Donnell and Dachs and Rea argued that 1962 and the committee of inquiry signaled the death knell of the CA. Both say that membership peaked around 1960 and by 1962, the CA went into permanent decline, although O'Donnell did mention that in the Salisbury and Umtali dioceses the CA experienced "a renewal" in the late 1960s but was dead in Bulawayo and Wankie.[144] In point of fact, CAA membership first peaked in 1958, not 1960 or 1961, with 5,300 paid members. Not surprisingly, that number declined in the face of violent opposition from the nationalist parties. Bulawayo continued to send representatives to the territorial council until 1964 and Gwelo until 1973. Although the CA was no longer a national organization in the sense that it had members participating from all five dioceses (six following the erection of the Sinoia prefecture apostolic from the northern part of the Salisbury archdiocese in 1973), what is most significant about the "renewal" in the late 1960s and early 1970s is that membership exploded in those areas—particularly in the Salisbury archdiocese—where the second *chimurenga* was becoming most intense. It would be most interesting to study whether there was a correlation between these two phenomena or if it was merely coincidental. Regardless of the answer, the issue raises a further question of the extent to which and reasons why people in times of war have recourse to religion.

Hugh O'Donnell concluded that the CA's achievements included fostering a sense of unity through the congress, raising particular subjects and problems for discussion during the congress' lectures and question and answer sessions, and providing basic leadership training and opportunities for leadership; and that its failures included a lack of action after congresses, vague aims, poor leadership, a lack of support on the part of clergy, constantly revising its constitutions, missionaries imposing external ideas without a clear understanding of the local situation, and the inability to reconcile with parish councils.[145] It is significant to note that Hugh O'Donnell was an Irish Franciscan missionary who served as a spiritual adviser to the CA. Accordingly, his preponderantly negative view and grim outlook for the future of the CA are informed by the perspective of the missionaries who were the CA's critics.

Jesuit John Dove, the Salisbury regional council's spiritual adviser from 1964 to 1971, had a much more positive perspective on the CA and its activities. When asked whether the CA was in fact a "do-nothing organization," Dove responded that he thought that to be "an unfair criticism:"

> [The CA] was started for a Christian influence in village life: take marriage, for example, what if a man wanted a second wife, or if she were forced into it? . . . There was also information about agriculture: knowledge of fertilizers and cooperative farming, sharing scotch carts and tools, bulk purchases—but money was always paid to the individual. . . . It was a general movement to Christianize a village: how to handle local problems . . . The problems and questions [they dealt with] show how they related to life every day. The CA went on and people went to the CA person. They were very effective—they weren't necessarily parading on Sundays, but they had the CA meetings at the local level. . . . People preferred spiritual topics and accepted agriculture and education. It held together in a very strange way: dealing with traditional problems in confrontation with Christianity.[146]

And that, perhaps, is a fitting image: of people caught in the crucible of being "traditional" Africans in very concrete circumstances in specific times confronted with and trying to integrate constantly contested understandings of Christianity into their lives and the worlds around them. The Catholic Association may not have done monumental things that are recorded as the great deeds of great people, but the men and women who joined its ranks, attended its congresses, gave their money in support of its projects, and supported one another in the mundane activities of daily village life certainly did something: and that something was a careful and successful negotiation of the complex and constantly shifting relationships in which these African Catholics found themselves with the church's hierarchy, and with the nationalist movements that placed unusual pressure on them as collaborators with the settler regime. They pushed the church's clerical leaders, both European and African, to recognize and address the laity's interests. They adapted to complex structures and difficult situations, often used oppressively against them. And they learned to use those structures and situations to their own advantage, and that of their African understandings of Christianity.

5 Until Death Do Us Part? African Marriage Practices and the Catholic Church, 1890-1979

> *Francesca Misodzi rejects the claim of Vale Mupunga though she is the mother of his child. She declares that in marrying again, she will observe the rites of the Faith; the Catholic church. She desired her children to remain at Chishawasha when requested to express her opinion on their being removed to Hartley. It is the known wish of her late husband, Henry Muronda, that she and her five children should remain [in] a position where they can be instructed in their faith. He gave the eldest daughter over to the care of the [Dominican] Sisters for her protection. The children are: Clara Chitima, born 28th November, 1903; One, a boy died; Francis Chirenda, school boy; Rosa Nyorergwa; Joseph Musiwa; one illegitimate child by Vale Mupunga.*
>
> Fr. Richartz Letter Book, April 10, 1919

For most of the colonial period, the Catholic Church's hierarchy in Southern Rhodesia presumed the superiority of Western Christian marriage and made no efforts to integrate African and Western Christian marriage practices, showing more concern with regularizing canonically invalid unions of African Catholics by various means available within canon law. African Catholics generally disregarded the church's canonical requirements, marrying according to "customary law." By 1967, approximately 80 percent of African Catholics were not marrying in the church according to canonical form. Consequently, the bishops formed two commissions to study the problem. The commissions recommended, against the opinion of Jesuit canonists, that the bishops recognize African customary unions as the basis for canonical marriage within the church, which they accepted. The recommendation was largely ineffective, thus, in 1975, the bishops petitioned Rome for permission to allow elder lay Catholics to preside at Catholic weddings as a means to integrate African and church practices. Although they apparently did not receive authorization, the request itself, as well as the marriage commissions' recommendation to recognize African customary unions, indicates a significant change in the church leadership's understanding of African marriage practices, and an unprecedented openness to experimentation to incorporate African marriage processes formally into church structures.

VaShona Marriage Practices and the Making of "Customary Law"

Early in the colonial period, sexual and marital relations between African men and women derived meaning and function within a broader social context. Marriage entailed the joining of two families as well as the union of two individuals. During this period no single wedding ritual signaled the beginning of marriage. Marriage involved a process of negotiation between the families, and a man and woman were considered married either when the first part of the bride price (*lobola*) was paid to the woman's family in cattle or crops, when the woman was accompanied to her husband's homestead (*kuperekedzwa*), or when the woman bore her first child. The *munyai*, an intermediary engaged by the prospective husband's family, usually arranged preliminary negotiations between the families, including the *vhuramuromo*, or payment to the woman's father or *tezvara* (father-in-law), to encourage him to specify the *lobola* price. Elopement (*kutiza*), however, was a common means to begin the negotiation process, usually having the tacit knowledge and approval of the woman's paternal aunt, or *tete*.[1]

Following the 1896–97 *chimurenga*, and prior to the colonial African economy's monetization, matrilocal service marriages in which the prospective husband, or *mukuwasha* (son-in-law), agreed to work for the *tezvara* for a number of years rather than pay *lobola* became more common. By the 1920s, as more young African men entered the colonial economy as laborers in towns or mines, *vadzitezvara* (fathers-in-law) began to require *lobola* payments in cash, and increasingly "in a single transaction, or at least a significantly large first payment. This was a wholly different kind of transaction from the long-term transfer of goods which had characterized the marriage alliances of the 1890s, involving a lifetime of exchange and obligation linking families across generations."[2] It was also during this period that *vadzitezvara* began to exact *rutsambo*, or a large initial cash payment payable by the suitor himself rather than his family, first as protection against the bad faith of African migrant workers but subsequently as a means of income. Payment of cattle continued to be associated with the birth of children.

In order to prevent another rebellion akin to the *chimurenga*, the British South Africa Company (BSAC) and settler administrations adopted a limited noninterference policy with African culture during the colonial period. This entailed members of the Native Affairs Department consulting with wealthy senior African men as to what constituted legitimate African "tradition" or "custom," and enacting it into law. These consultations resulted in the development of African "customary law," or the promotion and protection of wealthy African men's interests so long as those interests did not conflict with the interests of BSAC or, from 1923, the settler administration.[3] The 1898 order in council provided that in civil cases between Africans the courts "shall be guided by native law so far as that law is not repugnant to natural justice or morality."[4] Thus, marriage legislation allowed *lobola* and polygyny to continue, but it banned child pledging and forced marriages.

Southern Rhodesian authorities passed several laws to regulate African marriages. The 1901 Native Marriage Ordinance (NMO) allowed for polygynous marriages, required payment of *lobola* within twelve months of the date of marriage (to prevent pledging of young girls), limited *lobola* to four head of cattle (five for the daughter of a chief) or the cash equivalent, and required registration of the marriage at a native commissioner's office to ensure that the woman had given her consent (to prevent forced marriages) and recording of the *lobola* payment to prevent excessive payments or nonpayment. The 1901 NMO exempted Christian marriages from its provisions. The 1901 ordinance was based on an "extremely limited understanding of African marriage processes," and aimed more at preventing than encouraging marriages, for example, by not recognizing elopement marriages.[5]

The 1901 NMO presumed marriage was a discrete event requiring official sanction. This Western notion of marriage did not account for African beliefs and practices that marriage alliances could be contracted between the families involved without official sanction, or without payment of *lobola* (for example, in service marriages). The 1905 Native Marriage Ordinance unintentionally encouraged "technical concubinage," or unions that Africans accepted as marriages but were illegal according to European norms because they were not registered at a native commissioner's (NC) office. Christian marriages also encouraged technical concubinage because they forbade African Christian men from contracting second marriages under the penalty of bigamy, thus they could not register any marriages contracted according to African practice, which rendered such wives concubines according to European law.[6] Thus, in 1912, colonial authorities passed another marriage ordinance outlawing child pledging, mandating registration of all African marriages regardless of whether or not *lobola* was paid, removed the limit on the amount of *lobola*, and allowed African men who married according to Christian rites to contract polygynous marriages according to African practices. Such marriages would be registered and recognized according to civil law only.[7] According to historian Diana Jeater, these laws did not "fundamentally alter [African] marriage practices," since Africans frequently chose to ignore the requirements to register their marriages.[8]

In 1917, BSAC passed another marriage ordinance. The 1917 NMO resulted from disputes between the administration and Christian missionaries. The latter opposed polygyny's continuance, and the 1912 NMO provisions allowing African Christians to contract polygynous marriages according to African practices. Native commissioners disliked missionaries who frequently refused to obtain a *tezvara*'s consent before performing Christian marriages, which the law did not require but African practice demanded. Christian marriages were subject only to English common law. Thus, a twenty-one-year-old African woman did not need parental consent to marry. The administration was also concerned that African men who contracted Christian marriages frequently did not register non-Christian polygynous marriages, and because the courts did not recognize unregistered marriages, the women technically became concubines before the law and the man in question could not be held liable for bigamy. The 1917 NMO thus considered any unregistered marriage invalid (per the 1901 NMO, a woman had to give her consent to marriage at a NC's office to register a marriage); outlawed pledging and forced marriage (previously forced marriage was only considered as grounds for disallowing a marriage); and required a woman's parent or guardian give his consent before the marriage occurred. Historian Elizabeth Schmidt claimed that the 1917 NMO allowed a woman to appeal her guardian's refusal of consent if she thought he had done so unreasonably, but she was allowed to marry without his consent only provided that the territorial administrator gave his: "In other words, her tutelage was transferred from an African guardian, deemed incompetent by the state, to a substitute European patriarch." Jeater argued that the 1917 NMO established an African "customary" marriage: by requiring that registration occur after *lobola* payment and before consummation native commissioners could distinguish between lawful marriages and informal sexual unions; by expanding registration requirements it ensured a woman's consent. The 1917 NMO's definition of African custom invalidated elopement as a way to contract a lawful marriage. As with previous marriage legislation, however, the 1917 NMO was largely ineffective: Schmidt noted that into the 1930s child pledging was "prevalent" and forced marriages were still "widely practiced." According to Jeater, several NCs complained that the legislation criminalized over half of Southern Rhodesia's African population.[9]

The 1929 NMO maintained the criminal offense for not registering marriages, but no longer invalidated them. Additionally, African men married by Christian rites were legally obliged to remain monogamous regardless of whether they registered additional marriages.[10] To curb increasing *lobola* amounts that *vadzitezvara* required, the 1951 African Marriages Act limited *lobola* to £20. It required a couple to apply in person for a certificate from a district commissioner stating that the *tezvara* did not object to the marriage. In 1962, the Southern Rhodesian parliament repealed the £20 limit.[11]

The 1964 African Marriages Act appointed a registrar of marriages to oversee the registration of all African marriages within the colony;

required the written consent of the parent or guardian of any person under twenty-one years of age wishing to marry, and forbade African boys under eighteen and African girls under sixteen from marrying; removed the ban on a person marrying the brother or sister of a spouse from whom she or he had been divorced while the spouse was alive; and required a couple to obtain an enabling certificate to marry according to Christian rites.[12] The legislature consulted the Catholic bishops during deliberations on the 1964 African Marriage Act, and apparently deferred to them on a number of points. Archbishop Francis Markall noted although the bishops disagreed with several parts of the legislation, on the whole "they feel that the new Act is as well-conceived and effective a piece of legislation as could have been hoped for in this important matter."[13] An example of evident consultation with the Catholic bishops and their pleasure with the new marriage law is in the section on the requirements for the publication of marriage banns. The law stipulated a couple could publish or verbally announce the wedding banns at a worship service on three Sundays prior to the wedding date (not necessarily on successive Sundays), or publish a notice of intent to marry fifteen days prior to the wedding date, or obtain a marriage license from a district commissioner. According to the regulations accompanying the promulgation of the marriage act, a couple had to pay two shillings and six pence for a notice of intention to marry or £5 for a marriage license.[14] There were no fees required to publish wedding banns, which was canonically prescribed for Catholics.

The Catholic Church's Canon Law of Marriage in Colonial Zimbabwe

The Catholic Church teaches that marriage is a permanent, indissoluble, sacramental union between a man and a woman that God instituted in the person of Jesus Christ (Mark 10:2–12; Matthew 19:3–12). According to Catholic doctrine, divorce is impossible, although an ecclesiastical court may issue a decree of nullity, or annulment, if it determines grounds for a given marriage were defective or invalid.

Regulations concerning the validity and licitness for marriage within the church are found in canon law. While the first collection of the *corpus iuris canonici* dates to 1190, the church did not promulgate a single, unified code of canon law for the entire church throughout the world until 1917. In 1963, Pope John XXIII established a commission to revise the code in light of the changes brought about by Vatican II. Pope John Paul II promulgated the revised code in 1983.

As early as 1563, the Council of Trent issued "Tametsi," a decree that required a man and women to publish wedding banns publicly and to marry in the presence of a priest and at least two witnesses for a valid marriage within the church. For a variety of reasons, "Tametsi" was not universally promulgated throughout the church, so Pope Pius X issued the decree "Ne Temere" in 1907, which reiterated the canonically valid form of marriage found in "Tametsi." The provisions of "Ne Temere" were subsequently incorporated into the 1917 code.[15] Canon 1098 of the 1917 code, however, provided two exceptions to the canonical form: marriage could be contracted licitly and validly in the presence of two witnesses only (that is, without the presence of a priest) in danger of death, or if a couple could not go to a priest "without great inconvenience" (*sine gravi incommodo*).[16]

From the third century, the church opposed marriage between a Catholic and a "schismatic or heretic" (that is, non-Catholic) and considered a union between a Catholic and a non-Christian canonically invalid, so that the bond of matrimony does not exist, and an impediment to valid canonical marriage within the church (a diriment impediment). Marriage between a Catholic and baptized, non-Catholic Christian was considered canonically valid (that is, the bond of marriage exists) but illicit (an impedient impediment), or invalid and illicit without a valid dispensation.[17]

The documentary evidence in the Jesuit archives and the Harare archdiocesan archives supports Schmidt's and Jeater's arguments, and it also raises issues that bear on the church's lack of effort to adapt its marriage practices to those of its African constituents. According to Schmidt, Jesuit and Wesleyan Methodist missionaries did not allow African women to use "the custom of elopement, which would have entailed sexual relations before a church wedding."[18] While Jesuits at

Chishawasha may not have allowed resident Christians to elope, they apparently recognized elopement as an accepted VaShona marriage practice and as a preliminary basis for contracting Christian marriage. In 1905, Jesuit Emil Schmitz expressed a commonly held view that eloping

> is the only *native proof* that a girl wants a boy. As long as this is not done, there is no real proof of her love or will in the eyes of the natives. This custom exists all over the country. In the past, when complications were likely to follow—as the result of running away, we always sent the boy to the N.C., and Capt. Nesbitt after questioning the girl, always allowed her to stay at Chishawasha for six months to see if she was fit for a Christian marriage. I may mention here, that "Christian marriage" is an important step for both parties concerned since it means "union for life with one wife." Therefore, we think the girl should get a chance of at least six months instruction before marrying. . . . May I add that for Christian marriages, we cannot possibly follow the routine followed for Pagans. And this Capt. Nesbitt understood and accordingly helped as far as he could to be instructed and made fit for Christian marriage once a girl had shown proof of her wish by running away from home. This I should say is quite a natural view to take for a civilising Christian government.[19]

This passage from Schmitz's letter also shows the cordial and informal arrangement that Jesuits at Chishawasha had with the NC Goromonzi district and the implicit assumption of the superiority of Christian marriage to African marriage.

Schmidt noted that "while the state appreciated missionary values, it resented their interference in state affairs," including the adjudication of non-Christian marriage cases.[20] In one such case, Jesuit Edward Biehler referred the case of Chief Usiku's son, Chinyani, to fellow Jesuit Charles Bert rather than a NC. Evidently the child of Chinyani and his second wife, Mushonga, died, and about a month later Mushonga's mother, Pabiri (variously spelled Vabiri) took Mushonga back to her kraal in Mazoe district even though Chinyani had paid five head of cattle in *lobola*. According to Usiku, Pabiri threatened to poison Chinyani "if he came to her kraal to fetch his wife." Biehler advised Bert that

Osiku [sic] is afraid of Nesbitt [NC Goromonzi] sending Chinyani to fetch the woman. If so, Osiku says Chinyani will be poisoned and killed. It will be good to let Capt. Nesbitt know this, since the old Vabiri is [a] dangerous woman.... Therefore, it would be necessary in order to settle the case, to call for the [tezvara], Kudjgachete (in Shopo's kraal, Mazoe district), the wife of Chinyani, Mushonga, and the little girl Maria Mwera (in Mangewe's kraal also), and the baby Sheniwo on Mushonga's back. Of course Capt. Nesbitt would get these people through Mr. Kenny, NC of Mazoe. The old Vabiri deserves a good punishment.[21]

Given the apparently cordial relations between the Jesuits at Chishawasha and their local NC at Goromonzi, it is probable that Captain Nesbitt would have appreciated Biehler and Bert's involvement, though officials at the Native Department headquarters in Salisbury, such as W. S. Taberer and J. A. Halliday, would have perceived such involvement as meddling.

On two occasions Bert inquired into the status of African Christian widows.[22] Precolonial and early colonial VaShona marriage practices provided for the inheritance of a widow by another man in her deceased husband's family.[23] Church teaching from the Council of Trent (and the 1917 code of canon law) simply stated that though "chaste widowhood is more honorable," second marriages were permissible so long as the first marriage bond was proven dissolved and that there were no impediments to a valid marriage.[24] In one instance Chief Native Commissioner Taberer informed Bert that a Christian widow could not be forced to become "the property and wife of a pagan against her will," because even though an inherited wife did not necessarily have the right to exercise her free will as a woman who married for the first time, "the absolute forcing of any woman to cohabit with a man against her will, whether she be pagan or Christian, is repugnant to natural justice and morality, and any custom enforcing such a submission is insupportable in our law." Furthermore, such a woman was not liable to taxation unless she became the second wife of a man "with her consent."[25] In the second instance, NC Nesbitt advised Bert that "native law" required the payment of *lobola* to a Christian widow's father or guardian just as "for a woman on the occasion of her first marriage," and the widow's parent or guardian would be liable to the decedent's next-of-kin if he demanded the return of the original *lobola*.[26]

These cases provide examples of the manufacture of African "customary law": African Christian women expressed concern about their status upon the death of their (presumably) Christian husbands and caused Bert to consult Native Department officials. Bert's desire to protect his African Christian women charges made Taberer invoke and interpret the 1898 order in council concerning "repugnance to natural justice and morality," and likewise Nesbitt to impose Western logic on a previously fluid African social practice. Presumably Bert would have reiterated the church's teaching concerning the indissolubility of Catholic marriage as well as its monogamous and sacramental nature to the widows and their intended husbands prior to issuing wedding banns and presiding at the marriage ceremonies.

In light of the discussion of African Christian widows' status, Jesuit John Apel should have received an affirmative reply to the following case: "A Native Christian widow wants to be married to a Native Christian widower, who is the brother of her former husband. Kindly inform me if the law allows the marriage. In this case the union is very desirable, as both have small children."[27] This case could be considered an early African effort to adapt church practices to local African practices: as Apel described the situation, the African couple took the initiative to seek to marry according to the rites of the church, but significantly they applied ecclesiastical practice to a distinctly African way of proceeding, the inheritance of a widow by a man in her late husband's family. While the degree to which principles of a specific case could be generalized into church policy is debatable, the lack of any discussion of the possibility in Chishawasha's documentary records indicates a failed opportunity for the Jesuits to have mitigated what they saw as a pernicious practice among their African residents.

The Chishawasha Jesuits apparently took careful note of the frequent changes in marriage legislation and carefully explained the contents of the marriage ordinances to their African residents.[28] In 1913, following passage of the 1912 NMO, Zambezi Mission Superior Richard Sykes sent a circular letter to the mission priests summarizing the legislation's main provisions. Noting that even those African men who married according to Christian rites could legally contract subsequent polygamous marriages according to "native custom" and have them registered and recognized by the BSAC administration, Sykes ordered that

> the following directions should be carefully observed. Although the natural marriage of Pagans becomes a Christian marriage on the reception of Baptism by the parties, it will be advisable and even necessary, in order to protect as far as possible neophytes against themselves and to do away with the temptations of polygamy, to impart full solemnity to their Christian marriage by observing the customary celebrations, including publication of banns and regular marriage rites, so as publicly to stamp the previous native marriage with the full celebration of a Christian sacrament [and thus] render the parties liable to criminal proceedings for bigamy should they proceed to another attempted marriage. Consequently the parties should not merely renew their consent and receive an informal blessing when they become Christians but the recognised marriage ceremony of the Ritual should be performed, and the now Christian marriage entered in the Government register and the legal certificate forwarded to the proper quarters. . . . The proper thing, that *long before the marriage*, in Christian instruction, this effects [sic] of the Christian marriage should be made clear to the catechumen, that it may even prevent him from joining the Christian religion if he does not feel able to fulfill the conditions.[29]

Sykes described what canon lawyers call "convalidation," or the removal of an impediment to valid marriage by the conversion of the non-Catholic partner followed by the public renewal of their marriage consent before a priest and at least two witnesses in "the recognised marriage ceremony of the Ritual." Sykes also expressed views that were common for missionaries of his time: the need to protect recent Christian converts from themselves and the dangers of polygamy, even to the point of discouraging potential converts from joining the church, and the necessity of registering Christian marriages according to civil law.

The following case shows that the Jesuits more than likely taught the Christians in their charge the contents of the various civil marriage laws as well as the church's law. In May 1920, John Apel wrote to the NC of Mrewa District informing him that the woman Mambidzeni had married Muvirimi in the district office.

> They had two children, one is dead and the other has been taken by Muvirimi.
> Muvirimi received baptism, after which he dismissed his wife, advancing the plea that she was a heathen. Still, the woman has ever since been anxious to stay with him because she loved him. In fact, she has gone to Fr. Burbridge at [St. Peter's Church] Salisbury and has come to me here with the idea and in the hope that we could induce Joseph Muvirimi to take her back. Our efforts have been unsuccessful. Joseph even contemplates contracting another marriage with a girl called Katarina Kupara, living at Brown's Farm, Salisbury.
> According to church law, Muvirimi ought to take back Mambidzeni as his wife, seeing that she wants to live with him in peace.
> May I suggest that you call Muvirimi and arrange matters between the two.[30]

Muvirimi was familiar with the civil law that allowed him to marry and divorce, and even to contract multiple marriages so long as he did not marry junior wives according to Christian rites. More significantly, he was also evidently aware of the church's teaching that when two non-Christians become Catholic, the church recognized the canonical validity of their marriage, and that if a non-Catholic married to another non-Catholic converted, the neophyte Catholic's marriage to the non-Christian was null in the church's eyes. Thus, according to the 1917 Code of Canon Law, presuming there were no other impediments, Joseph Muvirimi could have licitly and validly married Katarina Kupara according to Catholic rites and raised his child by Mambidzeni (whose custody he could claim according to VaShona marriage practice by virtue of his having paid *lobola*, a requisite for the civil registration of an African marriage according to the 1912 marriage ordinance) within the church. Strictly speaking, Apel's claim that "Muvirimi ought to take back Mambidzeni as his wife" contradicted Canon 1070 of the 1917 code, his good will toward Mambidzeni notwithstanding.[31] This is a rare instance in which a Jesuit supported the case of an unbaptized, "pagan," African woman against the dictates of Catholic canon law.

Marriage cases in St. Peter's parish's records in the Archdiocese of Harare's archives show the church's primary concern with canonically regularizing African Catholics' marriages, rather than finding ways to adapt church practices to African practices. They also show African Catholics' faith and desire to put their marriages right in the church's eyes.

In one case, Agnes, a Catholic, married Felix, a Methodist "from outstanding Methodist parents" in 1957. According to the African diocesan priest promoting their case, from the time of their marriage, Agnes

has been living with him peacefully. All her children, Campion, Felix, Regis, Godfrey, and Stephen are baptised and they received the sacraments. She goes to church herself [with] the children and [Felix] sometimes takes them there. I and some of his friends have been encouraging him to become a Catholic. [He replied] "I shall be the only one from my family becoming a Catholic and to me it means abandoning my family. But I am very sorry for my wife, who cannot receive the sacraments because of me. I wish something could be done." He says this quite sincerely.[32]

Fr. Chifeya believed the family was "quite stable," and thought there was no "danger of divorce at all." He requested permission for and received a mixed marriage dispensation from Archbishop Markall.[33]

By contrast, the case of Joseph and Agatha was more complicated. Joseph married a "pagan" woman in 1930 at the NC of Selukwe's office, but he had no civil divorce documents. Agatha also married a "pagan" according to "African custom" but did register it. Joseph and Agatha had a civil marriage in 1946, and by 1966 had five children. Joseph's first wife and her parents had been living in Selukwe while they were married, but by the time Fr. Chifeya presented the case to Markall (1966) Joseph thought she was either dead or remarried "because 1930 is such a long time for anyone to wait." Joseph and Agatha "want[ed] to marry properly according to Christian rites in the Catholic church" because "they are both quite old now [and] they think it's now time they put themselves in the hands of God."³⁴ Fr. McNamara asked Chifeya for more information, specifically for Joseph's and Agatha's baptismal certificates, and whether there was any evidence that "Joseph's first partner is dead. . . . 1930 may be a long time ago but Joseph himself is not dead so we cannot presume that [she] is without some evidence."³⁵ There was no documentation in the general files whether Joseph and Agatha received a dispensation and were allowed to marry in the church.³⁶

One of the more interesting marriage cases in the St. Peter's parish records involved Charles Mzingeli, a member of the Industrial and Commercial Workers Union (ICU) in the 1920s and 1930s, and a leader of the revived ICU in the 1950s. When Mzingeli joined the ICU in the 1920s, the South African Catholic bishops had condemned it.

On these grounds the priest at St. Peter's [Fr. Alfred Burbridge] obliged him to leave it under pain of excommunication. He [Mzingeli] was so upset by this that he had several talks with Monsignor [Robert Brown, the prefect apostolic of the Zambezi Mission] who he said could only rely on the other Bishops' decision. Fr. Johanny was also asked if he could smooth the matter out. Fr. Johanny told me he could not manage to get the matter settled. Mr. Mzingeli believes that because the Government of South Africa did not like the Union assisting Africans to Trade Unionism the Church followed the Government in place of defending people's rights. He believes he was never excommunicated by the Church, but by his priest.

Deprived of the Sacraments and wishing to marry, he married at the NC's office with a Methodist. From the time of the "excommunication" until about 1950 he has not been a practicing Catholic. He has walked in processions and on several occasions has publicly testified to his adherence to the Catholic faith, during the period 1950 to the present [1954]. He has also been to Mass sometimes. I put the [times] such that Mass could be attended before the frequent meetings held on Sunday mornings. He is, however, often away addressing meetings.

Mrs. Mzingeli was a Methodist and with some help from her husband and two women she has been won over to the Catholic Faith. She is an invalid and could be received in the near future.

Today I spoke with Mr. Mzingeli about putting the marriage in order. He is willing to do this but says he has been so hurt by the treatment he received that he would first like an assurance that he was not wrong in seeking the aid of those who would help Africans towards trade unionism.[37]

Clearly, Mzingeli was aware of Burbridge's violation of church teaching in denying him access to communion, since only a bishop has the power to excommunicate. Despite the personal affront that hurt him deeply and the hierarchy's failure in proclaiming and implementing the church's teaching on social justice,[38] Mzingeli was willing to submit his marriage for canonization in the church provided that Chichester and his minions acknowledge that the labor leader had done no wrong. There is no record of a response from Chichester or of a resolution to the case.

Collectively these three cases show the church's hierarchy, including African priests, operating according to Western legal norms. Agnes and Felix received a dispensation from the impedient impediment of a mixed marriage so that Agnes could receive communion at mass. Joseph and Agatha's baptismal certificates were necessary to determine whether and what type of dispensation they needed to allow them to marry within the church: if either of them had been baptized Catholic before their respective first marriages to non-Christians, technically she or he would have been required to seek the bishop's permission to marry a non-Christian, which would have necessitated a dispensation from disparity of cult, which (as with a dispensation from mixed religion—that is, with a baptized non-Catholic Christian) would have required the non-Catholic partner to promise "to remove all danger of perversion of the Catholic party," and both partners to promise "that all their children shall be baptized and brought up as Catholics."[39] If neither had been baptized prior to marriage but converted to the church subsequently then "the valid marriage of unbaptized persons [could be] dissolved in favor of the faith by the Pauline privilege."[40] The Pauline privilege refers to the freedom of the non-Christian partner to leave the marriage and the nonobligation of the Christian neophyte to be bound to remain in such a marriage (1 Cor. 7:12–15). If Joseph's first wife had been alive when Fr. Chifeya promoted the case, either he or Joseph would have been required to interpellate the first wife before Joseph could marry Agatha; that is,

> to ask (1) whether the [non-Christian] party wishes to be converted and baptized, (2) in case the [non-Christian] party does not wish to be baptized, whether he, or she, is willing to live in marriage without offense to God, which is to say that he, or she, will not interfere with the religious obligations of the convert [i.e., the practice of the Catholic faith and Catholic upbringing of their children].[41]

Since Mzingeli's wife was apparently willing to convert, after her formal reception into the church their marriage could have been regularized by convalidation, or the public renewal of marital consent in the presence of a priest and at least two witnesses. If she had not been willing to become a Catholic, however, then—presuming the stability of the marriage (that is, the likelihood that the partners would not separate)—the marriage could have been regularized by means of a *sanatio in radice* (cleansing at the root), which is the validation of marriage "which imports, besides dispensation from, or a cessation of, an impediment, a dispensation from the law of renewing consent, and a retro-action by fiction of law [*per fictionem iuris*], in reference to the canonical effects in the past state while the union was invalid."[42]

These cases also show the deep faith of many African Catholics and the consequences of the church's failure to consider accommodating its marriage practice to African practices in some form prior to 1967. Many Catholics knowingly married non-Catholics according to "African custom" or civilly without the clergy's consent or approval. Yet Mzingeli, and no doubt others like him, felt "deprived of the sacraments." Joseph and Agatha wanted "to put themselves in the hands of God." There was no evident material gain to be had in regularizing marriage according to the church's norms, except for being able to receive communion at mass: Catholics in canonically invalid unions could still attend mass and otherwise participate in the life of the church and their parochial communities. The spiritual benefits according to their beliefs, however, were tremendous in that they would be allowed full participation in the life of the church and the reception of the body of blood of Jesus Christ sacramentally present in the form of bread and wine. This shows a distinct commitment to faith on the part of those African Catholics who sought to enter more deeply into the church's fold.

The Debate Over Adapting Canon Law to African Practices

The 1967 Marriage Commission

Despite the bishops' relative pleasure with the 1964 Marriage Act, they faced a situation in which four in five African Catholics were not marrying in the church, much less according to canonical norms. Thus, in January 1967, they established a commission with representatives from each of the five dioceses in the territory to study the causes of this problem and recommend possible solutions.[43]

The commission sent a circular letter to all priests in Southern Rhodesia asking for opinions on several questions concerning the marriage situation, and asking them to consult with "interested lay people." The commission members wanted to know: whether the clergy (and laity) thought that civil legislation was responsible for the high rate of canonically invalid marriages and if so to what degree, particularly provisions for obtaining an enabling certificate; at what point in the African marriage process the couple was considered married; if the church were to recognize African "customary" marriages what effects it would have, and if it were possible for the church to do so how it should be done and "what safeguards would be necessary"; whether they thought *lobola* was "the main obstacle to the convalidation of African marriages"; whether pubic opinion was helpful in convalidating marriage; and whether "the Church [paid] sufficient attention to instructing the people with regard to the Sacrament of Matrimony."[44]

The commission received seventy-three replies and submitted a report based on them to the bishops' conference in January 1968, with two recommendations: first, the church recognize African "customary unions" as the basis for canonical regularization, and "that the matter should be submitted to a canonical study." The bishops, however, considered the report insufficient and "requested the Commission to continue its study."[45] Archbishop Markall apparently then asked Jesuit canonist Lachlan Hughes, who was not a member of the commission, to write a canonical evaluation of the commission's report—though this was not the official report recommended by the commission—and circulated Hughes's private opinion to the bishops and commission. This sparked a debate between Hughes who supported the Jesuit minority opinion on the commission and Bethlehem Missionary Joseph Suter, who represented the majority.[46] The debate concerned differing interpretations of canon law and its application to African culture. Whereas Suter and the majority of the commission were willing to admit elements of African practice as necessary preconditions to valid canonical marriage within the church, Hughes and a minority of the commission saw those elements as impediments to valid marriage that either had to be abolished or ignored in order to regularize African Christian marriages.

The marriage commission recommended that African customary unions be recognized as the basis of marriages that required canonical regularization, and three elements were necessary to verify the existence of an African customary union: the consent of the woman, her guardian (*tezvara*), and the *mukuwasha* (groom/son-in-law); the mutual agreement to payment of *lobola* by the *mukuwasha* and its acceptance by the woman's family; and the formal handing over of the bride.[47] The commission further recommended that the church develop a rite centered on the VaShona *kuperekedzwa* ceremony, the time during the marriage process when the woman is handed over to her husband, and suggested that "undertaking" to pay *lobola* (versus payment in full) was sufficient grounds to allow marriage according to Christian rites.[48] A dissenting minority opinion put forth by Jesuit John Diamond, however, held that African elders recognized no uniform customary marriage and that the church could not use customary unions as the basis for canonical regularization because they lacked stability, allowing polygyny and divorce, and the stability they possessed was guaranteed only by the payment of *lobola* and the birth of healthy children.[49]

Lachlan Hughes's Critique of the Marriage Commission

Hughes's memorandum primarily addressed canonically valid marital consent. Hughes argued that the commission failed to distinguish between *matrimonium in fieri* (the moment of consent) and *matrimonium in facto esse naturale* (the marriage lived out following the exchange of consent),⁵⁰ and that the lack of distinction "induce[s] a confusion into the [commission's] recommendations." In his view, African customary law was unsuitable and inadequate as the basis for Christian marriage, but that customary unions were valuable as preparation for canonical marriage. He believed that it was not possible to canonize customary law because it required the consent of a third party (tezvara) to marriage under pain of nullity; it was "conditional in [marriage] consent"; and its requirement of full payment of *lobola* to the *tezvara* was an "invalidating impediment" to canonical marriage which caused "significant delay of marriage" and "lengthy concubinage." Furthermore, he opposed the church recognizing and canonically regularizing unregistered customary unions because doing so would "introduce two classes of [African] marriage": marriages registered at a district commissioner's office and thus afforded protection under civil law, and unregistered marriages that would not have legal protection from the government.⁵¹

Hughes addressed what he perceived to be the inadequacies of the three elements that the commission stipulated as constitutive of an African customary union at length. With regard to consent, Hughes claimed that the commission's recommendation to recognize customary unions was flawed because canon law does not recognize the consent of anyone but the two people intending to marry as necessary, and the consent of either of the two people concerned cannot be conditional upon the consent of a third party (say, a *tezvara*); thus, "the customary union is not apt for the canonical consent."⁵²

Similarly, Hughes objected to the commission's provision for an agreement to pay *lobola* because it was not required canonically, and if it were a "subjective requirement of [the] Tezvara before he consents," then the marriage could not be validated due to the conditional nature of a third party's consent. He further questioned the commission's position that only an agreement to pay *lobola* was sufficient by referring to the "fact" that *vadzitezvara* (fathers-in-law) frequently withheld permission to marry "until full lobola has been paid—and sometimes beyond the agreement."⁵³ Accordingly, "even the agreement to lobola cannot be accepted as a constituent element of customary union. Therefore customary union as such is not apt for canonical consent or form."

Although Hughes did not object to the development of a Catholic rite to be performed at the time of the *kuperekedzwa* ceremony—in fact, he extolled it as "a sufficiently direct symbol of itself to be acceptable as the 'locus' for canonical form," namely the public exchange of vows before a priest and two witnesses—he questioned whether the *tezvara*'s handing over of the woman was absolute or contingent upon fulfilling certain conditions such as the completion of *lobola* "in such a fashion that if the conditions are not fulfilled the handing over is 'rescindible [sic],'" and if so, then validation was not possible.[54]

Hughes then discussed at length the relation of *lobola* to canonical requirements for consent, and concluded that the conditions associated with bride-price payments effectively negated the possibility for valid consent to a canonical marriage, and that therefore the "consensual element of customary union is not very apt to be the basis" of Christian marriage. He included a series of five objections to his argument concerning *lobola* and consent with responses to each objection.[55] Apparently one of the Jesuits on the marriage commission informed Hughes of the contents of their deliberations, for he described responses to the commission's circular to the clergy as "wild" and "simplistic,"[56] and this was Hughes's effort to respond to those members of the commission who favored recognizing African customary unions. Hughes taught at the Chishawasha seminary, and John Diamond, the seminary rector, was one of the Salisbury archdiocese's two Jesuit representatives to the commission.

Hughes concluded the three elements the commission suggested as constituting a customary union would be useful to determine the stability and other requisite elements for a valid canonical marriage, but that they could not be required for the regularization of marriage because "this would allow that other agencies than the Church can establish diriment impediments for Christians."[57] He also concluded since African customary unions were neither "suitable" nor "adequate" for regularizing marriages they could not be used as such unless they were "so modified" that people would no longer recognize them as customary unions. Customary unions, thus, could be used "as a means of preparing the marriage," which should include the "exchange of proper canonical consent," and that while consent could be exchanged at the *kuperekedzwa* ceremony, the "difficulties . . . arising from distance from a Church, attendance of the priest, etc., in kuperekedzwa, should not be underestimated."

Hughes next proposed "practical steps" to regularize registered and unregistered customary unions. He first thought it necessary to verify that customary marriages "are actually subsisting" and only lacked canonical form. If so, then there would be "comparatively little difficulty" to validate them by "complete full marriage," convalidation, or *sanatio*, that is, the ordinary means that the church used to canonize marriages. Hughes believed that the *tezvara*'s approval of church marriage was evidence of a "subsisting" customary union, and his refusal would be "evidence that the union was not a genuine customary law marriage."[58]

Hughes recommended the same verification and validation process for unregistered customary unions, suggesting that it would be possible either to marry within the church couples with customary unions that were unregistered due to the *tezvara*'s opposition or to validate the marriage via *sanatio* after the inquiry into the couple's continued consent. He thought this "a very radical solution," because it would introduce "two classes of African marriage" one protected by civil law and the other not.[59]

Last, Hughes addressed "the problem of how to go about securing good Catholic marriages from the beginning." Briefly acknowledging the need for the church to provide "education and formation," and the need to maintain "traditional observances" (noting that *kuperekedzwa* would be ideal for including canonical consent in the customary marriage process), he addressed the issue of what to do if the *tezvara* refused a church wedding. Hughes believed that the *vadzitezvara* agreed to help a couple obtain an enabling certificate only after *lobola* had been paid in full; thus, the church had two options if the *tezvara* did not accept the "undertaking" to pay *lobola* "as sufficient to proceed to the Church marriage": "either admit that the problem was insoluble or "disregard the opposition of the vadzitezvara." The danger of disregarding the *vadzitezvara*, however, would leave couples so married without the protection of the civil law, "and indeed it might be possible that the vadzitezvara would invoke the help of the government to recover control of their women," a situation Hughes felt capable of producing "a greater evil." Accordingly, Hughes recommended invoking a law for appeal against "ridiculous sums set as lobola," but he thought that it was the *vadzitezvara*'s "tendency to ever-increasing exactions which bodes so ill for the future of Christian marriage."[60]

Joseph Suter's Response to Hughes's Memorandum

Joseph Suter, a Swiss Bethlehem priest and member of the commission from the Gwelo diocese, structured his response to Hughes around three questions: whether it was possible to "raise" customary unions to church marriage, whether there was consent in customary unions, and why were African Catholic couples not obtaining enabling certificates in order to marry within the church. Regarding the possibility of canonizing customary unions, Suter observed that Hughes's distinction between *matrimonium in fieri* and *matrimonium in facto esse naturale* was useful, but secondary to the question of which unions were marriages (*matrimonium*) capable of becoming church marriages versus "concubinage" (*contubernia*), which was incapable of being "raised" to church marriages.[61] Suter listed four categories of unions that could not become church marriages: (1) unions containing a diriment impediment,[62] whether absolute (that is, with no possibility of granting a dispensation) or relative (that is, a possible dispensation had not yet been granted); (2) polygamous unions that violated the unity of marriage (a man and his first wife are validly married, and all subsequent unions while both partners remain alive are invalid and incapable of regularization); (3) unions that violated the indissolubility of marriage (if either or both partners do not "want to enter a permanent union for life"); or (4) unions that lacked the consent of the husband or wife, or that contained consent conditional upon a future act.[63] Suter believed the greatest "leakage" was in unions violating the indissolubility of marriage. Concerning *lobola* and consent, Suter responded directly to Hughes, arguing that whereas Europeans saw *lobola* as a business transaction, Africans saw it as establishing "new personal relations."

A whole new kinship system is established by lobolo [*sic*] and a whole pattern of behaviour among the various groups. For the girl the decisive question is: Is my beloved accepted as mukuwasha? If that is so, tangibly proved by accepting money and cattle, then her interests of being protected by her family are safeguarded, and that is all she wants. Therefore, if a lobolo arrangement is made, the woman understands the following steps as leading to a proper marriage to which she fully cooperates with her consent, as she wants the man to be her true husband. If no lobolo arrangement is made, the woman knows very well that this union does not mean marriage, at least not yet. Consequently there is no marriage consent and no basis for a Church marriage. Therefore matrimonial consent is absent or at least very doubtful where there is no lobolo arrangement made.[64]

Suter defined *matrimonium in facto esse naturale* as a couple not prevented from marriage by a diriment impediment that lives monogamously and intends to remain so for the rest of their lives, in which "a real and true consent is expressed and still exists, but they did not comply with Canon 1094 due to grave and serious reasons,"[65] and that only those cases could and should be rectified. He further defined *matrimonium in fieri* as "pathetic cases of intended marriage. The two engaged people wait for years, sometimes almost heroically, till the young man has saved enough money to complete the lobolo payment, which may be raised at will by the tezvara."[66]

Suter directly confronted Hughes's contention that the "customary union as such is not apt to canonical consent or form"[67] by proposing "a solution" that first required verification: of a customary union for the validity of consent; that the union did not fall into one of the four categories that were incapable of regularization; and of a valid reason for the couple not having obtained an enabling certificate. If the case was one of a civilly registered customary union in *matrimonio in facto esse naturale*, then the marriage could be convalidated. If the case was one of a civilly unregistered customary union in *matrimonio in facto esse naturale*, then the marriage could receive a *sanatio in radice* because the "radix [root] exists and consent continues."[68] In cases of *matrimonium in fieri*, presuming verification of the aforementioned three elements, Suter recommended that "the couple should be adviced [sic] to make use of the extraordinary form of can. 1098."[69] Canon 1098 allowed a couple to marry in the presence of two witnesses only provided that they could not go to a priest "without great inconvenience."[70] This was a significantly innovative application of canon law to an African context.

Suter reiterated the commission's view on the three elements that constituted a customary union, that is, the consent of the woman, the man, and the *tezvara*; the mutual agreement to pay *lobola*; and the formal handing over of the bride. Concerning the *tezvara*'s consent, Suter distinguished between consent to cohabitation, which was necessary for a legal claim to *lobola*, and consent to civil or church marriage in a district commissioner's office, implying that the *tezvara* had received enough payment and was not expecting much more as debt against the enabling certificate. Citing the VaShona proverb that a *mukuwasha* was like a fig tree to be eaten without end, Suter noted that the *tezvara* would be willing to grant consent to cohabit but reluctant to consent to an enabling certificate. Thus, "As only the right for cohabitation is essential for marriage, but not the customary transfer of wealth, the first consent is only essential and is sufficient to the marriage contract."[71]

Addressing the mutual agreement to pay *lobola*, Suter noted that the amount frequently was not fixed for many years, and argued that arrangements were "in the first place not a question of wealth, but a question of person":

The tezvara group has to decide: Do we accept this young man as our mukuwasha? Can we trust him? Are we ready to enter into a marriage agreement with him, to establish a new kinship relation with him and his relatives? Will this young man and his family group behave toward us as expected by tradition, paying proper respect and providing help in case of trouble and death? Can we trust that he will fulfil all his obligations as mukuwasha? (One of these obligations is to pay the due lobolo). The traditional ceremony of "kupinza mukuwasha kumusha," i.e., to receive him into the village, is the tangible answer that he is in fact received as son-in-law. Thus the . . . condition is fulfilled when the ceremony kupinza mukuwasha kumusha has taken place.[72]

Suter further argued that handing over the woman was done normally during the *kuperekedzwa* ceremony, or during the *kupinza mukuwasha kumusha* in the case of elopement (*kutiza*). According to Suter, the customary union was "the only way . . . at present and in all likelihood in the near future the African people *express their marriage consent*," thus, a sine qua non for consent as opposed to an essential requirement for marriage: "Any sanatio or convalidatio or any new marriage can only be arranged on the foundation of a customary union. Disregarding this foundation would inevitably bring about a vast number of invalid and doubtful marriages."[73]

Though Suter conceded Hughes's point that unregistered marriages would not receive protection under the civil law, he disagreed that they were unstable unions. Suter noted the general interest on the part of both families to maintain the marriage and the *tezvara*'s reluctance to have a marriage dissolve because he would be obliged to return *lobola*: "This explains somehow the happy fact that the stability of customary unions and proper marriages among [the] African population in this country is remarkable."

According to [African] customs no marriage is ever broken up against the will of at least one of the spouses. The vakuru never divorce a couple, they only accept the fact that two married people have rejected each other. . . . Comparing the efforts of the government to save endangered marriages by counselling or by its courts, I must say that the African customs are much better to iron out marriage difficulties. But if all efforts according to customs have failed, the marriage is simply taken as dissolved. No European court-ruling will make any difference. It can only confirm the de facto divorce or it will be ignored.[74]

While Suter thought it "highly desirable" for church marriages to have civil protection, he thought that if obtaining such protection proved "too cumbersome, it can be dispensed with," because the marriage's stability rested on the customary union, not the marriage registration certificate. Thus, he considered the customary union "essential for a valid consent [and] essential for the stability of marriage, and therefore indispensable."[75]

Turning to the last of his three questions (why African Catholics were not obtaining enabling certificates), Suter took issue with Hughes's assertion that *vadzitezvara* opposed church marriages because of their permanence. Suter argued that *vadzitezvara* welcomed stable, permanent marriages because if the marriage were to fail they would have to return *lobola* to the *vakuwasha,* and so the *vadzitezvara* frequently used the enabling certificate as a means to put pressure on the young couples to ensure that payment would be forthcoming.

The reason for not marrying the couple in the [district commissioner's] office by the tezvara is to leave the couple somehow in a somehow awkward and often embarrassing situation, so that the couple realizes that to finish lobolo may be the lesser evil. . . . He wants by no means the marriage union to be broken. If that should happen, he would have lost the whole game, would be called a fool, who overreached himself, because he did not know when to give in. But he uses the natural desire of the union to squeeze out the last of his lobolo claims.[76]

Suter countered Hughes's argument that the government would assist *vadzitezvara* to reclaim their daughters if there were no civil protection, claiming that such a situation would be "certainly out of the question" for any African woman twenty-one years of age or older (the age of majority in English common law). Further, a *tezvara* could not take a *mukuwasha* to a European court for *lobola* if the marriage was not registered: in such a case, the parties would have recourse to a chief's court unless a marriage certificate had been issued. In cases of last resort where the *tezvara* could demand the *lobola* of his daughter's daughter, this was permissible only in a situation where no permission to cohabit had been given, and thus no customary union existed. Suter opined that the reason for the sharp fall in canonical marriages resulted from a mutual mistrust of the younger and older generations of African Christians. [77]

Suter was not surprised that for many young African men who earned relatively low wages it was "impossible to complete lobola [payments in the range of £100–250], soon." Nonetheless, poverty "should not be a reason to prevent the couple from the basic human right to marry," and deserved the "sympathetic concern of the Church."[78]

Responding to Hughes's suggestion that the church should invoke civil laws against increasing amounts of *lobola*, Suter argued that it was "simply impossible" for a *mukuwasha* to take a *tezvara* to a European magistrate because "the whole lobolo system is in spite of all something of a gentleman's game. The enabling certificate cannot be forced in such a way." The church, thus, had a responsibility to act "courageously" in proving the impossibility of a *mukuwasha* to pay *lobola* in full prior to marriage, and then either convalidate, sanate, or use the extraordinary form of Canon 1098 to regularize African marriages, particularly cases of *matrimonium in fieri*. Suter mused whether

> the Council of Trent laid down the best form of marriage for African people in the 20th century ["Tametsi"]. Previous forms seem to fit much better into our situation. . . . In many respects we are somehow facing problems of the early Church, are in an extraordinary situation for which the Church provides the extraordinary form of marriage according to can. 1098. . . . In our previous [marriage commission] meetings we discarded the solution with the remark: Exceptional cases. But these exceptional cases have been the ordinary way for 1000 years. The argumentation against can. 1098 was that it may open the way to clandestine marriages. But can. 1098 is a public affair, only without the priest being present, but at least two witnesses are required ad validitatem, who together with the marriage partners are responsible, that the marriage be reported to the priest. . . . If kuperekedzwa ceremony were accepted as the time of applying can. 1098, there should always be plenty of witnesses as it is a public affair.[79]

Hughes's Application of the Extraordinary Form in Canon 1098

Hughes responded to Suter with an extended point-by-point refutation of the latter's recommendations, arguing while the elements the commission proposed as constituting an African customary union were significant for determining the existence of such a union, they were unnecessary for canonical marriage in the church or as requirements for a marriage to be regularized. He reiterated his objection to requiring the *tezvara*'s consent for valid marriage, noting that Christian marriage was not a "group affair," as well as his position that *lobola* could not be considered a valid requirement for marriage.[80]

Hughes gave extended consideration to Suter's suggestion to use the extraordinary form of marriage available in canon 1098. This was a rare instance in which Suter and Hughes agreed, and Hughes's reflections were a practical application of Suter's idea. The commission gave serious thought to incorporating Hughes's recommendation into its final report.

After briefly summarizing and analyzing the historical developments that led to the inclusion of canon 1098, as well as several of its interpretations by noted canonists, Hughes determined that the extraordinary form was "a potentially acceptable solution to the problem of *matrimonium in fieri*" and examined its ramifications on four levels: "in itself" and in its consequences, applications, and limitations.[81]

Hughes first noted that the use of the extraordinary form would result in canonically valid marriages and that it could be used in situations where there was a civil impediment that the church did not recognize (for example, the requirement of the *tezvara*'s consent or agreement over *lobola* for a valid customary union) or a lack of documents required by the civil authority (for example, an enabling certificate or registration of the customary union). The great inconvenience to the priest was that he would be subject to a £500 fine and/or five years in jail for functioning "as a marriage officer to produce a civilly valid marriage."[82] The "grave moral inconvenience" to the couple was "automatic" if they wished to marry but "in the concrete circumstances" could not have a priest be present. "Hence the priest cannot be compelled to marry them: they cannot be *compelled* to remain unmarried."[83]

Reiterating the canonical validity of marriages effected according to canon 1098 as well as his opposition to the *tezvara*'s consent for a valid Christian marriage, Hughes argued that one of the consequences of the extraordinary form was that

> there could be no absolute requirement that the man, *now validly and licitly married,* should continue to make lobola payments. . . . This does not mean

that the newly married man may not pay lobola as long as he likes: but simply that the Church in these circumstances cannot support that there is a moral obligation to do so.[84]

While the priest who would have been "the proper officiant" would be free from any penalties, since he was not acting as a marriage officer, the "canonically valid and sacramental marriage" would be civilly invalid. Hughes thought that such a situation could result in a *tezvara*'s either refusing permission to cohabit or refusing to receive the *mukuwasha*, or attempting to recover control over his daughter, which would be likely as the couple would not have any civil protection. This latter situation, in Hughes's opinion, would be proof that permission to cohabit was not permission to marry, but were the couple allowed to use the extraordinary form and to cohabit, then the *tezvara* would effectively have little legal recourse except against his married daughter.[85]

Hughes also saw as consequences of using canon 1098 potentially negative effects regarding the civil administration, specifically, that were a priest to become involved at any point in the process he could be accused of acting as a marriage officer or of marrying people without a declaration of intent or civil banns. More significantly, the invocation of the extraordinary form could result in complaints from *vakuru* that the church was treating couples as "fully married, permitting them the Sacraments," and that while that in and of itself would not be a problem for the government, "the disturbance of custom would," and could result in government intervention.[86]

Turning to practical applications, Hughes stated the local bishops would have to approve the general application of the extraordinary form and grant permission to use it in every case. The regular canonical investigation "to ensure freedom to marry, absence of or dispensation from impediments, etc." would still be required, as would the careful instruction of the faithful to prevent "the danger of immense confusion," and "an explicit form of exchange of consent before witnesses who would record the fact and have the record transferred to the priest." Two "definite" witnesses would have to be commissioned to confirm the exchange of consent: "it would not be acceptable that a crowd of guests should be asked to affirm the fact of consent exchanged." Accordingly, Hughes suggested the development and use of a "definite formula printed in cautious terms." The couple could receive no form or certificate that could give them the ground to say, "The church married us." This would cause government intervention because couples married by the extraordinary form would more than likely use such a form for civil purposes (for example, obtaining married family housing in urban areas). A diocese would have to keep a "special book" for such marriages "most scrupulously." The church would have to instruct the couple and families of the definitive effects of marriage in this form: they would have to determine if it were "prudent" to inform *vadzitezvara* of permission to cohabit plus canonical consent "in all cases" as doing so could decrease the frequency of permissions, and not informing them could result in "serious indignations." The church would also have to educate people that the extraordinary form was not permission for the unmarried to go to sacraments: this was one of "gravest difficulties" of the scheme in Hughes's opinion.[87]

Suter and Hughes disagreed in their interpretations of canon law and its application to African marriage practices, most significantly over the inclusion of elements of an African customary union as prerequisites for the canonical validation of African Catholics' marriages, or more specifically the very limited incorporation of African marriage practices into those of the Catholic Church. Suter favored such a move and Hughes did not. Suter's tone was much more pastoral, showing concern for the spiritual well-being of the African Catholics in his care, whereas Hughes's writings were more juridical and more concerned with upholding the letter of the church's law. Whereas Suter saw the extraordinary form as a means to help Catholics put their marriages right in the church's eyes—an expression of the church's "sympathetic concern"—Hughes saw canon 1098 as a way for the church to confront "the whole complexus of unjust demands occasioned by the present decadence of the lobola system," as well as a means to stifle the criticism that the church "manufactured . . . obstacles to Christian marriage . . . because those who wished to marry correctly by the extraordinary form would have it in their power to do so, provided they were willing to join issue with the family difficulties which it might produce."[88]

The marriage commission appreciated Hughes's application of Suter's idea to use the extraordinary marriage form in canon 1098, for its members apparently asked the Rhodesian Catholic bishops to request a legal opinion on its repercussions regarding the 1964 Marriage Act. The bishops' counsel advised that "to avail oneself of the provision of Can.1098 would be to solemnise or to purport to solemnise marriage: the clergy who counselled, incited, or advised Catholics to follow this expedient would be in conspiracy and as *socii criminis* [friends of the crime] punishable as principals."[89] This legal finding ended further discussion of the use of the extraordinary form of marriage.

The Marriage Commission Report

The marriage commission submitted its final report to the bishops in April 1970. Although the commission suggested causes such as a "lack of real faith in God and in the Sacrament of Matrimony," or a "lack of real mutual love," or a "reluctance to commit oneself to an exclusive and permanent union," or social and economic changes brought about by "the whole process of 'westernization'" contributed to the low rate of canonical marriages within the church, "the main reason," in its opinion, was "the present exorbitant demand" for *lobola*, "which enables the guardians to prevent the young couple obtaining an Enabling Certificate" as required by civil law. The commission held customary unions meeting Suter's definition of *matrimonium in fieri* (free from canonical diriment impediments, monogamous, permanent, "contracted by a real and true consent," and lacked an enabling certificate from the *tezvara*) "are apt for convalidation by the Church and registration by the State." Further, the commission decided it would be "disastrous" to marry African couples according to canonical requirements only, and considered the triple consent of the woman, *tezvara*, and *mukuwasha*, the mutual agreement to pay and accept *lobola*, and the formal handing over of the woman by her family to her husband and his family as "essential requirements which establish the fact of a customary union" as expressed in either the *kuperekedzwa* ceremony, or the *kupinza mukuwasha kumusha* ceremony in the case of elopement.[90]

The commission suggested if the "essential" elements were present, and if the couple met the canonical requirements then they could "validly and lawfully contract a Church marriage," although such a marriage while in accord with customary law would not have legal standing according to civil law, and the couple would thus "forfeit certain rights and privileges attached to civil marriages." The commission thought the benefits of this policy were: putting Christian marriage "within reach of many more couples than formerly"; such marriages would accord with canonical and customary requirements and would have the protection of customary law by virtue of African communities recognizing them. The disadvantages included depriving couples of "the civil effects which follow registration," and the perception of the church acting contrary to public policy, thus confirming Hughes's position that they were creating two classes of marriage. To implement the policy, the commission recommended that "the priest who investigates such marriages should thoroughly understand the nature of the customary union" and be able to determine whether the conditions for a customary union existed, and in order to facilitate such investigations that a "customary union addendum" be added to the prenuptial forms.[91] Finally, the commission recommended abolishing the enabling certificate, saying that "for the sake of clarity, [the civil law should] specifically state" that while the agreement to *lobola* is essential for marriage, "the actual details of the agreement and the payment or non payment of [*lobola*] have no effect in law on the validity of marriage."[92]

While the marriage commission acknowledged Lachlan Hughes's contributions to its deliberations, its recommendations followed Joseph Suter's position. The commission in its deliberations and recommendations also belatedly established ecclesiastical "customary law": the priests on the commission deferred to African "custom" so long as it was in accord with the institutional church's interests. As with the early BSAC and settler marriage legislation, there were notable differences of opinion as to what constituted the church's interests. Nevertheless, the commission's deliberations were unprecedented in engaging African culture positively, and they departed significantly from the church's policies and practice concerning African marriages.

The Bishops' Conference adopted some of the commission's recommendations, as evidenced by the requirement of "a completed customary union addendum in those cases where the parties [do not] possess a marriage certificate issued in terms of the Marriage Act of 1964."[93] Despite this step toward engaging African marriage practices, the situation did not improve significantly. This was more than likely because the bishops decided that the preferred practice was still to ask the bride and groom to go to the district commissioner (DC) for an enabling certificate and for the priest to marry them according to the Marriage Act (1964) when they had got such a certificate.[94]

Because so many African Catholics were not marrying in the church by 1972, the bishops established another commission to investigate the problem.[95] There is no record of the second commission's final report or recommendations in the Jesuit archives. There is a 1975 letter from the Rhodesian bishops to the cardinal prefect of the Sacred Congregation for the Evangelization of Peoples requesting "with the grave urgency of the situation before us . . . that the faculty be granted by the Holy See to this conference [of bishops] whereby individual, selected Catholic laymen may be appointed by local ordinaries to officially witness and record marriages in accordance with the terms and conditions of the instruction 'Sacramentalem Incolem.'"[96] The absence of any discussion of an African layperson presiding at a Catholic marriage ceremony in subsequent marriage regulations of the Archdiocese of Salisbury indicates that the bishops did not receive the Vatican's permission.[97]

Conclusion

Throughout the colonial period, the Catholic Church did very little to engage African marriage practices in Zimbabwe. It took crisis proportions to spur the bishops to establish a commission to investigate the problem in 1967. Although the commission eventually recommended recognizing African customary unions as the basis for marriage within the church, a significant departure from the hierarchy's previous stance, and five years later the bishops went even further to request that select African laypersons be allowed to preside at wedding ceremonies, the situation did not improve appreciably. The commission's deliberations can be likened to the process of the formation of African "customary" law decades earlier by the Southern Rhodesian colonial administrations: of taking selected elements of once-fluid social practices and enshrining them into relatively inflexible legislation.

6

"Thou Shalt Not Take My Name in Vain": The Mwari Controversy, 1911-1961

> *I had a second letter from Fr. Apel; the last idea is, that Mwari means as much as: he, who is! is, qui est. Against stupidity even Gods fight in vain!*
>
> Andrew Hartmann, S.J., to Francis Richartz, S.J., July 26, 1921

Fr. Ignatius Chidavaenzi and his colleagues on an interdenominational team preparing a more recent and more accurate translation of the Bible into ChiShona presented a theological explanation for the meaning of the name Mwari.[1] Claiming that of all the ChiShona names for God, "'Mwari' alone does not seem to mean anything," the biblical scholars proposed two possible meanings based on linguistic evidence. The first proposal held that Mwari was a contraction (and incorrect spelling) of Muwari, which is derived from the ChiShona verb *kuwara*, "to spread" (as in a blanket on grass). This conveys the idea that Muwari "is the being that has put in the world everything we see, 'Ndiye akawaridza zvose zvatinoona panyika.'"[2] This implies that God is the creator of all that exists, and is akin to the ChiShona names Musiki, "creator," or Musikavanhu, "creator of people." Chidavaenzi and his colleagues rejected Muwari because the tone patterns of "Muwari" and "Mwari" were different in ChiShona, which, like most Bantu languages, is tonal (the former being low-low-low and the latter being low-high), and did not conform to ChiShona's ordinary rules of contraction or patterns of sound change.

The second proposal held that Mwari was a contraction of Muari, which derived from the third person singular of the irregular verb "to be" in ChiShona. This translates literally as "the one who is," has the same tone pattern, and follows ChiShona rules for contraction and patterns of sound change, as well as rules for denoting a personal agent. Similarly, in normal speech patterns there would be no significant aural difference between Mwari and Muari.

The VaShona biblical scholars noted, "there exists a very interesting similarity between the name which God gives Himself in Exodus 3:14, and the name which the Shona people give to God."[3] In comparing the various names of God found in the Bible with the various names of God in ChiShona, they further noted, "God is known by various names which convey to us some insight into the nature of God.... Shona translators have to make an effort, therefore, to translate the various names of God by suitable and appropriate names in Shona. We would not be right, surely, if we translate two or three names by the same name or attribute."[4]

Thus, Chidavaenzi and his colleagues recommended not changing the spelling of Mwari to Muari so as not to lose one of "the rich aspects" of "the name of God in Shona . . . namely, that God is the one who caused things to be—MUWARI—the Creator."[5] Rather, they preferred using both forms of spelling the God's name "to preserve the envaluable [sic] riches in both forms of the same name. We can use MWARI to translate 'El' and 'Elohim' which mean simply 'God,' and we can use MUARI to translate the unique and personal name of God, YAHWEH," and *tenzi* to translate the Hebrew title *adonai* (Lord).[6] The biblical scholars further maintained

> even if the reasons given for thinking that the word Mwari comes from the verb "to be" were not persuasive, we should still adopt MUARI to translate YAHWEH because if other languages go so far as to coin names which are not at all close to the meaning of God's unique name we are more fortunate to have a name which is Shona in sound and form and can be explained to people and has the same meaning and explanation as the Hebrew name. Some of the translation committees in East Africa envy us for having even the possibility of such a name.[7]

The diametrically opposed views of Muari and Mwari—that of two German Jesuits in the 1920s and that of a MuShona biblical scholar writing in the latter years of the twentieth century—show the changes in Catholic understanding of the ChiShona name for the Christian God. Initially used by the first Jesuit missionaries in the 1890s, officially banned by the Jesuit superior of the Zambezi Mission in 1923, by the 1960s, Mwari had come full circle to be accepted as the name for the Christian God in the Catholic Church. Historians, however, have shown the name Mwari has a much longer history than its use by Western Christian missionaries. Within this context, what has come to be known as the Mwari controversy can be seen as the continuation of a debate between ChiShona-speaking Africans under a Christian guise.

What's in a Name: Histories of Mwari

Several scholars have investigated the antiquity and use of names for deities in the territory between the Zambezi and Limpopo rivers, and their reflections on the history of the name Mwari have implications for understanding the controversy between Jesuit missionaries and their African adherents in the early twentieth century. Zimbabwean historian S. I. G. Mudenge analyzed the interactions between various religious cults and the relationships between the cults and the Munhumutapa (Great Zimbabwe) state's court from the tenth to fifteenth centuries.[8] Linguist George Fortune and historian Terence Ranger wrote histories of the name of the deity that has come to be known as Mwari.

What is clear from a brief review of the literature and their respective analyses is that the name Mwari is ancient among VaShona, dating anywhere from one to three millennia; the oracular Mwari cult probably originated in but was definitely based in the Matopos hills of southwest Zimbabwe and exerted its influence through an extensive tributary network, and that amidst the extensive interactions between and among ChiShona-speaking, (historical) Karanga-speaking, Kalanaga-speaking, and Korekore-speaking groups between the Zambezi and Limpopo rivers theological categories and vocabulary were very fluid and highly adaptive, as the extent of the territory in which Mwari's name came to be known as the high god shows, as well as the spread of the *mhondoro* cult system. Despite the breadth of the use of Mwari's name throughout the area between the Zambezi and the Limpopo, there seems to have been no consensus among different ChiShona-speaking groups as to whether Mwari was the high god: speakers of Kalanga, Karanga, Manyika, and Ndau in the southwest, south, and east respectively apparently accepted Mwari as the supreme being/creator, whereas speakers of Zezuru and Korekore in the central and northern regions did not. Thus, what came to be known as the Mwari controversy in Catholic missionary circles during the early decades of the twentieth century was more than likely a continuation of a millennia-old debate among ChiShona speakers within a Christian context.

According to Fortune, despite "successive and prolonged influences" from Southern VaShona institutions, central and northern VaShona seemed hesitant about "accepting the divine status of Mwari and agreeing that the name Mwari" was acceptable for the creator/high god. Fortune thought that perhaps northern VaShona demurred because "an alien power" brought the name and cult with them, or perhaps because VaZeruru believed Mwari "too particularized and concerned with things of the earth to qualify him to be God. He is a *mwea wepasi* [spirit of below], whereas the Supreme Spirit is *NyaDenga* [of heaven]." Fortune further suggested that Western Christian missionaries chose Mwari as the name for God from among the many names and titles for a supreme being found in ChiShona, due to "the widespread acceptance by the Shona people of Mwari as Creator before the missionaries identified him as such. This belief may have been disseminated at the time when the cult of Mwari was associated with the Rozvi dynasty and, possibly that of the Torwa before them. But this belief existed somehow unreconciled with the more spiritual notions of the Central and Northern Shona."[9]

This difference in theological opinion throughout several centuries of VaShona religious history had significant implications for VaShona Catholics during the period of contact with European missionaries beginning in the nineteenth century. Among the eastern Manyika-speaking and Ndau-speaking VaShona, Anglican, Methodist, Catholic Mariannhill, and American Board Mission missionaries almost exclusively used Mwari for the name of the Christian god from as early as 1898. In the ChiZezuru-speaking central areas, the different churches used different names for God: the Lutherans from 1899 to 1912 employed Mudzimu (an ancestral spirit); from 1909 to 1941 the Dutch Reformed Church used Wedenga (of the sky/heaven), as did the Church of Sweden until it switched to Mwari in 1928. According to Fortune, from the founding of Chishawasha mission in 1892, the Jesuits translated God's name as Yave, a rendering of the Hebrew Yahweh.[10]

Mudenge, Fortune, and Ranger all describe the religious changes associated with the Mwari cult as functions of larger sociopolitical changes, not necessarily because of changes in African understandings of the sacred, or what would appear to be highly adaptive theological transformations. Where they studied social aspects of religious change, anthropologist David Lan provided theological explanations of socioreligious changes that occurred in the *mhondoro* spirit cults during the colonial period and resulted in the transference of African peasant allegiance from chiefs appointed by the colonial state to spirit mediums during the war, and consequently greater support for the nationalist movements.[11]

The Mwari Controversy

It is unclear how much of the foregoing Francis Richartz and his Jesuit confreres who founded Chishawasha mission would have known in the early 1890s. Richartz and his fellow Jesuits at Chishawasha, in the north-central ChiZezuru-speaking area, had sufficient doubts as to whether Mwari referred to the Christian God that they chose to translate God's name into ChiShona as Yave, from the Hebrew name Yahweh found in the book of Exodus.[12]

Reasons for abolishing that heathen name [Mwari]:
  1) Our doubts *about the meaning* of that name *quite in the first years*—girls got *that name*. Natives honoured only vadzimu [ancestral spirits], Mwari was only asked for rain.
  2) *The Natives had no clear idea about God* so we had to fear that with our keeping the name Mwari, they would join their wrong ideas with that name, in spite of instruction, as experience proved.

3) By introducing *Yave* the Natives were dependent on *our* explanation and were convinced that we gave the highest Being other qualities of which they had not heard before—like Creator, Preserver, Saviour, and especially an *almighty, eternal omniscient Judex* [judge]. . . . *Mwari has not been seen or is not being seen* except by the so-called va*Mbuya* (Mbuya = grandmother and woman who came from Mwari) *VaMbuya* vanotaura kuti vanobva kwa Mwari [VaMbuya speaks because she comes from Mwari]—they bring the orders of Mwari = uyai ne mombe kana nembudzi [come with cattle or goats]—(last year the people refused (3 months?) [sic] Bonga Mandara was sent to Mwari and became by and by "Vambuya"—some are called Mwari. Last year's Mbuya was refused, people saying "We know you, you have been born in our country—(The VaMbuya, maintain to be made or created by Mwari).[13]

Significantly, when Richartz wrote the foregoing in 1923, he had been assigned to the Jesuit mission at Gokomere, in the south of colonial Zimbabwe, an area dominated by ChiKaranga speakers. Richartz was the founding superior of Chishawasha mission from 1892 through 1904, and superior again from 1909 to 1920, whereupon he was transferred to Gokomere. He more than likely encountered the women who served as Mwari shrine officials after his transfer.

Evidently, Richartz and his confreres tried to use the name Mwari to refer to the Christian god and only subsequently introduced Yave:

Soon after our arrival at this mission . . . we found that the heathen name Mwari had no definite meaning besides "Rainmaker" and we were in this important case, like in general, very much impressed by the sorcery, want of clearness and straightforwardness with which all actions of the natives were surrounded, especially everything that could be supposed to be in connection with "religious" ideas such as prayer, sacrifices, etc. and at occasions like childbirth, marriage, fieldwork, war, etc.

Most of all was our teaching hampered by using existing words and finding expressions for theological terms which occur in religious instruction.

The very doubtful meaning of Mwari forced us soon to avoid this dangerous word and replace it by another word which meant exactly the True God, and fitted well in the Native languages (Chizezuru and Chikalanga)—Yave.[14]

Furthermore, when the Mwari controversy reached its most critical and intense phase, Richartz wrote against "the *reintroduction* of the heathen name Mwari for God, which after due and long consideration and consultation, with the consent of our Superiors and the Christian part of our Natives, *was replaced* by the old and venerable name Jahweh, or Yave."[15]

Beginning in 1898 with the Anglicans, several Western Christian groups used the name Mwari to translate God's name in their prayer books, hymnals, and Bibles.[16] Fortune suggested that they chose Mwari due to its long standing as God's name. Richartz argued beginning in 1900, Jesuits at Chishawasha published several prayer books, catechisms, and dictionaries using Yave for god.[17] Fortune noted also that Jesuits Andrew Hartmann and Edward Biehler omitted Mwari in favor of Yave in their respective Shona-English dictionaries published in 1894 and 1898.[18]

Opinions vary as to when the Mwari controversy began. Fortune referred to the period from 1921 to 1924 as the time when "there was a discussion in Roman Catholic missionary circles as to whether the Shona word *Mwari* should not replace *Yave*." Although Fortune cited Mariannhill Fr. F. Mayr's *Katekisima re Makristo e Sangano Rekatolike*, published in 1910, as evidence of Catholic usage of Mwari in eastern colonial Zimbabwe, he did not link it specifically to the controversy of the early 1920s. Further, Fortune noted, "there was a difference of opinion [among the Jesuits], and the majority favoured *Mwari*;" in his article, he only presented the arguments of the minority that preferred Yave and opposed Mwari.[19] Terence Ranger traced the beginning of the controversy to 1911, following the publication of Mayr's catechism. Ranger placed his discussion of the Mwari controversy in the context of the formation of Manyika identity and presented the debate as one between Mariannhillers, who supported the development and use of ChiManyika, and Jesuits, who preferred and uniformly imposed the use of ChiZezuru. Like Fortune, Ranger did not discuss the opinions of the pro-Mwari group, except insofar as they preferred the use of ChiManyika.[20] Neither Fortune nor Ranger gave a sense of the magnitude of the division between Jesuit missionaries. The redactor of the Mwari Controversy Typescript in the Jesuit Archives of Zimbabwe, however, did so when he noted, "the controversy split the [Zambezi] Mission into two groups, to the detriment of religious charity and unity."[21]

Documents in the Jesuit Archives of Zimbabwe link the beginnings of the controversy to the publication of Mayr's 1910 catechism. According to Francis Johanny, writing as pro-prefect apostolic and de facto superior of the Zambezi Mission to the Jesuit superior general in Rome, in May 1922,[22] Mayr's catechism, as well as subsequent books Mariannhill published, "used the name MWARI to designate God."[23] With time, and in part due to a drought, Catholic neophytes from the Mariannhill missions migrated to Salisbury, "bringing with them their prayer books and their use of the name, MWARI. Hence arose some confusion, and for parish priests in native townships a difficulty, since now some of their flock called the God of the Christians JAVE, and the God of the pagans, MWARI; others, taught by the Trappists [Mariannhillers], said that MWARI and JAVE were one and the same God."[24]

According to Johanny, in 1918, amidst preparations to revise and publish a third edition of the Chishawasha Prayer Book, the prefect apostolic, Richard Sykes,

> gave to a committee of three Fathers the task of correcting and amending the book. These Fathers, who could not agree among themselves, were discharged from the duty [and a] fourth Father [John Apel] was chosen who was ordered to complete the work by himself. He weighed the diverse opinions on many points and especially as to the use of the name for God. The new editor tried to steer a middle course by keeping YAVE in the body of the book, but using MWARI, especially in the Appendix where extracts from the *Imitation of Christ* were translated into the Native language.[25]

Sykes apparently submitted the book to be reviewed by censors, but clearly gave his imprimatur in 1919, allowing the book to use Mwari for the name of God and to be printed and published as *The Prayer Book Edited by the Fathers of the Society* [of Jesus] *in the Chishawasha Mission: The Third Edition, Revised and Enlarged.* Apel, however, was not named as editor, and this infuriated Francis Richartz, then superior of Chishawasha Mission, who "regretted the many innovations and especially the use of the name MWARI."[26]

In 1919, Edward Parry succeeded Sykes as prefect apostolic, and in 1920, appointed a committee of four—chaired by Apel—"to review, write and amend the language used in the publications in the Native languages." Also in 1920, Parry appointed Apel as superior of Chishawasha.[27] Apparently the other members of the committee disagreed with Apel, resigned from the committee, and proposed taking the matter to Rome.[28] Parry forbade Jesuits gathered for a conference in Bulawayo in early 1922 to discuss the question. He further decided not to approve the publication of any books until the question was resolved.[29] His successor, Robert Brown, apparently continued that policy, as is seen in a July 1923 letter from Apel:

I am sending you a copy of the Child's Bible History in Chiswina [ChiShona]. The text as it stands was passed "cum laude" by four censors under the late Mgr. Parry. His Reverence however did not give the Imprimatur on account of the divergence of opinion about the word *Mwari*. Nor did he consent to allow it to be printed when I offered to put *Yave* instead, because the question of Yave vs. Mwari was to be decided elsewhere.[30]

As Parry's alleged response to Apel implied, and Johanny's letter to Jesuit Father General Ledochowski clearly stated, Parry referred the matter to the Jesuit superior general. Ledochowski referred the question back to Robert Brown with instructions "to look into the matter with great care, taking into account the usage of missionaries in neighbouring Prefectures," and gave him authority either to decide to resolve the conflict himself or to refer it to Propaganda Fide.[31] Brown decided to settle the matter without reference to Propaganda Fide. In August 1923, he posted a circular letter to all Catholic mission stations in Northern and Southern Rhodesia that read, in part:

In recent years there has arisen a controversy amongst Ours [i.e., Jesuits] as to the Native name to be used for God. The matter was referred to Rome and Very Rev. Fr. General commissioned me to go into it and decide the question. After much serious consideration and consultation with Ours of the different mission stations and with theologians in Rome, it has forced itself upon me that the introduction of the doubtful word "Mwari" is wrong, and that the word "Jahve," which has been in possession for so long is the better word to use. Hence, in future, the word to be used to express the name of the One True God is "Jahve."

In the revision of prayers and catechisms etc., care must be taken that the old terms be retained as far as possible, otherwise confusion and distrust will be caused in the minds of the Natives.[32]

But the controversy did not end there. More than a year later, in September 1924, Brown wrote to Bishop Adalbero Fleischer, the superior general of Mariannhill in Natal, South Africa, and to Fr. Ignatius Arnoz, the superior of Triashill Mission, threatening to suspend Arnoz and to close Triashill "unless Mwari is eliminated and Jahve substituted."[33] Evidently Arnoz must have been particularly recalcitrant in his opposition as Brown's letter was apparently the second sent insisting on the change from Mwari to Yave. Additionally, Fleischer also sent Arnoz a letter "which mention[ed] the introduction of Yave," but Arnoz claimed that "Mwari had ceased already and that people are praying and singing better than we ourselves the new form of God."[34]

As Fortune noted, the pro-Yave/anti-Mwari faction held a minority position. A document in the Mwari controversy file lists eleven Jesuits as being "for Mwari" and seven against (subsequent correspondence, however, shows two others—Andrew Hartmann and Edward Biehler—who were not listed but who were also against Mwari, making the total nine). Thus, the Jesuits of the Zambezi Mission were almost evenly split over the question. The document further noted that Monte Cassino Mission (under the direction of Mariannhill) used both Mwari and Yave, and that Triashill, "all the Protestant denominations except the Dutch Reformed Church, Victoria District, who use Wedenga [of the sky/heaven]," and "the people of Mashonaland [who] know only Mwari," used Mwari for the name of God.[35]

The preponderance of the documentary evidence supports the pro-Yave/anti-Mwari side, much of it written by Francis Richartz. The arguments generally fell into practical and theological categories. Of the practical reasons for keeping Yave, the most frequently invoked was that Yave was "in possession," that is, that Jesuits at Chishawasha introduced the name in 1892, their African Christians had accepted it without complaint, and there was no reason to revert to Mwari after almost thirty years. Additionally, Richartz believed that making the switch would create a "bad impression" on those African Christians who were accustomed to using Yave in their prayers, as well as give "the sects" (Protestant churches) the impression of Catholic inconsistency on the matter and the idea that Catholics were "coming over" to their perspective. Further, using Yave would make African Christians dependent on the Jesuits for an explanation of the name, whereas they would be able to infer pre- or non-Christian attributes associated with Mwari, thus Richartz's categorization of Mwari as a "dangerous" word.[36]

Richartz thought Mwari was dangerous theologically because in his estimation it was a "'nomen Dei pollutum' [polluted name of god] and as such to be avoided, if only because of scandal to little ones, to which class all our Natives belong!" According to Richartz, the first Jesuits at Chishawasha

did not refuse Mwari maintaining that it was no name for God—we left that question open and undecided (and we *want to prove* that he, Mwari, is the Deus Verus, the Eternal Judge of the living and the dead, and the Rewarder—without which beliefs the knowledge of and belief in God is of no use to anybody). We explained always to our people that we chose the word Jave because we are *not* sure about the being Mwari. Further we had, and have still more, reasons to be sure that Mwari (even if originally a name of God, *which is not proved*) was and is a nomen Dei pollutum . . . by all the many superstitions, immoral and barbaric customs practised by the people who, though calling perhaps Mwari the Creator, all powerful Ruler of the Universe, etc., *do not care for him, do not pray to him (Gabriel and Peter, etc.), have only a hazy idea about him, where he comes from and absolutely no idea about an eternal existence and his relation to mankind as Omniscient Judge, who after the death of men and on the General Judgment Day, rewards the good and punishes the wicked for all eternity.*

Yet this is essential for the notion of God required of those who receive baptism. "Without faith it is impossible to please God. One must believe that

God exists and that He is the rewarder of those who seek him." Heb[rews] 11:6.[37]

Thus Richartz followed "the Holy Writ [that] says: 'Dii gentium daemonia' [The gods of the nations are demons]."[38] Though he did not state it definitively, he certainly implied he believed Mwari was a false god. Yet, the theological pollution that he attributed to Mwari was rooted in what he and his confreres perceived as VaShona (Christian and non-Christian alike) moral and theological degeneracy:

The important truth, that we do not appreciate enough the deep and low state in which *our* Natives live with regard to religious ideas, not to speak of supernatural knowledge, impressed me very much whilst repeating the parts of theology (de Deo Vero, Aeterno, Remuneratore, etc.).[39]

If the people bring limbo, sadza, doro, even cattle and girls to Mwari . . . they do not see him, but they hand his presents to a representative of Mwari called Mungai [sic] we Mwari (a man) who also pretends to have the same powers as Mwari, and even to be Mwari. Also women, especially widows (from another country prudently) pose as Mwari's, are called Mbuya, wife or wives and also daughters, of Mwari. They go about the country, are solemnly revered, and know how to get out of the people what they want. A special kind of asking questions . . . is used to get prophecies out of the Mwari's [sic].

Those men or women pretending to work for or with or as Mwari—swindlers, of course—tell people what Mwari has said, or that he has received the presents, eaten the food, drunk the beer, etc. and the stupid Natives believe all that. They ask as a rule only material help, rain, crops, health, etc. The Mwari says, "He will think," and the people do not have to ask why, e.g., no rain is coming, etc.—they are afraid and believe that he is still thinking.[40]

On the practical level, the pro-Mwari/anti-Yave faction replied to the argument that Yave was "in possession" that "In Chishawasha books, yes; in St. Triashill books, which are more numerous than ours [Chishawasha Jesuit books], no; in the country generally both pagan and protestant, no, Mwari is in possession."[41] Similarly, they felt that switching to Mwari from Yave would be a positive change because it would foster unity with the Mariannhill missions, as well as with

Protestant churches and "pagan" Africans. Additionally, they argued because Ignatius Gartlan and Richard Sykes, as prefects apostolic, had given their respective imprimatur to books published using Mwari, "The conclusion seems to be that we may lawfully use either—unless it can be proved that Mwari is not the equivalent for God."[42] Furthermore, they argued that if Yave were retained, then other errors in translation would have to be retained as well:

The argument applies equally well to all the other errors which were unavoidably made 25 years ago for lack of dictionaries and teachers who understood English. If its conclusion is to stand we must go on baptizing: "In the name of the Father and of the *Boy* and of the Holy Ghost," and saying, "Thou art prayed to the woman," in the Hail Mary; "You not killing," or "(If) you do not kill," "You not stealing," etc. in the Commandments; "Jesus Christ is in the *pictures* of bread and wine" in the definition of the Holy Eucharist, etc.[43]

At the theological level, they argued that Mwari was preferable because African Christians frequently had "no idea of the meaning of Yave whilst they know Mwari quite well"; that Yave was a foreign name for God (although they argued that Mwari might have been the ChiShona translation of Allah or Ali, coming from commerce with Arab traders on the East African coast before the imposition of European colonial rule[44]); and that VaShona "all over the country speak of Mwari as the Creator, All-powerful and the Ruler of the Universe. To them he is the Lord who made heaven and earth."[45]

A significant point in the theological debate concerned differing opinions of what was correct missiological practice within the context of the church's tradition. The pro-Yave/anti-Mwari side argued that no "civilized" (that is, Western Christian) nation used an indigenous word for the name of the supreme being, and cited the example of Francis Xavier's refusing to use a Japanese name for God while evangelizing Japan:[46]

I feel the strongest point against Mwari is that (as far as I know) not one civilized people used a word of their own language for "God." Dieu, Dios from Deus, Deus from Greek and I do not know the Greek from where. Is that accidentally or intentionally? . . . Did all the Romanic people not have a word in their language for the highest being? Why did they all choose "Deus" or a variety [of it] and why not the word from their own language? Was the church against it? It looks like [it].[47]

Richartz used this argument in his extended reply to Apel, as did Johanny in his letter to Fr. General Ledochowski:

The big nations which used these names [Theos, Deus, Gott, God], knew and believed at least that those names designated the highest Lord among many Dii and Gods, and so it was relatively easy for the first preachers of the Gospel, after doing away with the latter (Gods) to explain to those civilized nations the nature of the One God, Deus, and that He was designated with the same name. . . . What the missionaries all over Africa do is their business—let them mind it. Are all African tribes alike, or in such a low state as our people?[48]

In such a matter it is not the sound of the word that matters, but the mental concept that accompanies the word. But it is clear to all that in the words Deus and [Theos] there is no connotation at all unworthy of God, as there is in some Native words, as has often been vehemently asserted by the experts in the Native languages; which are rightly suspected to exist in the name MWARI; further, the names Deus and [Theos] signified and were understood to mean, by the more cultured Romans and Greeks, and the philosophers, the Supreme Being, the Creator and Ruler of the Universe, wholly distinct from the minor gods imagined by the pagans, such as Jove, Apollo, Venus, etc.

The same could hardly be maintained of our Natives, untaught, ignorant, immersed in superstition. They would not have that concept, free of all crudity and elements alien to the Godhead, when they used the name MWARI.[49]

Ledochowski sent Brown correspondence from the Missionaries of Africa supporting this position, according to which, the White Fathers in Nyasaland (colonial Malawi) introduced the KiSwahili name for the Christian god, Mulungu, "even though the language, Ki-Swahili, was not spoken in Nyassa."[50]

The pro-Mwari/anti-Yave faction argued it was long established Catholic tradition to use an indigenous word for the name of god, and that Francis Xavier's example, however much revered by his brother Jesuits, was more an exception than the rule:

From St. Peter & St. Paul down to modern African missionaries there seem[s] to be no instance on record of any mission using Yave, except Chishawasha. St. Peter found "Deus" used by pagans as a generic name for all pagan gods and he adopted it; St. Paul did the same with "[Theos]"; the apostles of England, Germany, Spain etc. all adopted the name for pagan gods; in Natal they use Unkulunkulu, in the Cape uTixo, Basutoland Modimo, Matabeleland Umlimo, Batongaland Reza, Zambesi & Nyasaland Mulungu, Congo Nzambi & Nyambi, Sud-Sansibar [sic] Mungu.

As far as the MaKaranga [sic] are concerned Mwari has never been used to denote pagan gods, though of course He has been the object of pagan worship. So it seems to have a better claim than many other names of God, including Deus and [Theos]. . . . It appears that the Japanese had many "local names for God," the VaKaranga have only one, Mwari. Had the Japanese a name for the true God as the VaKaranga certainly have? The practice of our greatest missionary in this matter looks singularly exceptional & suggests that circumstances also must have been singularly exceptional.[51]

Apel used this argument in his letter to Richartz, which the redactor of the Mwari Controversy Typescript described as "a key letter in this controversy."[52] There was no similar controversy among Jesuit missionaries working in AmaNdebele missions in western Zimbabwe.[53]

There is very limited documentary evidence of African perspective on the Mwari controversy. African Christians, however, played significant roles, principally as the translators of the works that sparked the controversy in the first place. Terence Ranger noted Mariannhill missionaries consulted their African catechists and teachers in developing "missionary Manyika," and that "the Jesuit critics of Triashill objected precisely to such consultations and to the indigenous input into the formulation of Manyika."[54] Ranger did not include African participation in the preparation of the controversial Jesuit text:

At present we are giving the last touches to the new translation [of the third edition of the Chishawasha catechism]. Emmanuel made the translation in the first instance. Then he and Fr. Daignault [pro-Mwari] went over it together. Then it was revised by the outschool teachers in conjunction with Fr. Daignault last October [1920]. After that, Fr. Marconnes [pro-Mwari] took it in hand. Finally, Lorenzo Sawada corrected it at Empandeni. It should soon be ready for the printer.[55]

Thus, African Christians had a hand in almost every phase of the preparation of the revised catechism, from initial translation to final editorial corrections, subject to the approval of Jesuit oversight and approval, which evidently was forthcoming.

Both sides of the debate cited African support for their respective positions. Richartz claimed "all" of the African Christians at Chishawasha and other Jesuit missions preferred the second edition—which used Yave—to the revised edition that used Mwari.[56] He further argued that reintroducing Mwari "did great harm to our Native Christians . . . so much so that they wrote to me, 'did you teach us wrong?' and 'The present vafundisi use the language of the sects!'"[57] The anonymous author of the "Notes on Mwari" countered,

Intelligent native Christians are well aware of many glaring mistakes in our books. A clever and good teacher stated in a letter dated 2/10/1912: "All the books translated are all wrong. They want to be colected [sic] again."; and he went on to give examples that fully proved his statement. . . . We may reasonably hope that the satisfaction produced by the correction of our many glaring mistakes will go a long way towards reconciling our native Christians to Mwari and to help them to overcome a certain feeling of repugnance that some of them may have at first. This hope is based on the hearty approval which they show on hearing the new version of the catechism with Mwari in it read to them; a hearty approval manifested in remarks such as the following: "Pa ka naka pese!", "It's all good"; "Ma zwhi aya a no baya," "these words cut to the quick"; "Catekisimo iyi ino tahura yega," "This catechism speaks itself" i.e., is quite clear. "Chi swina kwa cho ichi," "This is real chi swina." This being the case no serious difficulty should arise from the part of our native Christians in the making of necessary corrections and changes.[58]

More significantly, oral evidence suggests while African Christians prayed to Yave at mass and in public prayers with Jesuits present, in private and in personal prayers many people prayed to Mwari.⁵⁹ This indicates the probable presence of a hidden transcript favoring Mwari among African Christians at Chishawasha, the ostensible bastion of the pro-Yave camp.⁶⁰

Official church approbation of Mwari began in the Gwelo diocese (among predominantly ChiKaranga speakers) under Swiss Bethlehem missionaries' guidance. On May 19, 1961, Bishop Aloysius Haene "permitted the use of the word Mwari."⁶¹ The reversal was part of a process to "clear the catechism and devotional texts of Latinisms." The changes in terminology were based on discussions with African teachers and catechists, and eventually led to the first ChiShona mass in Southern Rhodesia being said in the Gwelo diocese. There is no documentary evidence of approval of the change more broadly in colonial Zimbabwe in the bishops' conference or archdiocesan archives. George Fortune, based on communication with Michael Hannan, noted,

The chief reason for the change was that the African clergy thought that there was an implied discrimination in not using a traditional [sic] African name for God, a practice that had been allowed to pagans of the past who had their own names applied to the Christian God, for example Zeus in Greek, Deus in Latin and the Romance languages, and Gott in German and related languages; also the use of African names, such as *Mulungu* in Nyanja and *Leza* in Tonga, had become an accepted practice long before the 1960s.⁶²

Although Hannan suggested the change from Yave to Mwari occurred around 1966, Jesuit Oscar Wermter recalled the that use of Mwari was widespread on his arrival in Southern Rhodesia in 1963, prior to the promulgation of the decrees and other documents of Vatican II.⁶³

It is not helpful to attempt to ascribe blame or responsibility for the Mwari controversy: any answer would leave the discussion at the level of a debate between European missionaries, albeit a serious and intense one. It is far more useful to examine the debate within the broader context of African religious developments. Fortune and Ranger both suggested the antiquity of the use of Mwari's name among ChiShona speakers dating from one to three thousand years. Fortune further noted Mwari never really gained acceptance as the supreme being's name among speakers of ChiZezuru on the central plateau between the Zambezi and the Limpopo rivers, whereas it did in other areas of what eventually became colonial Zimbabwe.

When Francis Richartz and his confreres arrived at Chishawasha, at the heart of the ChiZezuru-speaking area, in 1892, regardless of the Jesuits' apprehensions whether Mwari was a *"nomen Dei pollutum,"* it is not surprising that VaShona who became Christians and resided on the Jesuits' mission farms would not be averse to the introduction of Yave for the name of the Christian god, given their purported hesitance concerning Mwari. Mariannhill missionaries established their missions in the east, among ChiManyika speakers who evidently accepted Mwari as a name for the high god. Thus, there would be little complaint from African converts to Christianity about using Mwari to identify the Christian god. Within this context, the Mwari controversy was not only a bitter debate between and among European missionaries, but also appears to have been the manifestation in modern Christian form of a millennia-old debate between and among ChiShona-speaking Africans as to what names are appropriate for the supreme being or creator god.

7
Bread and Wine, Beer and Meat: The *Kurova Guva* Controversy

> *September 20, 1931: Mass. No communions, no Benediction, no procession, [or] Stations of the Cross because of two cases of* Kurova Guva *with all their incidental heathenism.*
>
> Chishawasha Historia Domus

VaShona cultural practices of honoring the spirits of the dead, or *kurova guva*, were initially banned by Catholic missionaries shortly after their arrival in Southern Rhodesia in the early 1890s. An important ritual, however, it persisted clandestinely on mission farms throughout the twentieth century. Largely at the urging of the Catholic Association and with the support of the African clergy, discussions about lifting the ban and adapting *kurova guva* to the church began in the 1960s and culminated in 1978 with the Catholic bishops approving a modified form of the ritual, called *kuchenura munhu*, which subsequently received the Vatican's approval on an experimental basis in 1981. In the late 1990s, several African bishops and priests renewed debate about the validity of *kuchenura munhu*.

Because *kurova guva* was banned, VaShona Catholics had to perform it secretly; thus, there is very little documentary evidence of its practice in the Jesuit Archives of Zimbabwe or the Archives of the Archdiocese of Harare.[1] Additionally, political violence following the February 2000 constitutional referendum's defeat made it virtually impossible to conduct oral research at various mission stations. Thus, the narrative of the process of the development and approval of *kuchenura munhu* is taken largely from an article by Paul Gundani.[2] This is supplemented where possible by documentary evidence from Chishawasha Mission and followed by a brief analysis of recent debates over rites to honor ancestor spirits in the Catholic Church in Southern Africa.

Bringing Home the Spirits of the Dead

VaShona theology holds that when a person dies, the spirit leaves the body and the homestead (*musha*) in which the person lived.[3] This is sometimes referred to as "wandering in the forest." *Kurova guva* is performed to bring the spirit of the deceased back to the homestead so that it can take its place among the ancestral spirits (*midzimu* or *vadzimu*; sg., *mudzimu*), and assist in protecting the living from evil. Prior to the ceremony, which is performed six months to a year after the person's death (usually during the dry season, from May to October), the deceased's family often consults a *n'ganga* (healer/diviner) to determine the cause of death, specifically whether an evil spirit (*ngozi*) was responsible. The ceremony is also associated with the final dissolution of the person's property (*nhaka*). The rite usually involves slaughtering an animal (ox or goat) and offering the meat and millet beer to the spirit, and sometimes the libation of the animal's blood on the deceased's grave. The remainder of the meat and beer is consumed in a feast welcoming the spirit home.

Michael Gelfand described the significance of *kurova guva* as follows:

The purpose of *kurova guva* is to bring back the spirit of the deceased from the grave to his hut to be in the midst of his descendants. . . . This ceremony illustrates the close bond which exists between the living and the dead in Shona family life. The proximity of the grave to the living quarters and the bringing back of the spirit to the home continually reminds the family of the dead man. They felt his presence amongst them and since the spirit is endowed with supernatural powers of protection, it is evident how strong a hold he and the other ancestral spirits must have in the daily activities and actions of the family. Nothing is more serious than to forget the *vadzimu* for this will provoke them to anger and retribution must surely follow. As the *vadzimu* keep a watchful eye on their descendants, the latter must be very careful to carry out all that is prescribed.[4]

From the beginning of the Catholic mission in colonial Zimbabwe, Jesuits decided that *kurova guva* violated the first commandment by offering sacrifices to false gods.[5] "With regard to *kurova guva*, the early [Jesuit] missionaries taught that to take part in it was a grave sin. Taking part in the ceremonies was understood to be participation in "ancestral worship" and therefore contrary to the first commandment."[6] Yet, according to Gundani, despite the prohibition on performing *kurova guva*, "the practice continued unabated. Such a lapse into the non-Christian ('pagan') habits was met with austere measures such as expulsion from sacraments, prohibition from entering the church during mass, or relegation to the back of the church when admitted. The strongest disciplinary measure taken against those who did not obey the mission regulations was eviction from the mission farm."[7]

Gundani claimed that many African Catholics saw the missionary ban on *kurova guva* "as the negation of 'the very essence of their (Shona) understanding of the spiritual world.'"[8] Accordingly, their resistance took a variety of "subtle secretive forms," including: "compromise rituals which were held publicly, camouflaged by new rites, commonly called '*musande*,'" in which the priest would lead "a service of Christian prayers, mostly extemporaneous, and hymns" as well as "bless the grain for the beer which was to be brewed for the participants' consumption" at a feast to honor the spirit of the deceased; and the practice of *kutora mudzimu* (to take the spirit of the deceased), that is, rather than perform *kurova guva* on the mission farm, the family took some soil from the deceased's grave in the mission cemetery to the African communal areas, killed a goat and severed its head, and then buried the head with the soil from the mission cemetery.[9] According to Gundani, before the arrival of the Christian missionaries, Va-Shona emigrants performed this ritual:

The idea was to have their ancestors emigrate with them to the new place where they were going to settle. . . . The ritual was a sign that the [family] members still cherished the ancestor's protection. Taking away the spirit from the mission cemetery to their original homes for a second burial enabled Catholics on the mission farms to honour their dead without incurring the wrath of the missionary priests, which invariably led to eviction. The *kurova guva* ceremony would take place in the communal lands over the weekend and the priests at the mission were left in the dark regarding the ceremony.[10]

Evidence from the Jesuit archives from the first three decades of the twentieth century and oral testimonies from current and former residents of various Jesuit mission farms confirms that *kurova guva* and the practice of *bira*, or the invocation of a senior ancestral spirit to possess a medium (*svikiro*), continued throughout the twentieth century.[11] The frequent references to "beer drinks" and the like refer to *bira*, which is usually held at night until dawn the following morning.

In the middle of the night there was an obscene dance at the house of Theo . . . and so the boys, at the order of Fr. Richartz, totally destroyed the house.[12]

Seven Mt. Darwin boys, hitherto most trustworthy, returned tonight from a kraal dead drunk and fighting. We spent some time in clearing them out of their sleeping quarters and putting them elsewhere—a revolting task. They are to kneel at the church doors and abstain from the sacraments and do other penances until further notice. Half the men of the congregation were drunk this morning after a big beer drink (a *kurova kwe guva*); further investigation to be made. . . . Fr. Seed went off and overturned the rest of the beer. The police made two arrests yesterday. [Fr. Seed went] to Goromonzi. . . . Discussed yesterday's affairs with the Police and discovered the two Police boys [African policemen] had arrested seven, two strangers only being liable for punishment. These two got away before arriving at Goromonzi—the two Police boys were also somewhat fuddled. The Police took a statement from Fr. Seed. Patrol Knill arrived to obtain witnesses re drinking by the Police boys. Apparently the law forbids natives to brew beer without permission from their master.[13]

Evidently, the Jesuits were not necessarily opposed to the brewing of beer or dancing in and of themselves; rather they were opposed to beer brewing and dancing associated with the *midzimu*:

Celebrations for the name day of Fr. Richartz. 36 baptisms by Fr. Sykes. . . . At 9:30, the whole parish congratulated Fr. Richartz; great parade; boys, young men, married men followed 112 women and girls carrying on their heads big pots of beer; also some 700 non-Christian adults, not counting the children.

The boys put on a fantastic dance [for the visiting Chief Native Commissioner].

Two eldest children (John and Cecilia) of Simon Taoneyi married Nuptial mass. Great jubilation at Nazareth. [Jesuit] Community invited there for tea in afternoon. We went. Big crowd. They ate an ox and four bags of mealies [corn-meal]. How much was drunk is not known.

December 25, 1931: No midnight mass—punishment for the prevalence of drink and immorality. Midnight mass for the Sisters, Candidates, and Brothers in the Convent.[14]

According to C. L. Muringayi, a lifelong resident of Chishawasha, priests did not try to stop beer drinking or brewing, but the *midzimu* and *kurova guva* were forbidden. If anyone were found out, he or she would be expelled. In the early 1920s or 1930s, Michael Shambare's *baba mudiki* (father's younger brother) was expelled for invoking the midzimu. According to Muringayi, people would tell the missionaries. He further claimed that Shambare's mother was a *svikiro*, and "when she was possessed she said that the midzimu didn't want him to become a priest."[15]

In one instance the priests at Chishawasha had "all the chiefs" in and around the mission "summoned" by the local native commissioner and "detained for three weeks" for "dealings with a witch-doctor [*n'ganga*]."[16] In another, allegations of activity involving spirits resulted in the Jesuits keeping a watchful eye on one specific resident:

Fr. Schmitz hear from *all* sides that the wife of Goto Marege has a *shave* [healing spirit] and that pagans and Christians visit her, and this is going on for many years. Goto and his wife deny everything. . . . [Four years later] Last night Frs. Seed and Gits made a raid on Goto Marengi's kraal where much drinking was in progress. Took the names of many drunkards from other kraals—caught one of the teachers (undergoing the [teacher-training] course, here) on the veld with another man's wife—both drunk.[17]

Oral evidence also testifies to the Jesuits' opposition to *kurova guva*. One Jesuit brother stated that his maternal grandfather invoked the *midzimu*, "and he got chased out of there. There were lots [of people who did so]. Not only him."[18] Sr. Bernadette Garatsa said that many people at a Catholic mission near her home in Mutambara in Mukoni District both engaged in Christian rites and practiced *bira*. She claimed that the priests knew, and recalled an incident in which a priest "covered himself and participated [in *bira*] one night. The next Sunday he forbade the participants to receive communion."[19]

Even residents at Kutama Mission, famous for the Christian village founded by Jean-Baptiste Loubière ("the enclosure," according to one resident), admitted that African Christians performed *kurova guva*, though they were apparently few in number. According to Boniface Gumbo, the Jesuits "had to be cautious with tribal [sic] dances and rituals. The church didn't want to hear of this." Because of church opposition to VaShona rites, which "slowed [evangelizing] penetration into the elders, [the Jesuits] established the Christian village: Christians in and non-Christians out." Missionaries set policy and African lay leaders, such as Joseph Dambaza Chikerema, implemented it. Gumbo admitted that his father "snuck off to beer drinks . . . [but] not many snuck out because there was a lot of intimidation. [Fr. Jerome] O'Hea would go out and fight if he heard drums, etc. [People] couldn't expose themselves easily. . . . There was freedom, there was beer, music, and dancing, but they couldn't expose themselves as people speaking out."[20]

Teresa Joe similarly acknowledged that "some [residents in the Christian village at Kutama] used beer and the *midzimu* privately," though she was not sure how many. Because *kurova guva* was forbidden, the residents "had a big dinner and a mass. [The body] was taken to the church [for a] whole night wake [during which] there was the rosary and singing hymns. This was followed by burial the next day." One of the changes in the Christian village that Fr. Jerome O'Hea implemented following Loubière's death in 1930 was to allow people to brew beer openly. Despite this relative relaxation of discipline within the Christian village, there are "few Christians doing *kurova guva* or using the *midzimu* [at Kutama] even today."[21]

As Boniface Gumbo noted, the Jesuits in colonial Zimbabwe were "cautious" regarding African rituals and their willingness to adapt them to church practices. While feelings of Western cultural superiority more than likely figured prominently in their thinking, rituals dealing with ancestors and incorporation of local practices were the same issues in China and India from the sixteenth to the eighteenth centuries (known as the Chinese rites and Malabar rites controversies respectively) that contributed significantly to the decision of Pope Clement XIV to suppress the Society of Jesus in 1773. The Chinese rites controversy, in particular, centered on whether Christian converts could participate in rituals honoring Confucius and ancestral spirits. Jesuits such as Matteo Ricci claimed that because they were civil ceremonies, Chinese Christians could participate without fear of violating the first commandment. Others in the church, including the Dominican fathers, argued that the ceremonies were religious and constituted sacrifice to a false deity.[22] The suppression of the Society of Jesus for over forty years indicates that the Jesuits were on the losing side of the debate, and this figured prominently in the long corporate memory of the Jesuits in Southern Rhodesia.

Writing to Edward Parry, the prefect of the Zambezi Mission, concerning a debate among the missionaries about "encouraging wicked pagan customs" in February 1920, Francis Johanny suggested careful study of the question and invoked the specter of the Chinese rites controversy:

> Frs. Casset, Daignault, and Loubière may be right, and yet even then obviously Frs. Moreau, Richartz, and Hess are not encouraging wicked pagan customs, because obviously also these customs, *in their eyes* and *in their opinion* are neither wicked in themselves nor of pagan significance. If the point of view of Frs. M[oreau], R[ichartz], and H[esse] is right then Frs. C[asset], D[aignault], and L[oubière] are wrong; but the latter's contention would be precisely that these customs are tainted with pagan superstition and therefore wicked. That precisely is the question which needs looking into. In fact, I think we are here face to face with a question which, because of the divergent, even opposite, views held by the Missionaries about it, and because of the warmth of feeling its discussion is apt to develop, will require at no distant date, a close and

minute study by a competent, impartial, third party. The reason is plain: opposition of views in these matters will lead to difference of action (where uniformity is essential) and to confusion of the Natives' mind. Hence I should consider it a most regrettable thing if Your Reverence who, of course, will have to act as arbiter and judge, happened to let either party feel or suspect that you side with the other, on that subject of pagan customs. . . .

The question appears to me most interesting because it affords a parallel case with the question of the Malabar and Chinese Rites. The latter especially has points not unlike those which vex our missionaries—e.g., honours paid to ancestor spirits, the name used for God, etc. And the history of the Society [of Jesus] throws a light on the cautious course we should follow. For, as Your Reverence will remember, though our missionaries were almost unanimous in their view that those rites were purely civil ceremonies and that they had no religious significance—what Fr. Moreau would maintain of Tonga customs—and though the men who held these views were eminent for learning and holiness, yet others, Dominicans, Bishops, etc. held the opposite view and in the end Rome's decision, both through its Legate, Cardinal Tournon, and through the Popes themselves, went against us.

For obviously, though condescension to Native weakness may be adopted up to a certain point, Rome will value and maintain above all things the unity of the Faith, and therefore one cannot a priori lay down any rule until the matter has been thoroughly sifted, to make sure that the superstitious practices are not really carried out by our Christians.[23]

Although the memory of the Chinese and Malabar rites figured in the minds of members of the Zambezi Mission, curiously, they apparently did not take note of either of the documents that formally ended the controversies by allowing for the adaptation and admission of local customs to church practice in 1935,[24] or of a similar 1938 letter to the apostolic delegate in the Belgian Congo allowing for the adaptation of local funerary practices.[25] The cardinals at the head of Propaganda Fide decided to leave approbation of adapted rites to the discretion of the apostolic delegate and local ordinaries.

As with the Mwari controversy, Jesuits were split over the practices in which African Christians engaged. That the debate erupted among Jesuits points to the fact that Christians living on the mission farms were very selective as to which parts of the Christian message they accepted, which parts they adapted, and which parts they rejected. Also, as with the Mwari controversy, not all African Christians accepted and practiced *kurova guva*. Joseph Munyongani Mutoko, the first convert at Chishawasha, clearly demonstrates this:

[Munyongani's first wife] Maria took ill in childbirth. The [Jesuit] Fathers tried to help her and had her brought in to Harare hospital. She gave birth to the child without trouble. But on the way back to Chishawasha Maria died. . . . Then the child died, too, just as the sun was coming up.

Maria had a fine funeral, with the people at the Mass, which was the first Mass for the Dead at Chishawasha. . . .

When on his deathbed [in 1919], "Finally the father [Munyongani] addressed his children: 'You must continue to behave well as you did when I was alive. No quarrelling or grumbling. And see to it that your own children get married, just as you did for my sake.

'I warn you, I do not want the "kurova guva" ceremony done for me. If you do, I shall hold it against you. Nor are you to go (to the witchdoctor) [*n'ganga*] to find out what (or who) killed me. Can you not see, my years on this earth are at an end?'"[26]

Canonizing the Spirits: The Kuchenura Munhu Rite

The Catholic Association territorial council's request to study the possibility of adapting *kurova guva* pushed the bishops to establish a commission of inquiry. Paul Gundani noted that several African priests, most notably Fr. Joseph Kumbirai of the Gwelo diocese, took the lead in promoting adaptation and experimentation.[27]

In 1968, the bishops' conference established an interdiocesan committee to investigate the issue further. In 1969, the committee presented a report that "argued that *kurova guva* and similar ancestral rites were to be understood in the context of the fourth Commandment ('Honour thy father and mother') rather than the first (against false gods). Thus, such practices were not idolatrous nor against the Catholic faith. The committee therefore recommended lifting the ban on *kurova guva* for pastoral reasons." Fr. Emmanuel Mavudzi of the Salisbury archdiocese submitted a minority report "reject[ing] *kurova guva* and ancestor veneration in general. [Fr. Mavudzi] called upon Catholic members and their relatives to engage in a simple ceremony of comforting the bereaved—*nyaradzo*.[28]

The conflicting reports led the bishops to recommend further study, and to highlight the need for general instruction of the laity on the significance of inculturation following Vatican II. Thus, no progress was made until after the establishment of the National Association of Diocesan Clergy (NADC) in 1973, when the African priests "supported the recommendation of the majority report of the inter-diocesan committee to lift the ban on *kurova guva*." In June 1974, the bishops accepted the recommendations of the interdiocesan committee and the NADC to remove the ban on *kurova guva*, and they tasked a new theological commission to develop "a theological argument" for the rite while also considering Fr. Mavudzi's minority report.[29]

According to Gundani, the majority of the theological commission defined sacrifice as "a special act of external worship by which something can be perceived by the senses, is legitimately offered to God . . . the action of offering involving a certain change in the thing being offered—to show recognition of His supreme majesty," and argued that performing *kurova guva* was "doing one's duty to the departed spirit and fulfilling one's family obligation." Furthermore, they contended that in this light, the ox and goat "should not be viewed as sacrifice in the theological sense but as food for the invited guests and all participants and that it symbolized the honour and respect paid to the deceased."[30]

As with the interdiocesan committee, a single priest submitted a minority opinion. Fr. Bernard Ndhlovu contended that VaShona, AmaNdebele, and VaKalanga practices of reinstating the dead "was at best a form of religious sacrificial act . . . directed to the spirit of the deceased and not to God," and that the ceremony contravened the first commandment. He further argued that "people performed the ceremony out of fear based on the assumption that the spirit of the deceased had power over the living if they did not perform the rite. If the overall motive then was to pacify the spirit, Fr. Ndhlovu argued, the practice was not only evil but also incongruous with the Christian faith.[31]

According to Gundani, the theological commission saw *kurova guva* and other practices related to the *midzimu* as compatible with Christianity. The majority of the commission "endorsed the Inter-diocesan Committee's position that kurova guva and the overall Shona belief in communing with and depending on the ancestors provided fertile soil for the church's teaching and belief in the communion of Saints. The Church teaches that Saints have communion with the living and intercede on behalf of the living to God. The majority members therefore viewed the status of ancestors as comparable to that of the Saints since the spirit brought back home to protect the family is also expected to intercede to the senior family ancestors (*madzitateguru*)."[32]

Evidently Fr. Ndhlovu also raised concern regarding the status of the spirit after death and before reinstatement. The majority took the position that the VaShona understanding of purification associated with *kurova guva* was also compatible with the Catholic doctrine concerning purgatory. According to the church, the souls of those who retain the effects of unrepented sin must be purified before attaining salvation. They require the prayers of the living faithful to help them in the process of purification. Similarly, according to VaShona belief, death "inflict[ed] a 'black spell' on the spirit of the deceased" necessitating purification. The "duty and responsibility of the living to the dead performed in the hope that the spirit would be given a place in the other world" was an integral part of this belief.[33]

Accordingly, the commission recommended that the bishops not only lift the ban on *kurova guva*, but "that it be Christianized for liturgical purposes." The bishops then referred the matter to Bishop Patrick Chakaipa, the recently appointed first African bishop, to consult with the National Association of Diocesan Clergy. The NADC held meetings in 1977 and 1978, and ultimately decided that Christianizing *kurova guva* was a matter of urgency; approved the offering of grain, beer, and animal victims; and rejected the role of the diviner (*n'ganga*) in determining the cause of death (*gata*) and the singing of war songs (*ngondo*) when returning from the grave to the homestead.[34] They submitted their report to the bishops in March 1978, and in June the bishops asked the NADC to develop a catechism for the new rite to be called *kuchenura munhu* (to purify the person). After extensive grassroots consultations, the NADC committee submitted its draft of the catechism on *kuchenura munhu* to the Commission for Christian Formation and Worship, which then forwarded it to the bishops for adoption in early 1980. The bishops, in turn, sent the catechism and rite to Rome, and on April 9, 1981, they received approbation *ad experimentum* for three years. Mambo Press published the rite with the catechism "for use by all members of the Church" in 1982.[35]

Paul Gundani attributed the Zimbabwean Catholic hierarchy's adaptation of *kurova guva* rites "as official liturgy" to the radicalization of the Catholic Association caused by "the growing consciousness expressed in African nationalism" and the support of "the few Black clergy" who "became a force to reckon with in the Roman Catholic Church in Zimbabwe, from 1972 when they formed" the NADC. He further argued that *kurova guva* represents a "classic case" of inculturation, adding that "the process of change which resulted in the new liturgy was unique in the 'historical' churches" because it sprang up from the grassroots, not from the top down.[36]

The development of the *kuchenura munhu* rite highlights the roles that the Catholic Association and the African clergy played (coupled with the new theological dispensation of Vatican II) in opening discursive space in which to discuss adaptation of *kurova guva* to a form acceptable to Catholic belief and practice. It also clearly demonstrates African Christians' ability to discern their own interests, and not only negotiate successfully the contested bounds of Catholic theological discourse, but also to expand them to include distinctly African forms of Christian belief and practice into the universal church's doctrinal and liturgical corpus.

Kuchenura Munhu Reconsidered

Over the last decade there has been significant rethinking of the nature and role of ancestor rites in the Catholic Church in Southern Africa. In December 1997, the issue of the nature of *kurova guva*, specifically whether it was a sacrifice that derogated from the worship due to God alone, came to the fore of Zimbabwean Catholic theological discourse.[37] One of the bishops called for a renewed investigation of the *kuchenura munhu* rites (which were still approved *ad experimentum*) when allegedly several of his priests claimed that they were "confused" regarding the theology surrounding the rites.[38] This touched off a flurry of articles in the Catholic press in which Emmanuel Mavudzi restated his opposition to the Christianized form of *kurova guva* and Ignatius Chidavaenzi found the *kuchenura munhu* rite theologically objectionable.[39] In April 2007, using language that echoed the perspectives of the leaders of the Zambezi Mission in the early twentieth century, the Southern African Catholic Bishops Conference (SACBC) issued a pastoral statement, "Ancestor Religion and the Christian Faith," that effectively renewed the ban on African Catholic recourse to rites to honor their ancestors.[40] These developments highlight the fundamentally anti-African bias that circumscribes the discourse of inculturation within the Catholic Church.

Zambezi Mission superiors clearly opposed *kurova guva* prior to the Second Vatican Council, as most notably expressed in Francis Johanny's 1920 letter to Edward Parry invoking the specter of the Chinese rites controversy. African Catholics also opposed *kurova guva* dating back to 1919, when Joseph Munyongani died. Emmanuel Mavudzi dissented from the interdiocesan committee that recommended lifting the ban on *kurova guva*, and Bernard Ndhlovu opposed the majority opinion of the theological commission that developed *kuchenura munhu*.

Ignatius Chidavaenzi of the Diocese of Chinoyi examined the questions of whether *kurova guva* was a sacrifice and whether there was anything theologically objectionable associated with the *kuchenura munhu* rite.[41] Fr. Chidavaenzi opposed the assertion in the catechesis of the *kuchenura munhu* ritual that *kupira* (offering) is "a purely symbolic gesture without sacrificial connotations in the theological sense,"[42] and argued that *kurova guva* was a sacrifice akin to devil or angel worship, and that because sacrifice was a form of divine worship that ought to be reserved only for God (that is, *latreia*), it was not possible to inculturate *kurova guva*, only to retain "what is good in Kurova guva ... to enhance our faith."⁴³ At no point, however, did Fr. Chidavaenzi ever state what he thought was "good in *kurova guva.*"

The elements of *kuchenura munhu* that Fr. Chidavaenzi found "objectionable" included the use of blood in animal slaughter; libation of blood or beer; the offering of animals, beer, tobacco, or other goods to the spirit of the deceased rather than directly to God; what he perceived as the divinization of ancestor spirits (that is, the ascription of divine attributes to the spirits) in the *kuchenura munhu* rite; and the performance of the ritual only for married adults. According to Chidavaenzi, the sacrifice of Jesus Christ on the cross and its reenactment "in the Eucharist" (that is, the Mass) replaced "all these sacrifices (goats and cattle), offerings (beer and tobacco), [and] the libation (of blood and beer)."⁴⁴ Following the arguments of Frs. Ndhlovu and Mavudzi, Fr. Chidavaenzi also criticized the alleged fear that motivated people to perform either *kurova guva* or *kuchenura munhu,* as did the Southern African bishops.⁴⁵

At the back of the mind lingers the feeling that this ceremony is not really necessary for salvation but we must inculturate it because whether we inculturate it or not people will not relinquish it, not because of their love for the dead but because of the fear connected with not performing this ritual for their dead. . . . The whole ritual [*kuchenura munhu*] smacks [of] double allegiance in a bad sense to the spirits of the dead and [to] Jesus Christ. One has to remember, though, that God is a jealous God.⁴⁶

The "ray of hope" that Fr. Chidavaenzi thought "the best way to adopt as a way of Kuchenura [purification] centered on the Eucharist" was "the practice of unveiling the Tomb Stone" because it was performed for all people ("adults, teenagers, married, and the unmarried") by "all cultures in Zimbabwe" and by "all the churches"; the *n'ganga* had no role; and there was no sacrifice associated with it, but there was a ceremony that "makes people feel they have done something for the dead relative." The only alternative, according to Chidavaenzi, was "to modify drastically the Shona ritual by removing all objectionable aspects of the present Rite (the sacrificial animals, the beer, tobacco, libation, and the implied consultation of the n'ganga and the fear attached to the non-performance of the Rite) and centralise this ritual on Jesus Christ the Saviour and the Eucharist."[47]

Fr. Chidavaenzi, although a Catholic theologian, did not write like one regarding *kurova guva* and *kuchenura munhu*. His interpretation of scripture was very narrow and literalistic. He provided his reader no sense of the historical development of Catholic tradition, and how that development bears on the theological point in question: he drew his examples and supporting evidence from Hebrew scripture (particularly dealing with Mosaic law and the ancient kingdom of Israel) and Christian scripture, comparing these directly with VaShona examples from Zimbabwe, but he did not provide any temporal specificity—that is, we are not sure whether he referred to contemporary VaShona practices, those of the colonial period, or even those of the time before the Europeans came. He provided no sense of historicization or religious (or more broadly cultural) change either as Christianity was adapted to Western cultures in Europe over two thousand years, or of cultural or religious change in Zimbabwe. For example, in "The Sacrificial Aspects of Kurova Guva," Fr. Chidavaenzi asserted,

in spite of the fact that *kurova guva* is held as very very important among us Shona Africans, no clan or tribe [sic] has as yet written a traditional ritual for themselves. When people perform the ritual, it is done according to the knowledge and memory of those who are present on that occasion. This, of course, explains why there are so many variations of the same ceremony, with differing understanding on what one tribe would think important and essential to the ceremony. To take on this method of doing things with regard to the inculturation of *kurova guva* is, again, unwise and will produce a chaotic situation in the Church like that recorded by the book of Judges which says, "In those days there was no king in Israel, and everyone did as he saw fit. (Jg. 21.25).[48]

Fr. Chidavaenzi did not take into account the variations of the written Catholic Mass that occur within a single country such as Zimbabwe; he did not compare the different styles of worship in a church that uses an organ in which the congregation sings English hymns with those of a church that uses drums and *hosho*, and the congregation sings Shona hymns, or—in the Gweru diocese—plays the *mbira*. Nor did Fr. Chidavaenzi consider the changes in the mass, even though written, from the pre–Vatican II Tridentine rite to the contemporary vernacular liturgies. Further, his gratuitous reference to premonarchical ancient Israel as a time of chaos does not consider that God perceived the establishment of the monarchy as a rejection of his authority: "Grant the people's every request. It is not you [Samuel, the last of the judges] they reject, they are rejecting me [God] as their king" (see 1 Samuel 8:7). Additionally, he did not consider the fact that biblical stories were transmitted orally for centuries before they were written; thus they—like VaShona rituals—are the products of oral traditions (consider, for example, the multiple creation stories in the book of Genesis, the alleged three authors of the book of Isaiah, or the various sources of the four Christian gospels) and redaction into "seamless" written narratives. Most significantly, Fr. Chidavaenzi did not address the fact that the kinds of uniformity and standardization that he espoused are relatively late developments in the history of the Catholic church in Europe, most notably associated with the Council of Trent in the mid–sixteenth century and the reactionary conservatism of the late nineteenth and early twentieth centuries associated with the reign of Pius IX (among them the index of forbidden books and the First Vatican Council, which bequeathed the doctrine of papal infallibility), the promotion of Thomistic philosophy as the standard for clerical formation, and the promulgation of a unified code of canon law for the entire Catholic Church throughout the world in 1917.

Both Fr. Chidavaenzi and the SACBC go to great lengths to show that *kuchenura munhu* (or ancestor veneration) is a form of sacrifice offered directly to the spirit of the deceased for the expiation of sin, rather than to Jesus Christ or God the Father. The prayers of the ritual, however, clearly show that where any sacrifice is made it is offered to God *via* the ancestor spirits *on behalf* of the deceased in much the same way that Western Catholics bring prayers of supplication or petition to God via the communion of saints:

The presentation of the animal (*nhevedzo*)

This animal [*nhdedzo*, killed for the burial ceremony] is presented to the dead person, that he presents it to the ancestors who present it to God with this prayer:

Presenter: [Name of Ancestor], tell also [name of ancestor], who tells too [name of ancestor], you tell each other until it reaches Christ, who himself brings to God, the Creator, that this animal is the one which enables your child, [name of deceased], to go, we are presenting him to you and his ancestors, that they may present him to you, the Creator. We have sprinkled this animal in your name and that of the Son and of the Holy Spirit.

He sprinkles with holy water.

Presenter: All you midzimu of his lineage, guide him to Jesus who opens to people the courtyard of his Father. It is he, who is the bridge we cross, when we go to the new country full of saints and angels . . . .

For those who pour beer at the grave

Presenter: You [name of deceased], tell [name of ancestor], who tells [name of ancestor], which goes like that until to Christ. He brings it to the Father too, that we pour this beer at your grave, that we are united with you, as the unity which was achieved for us by the blood of Christ.

The Presenter pours the beer saying:

Presenter: We do this in the name of the Father and the Son and the Holy Spirit.

All: Amen.[49]

Compare the extract of this *kuchenura munhu* ritual with the following extracts from Catholic novena prayers to Mary (Our Lady of Lourdes) and St. Raphael (guardian/archangel):

Ever Immaculate Virgin, Mother of mercy, health of the sick, refuge of sinners, comfort of the afflicted, you know my wants, my troubles, my sufferings. Deign to cast on me a look of mercy.

By appearing in the Grotto of Lourdes [in southern France in 1858], you were pleased to make it a privileged sanctuary, from which you dispense favors; and already many sufferers have obtained the cure of their infirmities, both spiritual and corporal. I come, therefore, with the most unbounded confidence to implore your maternal intercession.

Obtain, O loving Mother, the granting of my requests. Through gratitude for your favors, I will endeavor to imitate your virtues that I may one day share your glory.

Through your loving compassion shown to thousands of pilgrims who come to your shrine at Lourdes, and through your special love for your devoted client Bernadette, I ask you for this grace if it be the Will of God: *(Mention your request)*.

Our Lady of Lourdes, aid me through your prayers with your Divine Son, to be a true child of yours, as Bernadette was, and to grow daily into your likeness.[50]

Holy Archangel Raphael, standing so close to the throne of God and offering Him our prayers, I venerate you as God's special Friend and Messenger. I choose you as my Patron and wish to love and obey you as young Tobiah did. I consecrate to you my body and soul, all my work, and my whole life. I want you to be my Guide and Counselor in all the dangerous and difficult problems and decisions of my life.

Remember, dearest Saint Raphael, that the grace of God preserved you with the good Angels when the proud ones were cast into hell. I entreat you, therefore, to help me in my struggle against the world, the spirit of impurity, and the devil. Defend me from all dangers and every occasion of sin. Direct me always in the way of peace, safety, and salvation. Offer my prayers to God as you offered those of Tobiah, so that through your intercession I may obtain the graces necessary for the salvation of my soul. I ask you to pray that God grant me this favor if it be His holy Will: *(Mention your request)*.[51]

Significantly, unlike the *kuchenura munhu* ritual, the novena to Our Lady of Lourdes directs the supplicant to request a specific grace directly from Mary, presuming accordance with the Divine will ("*I ask you for this grace* if it be the Will of God"). Furthermore, at no point does the catechesis of the *kuchenura munhu* ritual claim expiation of sin as its intent. Rather it is "a continual reminder of the peoples [sic] sins,"[52] and as such a vehicle to ask for God's grace. "Unveiling a tombstone" is not a historically culturally significant symbol for honoring the dead in VaShona culture.

The SACBC's ban on ancestor rites is indicative of a chronic pro-Western and anti-African bias in the Catholic church's theology of inculturation. In the pastoral statement, there is no sense of appreciation of African experience or understanding of the African sacred world except to castigate it as Other, and thus wrong and inferior, according to Western norms. The statement does not, for instance, consider John Thornton's insight that African religious thought is premised on a dynamic continuity of divine revelation, or John Mbiti's theological proposition that God revealed himself to different people in different places at different times in ways that were different from those recorded in the Hebrew and Christian scriptures. It rejects the long-established Catholic tradition that teaches that "the seeds of the Gospel" are present in all cultures prior to their evangelization by missionaries.

Sadly, the Southern African bishops, in their pastoral statement, prove Cameroonian historian Achille Mbembe's contention that in order for Africans to be accepted by the West they must purge themselves of those elements that distinguish them as Africans.[53] For example, the bishops condemned several African practices, including fortune telling, divination, and witchcraft that have Western analogues.[54] They also proscribed simony, which they defined as "the buying or selling of spiritual things," yet did not consider the possibility that requiring and/or receiving "donations" or "offerings" (read: payments) to say a Mass for a given person's intentions could easily be construed as such. More significantly, the bishops used language—and expressed a mindset—that is virtually identical to that used (and expressed) by the superiors of the Zambezi Mission a century ago to condemn African ways of honoring their ancestors:

The first commandment forbids honouring gods other than the one Lord who has revealed himself to his people. It proscribes superstition and irreligion. Superstition in some sense represents a perverse excess of religion; irreligion is the vice contrary by defect to the virtue of religion. . . . In local cultures superstition abounds. This is also so when people have not purified their faith in Christ to the extent that they are able to pray "thy Kingdom come, thy will be done" . . . in the full acceptance of the supreme power of God who is without rival.[55]

Significantly, the Southern African bishops presumed the equation of "religion" with Western Catholic Christianity as opposed to "superstition" which "abounds" in "local cultures." Nor did they consider or integrate the more ecumenical theological proposition of the Zimbabwean National Association of Diocesan Clergy that honoring ancestor spirits could be considered an obligation of the fourth commandment ("honor thy father and mother") rather than an abomination of the first commandment.

Clearly, the application of Fr. Chidavaenzi's criteria for the abolition (or significant modification) of *kuchenura munhu*—as the Southern African Catholic bishops did with their pastoral statement concerning ancestor veneration—would raise questions as to the validity of many orthodox Catholic traditions, to say nothing of the admission or adaptation of meaningful non-Christian cultural symbols. He used a narrow interpretation of Hebrews 9 and 10 to argue that Jesus' sacrificial death on the Cross and its reenactment in the Mass replaced all other forms of sacrifice for the expiation of human sin.[56] The implication is that not only is it not necessary to inculturate *kurova guva*, but it is also impossible to do so, and thus there is no need for the *kuchenura munhu* ritual within the church. Applied more broadly—as in the South African case, Fr. Chidavaenzi's method and conclusions imply no need for inculturation at all.

From a functionalist anthropological perspective, it is clear that theology, like secular law, develops from practice in order to approve or proscribe specific social practices and provide justificatory explanations for the approval or proscription. From a theological perspective that views theology as the interpretation of divine revelation, however, the inculturation of *kurova guva* as *kuchenura munhu* represents a new human understanding of the divine will:

There is a sense of "homecoming" that symbolizes the journey that the deceased makes to God's kingdom, the "real home" of the departed Christian; home is no longer conceived in terms of the traditional "*Nyikadzimu*" (the land of the ancestors). Traditionally, *Nyikadzimu* did not refer to God's kingdom, but in these rituals God's kingdom accommodates all the righteous ancestors of the deceased and is the eternal home that the deceased aspired to since baptism. This change comes about because of the transposition of Christian eschatological views on traditional Shona eschatological views. The "homecoming" rituals dramatize a new religious phenomenon—the solidarity of the living and the departed as well as the enhancement of life in Christ, "the first born from the dead" (Col 1:18). By virtue of being the firstborn, Christ becomes the eldest ancestor of all families. He becomes the reference point in all relationships with God because of his proximity to Him [God]. It is Christ who should be called *"Mudzimu mukuru"* (the greatest ancestor), not God the Father, because He cannot be likened to a human ancestor.[57]

Thus, from functionalist anthropological and secular historical viewpoints, abolishing *kuchenura munhu* would return the Catholic church in Zimbabwe to a time when "people are bound to lead two lives: that demanded by the church and that by reason of the beliefs and ideas developed and fostered through culture for centuries."[58] From a Catholic theological standpoint, however, to retreat from the inculturated ritual would be to admit that either God the Holy Spirit failed to protect the church from error and/or that the people of God in Zimbabwe, their priests, and their bishops—with the explicit approval of the Congregation for the Evangelization of Peoples in Rome, which gave its formal approbation to the modified rite, even if only *ad experimentum*—knowingly and willingly chose to err and to embrace heresy.

Conclusion

In 1962, the Southern Rhodesian Catholic bishops appointed a commission to investigate the mission of the Catholic Association and its relationship to other Catholic organizations in the colony.[1] The organization had petitioned the bishops to delete the word "African" from its title and establish it as the "territorial administrative body for all Catholic Action within [Southern] Rhodesia."[2] While Catholic Association leaders at all levels "always show[ed] good will, a readiness to cooperate and to accept guidance," many felt "frustrated" by the lack of interest and support shown by the clergy." The bishops approved the name change with the proviso that it not "be implied that [the Catholic Association] is to be the parent body of all Catholic Action."[3] The bishops included the condition, which directly contradicted the will of the African lay leadership, because of their hesitation about requiring European organizations to affiliate with the Catholic Association "as the parent-body of all Catholic Action."[4] The confusion this contradiction caused resulted in the bishops calling the commission to investigate the Catholic Association.

During the inquiry commission's deliberations concerning the Catholic Association's mission and "what a good Catholic is supposed to do," one of the seven European priests in attendance noted that "a practicing witch-doctor" had been elected as a Catholic Association officer, contrary to a rule that forbade the election of non-Catholics.[5] Although it is not clear whether "the witch-doctor" or *n'ganga*, was elected to a local executive or the territorial council, this instance raises the issue of perspective, and different understandings of "what a good Catholic is supposed to do." Obviously the Jesuit missionary on the board of inquiry did not consider the *n'ganga* a good Catholic. But evidently, the *n'ganga* considered himself to be a good Catholic, and—more importantly—his peers in the Catholic Association must have thought him a good Catholic as well. This situation and the preceding chapters show the operation of two separate yet intersecting processes: the Africanization of the Catholic Church and the discourse of inculturation. To the extent that VaShona Catholics made the church their own it was generally over and above the objections of the Jesuit leadership of the Zambezi Mission and usually with their grudging acceptance.

Africanization of the church shows Africans, in this case VaShona, receiving Christianity from missionaries, interpreting it through the medium of their collective experiences through time—including their understanding of the relationship between the human and spiritual worlds, and practicing it more or less on their own terms. The discourse of inculturation represents the field of intellectual interaction and concomitant religious praxis between African Christians and Catholic prelates, priests, and theologians—both European and African—that the latter established to facilitate the integration of Catholic Christianity with VaShona cultures. Africanization certainly occurred apart from the control of the church's hierarchy, yet was also clearly influenced and circumscribed by it. Conversely, the church's hierarchy established the parameters of inculturation discourse, yet had to reconfigure them periodically in order to respond to pressures resulting from African Catholics perceiving and practicing (or not practicing, as in the case of marriage) Christianity within the context of their cultures. The categories "African Christians" and "Catholic prelates, priests, and theologians" are not mutually exclusive as several of the former entered the ranks of the latter and occupied both categories.

VaShona received the Catholic version of the Christian message from European Jesuit missionaries beginning in the 1890s, whether for spiritual and/or material reasons. Jesuits responded by establishing mission farms and laying down strict parameters for their African residents, including requirements that adults send their children to the mission schools, that they pray to Yave instead of Mwari, and that they not perform kurova guva or otherwise engage the VaShona spiritual realm. Violation of any of these requirements would frequently result in expulsion from the mission farm. Yet the historical record shows that VaShona Catholics frequently withheld their children from mission schools, prayed to Mwari, and performed *kurova guva*, among other rites. Recall that Goto Mareke's wife at Chishawasha in the 1920s was renowned for her *shave* spirit.

The formation of African religious and clergy shows that African Christians took the initiative to work their way up to the highest levels of the church's hierarchy in the colony. African women who first expressed the desire to become nuns in the 1920s frequently met opposition from the Jesuits and consequently had to pursue their vocations in one of the orders established in the 1920s at Mariannhill mission stations. Similarly, the results of Robert Brown's 1926 survey showed that the majority of Jesuits in the Zambezi Mission opposed the seminary training of African men. Thus, the first MuShona priest, Kilian Samakande, joined Mariannhill and was ordained in South Africa. In 1931, Aston Chichester expanded the bounds of inculturation discourse by establishing the LCBL Sisters and accepting African candidates for the priesthood. Given that nineteen women opened the LCBL novitiate at Makumbi mission and eleven men entered the minor seminary program at Chishawasha in 1934, Chichester was clearly responding to African initiatives and demands (however politely expressed) to enter religious life and the clergy. African women eventually took charge of their orders, as was the case for the LCBL Sisters in 1965, and as African men—many of whom received their early educations from African nuns—entered the seminary at Chishawasha, they began the process of incorporating themselves into the Catholic hierarchy, first as priests and, from 1973, as bishops. As women religious, bishops, priests, and religious brothers, Africans stood with equal footing in the church's hierarchy as any other sister, brother, priest, or bishop in the church throughout the world. Thus, Africanizing women's religious institutes and the priesthood expanded the parameters of the discourse of inculturation over and against the opposition of the majority of the Jesuits.

Similarly, the African laity organized itself into a significant body that expressed its concerns and interests to the (gradually) Africanizing hierarchy, beginning with the teacher's conference at Chishawasha in

1934 and culminating with the Catholic African Association having more than five thousand paid members in 1958 and the Catholic Association having more than eight thousand members in 1974 as the fighting of second *chimurenga* intensified. It was at the Catholic Association's urging that the Rhodesian Catholic Bishops Conference began the process that would ultimately lead to approbation of the *kuchenura munhu* ritual. Catholic Association leaders and members achieved their successes in Africanizing the church amid severe constraints from the hierarchy in the forms of unrelenting clerical domination in ideas of Catholic Action and glaring apathy on the part of many European missionaries, as well as from those missionaries that took the time to work with them. Their struggle as lay people working against clerical domination is more typical of hierarchy-laity relations in the Catholic Church throughout the world at various points in time.

The limits that church officials imposed on inculturation discourse concerning Mwari, marriage, and *kurova guva* were even more restrictive than those placed on African nuns, priests, brothers, and laypeople, and show the struggles that VaShona Catholics had to endure in order to bring elements of their culture into "dialogue" with the Catholic Church as mediated primarily by the Jesuits. Even with African personnel in place, integration of culture into the church's corpus of symbols and ideas was not given. For forty years, Jesuits banned the use of Mwari in Catholic books and liturgies, and similarly forbade honoring ancestor spirits with kurova guva throughout the colonial period. Despite the bishops' acknowledging and incorporating the consent of the *tezvara* (father of the woman) and the requirement to pay *lobola* (bride price) as part of the marriage process, relatively few Africans married according to canonical form in the church. In significant measure, however, African Catholics ignored these prohibitions and continued pray to Mwari, honor their ancestor spirits, and marry according to "African custom." Thus, VaShona efforts to Africanize the church forced the hierarchy to renegotiate the bounds of inculturation discourse and quietly "baptize" Mwari as a legitimate name for the Christian god in the 1960s, to acknowledge the role of the *tezvara* and payment of *lobola* in marriages in the church, and to authorize a modified *kurova guva* ritual in the form of *kuchenura munhu*, which ultimately received approbation, first from the Zimbabwean bishops, and then from Rome. This once again recalls David Newbury's distinction between African recognition of European power over them and their refusal to recognize European authority.

Presuming Basil Davidson's contention that African nationalism was more concerned with social liberation from the depredations of racism and colonialism than with forming nation-states, then the Catholic Association's efforts can be seen as an expression of moderate African nationalism and a critique of and opposition to racism within the church, especially as expressed by Jesuits and other members of the hierarchy. The seminary rebellions and concomitant acts of disobedience, along with the Catholic Association's request to be "the parent body of all Catholic Action," can be seen as more radical expressions of a maturing VaShona Catholic nationalist identity.

At one level, it could be argued that the case studies presented show that the Catholic Church's efforts at inculturation were fairly successful: VaShona marriage "customs" were incorporated into church practices; Mwari has been recognized as the name of the Christian god for almost fifty years; and *kurova guva* has been adapted and received temporary approbation from the Zimbabwean bishops and the Vatican as *kuchenura munhu*.

These developments, however, along with the translation of liturgies and prayer books into ChiShona and the incorporation of VaShona musical forms (including the use of the *mbira* in the Gweru and Masvingo dioceses) and prayer postures into Catholic liturgies still represent what Eugene Hillman called the "literal and literalistic transliteration" of Catholic Christianity in a Zimbabwean context. The only notable exception to this is the *kuchenura munhu* rite. That it has not yet received definitive (that is, permanent) approbation—especially from African bishops—speaks to the weakness of the discourse of inculturation that prevailed at Jesuit missions during the colonial era in Zimbabwe.

This is because a significant idea that the Jesuits adapted and incorporated into their discourse and practice was a belief in the inferiority of African culture. Further, as the 1926 survey of Zambezi Mission personnel indicated, several Jesuits also believed in the inherent incapacity of Africans to begin—much less complete—the requisite studies necessary for seminary training and ordination. Consequently, they provided inferior education to their African students, part of which included maintaining the ban on *kurova guva*. Recall that Christopher Gardiner felt it necessary to leave Chishawasha in order to receive adequate academic training at St. John Vianney Seminary in Pretoria, and that Chishawasha seminary staff thought that they were training "simple parish priests" (they told African students not to engage in-depth philosophical questions).

Further, consider the implications of Jesuit failure to implement Vatican directives, such as *Maximum Illud, Rerum Ecclesiae,* and the 1938 Propaganda Fide directives on death rites in the Belgian Congo: had Chichester and his religious brothers considered listening to African Christians and applying the contents of the 1938 letter, quite possibly adaptations of kurova guva may well have been developed and approved prior to the 1970s. That more than half of the clergy in Zimbabwe at the turn of the millennium—including Zimbabwean members of religious orders—were foreign missionaries speaks to the failure of the Jesuit inculturation discourse, and the long-term consequences of their having ignored directives from Rome, and violating their spirit, if not necessarily their letter.[6]

Thus, the superficial inculturation of the Catholic Church in Zimbabwe is a partial decolonization of the church in much the same way that political independence has only effected a partial decolonization of Zimbabwean society more broadly.[7] Power and authority have been transferred to local leaders, but they lack the ability to change the global institutions controlled in the West that ultimately dictate the parameters of the center-periphery relationship. Or, to put it another way, the archbishop of Harare has about as much influence on the policies of the Vatican curia as the president of Zimbabwe has on the policies of the International Monetary Fund. Thus, the Catholic Church in Zimbabwe finds itself living in a decidedly postcolonial situation.

Within the Catholic context, a two thousand year history points to moments when Christianity was more tolerant and willing to adapt and incorporate different cultural symbols. The mark of catholicity ostensibly and ideally allows for local cultures to influence the church universal by taking elements of broader Christian culture and incorporating them into their respective cultural contexts, while simultaneously offering their respective symbols to enrich the Christian context. The nature and terms of such an exchange ought to be the stuff of the dialogue between Christianity and culture. Again, within the Catholic context, Rome has unfortunately taken the model of a top-down monologue, as symbolized by the decision to hold the 1994 and 2009 meetings of the synod of African bishops in Rome rather than allow them to take place on the African continent.

If there are certain nonnegotiable elements of Christianity that cannot be compromised in the "dialogue" of inculturation, as Catholic theologians presume, then this study indicates that there are also nonnegotiable elements of VaShona culture that cannot be—and have not been—compromised, including the payment of *lobola* and the *tezvara's* consent for marriage, and the appropriate recognition and honoring of Mwari and ancestor spirits. Or, to borrow from James C. Scott, there were several "hidden transcripts" among VaShona Catholics at Jesuit missions.

If inculturation is to be a dialogue—that is, a conversation between equals—then not only must the church recognize that there are certain nonnegotiable elements of culture that cannot be compromised, but similarly, that adherents of a given cultural group must have not only the right not to receive the gospel message,[8] but also the right to purify the Christian message, that is, to select those aspects of the corpus of the entirety of two thousand years of Christian traditions and adapt them to their culture. Clearly, missionaries did not impart to Africans all of the Christian traditions that developed across the world over two millennia.[9] Rather, they selected those elements which they believed to be central and expected local cultures to adapt themselves to those elements (for instance, belief in one God, monogamous marriage, denial of ancestral spirits, and the like). Or to put it in Eugene Hillman's words, the church—particularly in Rome—must overcome its fear of innovation at the grassroots level. Consequently, many of the innovations and adaptations that developed did so underground, and away from formal ecclesiastical approbation, which would indicate some merit in Humphrey Fisher's contention that African independent churches point to "mixing" in an African context.

It remains to be seen whether inculturation as a dialogue between church and culture, as espoused by Catholic theologians, can be successful as a dialogue between equals. What is clear from the evidence presented here, however, is that at missions entrusted to the care of the Society of Jesus in Zimbabwe during the colonial era inculturation was less a dialogue of equals than a lecture (or sermon) replete with admonitions that the audience/congregation heard, listening to some parts and ignoring others. Or, in other words—referring back to Robin Horton and Lamin Sanneh—VaShona Catholics were consciously selective in receiving and incorporating elements of the Christian message from Western missionaries. The elements they chose to receive and incorporate made sense to them in the context of their historically developed and living cultures.

Inculturation as a dialogue of equals between the church and culture requires the boldness and broadness of vision of Paul of Tarsus, who preached the Christian message among first century gentiles of the Mediterranean basin; or Pope Gregory I ("the Great"), who, Bede the Venerable tells us, instructed Augustine of Canterbury to allow the continued use of early-seventh-century pagan English temples (after their cleansing with holy water) and feasts, including the slaughter of cattle, provided that they were offered to the Christian God; or Jesuit Matteo Ricci, who adapted the Christian message to Confucian philosophy and succeeded in preaching Catholic understanding of the Christian faith to the imperial court and in the city of Peking in early-seventeenth-century China; or Vincent Donovan, who attempted to preach the Christian message to Maasai during the twentieth century in Tanzania without the accretions of two millennia of Western culture.

Perhaps at one level the model of dialogue between church and culture is a useful one, and the only element necessary to make it effective is the will to respect culture as an equal partner in the dialogue on the part of church leaders. It was this lack of will, which closed the possibility of expressing Christianity in an African idiom, that led the Jesuits to ban the practice of *kurova guva* more than a hundred years ago and inspired members of the Zimbabwe Catholic Bishops' Conference—who were trained by the Jesuits at the one major seminary in Zimbabwe—to reexamine the approbation of the *kuchenura munhu* rites. Thus, the bishops, in discussing the possible revocation of one of the few inculturated Catholic liturgies in Zimbabwe, show the need for theologians to reevaluate and rethink the meaning, methods, and implications of inculturation. This is an instance where John Thornton's model of divine revelation as the basis of religious knowledge could be useful to Catholic theologians.

Thornton's model of interaction between African Christians and European missionaries as "a complex examination of revelations" conducted by both African and European Christians that was neither "a meshing of cosmologies" (that is, syncretism) nor simply "an intellectual enterprise" at once takes the reality of religious faith seriously and presumes a relative equality of both parties involved in the dialogue: both believe in a series of divine revelations; both examine the respective contents of the other's beliefs; and both are free to accept or reject elements of the other's beliefs as valid revelations of the divine on the human plane. Thornton developed his model from actual historical case studies, thus it simultaneously highlights VaShona Christians' successes in Africanizing the church and the Jesuits' failures to inculturate the church: because the Jesuits did not believe God had revealed himself to VaShona they ignored a long-standing teaching that "seeds of the Word" precede missionary arrivals.[10] Thornton's model of revelation ought to be extremely valuable for church theologians because it will push them to consider the respective historical contexts in which Christianity was adapted to various local cultures across the globe prior to the centralization of ecclesiastical power in Rome during the nineteenth century, amid an efflorescent European ethnocentric imperialism.

For the last two decades, however, many African theologians and Western theologians in Africa have been calling for "a new evangelization" of the African continent and the development of new methods of inculturation, including ones that respect and emphasize cultural plurality or pluriformity within the church's unity.[11] Some have even gone so far as to ask forgiveness from African Catholics for their failures and have called on the "universal" church to do the same.[12] This highlights inculturation discourse's limited success across the African continent. New methods of evangelization are necessary for the continent, but the prospects for any progress with inculturation are limited because the church's hierarchy suffers from "congenital and chronic ethnocentrism at the higher levels of ecclesiastical management" and a concomitant "fear of innovation at the grassroots level."[13] European ethnocentrism and fear of innovation at the African grassroots are also the primary causes of the general ineffectiveness of the church's inculturation theology. In this book, we have seen ample evidence of how the church's hierarchy—from the Vatican to local bishops, missionaries, and African clergy—narrowly circumscribed the conditions of possibility for inculturation in one African context, colonial Zimbabwe. More broadly, European ethnocentrism and racism remain constitutive elements of inculturation theology and foundational intellectual pillars in the church's present discourse on Africa.[14]

Several Catholic theologians have defined inculturation as a dialogue between Christianity (the church) and culture, but then say there are certain nonnegotiable elements of Christianity that cannot be compromised, and that as the church enters a culture, it is supposed to purify that culture of its imperfections, and once that has been accomplished the church can then implant itself and develop within the culture.[15] While this model of dialogue does not represent the entirety of the theological discourse on inculturation, and even though "the inculturation literature recognizes that 'culture' and 'church' are both abstractions, so that those in dialogue are always people who claim to be representing each of these realities, even though all such persons are shaped by each of them in very particular ways,"[16] the trope of African difference undergirds this intellectual formation.[17]

The *Instrumentum Laboris* (working document) for the October 2009 Synod of African Bishops called on the church in Africa "to make an examination of conscience,"[18] or "a review of one's past thoughts, words and actions for the purpose of ascertaining their conformity with, or difformity from, the moral law."[19] The examination of conscience is frequently associated with the Sacrament of Reconciliation (formerly "Penance" or "Confession"), which requires the penitent to confess his or her sins—which, according to the *Confiteor*, include acts of omission—and express contrition for them to a priest, who has the power to grant absolution. Despite some reasonably good social analysis of the contemporary socioeconomic context of the African continent, the drafters of the document make no acknowledgment of the failure—the sin of omission—of the church hierarchy or missionaries to recognize the "seeds of the Gospel" in African cultures and better inculturate the church in the past. Neither do they acknowledge the complicity of the church in supporting and benefiting from the transatlantic slave trade, or the European imperial conquest and colonial occupation of Africa during the nineteenth and twentieth centuries.[20] Neither do they express an act of contrition or *mea culpa* for the continued presence of European ethnocentrism and racism within the church.[21] The document reiterates the Vatican curia's distrust of African culture, expresses the superiority of the (Western/European) church over African culture, and calls for the church to purify African cultures. Of the sixty-seven citations at the end of the document, thirty-four refer to texts written or presented by John Paul II, with twenty-seven from the post-1994 synod's apostolic exhortation, *Ecclesia in Africa*; ten cite texts of Benedict XVI, and nine refer to documents written by various organs of the Vatican curia, whereas there are only two references to statements written by African bishops' conferences, one to the South African Catholic Bishops Conference's pastoral institute, and three to two different African patristic theologians (Cyprian and Augustine). Thus, the 2009 Special Synod of Bishops for Africa seems destined to be another "African Synod without Africa."[22]

From an African perspective, inculturation seems less a dialogue of equals and more a form of ecclesiastical imperialism, especially considering the church's practice of co-opting and incorporating non-Christian symbols and practices and reinvesting them with meanings different from those found in the host cultures.[23] If inculturation is to be a dialogue—that is, a conversation between equals—there must be parity between church and culture that the church thus far has not allowed to exist.

Notes

Preface

1. See Martinus L. Daneel, *Quest for Belonging: Introduction to a Study of African Independent Churches* (Gweru: Mambo Press, 1991), 88–97.

2. For an excellent explanation and example of this methodology, see Ranajit Guha, *Elementary Aspects of Peasant Insurgency in Colonial India* (Delhi: Oxford University Press, 1983). See the Bibliography herein for a list of oral sources.

3. Basil Davidson, *The Black Man's Burden: Africa and the Curse of the Nation-State* (New York: Times Books, 1992).

4. Jean Comaroff and John Comaroff, *Of Revelation and Revolution: Christianity, Colonialism, and Consciousness in South Africa* (Chicago: University of Chicago Press, 1991, 1998).

Introduction

1. Aylward Shorter, *Toward a Theology of Inculturation* (London: Geoffrey Chapman, 1988), 10–12.

2. Louis Luzbetak, *The Church and Cultures* (Maryknoll, N.Y.: Orbis Books, 1988).

3. Ranajit Guha, *Elementary Aspects of Peasant Insurgency in Colonial India* (Delhi: Oxford University Press, 1983), 4, 8–9.

4. James C. Scott, *Domination and the Arts of Resistance* (New Haven: Yale University Press, 1991).

5. Henry Bredekamp and Robert Ross, eds., *Missions and Christianity in South African History* (Johannesburg: Witswatersrand University Press, 1995), 5.

6. J. F. Ajayi, *Christian Missions in Nigeria, 1841–1891: The Making of a New Elite* (London: Longmans, 1965); Roland Oliver, *The Missionary Factor in East Africa* (London: Longmans, Green & Co., 1952).

7. Greg Cuthbertson, "Missionary Imperialism and Colonial Warfare: London Missionary Society Attitudes to the South African War, 1899–1902," *South African Historical Journal* 19 (1987): 93–113; "'Cave of Adullam': Missionary Reactions to Ethiopianism at Lovedale, 1898–1902," *Missionalia* 19 (1991): 57–64; Paul S. Landau, *The Realm of the Word: Language, Gender, and Christianity in a Southern African Kingdom* (Portsmouth, N.H.: Heinemann, 1995).

8. Terence O. Ranger, "Religious Movements and Politics in Sub-Saharan Africa," *African Studies Review* 29, no. 2 (June 1986): 1–69.

9. See O. U. Kalu, ed., *The History of Christianity in West Africa* (London: Longman, 1980); O. U. Kalu, *African Christianity: An African History* (Trenton, N.J.: Africa World Press, 2007); Richard Gray, *Black Christians and White Missionaries* (New Haven: Yale University Press, 1990); Thomas Blakely et al., *Religion in Africa* (Portsmouth, N.H.: Heinemann, 1994).

10. Lamin Sanneh, *West African Christianity: The Religious Impact* (London: C. Hurst & Co., 1983), and *Translating the Message: The Missionary Impact on Culture* (Maryknoll, N.Y.: Orbis Books, 1989).

11. See Robin Horton, "African Conversion," *Africa* 41, no. 2 (1971): 85–108. See also Robin Horton and J.D. Y. Peel, "Conversion and Confusion: A Rejoinder on Christianity in Eastern Nigeria," *Canadian Journal of African Studies* 10, no. 3 (1976): 482.

12. Horton and Peel, "Conversion and Confusion."

13. See Emile Durkheim, *The Elementary Forms of the Religious Life* (London: Allen & Unwin, 1964).

14. Humphrey J. Fisher, "Conversion Reconsidered: Some Historical Aspects of Religious Conversion in Black Africa," Africa 43, no. 1 (1972): 27–40.

15. David N. Beach, *The Shona and Their Neighbours* (Oxford: Blackwell Press, 1994).

16. Ngwabi Bhebe, *Christianity and Traditional Religion in Western Zimbabwe, 1859–1923* (London: Longman, 1979); Gabriel Setiloane, *The Image of God Among the Sotho-Tswana* (Rotterdam: A. A. Balkema, 1976).

17. Paul S. Landau, *The Realm of the Word: Language, Gender, and Christianity in a Southern African Kingdom* (Portsmouth, N.H.: Heinemann, 1995), xvi.

18. Gray, *Black Christians and White Missionaries*.

19. David Lan, *Guns and Rains: Guerrillas and Spirit Mediums in Zimbabwe* (Berkeley: University of California Press, 1985); T. O. Ranger, *Peasant Consciousness and Guerrilla War in Zimbabwe* (Berkeley: University of California Press, 1985); Janice McLaughlin, *On the Frontline: Catholic Missions in Zimbabwe's Liberation War* (Harare: Baobab Books, 1996); Carl F. Hallencreutz and Ambrose M. Moyo, eds., *Church and State in Zimbabwe* (Gweru: Mambo Press, 1988), Volume 3, Part I, 29–194; Terence Ranger, *"Are We Not Also Men?": The Samkange Family & African Politics in Zimbabwe, 1920–1964* (Portsmouth, N.H.: Heinemann, 1995); Ngwabi Bhebe and Terence Ranger, eds., *Society in Zimbabwe's Liberation War* (London: J. Currey, 1996); Ngwabi Bhebe, *The ZAPU and ZANU Guerrilla Warfare and the Evangelical Lutheran Church in Zimbabwe* (Gweru: Mambo Press, 1999); Luzbetak, *The Church and Cultures*; David Maxwell, *Christians and Chiefs in Zimbabwe: A Social History of the Hwesa People* (Westport, Conn.: Praeger, 1999); David Maxwell, *African Gifts of the Spirit: Pentecostalism & the Rise of a Zimbabwean Transnational Religious Movement* (Athens: Ohio University Press, 2006).

20. A. J. Dachs and W. F. Rea, *The Catholic Church and Zimbabwe, 1879–1979* (Gwelo: Mambo Press, 1979); C. J. M. Zvobgo, *A History of Christian Missions in Zimbabwe, 1890–1939* (Gweru: Mambo Press, 1996).

21. See note 19.

22. David Newbury, "Missionary Arrival in a Fragile Polity: Rwanda, 1900–1926," paper presented at the American Catholic Historical Association Spring Meeting, University of Scranton, March 2003.

23. See Oyeronke Oyewumi, *The Invention of Women: Making an African Sense of Western Gender Discourses*, (Minneapolis: University of Minnesota Press, 1997).

24. Maxwell, *Christians and Chiefs in Zimbabwe*, 4.

25. E. E. Evans-Pritchard, *Theories of Primitive Religion* (Oxford: Clarendon Press, 1965), 14–15.

26. Ibid., 15.

27. Ibid.

28. Ibid., 17. Emphasis in original.

29. Ibid.

30. Ibid.

31. See http://web.utk.edu/~rhackett/durban.html for the IAHR 2000 Durban Congress Program; see http://www.iahr.dk for the IAHR more generally.

32. See James Cox, "Identifying African Methodologies in the Study of Religions," paper delivered at IAHR Congress, Durban, South Africa, August 2000.

33. E. E. Evans-Pritchard, *Nuer Religion* (New York: Oxford University Press, 1956), vii.

34. See, e.g., Philip Peek, ed., *African Divination: Ways of Knowing* (Bloomington: Indiana University Press, 1991).

35. Philip Gleason, *Keeping the Faith: American Catholicism Past and Present* (Notre Dame, Ind.: University of Notre Dame Press, 1987), 219.

36. Ibid., 220.

37. Thomas Spear, "Towards the History of African Christianity," conference paper presented at Africans Meeting Missionaries: Rethinking Colonial Encounters, University of Minnesota, May 1997, 8.

38. Ibid., 8, 17.

39. See Jacques Derrida, *Of Grammatology* (Baltimore: Johns Hopkins University Press, 1976).

40. John Thornton, *Africa and Africans in the Making of the Atlantic World, 1400–1800*, 2nd ed. (Cambridge: Cambridge University Press, 1998).

41. See Benjamin C. Ray, *African Religions: Symbol, Ritual, and Community*, 2nd ed. (New York: Prentice-Hall, 1999).

42. See, e.g., M. E. Chamberlain, *The Scramble for Africa* (New York: Longman, 1998); Thomas Pakenham, *The Scramble for Africa* (New York: Avon Books, 1992).

43. For the best analysis, see McLaughlin, *On the Frontline*.

44. See Jean Comaroff and John Comaroff, *Of Revelation and Revolution: Christianity, Colonialism, and Consciousness in South Africa* (Chicago: University of Chicago Press, 1991).

45. Cited in Oliver Alozie Onwubiko, *Theory and Practice of Inculturation (An African Perspective)* (Enugu: Diocese of Ahiara, 1992), 1–2.

46. See Shorter, *Towards a Theology of Inculturation*, 10–11. Onwubiko provided several examples of Jesuit usage of the term in Arrupe's speeches and letters, and in the writings of other Jesuits, including Karl Rahner, in *Theory and Practice of Inculturation*, 3–6.

47. Onwubiko, *Theory and Practice of Inculturation*, 7; Shorter, *Towards a Theology of Inculturation*, 10.

48. Cited in Shorter, *Towards a Theology of Inculturation*, 11.

49. Ibid.

50. The incarnation in Catholic theology refers to the belief that God became human n the person of Jesus Christ. In this context, it refers to the church continuing to bring the message of Christ to the nations (that is, peoples or ethnic groups) of the world in respective cultural idioms that each group will understand. See Frederick E. Chiromba, *Evangelization and Inculturation* (Gweru: Mambo Press, 1989), 4.

51. Vincent J. Donovan, *Christianity Rediscovered* (Maryknoll, N.Y.: Orbis Books, 1982), 70.

52. See Chiromba, *Evangelization and Inculturation*; Eugene Hillman, *Towards an African Christianity* (Mahwah, N.J.: Paulist Press, 1991).

53. Donovan, *Christianity Rediscovered*, 102.

54. Ibid., 119–121.

55. The existence of the eastern churches in communion with Rome points to the time in history when there was greater development of the local churches and, consequently, greater inculturation of the church (that is, prior to the schism of the eleventh century). See Luzbetak, *The Church and Cultures*, Chapter 3, for a concise history of the missionary activities and stages of missiological development within the church.

56. See Donovan, *Christianity Rediscovered*, 119–120. For an interesting historical critique of Donovan and the experiences of Catholic missionaries among the Maasai, see Dorothy L. Hodgson, *The Church of Women: Gendered Encounters Between Maasai and Missionaries* (Bloomington: Indiana University Press, 2005).

57. Hillman, *Toward an African Christianity*, 1.

58. Ibid., 3.

59. Ibid., 38. This was true of several subsequent declarations of Popes Paul VI and John Paul II, as well as several subsequent episcopal synods.

60. Ibid., 41.

61. Thornton, *Africa and Africans in the Making of the Atlantic World*, 235–236.

62. See Zvobgo, *A History of Christian Missions in Zimbabwe*.

1. A Failed Mission, Contesting Colonial Rule, and Ecclesiastical Developments

1. See David N. Beach, *The Shona and Their Neighbours* (Oxford: Blackwell, 1994); Beach, *A Zimbabwean Past: Shona Dynastic Histories and Oral Traditions* (Gweru: Mambo Press, 1994); S. I. G. Mudenge, *A Political History of*

Munhumutapa, c. 1400–1902 (Harare: Zimbabwe Publishing House, 1988); T. O. Ranger, *Revolt in Southern Rhodesia, 1896–97*, (Evanston, Ill.: Northwestern University Press, 1967); Elizabeth A. Eldredge, "Sources of Conflict in Southern Africa, c. 1800–1830: The 'Mfecane' Reconsidered," *Journal of African History* 33, no. 1 (1992): 1–35; Norman Etherington, *The Great Treks: The Transformation of Southern Africa, 1815–1854* (London: Pearson Education, 2001).

2. See António da Silva, *Mentalidade missiológica dos Jesuitas em Moçambique antes de 1759* (Lisbon: Junta de Investigacões do Ultramar, 1967).

3. See in particular Beach, *The Shona and Their Neighbours*; Beach, *A Zimbabwean Past*; Mudenge, *A Political History of Munhumutapa*.

4. Ngwabi Bhebe, *Christianity and Traditional Religion in Western Zimbabwe, 1859–1923* (London: Longman, 1979), xii.

5. Ibid., 1–2. See also Ranger, *Revolt in Southern Rhodesia*, and Beach, *The Shona and Their Neighbours*.

6. Bhebe, *Christianity and Religion in Western Zimbabwe*, 3–4, 19–20.

7. Ibid., 65–66.

8. For an excellent summary of the debate see Herbert Chimhundu, "Early Missionaries and the Ethnolinguistic Factor during the 'Invention of Tribalism' in Zimbabwe," *Journal of African History* 33, no. 1 (1992): 87–109. See also Ranger, *Revolt in Southern Rhodesia*; David N. Beach, "Ndebele Raiders and Shona Power," *Journal of African History* 15 (1974): 633–651; Julian Cobbing, "The Absent Priesthood: Another Look at the Rhodesian Risings of 1896–1897," *Journal of African History* 18, no. 1 (1977): 69–85.

9. See Bhebe, *Christianity and Traditional Religion in Western Zimbabwe*, and "Some Aspects of Ndebele Relations with the Shona in the Nineteenth Century," *Rhodesian History* 4 (1973): 31–38. See also Bhebe and Lawrence Vambe, *An Ill-Fated People: Zimbabwe Before and After Rhodes* (London: Heinemann, 1972), 58–72.

10. A. J. Dachs and W. F. Rea, *The Catholic Church and Zimbabwe, 1879–1979* (Gwelo: Mambo Press, 1979); see also William Eric Brown, *The Catholic Church in South Africa: From Its Origins to the Present Day* (London: Burns & Oates, 1960), 101–102.

11. The following is taken primarily from Dachs and Rea, *The Catholic Church and Zimbabwe*, 16–29. See also the introductions to Michael Gelfand, ed., *Gubulawayo and Beyond: Letters and Journals of the Early Jesuit Missionaries to Zambesia (1879–1887)* (London: Geoffrey Chapman, 1968), and Moira

Lloyd, trans., *Journey to Gubulawayo: Letters from Frs. H. Depelchin and C. Croonenberghs, S.J., 1879–1881* (Bulawayo: Books of Rhodesia, 1979).

12. Dachs and Rea, *The Catholic Church and Zimbabwe*, 19.
13. Ibid., 22–23.
14. Ibid.
15. Ibid., 23–24.
16. Ibid., 24–25.
17. Ibid., 27.
18. Ibid.
19. Ibid., 27–28. The treaty was deliberately misinterpreted to Lobengula, who was led to believe that he was allowing a limited number of gold prospectors into VaShona territory, whereas the actual document granted Rhodes and his associates control over extensive areas between the Limpopo River and the Great Lakes region of Central Africa.
20. Ibid.
21. Ibid., 25.
22. Gelfand, *Gubulawayo and Beyond*, 22.
23. Ibid., 19–21.
24. Archivum Britanicum Societatis Iessu, London (ABSI hereafter), Zambezi Mission Papers (ZMP hereafter), Weld letter, November 19, 1879.
25. Bhebe, *Christianity and Religion in Western Zimbabwe*, 61–63.
26. *Letters and Notices* (L&N hereafter), July 1882, 150–151, de Wit to Weld, January 16, 1882.
27. L&N, January 1882, 2–3, Depelchin to Beckx, October 5, 1880.
28. ABSI, W/11, Weld letter January 6, 1882.
29. ABSI, W/11, Weld letter July 6, 1882.
30. See William V. Bangert, *A History of the Society of Jesus* (St. Louis, Mo.: Institute of Jesuit Sources, 1986); Philip Caraman, *The Lost Paradise: An Account of the Jesuits in Paraguay, 1607–1768* (London: Sidgwick and Jackson, 1975).
31. Dachs and Rea, *The Catholic Church and Zimbabwe*, 24.
32. Ibid., 25.
33. Ibid.
34. Ibid. See also Gelfand, *Gubulawayo and Beyond*.
35. See Charles van Onselen, *Chibaro: African Mine Labour in Southern Rhodesia, 1900–1933* (London: Pluto Press, 1976); Robin Palmer, *Aspects of Rhodesian Land Policy, 1890–1936* (Salisbury: Central African Historical Association, 1968); Robin Palmer, "War and Land in Rhodesia in the 1890s," in

War and Society in Africa, ed. Bethwell A. Ogot (Portland, Ore.: Frank Cass, 1972), 85–107; Robin Palmer, *Land and Racial Domination in Rhodesia* (Berkeley: University of California Press, 1977); David Johnson, "Settler Farmers and Coerced African Labour in Southern Rhodesia, 1936–1946," *Journal of African History* 33, no. 1 (1992): 111–128; Terence Ranger, *The African Voice in Southern Rhodesia, 1898–1930*, (London: Heinemann Educational, 1970); Terence Ranger, *Peasant Consciousness and Guerrilla War in Zimbabwe* (Berkeley: University of California Press, 1985).

36. See Ranger, *Revolt in Southern Rhodesia* and *Peasant Consciousness in Zimbabwe*; C. J. M. Zvobgo, *A History of Christian Missions in Zimbabwe, 1890–1939* (Gweru: Mambo Press, 1996); Elizabeth Isichei, *A History of Christianity in Africa* (Grand Rapids, Mich.: Eerdmans, 1995).

37. J. D. Omer-Cooper, "Central Africa, c. 1900–1953" and "Central Africa Since 1953," in *The Making of Modern Africa*, ed. A. D. Afigbo et al. (Essex: Longmans, 1986), 2:233–293.

38. Janice McLaughlin, *On the Frontline: Catholic Missions in Zimbabwe's Liberation War* (Harare: Baobab Books, 1996).

39. Data from the Instituto dos Arquivos Nacionais/Torre de Tombo, Congregação das Missões, Lisbon.

40. Several German Jesuits had completed their religious formation in England during the 1870s and 1880s as a result of Bismarck's *Kulturkampf*. Similarly, the (Catholic) German Foreign Mission Society, or Society of the Divine Word (or SVD Fathers and Brothers), founded in 1870, was headquartered in Steyl, Holland, until the superior general moved to Rome.

41. Dachs and Rea, *The Catholic Church and Zimbabwe*, 3–4.

42. See M. E. Chamberlain, *The Scramble for Africa* (New York: Longman, 1998); Thomas Pakenham, *The Scramble for Africa* (New York: Avon Books, 1992).

43. Conversation with Fr. Karl-Ferdinand Schmidt, S.J., Jesuit Archives of Zimbabwe (JAZ hereafter), July 28, 2000.

44. JAZ, Box 109.

45. Dachs and Rea, *The Catholic Church and Zimbabwe*, 172–174.

46. Ibid. In 1986, Chinoyi (formerly Sinoia) became a diocese. Recker continued to serve as bishop until his death in early 2004.

47. Conversation with Fr. Clement Freyer, S.J., St. Ignatius High School, Chishawasha, May 24, 2000.

48. Based on several conversations with British and German Jesuits about a variety of issues, including potential candidates to succeed Fr. Conrad Lansberg, S.J., as provincial in 2002.

49. Dachs and Rea, *The Catholic Church and Zimbabwe*, 64–66.

50. Ibid., 65, 70–71.

51. Ibid., 68–71.

52. Ibid., 73–74.

53. Ibid., 74–77.

54. Ibid., 143–147, 181–182.

2. "The Struggle Approximated to the Heroic": African Catholic Women Becoming Nuns in Colonial Zimbabwe, 1922–1965

1. Terence Ranger, "Women in the Politics of Makoni District, Zimbabwe, 1890–1980." I am particularly grateful to Elizabeth Schmidt for providing a copy of this essay.

2. Elizabeth Schmidt, *Peasants, Traders, and Wives: Shona Women in the History of Zimbabwe, 1870–1939* (Harare: Baobab, 1992), 96–97, 136–137; Diana Jeater, *Marriage, Perversion, and Power: The Construction of Moral Discourse in Southern Rhodesia, 1894–1930* (Oxford: Clarendon Press, 1993), 250–251.

3. Ranger, "Women in the Politics of Makoni District," 15–16. The Sisters of the Precious Blood were allowed to return to Monte Cassino mission in 1918 to serve as nurses in the area around the mission, and the Mariannhill fathers and brothers returned in 1920. See A. J. Dachs and W. F. Rea, *The Catholic Church and Zimbabwe, 1879–1979* (Gwelo: Mambo Press, 1979), 73. Although Ranger refers to the Mariannhillers as "Trappists" throughout his essay, the Congregation of Mariannhill Missionaries separated from the Order of the Cistercians of the Strict Observance, or Trappists, in 1909.

4. Dachs and Rea, *The Catholic Church and Zimbabwe*, 139.

5. AAH, Box 545/B, C. L. Carbutt [Superintendent of Natives, Victoria], "Memorandum Concerning Native Girl Agnes alias Rowesai," July 16, 1922; Sr. M. Rudolfina, CPS to Fr. Prefect [Edward Parry, S.J.], September 12, 1922.

6. AAH, Box 545/B, Sr. Rudolfina to Fr. Parry, S.J., September 12, 1922.

7. Ranger, "Women in the Politics of Makoni District," 12–13. For the issue of pledging girls in marriage, see 7–10.

8. Ibid., 16.

9. AAH, Box 545/B, Annexure (September 28, 1922) to Charles Coghlan, "Rights of Native Girls to Remain Single and to Enter the Religious Life," April 30, 1923; see also Jesuit Archives of Zimbabwe (JAZ hereafter), Box 300, File 1 (300/1 hereafter), Coghlan to Francis Johanny, S.J., April 25, 1923. There is also a copy of the full text of Coghlan's opinion in JAZ, Box 300/1. In 1923, Coghlan was elected as the first prime minister of Southern Rhodesia.

10. AAH, Box 545/B, Charles Coghlan, "Rights of Native Girls," 3–4.

11. Ibid., 2, 4–5.

12. Ibid., 9–10.

13. See AAH, Box 545/B, F. Johanny to Reverend Mother Superior, Monte Cassino Mission, May 12, 1927; Declarations of Damiano Bamu, Dominico Chikanya, June 22, 1927; Box 546/A, Declaration of Willibald Tinargwo, April 27, 1928; Declaration of Raymond Bonga, December 20, 1928; Declaration of Karani Shoniwa, December 25, 1928; Declaration of Mashumba Chigara, April 28, 1929.

14. See, e.g., AAH, Box 545/B, correspondence dealing with the case of Clara Margwisa.

15. Dachs and Rea, *The Catholic Church and Zimbabwe*, 139.

16. Ibid., 139.

17. AAH, Box 556/B, "Copy and Approbation of the Rules for the Congregation of the Holy Trinity."

18. See B. Randolph, "Charity—Sisters of," *Catholic Encyclopedia* (New York: Universal Knowledge Foundation, 1913), 3:605.

19. JAZ, Box 195/3, Letter of J. Apel [to Edward Parry], November 18, 1920.

20. JAZ, Box 13, Robert Brown, S.J., to Francis Johanny, S.J., February 6, 1929.

21. JAZ, Box 100/3 Emil Schmitz, S.J., to Francis Johanny, S.J., July 15, 1926.

22. Ibid.

23. JAZ, Chishawasha *Historia Domus* (typescript), August 4, 1926.

24. Dachs and Rea, *The Catholic Church and Zimbabwe*, 139.

25. AAH, 545/B, Francis Johanny, S.J., to Reverend Mother Superior, Monte Cassino, Macheke, May 12, 1927: "Native Girls from Kutama Mission Who Desire to Join the Daughters of St. Francis"; AAH, 546/A, Declaration of Lucas Chiteka, August 15, 1931; Declaration of Veronica Chiteka, February

1932. In 1929, the Jesuits engineered their takeover of the Mariannhill missions in the eastern highlands of Southern Rhodesia in exchange for the Jesuits' missions in Matabeleland in the southwest of Southern Rhodesia. See Dachs and Rea, *The Catholic Church and Zimbabwe*, 74–77. Veronica Chiteka entered the Daughters of St. Francis; she had been received as a candidate at Triashill mission in 1928.

26. AAH, 545/B, Chief Native Commissioner to Fr. Collingridge, April 18, 1931.

27. AAH, 545/B, Chief Native Commissioner to Fr. Collingridge, July 3, 1931.

28. AAH, 545/B, Chief Native Commissioner to Chichester, November 12, 1931.

29. AAH, 545/B Chichester to Chief Native Commissioner, Salisbury, n.d.

30. AAH, Box 545/B, Aston Chichester, "The Native Sisterhood," December 1941.

31. Ibid.

32. Ibid.

33. Ibid.

34. Interview with Sr. Bernadette Garatsa, LCBL, Chichester Convent, Chishawasha Mission, May 23, 2000. I would like to thank Sister Illuminata Nyawata, LCBL, the superior of the Chichester convent, for her assistance in arranging and translating during the interview with Sister Bernadette.

35. AAH, Box 546/B, Adalberto Fleischer to Chichester, April 8, 1931; Chichester to Cardinal Prefect of Propaganda Fide, December 27, 1931.

36. AAH, Box 546/B, von Rossum to Chichester, February 2, 1932.

37. AAH, Box 546/B, Chichester to von Rossum, March 15, 1932; von Rossum to Chichester, April 8, 1932.

38. AAH, Box 546/B, Chichester to Alfred Burbridge, S.J., May 26, 1932. There is no evidence in the Chishawasha records in the Jesuit Archives of Zimbabwe of an African woman being received as a postulant as early as 1919. It is possible, however, that such a woman may have been admitted as a candidate for the Dominican sisters. Additionally, although it is not conclusive, it is probable that the four women admitted were part of the same group admitted as "postulants" and entrusted to the care of the Dominicans in 1926. See Ferrera Weinzierl, *The Dominicans, 1891–1991: A Story of Vision, Poverty and Courage, Faith and Hope, Service with Love* (Harare: Dominican Sisters, 1991),

24. On the Catholic liturgical calendar, June 3 is the memorial feast day of Saint Charles Lwanga and the Ugandan martyrs.

39. Dachs and Rea, *The Catholic Church and Zimbabwe*, 140; Interview with Sister Bernadette Garatsa, LCBL, Chishawasha Mission, May 23, 2000; AAH, Box 546/B, "The religious habit is taken by 19 Native girls at Makumbe on the Feast of the Immaculate Conception"; "18 Natives take vows as Nuns in South [sic] Rhodesia"; "An Historic Ceremony in Southern Rhodesia."

40. Interview with Sr. Bernadette Garatsa.

41. Among VaShona of the late nineteenth and early twentieth centuries, particularly in the southern and western regions of colonial Zimbabwe, unmarried women served as officials, or Bonga, at shrines dedicated to Mwari, the supreme deity in the VaShona religious system. According to the tradition that a Jesuit missionary received and noted, these women were "entirely devoted to a life of prayer and intercession," and their families received no bride price because it was considered an honor for their daughter to have been chosen. During the Mwari controversy of the early 1920s, Francis Richartz, one of the founders of Chishawasha mission, noted that some of the Bonga were called Mwari (their function was to serve as "the voice of Mwari," that is, to speak the oracles of Mwari to those who came to consult it), and as such they were tantamount to false prophets who were not to be taken seriously. Although the church's superiors followed Richartz's lead, one of the first LCBL sisters recognized the parallel. See M. F. C. Bourdillon, *The Shona Peoples: An Ethnography of the Contemporary Shona, with Special Reference to Their Religion* (Gweru: Mambo Press, 1987), 279–281; JAZ, Box 24/1, Jerome O'Hea, S.J., to F. A. Barry, April 9, 1937; JAZ, Box 260/2, Undated miscellaneous notes in Richartz's hand; see also Chapter 5; interview with Sr. Bernadette Garatsa.

42. Interview with Sr. Bernadette Garatsa. See also Dachs and Rea, *The Catholic Church and Zimbabwe*, 140.

43. Ibid.; conversation with Rev. Albert Plangger, S.M.B., Mambo House, Harare, May 16, 2000.

44. Ibid.

45. Ibid. Ninety-eight sisters professed final vows on January 6, 1960. See JAZ, Box 108, Seminary *Historia Domus*, January 6, 1960.

46. Interview with Sr. Bernadette Garatsa.

47. AAH, Box 544/A, Chichester to Bishop Francis Hennemann, n.d. but c. December 7, 1934.

48. See AAH, Box 544/A, Chichester Circular Letter to Superiors of Missions, November 11, 1934.

49. AAH, Box 544/A, Chichester to Bishop Francis Hennemann.

50. ibid.

51. AAH, Box 544/A, Rev. J. Brown to Chichester, December 28, 1932.

52. cf. JAZ, Box 300/1, "Draft Constitutions & Rules for the Poor Children of Our Blessed Lady, 1932" and AAH, 544/B(2), *Constitutions of the Little Children of Our Blessed Lady* (Gwelo: Catholic Mission Press, 1959).

53. AAH, Box 546, File B, Cardinal Pacelli to LCBL Sisters, January 3, 1935.

54. AAH, Box 546/B, LCBL Sisters to Chichester, n.d. [c. 1937]. Emphasis in the original.

55. ibid.

56. AAH, Box 545/B, V.L.P. Fowke [Secretary of the Catholic Council for International Relations] to C. C. Martindale, S.J. [addressed at the Jesuit Provincial Superior's residence in London], February 26, 1932; JAZ, Box 24/1, Jerome O'Hea, S.J., to Florence A. Barry, February 12, 1937, April 9, 1937, June 21, 1937; AAH, Box 545/B, O'Hea to Chichester, January 11, 1938; Chichester to Barry, February 25, 1938; Barry to Chichester, March 7, 1938.

57. AAH, Box 544/A, Chichester Circular Letter to Superiors of Missions, November 11, 1934.

58. Ibid.

59. Interview with Sister Bernadette Garatsa, LCBL; interview with Sister Catherine Mazorodze, LCBL, Chichester Convent, Chishawasha Mission, May 23, 2000; interview with Mother Rocha Mushonga, LCBL, Visitation Convent, Makumbi Mission, May 28, 2000.

60. Interview with Sister Catherine Mazorodze.

61. Interview with Sr. Hyacinth Gerbecks, O.P., Africa Synod House, Harare, May 15, 2000.

62. For more on *Rerum Ecclesiae*, see Chapter 3.

63. AAH, Box 546/B, Aston Chichester, "The Native Sisterhood," December 1941.

64. AAH, Box 546/B, Anonymous letter to Chichester, n.d. [c. 1943]: "Not that we are not satisfied with the treatment or that we are not happy. On the contrary, we are very happy and I must say that I often wish that our Lord could work a miracle and make me like [the] others. Now Dear Reverend Father, I was thinking that if there is a Congregation of the Coloured would it not be good that I join them? But I would not do anything of my own will. I do what you tell me to do.... I cannot pray, and I think of nothing else than that, therefore, dear Reverend Father, do help me if you can. I was always

looking forward that there would be vocations at St. John's [the predominantly "Coloured" parish in Salisbury] one day and that a congregation would be started there [and] that we could join them. And don't you think that there would be vocations alright if the girls would see one of their own there as a Sister because I always think that perhaps they don't know where to go. Once more not as my will but as your will." See also Sister M. Immaculata, LCBL, to Chichester, October 10, 1946.

65. Michael F. C. Bourdillon, *The Shona Peoples* (Gweru: Mambo Press, 1987), 36–49. See also Dominique Meekers, "The Noble Custom of Roora: The Marriage Practices of the Shona of Zimbabwe," *Ethnology* 32 (1993): 35–38.

66. Bourdillon, *The Shona Peoples*, 36–37.

67. See Schmidt, *Peasants, Traders, and Wives*, 97.

68. AAH, Box 544 (LCBL Sisters), File A, Declaration of Mashumba Chigara, April 28, 1929. I am grateful to Dr. Isabel Mukonyora for assistance in translating this document.

69. JAZ, Box 24/1, O'Hea to Florence Barry, April 9, 1937; Schmidt, *Peasants, Traders, and Wives*, 97; Dachs and Rea, *The Catholic Church and Zimbabwe, 1879–1979*, 141.

70. JAZ, Box 24/1, O'Hea to F. A. Barry, April 9, 1937.

71. AAH, Box 545/B, J. Apel to Chichester, August 10, 1935.

72. AAH, Box 545/B, Assistant Native Commissioner Bindura to Chichester, September 13, 1935.

73. AAH, Box 545/B, Chichester to A. Yardley [Assistant Native Commissioner Bindura], September 19, 1935.

74. AAH, Box 545/B, D.C.H. Parkhurst to Superior, Chishawasha Mission, June 7, 1940.

75. AAH, Box 545/B, Ferguson to Parkhurst, June 12, 1940.

76. AAH, Box 545/B, Parkhurst to Ferguson, June 12, 1940. Emphasis in the original.

77. AAH, Box 545/B, Parkhurst to Ferguson, June 14, 1940.

78. AAH, Box 545/B, Ferguson to Parkhurst, June 15, 1940.

79. AAH, Box 545/B, Parkhurst to Ferguson, June 15, 1940.

80. AAH, Box 545/B, Parkhurst to Fr. Burbridge, June 17, 1940.

81. AAH, Box 545/B, Parkhurst to Ferguson, August 16, 1940.

82. AAH, Box 545/B, Ferguson to Burbridge, August 17, 1940.

83. Ibid.

84. AAH, Box 545/B, Parkhurst to Chichester, August 19, 1940.

85. Ibid.

86. AAH, Box 545/B, Parkhurst to Chichester, August 26, 1940. Additionally, there is a note in Burbridge's hand: "Fr. Ferguson notified & girl Maria sent to Chishawasha 27.8.40."

87. AAH, Box 545/B, Baptismal Certificate of Catherine Mazorodze, No. 6477.

88. Interview with Sister Catherine Mazorodze.

89. Ibid.

90. According to the archival documentation, Catherine was baptized on May 28, 1953. Sister Catherine recalled that she was baptized in 1954. Given the suspect nature of the documentation, I follow Sister Catherine's chronology. See AAH, Box 545/B, Baptismal Certificate of Catherine Mazorodze, No. 6477; interview with Sister Catherine Mazorodze.

91. Ibid.; AAH, Box 545/B, Bevis Collings to Chichester, July 15, 1956.

92. AAH, Box 545/B, Chichester to S. E. Morris, July 25, 1956.

93. Ibid.

94. AAH, Box 545/B, Morris to Chichester, July 30, 1956. Emphasis in original.

95. Ibid.

96. AAH, Box 545/B, Chichester to Morris, August 5, 1956.

97. AAH, Box 545/B, Morris to Chichester, September 7, 1956.

98. AAH, Box 545/B, Chichester to Morris, September 10, 1956.

99. Interview with Sister Catherine Mazorodze.

100. AAH, Box 545/B, Chichester to Chief Native Commissioner, January 7, 1950.

101. Ibid.

102. AAH, Box 545/B, Secretary of Native Affairs to Chichester, February 6, 1950.

103. AAH, Box 545/B, Assistant Chief Native Commissioner A. G. Yardley to Chichester, February 11, 1950.

104. Ibid.

105. AAH, Box 545/B, Chichester Memorandum to File, February 11, 1950.

106. Ibid.

107. AAH, Box 545/B, Chichester to Yardley, February 15, 1950.

108. AAH, Box 545/B, "Statement by African Francis Morisi [sic]," n.d., 5.

109. AAH, Box 545/B, Francis Markall to Chichester, February 28, 1950.

110. Ibid.

111. AAH, Box 545/B, L.M.N. Hodson, "Opinion: In Re the Vicariate Apostolic of Salisbury," July 8, 1950, 2.

112. Ibid.

113. Ibid., 2–3. For an analysis of the different payments involved in the VaShona marriage process, see Meekers, "The Noble Custom of Roora."

114. Hodson, "Opinion," 3, 7. Emphasis in original.

115. Ibid., 4–5.

116. Ibid., 5–6.

117. AAH, Box 545/B, Chichester to A. G. Yardley, February 15, 1950.

118. AAH, Box 545/B, Notes from Maurice Rea, S.J., Superior of Makumbi mission, n.d.

119. AAH, Box 545/B, Chichester to Chief Native Commissioner Powys-Jones, December 4, 1951.

120. AAH, Box 545/B, Anonymous notes concerning Francis Morosi.

121. AAH, Box 545/B, "Statement by African Francis Morisi [sic]," 6.

122. Ibid.

123. Ibid., 7.

124. Ibid., 8.

125. AAH, Box 545/B, Secretary for Native Affairs to Chichester, December 13, 1951.

126. AAH, Box 545/B, Chichester to C.N.C. Powys-Jones, February 1, 1952.

127. AAH, Box 545/B, Secretary for Native Affairs to Chichester, January 31, 1952.

128. AAH, Box 545/B, Chichester to Secretary for Native Affairs, February 2, 1952.

129. Ibid.

130. AAH, Box 545/B, Chichester to Mr. Kerr, May 16, 1952.

131. AAH, Box 545/B, Clara Margwisa to Chichester, September 24, 1950; October 15, 1950, April 1, 1951; Chichester to Clara Margwisa, April 4, 1951. From appendix to "Statement by African Francis Morisi [sic],"Chichester to Clara, August 22, 1950; September 9, 1950; October 4, 1950; April 8, 1951; October 3, 1951; February 23, 1952; June 29, 1952; July 31, 1952; Markall to Clara, September 13, 1950; May 26, 1952.

132. AAH, Box 545/B, Clara Margwisa to Chichester, September 24, 1950.

133. AAH, Box 545/B, Clara Margwisa to Chichester, September 30, 1951; October 10, 1951; October 26, 1951.

134. From appendix to "Statement by African Francis Morisi [sic]," AAH, Box 545/B, Chichester to Clara Margwisa, October 4, 1950.

135. AAH, Box 545/B, Clara Margwisa to Chichester, May 30, 1952.
136. AAH, Box 545/B, Clara Margwisa to Chichester, June 22, 1952.
137. AAH, Box 545/B, Chichester to Clara Margwisa, June 29, 1952.
138. Reports of the exact date conflict. Francis Morosi's statement said that she arrived home on August 19 (p.8); the N.C. Goromonzi claimed that she arrived home on August 13 (AAH, Box 545/B, N.C. Goromonzi to Chichester, September 4, 1952); and Chichester approximated that she returned home around August 21, 1952 (AAH, Box 545/B, Chichester to N.C. Goromonzi, August 28, 1952).
139. AAH, Box 545/B, N.C. Goromonzi to Chichester, September 4, 1952; "Statement by African Francis Morisi [sic]," 8–9.
140. AAH, Box 545/B, "Statement by African Francis Morisi [sic]," 9.
141. AAH, Box 545/B, Clara Margwisa to Chichester, October 8, 1952.
142. AAH, Box 545/B, Chichester to Clara Margwisa, October 8, 1952. The normal course of formation for the LCBL Sisters at the time was to spend three years as a candidate, one year as a postulant, and then two years in the novitiate before being admitted to first vows.
143. AAH, Box 545/B, J. Friedrich, S.J., to Chichester, October 20, 1952.
144. AAH, Box 545/B, Markall to Chichester, November 16, 1952.
145. See Meekers, "The Noble Custom of Roora," and Bourdillon, *The Shona People*.
146. AAH, Box 545/B, Markall to Chichester, November 16, 1952.
147. AAH, Box 545/B, R.D. Lynch to Chichester, February 26, 1953.
148. AAH, Box 545/B, Chichester to Lynch, March 1, 1953.
149. AAH, Box 545/B, Chichester to Markall, March 1, 1953.
150. AAH, Box 545/B, Markall to Chichester, November 16, 1952.
151. AAH, Box 545/B, Sr. Mary Aquinatia, C.P.S. to Chichester, May 14, 1953.
152. Ibid.
153. AAH, Box 545/B, Markall to Chichester, May 23, 1953.
154. AAH, Box 545/B, Chichester to Clara Margwisa, June 4, 1953.
155. Interview with Mother Rocha Mushonga, Visitation Convent, Makumbi Mission, May 28, 2000.
156. AAH, Box 412, File C, Archbishop Francis Markall to T. Mudeke, June 11, 1965.
157. Interview with Mother Rocha Mushonga.
158. Interview with Sister Catherine Mazorodze.

159. Interview with Mother Rocha Mushonga; interview with Sister Catherine Mazorodze.

160. Mother Rocha did not elaborate on the specifics of what "culturally sensitive education" entailed.

161. See Ranger, "Women in the Politics of Makoni District," 17–18; Schmidt, *Peasants, Traders, and Wives*, 94–97; Jeater, *Marriage, Perversion, and Power*, 250; Dachs and Rea, *The Catholic Church and Zimbabwe*, 140–141.

162. Interview with Sister Bernadette Garatsa; interview with Sister Catherine Mazorodze; interview with Mother Rocha Mushonga. See also AAH, Box 545/B, "Negotiations: Parental Opposition to Girls Wishing to be Nuns, 1923–1956," passim.

163. See, for example, the experiences of Sor Juana Ines de la Cruz in *La Respuesta a Sor Filotea de la Cruz*; several American Catholics in Carol K. Coburn and Martha Smith, *Spirited Lives: How Nuns Shaped Catholic Culture and American Life, 1836–1920* (Chapel Hill: University of North Carolina Press, 1999); and several European women such as Saint Clare of Assisi and Saint Glodesind in Jo Ann McNamara et al., eds., *Sainted Women of the Dark Ages* (Durham, N.C.: Duke University Press, 1992).

164. Cited in Ranger, "Women in the Politics of Makoki District," 18.

3. "The Most Important Work on the Mission": The Seminary of Saints John Fisher and Thomas More, 1919–1979

1. See Roland Von Nidda, S.J., "Reflections on the Strike"; T. Page, S.J., "Observations on the Strike," both in JAZ, Box 117/3; and "Report of the Seminary Commission," December 22, 1974, in JAZ, Box 117/4.

2. Basil Davidson, *The Black Man's Burden: Africa and the Curse of the Nation-State* (New York: Times Books, 1992), 164. See 118–196 for a more complete explanation.

3. See Joy Brain and Philippe Denis, eds., *The Catholic Church in Contemporary Southern Africa* (Pietermaritzburg: Cluster Publications, 1999), 124–150. See also Joy Brain, ed., *St. John Vianney Seminary* (Pietermaritzburg: Cluster Publications, 2001); George Sombe Mukuka, *The Other Side of the Story: The Silent Experience of the Black Clergy in the Catholic Church in South Africa (1898–1976)* (Pietermaritzburg: Cluster Publications, 2008). For perspectives from north of the Zambezi, see Anthony Simpson, *"Half-London" in*

Zambia: Contested Identities in a Catholic Mission School (Edinburgh: Edinburgh University Press, 2003).

4. A. J. Dachs and W. F. Rea, *The Catholic Church and Zimbabwe, 1879–1979* (Gwelo: Mambo Press, 1979), 223.

5. Benedict XV, *Maximum Illud: Apostolic Letter on the Propagation of the Faith Throughout the World* (Washington, D.C.: National Catholic Welfare Conference, 1919), 4.

6. Ibid., 5–6.

7. Ibid., 7: "For no matter how wild and barbarous a people may be, they are well aware of what the missionary is doing in their country and of what he wants for them. They will subject him in their own way to a very searching investigation, and if he has any object in view other than their spiritual good, they will find out about it. . . . Such a situation could easily give rise to the conviction that the Christian religion is the national religion of some foreign people and that anyone converted to it is abandoning his loyalty to his own people and submitting to the pretensions and domination of a foreign power."

8. JAZ, Box 195/3, A. Reinhard, R.M.M. (Superior of Triashill Mission) to Parry, November 12, 1920.

9. JAZ, Box 195/3, Letter of J. Apel, S.J. [to Parry?], November 18, 1920.

10. Ibid.

11. JAZ, Box 195/3, Letter of J. O'Neill, n.d.

12. Ibid.

13. Pius XI, *Rerum Ecclesiae* in *The Papal Encyclicals*, ed. Claudia Carlen (Raleigh, N.C.: McGrath, 1981), 3:285–286.

14. Ibid., 287, 288.

15. See JAZ, Box 108, Robert Brown, "Questions," July 1, 1926.

16. Dachs and Rea, *The Catholic Church and Zimbabwe*, 134.

17. JAZ, Box 108, Emil Schmitz, Chishawasha: "It is my opinion that Native Christians, who have a vocation, are intellectually and morally fit to become priests. Selected boys will have no difficulty in making the necessary studies." Henry Quin: "That there are youths, who if encouraged are capable of developing a vocation for the priesthood, that intellectually it is only a matter of patient training and instruction, and morally there is no difficulty."

18. JAZ, Box 108, Jean-Baptiste Loubière; Thomas Esser; H. Seed; Andrew Hartmann; Thomas Gardiner.

19. JAZ, Box 108, John Apel; H. Kaibach; Francis Richartz; Anonymous; Anonymous (typed).

20. This does not include the responses of Loubière and an anonymous Mariannhill priest at St. Benedict's mission with references to "a few" and "some" respectively. Dachs and Rea reported only fourteen Africans expressing interest in the priesthood; see *The Catholic Church and Zimbabwe*, 134.

21. JAZ, Box 108, Reply of John Apel, S.J.

22. JAZ, Box 108, Reply of Francis Richartz, S.J.

23. JAZ, Box 108, Reply of Thomas Gardiner, S.J.

24. JAZ, Box 108, Reply of Henry Quin, S.J. See also Emil Schmitz.

25. JAZ, Box 108, Reply of Jean-Baptiste; Francis Richartz.

26. JAZ, Box 108, J. Moreau, S.J.; Edward Biehler, S.J.; John Apel; T. Esser; H. Seed; A. Hesse, S.J.; Andrew Hartmann; Jean-Baptiste Loubière; Anonymous Mariannhiller 1; Anonymous Mariannhiller 2; Anonymous [Jesuit] 2; Anonymous (typed) reply; H. Kaibach; Thomas Gardiner; Henry Quin; Emil Schmitz.

27. JAZ, Box 108, replies of Edward Biehler, S.J., Jean-Baptiste Loubière, John Apel, Andrew Hartmann, and Francis Richartz.

28. JAZ, Box 108, Reply of Emil Schmitz; Reply of J. Moreau, S.J.; Reply of H. Kaibach.

29. JAZ, Box 108, Reply of Henry Quin.

30. JAZ, Box 108, Reply of Thomas Gardiner.

31. JAZ, Box 108, Anonymous (typed) reply; replies of Francis Richartz and Anonymous 2; replies of H. Kaibach, Andrew Hartmann, Thomas Gardiner, J. Moreau. No explanation was given as to why this missionary presented the priesthood to African Christian parents yet not to the potential candidates themselves.

32. The full question asked: "Assuming, as a universal experience justifies one in doing, that vocations grow best in a thoroughly Christian home atmosphere, what means would you suggest as best calculated to create and spread such a home atmosphere?"

33. JAZ, Box 108, Reply of Henry Quin.

34. JAZ, Box 108, Thomas Gardiner: "The home atmosphere cannot improve so long as the stench of heathenism is free to come in by the door. Good pious Christian mothers are of more importance perhaps than good pious Christian men. You must begin with the parents—hence boarding schools for boys and girls are imperatively necessary. The girls should stay there till they are married to boys who have been brought up in *similar* schools. Only those who have passed their time cum laude 90% should be drafted into newly

formed Christian villages—these villages must be firmly isolated if possible. The practical way of ensuring such isolation would be to form Christian districts—large groups of Christian villages where pagans may not enter so that heathenism may not be introduced and practised on the sly. This does not hint at the extinction of the kraal school. But [it] must be lifted to a far higher plane, by means of far better catechists. The pick of the kraal schools, the very best, should be sent to the boarding schools. The pick of the boys boarding schools after four years of intense learning and piety should be drafted to the seminary." Emphasis in original. See also reply of A. Hesse, S.J.

35. See the replies of John Apel, Monte Cassino Mariannhiller, and Andrew Hartmann.

36. JAZ, Box 108, Reply of Edward Biehler.

37. JAZ, Box 108, Reply of Henry Seed.

38. JAZ, Box 108, Reply of Emil Schmitz. Emphasis in original.

39. Communication with author, March 3, 2001. The reference is to his 1990 University Sermon at Oxford University. See also Terence Ranger, *"Are We Not Also Men?": The Samkange Family & African Politics in Zimbabwe, 1920–1964* (Portsmouth, N.H.: Heinemann, 1995).

40. Dachs and Rea, *The Catholic Church and Zimbabwe*, 135.

41. Richartz and Hartmann replies.

42. See Chapter 6.

43. JAZ, Box 135/1, Robert Brown's 1928 Circular letter; JAZ, Box 135/2, "Kutama Training School, 1931," E. King, S.J., "The Training School at Kutama Mission," *Nuntii De Missionibus* 6, no. 1 (June 1933): 4–27; Dachs and Rea, *The Catholic Church and Zimbabwe*, 136.

44. JAZ, Box 108, Seminary *Historia Domus*, July 1, 1939; Archives of the Archdiocese of Harare (AAH hereafter), Box 528, File A (528/A hereafter), Kilian Samakande to Chichester, March 8, 1939. Apparently Chichester sent a cross to Samakande as an ordination gift. There is no mention of this or of Kilian Samakande in Dachs and Rea's chapter on the founding of the seminary at Chishawasha.

45. JAZ, Box 108, Seminary *Historia Domus*, October 24, 1962.

46. JAZ, Box 108, Rev. Isidore Chikore, "The Regional Major Seminary, Chishawasha," March 1973, 1; Dachs and Rea, *The Catholic Church and Zimbabwe*, 136–138.

47. JAZ, Box 108, Rev. Isidore Chikore, "The Regional Major Seminary, Chishawasha," March 1973.

48. See John Baur, *2000 Years of Christianity in Africa: An African Church History* (Nairobi: Daughters of St. Paul, 1998).

49. Dachs and Rea, *The Catholic Church and Zimbabwe*, 126–127.

50. AAH, Box 528/A, A.V.D. Peyssal to Fr. Rector, April 8, 1930; anonymous three-page letter concerning the White Fathers in Uganda, Tanganyika, and southern Sudan.

51. Dachs and Rea mentioned that Chichester visited Uganda, but one version of the rules for the Confraternity of the Sacred Heart was written on stationary from the Holy Ghost Training School in Morogoro, Tanganyika. See Dachs and Rea, *The Catholic Church and Zimbabwe*, 136.

52. JAZ, Box 108, Rev. Isidore Chikore, "The Regional Major Seminary, Chishawasha," March 1973, 1–2.

53. Ibid.; AAH, Box 528/A, Bishop Chichester's Notanda, October 9, 1933.

54. JAZ, Box 108, "Experimental Rules of the Confraternity of the Heart of Jesus," n.d.; AAH, Box 528/A, "Rules (Experimental) of the Confraternity of the Heart of Jesus," n.d.

55. JAZ, Box 108, "Experimental Rules of the Confraternity of the Heart of Jesus," n.d.

56. AAH, Box 528/A, Francis Ketterer to Chichester, November 25, 1933.

57. AAH, Box 528/A, Chichester to Fr. O'Rourke, February 5, 1935.

58. Dachs and Rea, *The Catholic Church and Zimbabwe*, 136.

59. JAZ, Box 108, Seminary *Historia Domus*, January 1, 1936; Memoriale Visitationis, P. L. Beisley, S.J., July 27, 1942: "We should be careful, as far as the primitive conditions admit, to give the Seminarians a good example in neatness of dress and such things." Interview with Rev. Bernard Ndlovu, Chancery, Archdiocese of Bulawayo, May 10, 2000.

60. Interview with Rev. Bernard Ndlovu. Fr. Ndlovu was the first IsiNdebele-speaking priest ordained in colonial Zimbabwe.

61. Ibid. See also interview with Mr. Laurence Masundire, Chancery, Archdiocese of Harare, May 18, 2000. Mr. Masundire, who entered the seminary in 1948, described the conditions as "pretty primitive," and the food as "pretty poor." He also corroborated the difficulties of collecting water "in a half drum" and firewood, and sleeping on the floor.

62. Sadza is the staple of the VaShona diet. It consists of ground cornmeal boiled in water until it becomes stiff. Usavi is a stew of vegetables and meat that accompanies sadza.

63. Interview with Rev. Bernard Ndlovu.

64. AAH, Box 528/G, Memorandum concerning food at the Seminary, May 10, 1962.

65. Interview with Rev. Christopher Gardiner, St. Elizabeth Ann Seton Church, Bark River, Michigan, July 8, 2000.

66. JAZ, Box 108, Rev. Isidore Chikore, "The Regional Major Seminary, Chishawasha," March 1973.

67. AAH, Box 528/ D, Chichester to Hugh Boyle, bishop of Johannesburg, August 17, 1955.

68. JAZ, Box 108, Seminary *Historia Domus*, February 3, 1940; February 1, 1944.

69. Interview with Patrick Moloney, S.J., Prestage House Jesuit Community, Harare, May 29, 2000. See also Seminary *Historia Domus*, July 30, 1945: first public disputations in philosophy and theology.

70. AAH, Box 528/C, Chichester to N.E.D. Director Stark, March 7, 1949.

71. AAH, Box 528/C, Stark to Chichester, June 14, 1949.

72. AAH, Box 528/C, Chichester to N.E.D. Director Stark, March 7, 1949.

73. AAH, Box 528/C, Cedric Myerscough, S.J., "Seminary Jottings, 1953."

74. AAH, Box 528/E, N.E.D. Director, H. Finkle to Archbishop Francis Markall, S.J., March 25, 1958; Markall to Francis McKeown, March 28, 1958.

75. AAH, Box 528/ D, Chichester to Hugh Boyle, August 17, 1955.

76. JAZ, Box 108, Seminary *Historia Domus*, January 28, 1940.

77. JAZ, Box 108, Seminary Rule Book, 1938–1949.

78. Ibid.

79. Interview with Rev. Christopher Gardiner.

80. JAZ, Box 108, Seminary Rule Book, 1938–1949.

81. Ibid.

82. AAH, Aston Chichester, "The Seminary of Saints John Fisher and Thomas More," n.d.

83. AAH, Box 528/ D, Chichester to Hugh Boyle, bishop of Johannesburg, August 17, 1955.

84. JAZ, Box 116/5, "Extracts from the Historia Domus of the Seminary: Chishawasha, 1937–1975" (typescript), 14.

85. JAZ, Box 117/8, Constantine Mashonganyika, "The Seminary at Chishawasha," 24–25.

86. Ibid., 14, 24–25.

87. AAH, Box 528/B, Francis C. Barr, S.J., to Chichester, December 20, 1943. See JAZ, Box 116/5, W.F. Rea, "Extracts from the Historia Domus of the Seminary: Chishawasha, 1937–1975" (typescript), 27.

88. AAH, Box 528/B, Francis C. Barr, S.J., to Chichester, December 20, 1943. Emphasis in the original.

89. Ibid. Emphasis in the original.

90. Dachs and Rea, *The Catholic Church and Zimbabwe*, 136.

91. Interview with Archbishop Pius Ncube, Chancery, Archdiocese of Bulawayo, May 10, 2000; interview with Rev. Charles Mafurutu, Chancery, Archdiocese of Bulawayo, May 10, 2000; interview with Rev. Hebron Wilson, St. Patrick's Church, Bulawayo, May 11, 2000.

92. JAZ, Box 108, Seminary *Historia Domus*, October 26, 1947; December 22 and 28, 1948. Alois Nyanyete was ordained on October 29, 1950; Joseph Kumbirai and Regis Chigwedere on October 26, 1952; and Peter Claver Marimanzi and Thomas Marumbgwa on October 25, 1953.

93. AAH, Box 528/D, Chichester to Hugh Boyle, Bishop of Johannesburg, August 17, 1955. See also AAH, Box 528/C, "Provisional Arrangement Between the Bishop and African Priests," March 2, 1948.

94. AAH, Box 528/D, Chichester to Boyle, August 17, 1955.

95. Interview with Archbishop Patrick Chakaipa, Chancery, Archdiocese of Harare, May 5, 2000; interview with Rev. Walter Nyatsanza, Africa Synod House, Harare, May 15, 2000; interview with Mr. Laurence Masundire, Chancery, Archdiocese of Harare, May 18, 2000; interview with Rev. Ignatius Chidavaenzi, Bible House, Harare, May 18, 2000. A similar process obtained in the Bulawayo diocese. Archbishop Pius Ncube recalled being inspired to become a priest by the example of Rev. Bernard Ndlovu, the first isiNdebele-speaking diocesan priest to complete the course of study at Chishawasha. Similarly, Fr. Ncube inspired and encouraged Hebron Wilson. Interview with Archbishop Pius Ncube, Chancery, Archdiocese of Bulawayo, May 10, 2000; interview with Rev. Hebron Wilson, St. Patrick's Church, Bulawayo, May 11, 2000.

96. JAZ, Box 108, Seminary *Historia Domus*, February 2, 1937; February 2, 1938; May 9, August 1, 1939; January 22, January 23, February 2, 1940; February 2, 1942.

97. JAZ, Box 108, "The Common Rules of the Brothers of St. Peter Claver." There is apparently no documentary evidence of the existence of the Brothers of St. Peter Claver beyond this set of rules. The author was not able to locate anything concerning their existence as a religious congregation in the archives of the Archdiocese of Harare or the Jesuit Archives of Zimbabwe papers for Chishawasha and Kutama missions or the parish of St. Peter in Harare.

98. Interview with Rev. Francis McKeown, S.J., Canisius House, Harare, May 15, 2000; interview with Br. Herman Toma, S.J., Old St. Peter's Church, Mbare, Harare, May 18, 2000. Due to the political violence in the run-up to the June 2000 parliamentary elections, several former members of the Brothers of St. Peter Claver declined to be interviewed.

99. JAZ, Box 108, Seminary *Historia Domus*, January 27, 1958.

100. Interview with Archbishop Patrick Chakaipa, Chancery, Archdiocese of Harare, May 5, 2000; interview with Archbishop Pius Ncube; Interview with Rev. Bernard Ndlovu, Chancery, Archdiocese of Bulawayo, May 10, 2000; Interview with Br. Herman Toma.

101. AAH, Box 528/A, "The Seminary of Saints John Fisher and Thomas More, Salisbury Vicariate, Southern Rhodesia," n.d.

102. Conversation with Rev. Stephen G. Buckland, S.J., Arrupe College, Harare, December 15, 1999.

103. JAZ, Box 357/1, "Agreement Between The Right Rev. Aston Ignatius Chichester and the Institute of the Marist Brothers for the Acceptance of the Native Teacher Training School at Kutama," notes 4, 6.

104. Conversation with Rev. Ignatius Zvarevashe, S.J., St. Francis Xavier Church, Braeside, Harare, May 19, 2000.

105. JAZ, Box 108, Seminary *Historia Domus*, February 16, 1955; April 24, 1955; May 21, 1956; September 8, 1956.

106. Interview with Francis McKeown, S.J.; JAZ, Box 117/8, Constantine Mashonganyika, "The Seminary at Chishawasha," 21.

107. AAH, Box 528/E, Sacred Congregation for Propagating the Faith Decree, March 25, 1958.

108. AAH, Box 528/E, "Visitation of Seminaries," August 28, 1959. See also the 1918 Code of Canon Law, canon 1357.

109. See, e.g., AAH, 528/F, Francis McKeown, "Memorandum: Date & Place of Ordinations," June 21, 1960; McKeown to Markall, June 21, 1960; Francis McKeown, "Memorandum for Discussion at the next meeting of the Board of Bishops," n.d. The subject of the memorandum was "The Date of Major Ordinations."

110. From 1936 to 1938, several Dominican sisters taught at the seminary. Chichester "sacked" them despite their "good teaching" because they apparently had "little influence." See AAH, Box 528/D, Chichester to Hugh Boyle, August 17, 1955. There were also always one or two Jesuit brothers who supervised maintenance of the physical plant and grounds. See JAZ, Box 116/5,

W. F. Rea, "Extracts from the Historia Domus of the Seminary: Chishawasha, 1937–1975," 27–28 and JAZ, Box 117/8, Constantine Mashonganyika, "The Seminary at Chishawasha," 18; "Some Reflections on the Seminary, March, 1960."

111. AAH, Box 528/C, Governor of Southern Rhodesia to Chichester, May 25, 1950. Chichester had applied for a £25,000 grant from the Beit Trust for seminary construction. AAH, Box 528/D, Chichester to Fr. Miles, November 21, 1954. Chichester was seeking sponsorship of £15 per year per seminarian for fifteen years or a lump sum of £495.

112. AAH, Box 528/C, Cedric Myserscough, "Seminary Jottings, 1953."

113. AAH, Box 528/D, Chichester to Hugh Boyle, August 17, 1955.

114. AAH, Box 528/D, Cedric Myserscough, "Seminary Jottings, 1956."

115. Ibid.

116. JAZ, Box 108, Seminary *Historia Domus*, May 21, 1956.

117. AAH, Box 528/E, McKeown to Markall, July 23, 1958; interview with Francis McKeown, S.J.

118. JAZ, Box 116/5, Francis McKeown, "Seminary Jottings, 1962"; "Seminary Jottings, 1963"; Box 108, Seminary *Historia Domus*, January 1963.

119. Dachs and Rea, *The Catholic Church and Zimbabwe*, 144–148.

120. Conversation with Rev. Albert Plangger. See also the numerous publications of Mambo Press in both English and ChiShona on a variety of topics related to the Church and African culture.

121. Chichester invited Irish Carmelites to take charge of the eastern districts in 1946, and in 1953, the Vatican erected the prefecture apostolic of Umtali, which became a diocese in 1957. See Dachs and Rea, *The Catholic Church and Zimbabwe*, 181–182.

122. See Terence Ranger, *The African Voice in Southern Rhodesia* (London: Heinemann Educational, 1970), and *Peasant Consciousness and Guerilla War in Zimbabwe: A Comparative Study* (Berkeley: University of California Press, 1985).

123. JAZ, Box 109, Seminary House Consultations Minutes, August 18, 1958. By this time the seminary staff had decided that corporal punishment was no longer appropriate given the age of the seminarians. AAH, Box 528, File E (1958–59), Archbishop Markall to Francis McKeown, January 18, 1958. JAZ, Box 116/6.

124. AAH, Box 528, File E (1958–59), Archbishop Markall to Francis McKeown, January 18, 1958.

125. JAZ, Box 109, Chishawasha Seminary House Consultors' Minutes Book, March 6, 1961, September 2, 1963.

126. AAH, Box 528, File G (1962–66), McKeown to Markall, December 6, 1961. See also JAZ, Box 116/3, "Seminary Custom Book, January 1963, nn. 74–79.

127. JAZ, Box 109, Chishawasha Seminary House Consultors' Minutes Book, November 6, 1961.

128. JAZ, Box 108, Seminary *Historia Domus*, May 4, 1959; February 7, 1960; June 6, 1960; February 24, 1962; November 4, 1962.

129. Interview with Patrick Moloney, S.J.

130. JAZ, Box 108, Memoriale Visitationis, T. E. Corrigan, March 27, 1961.

131. Ibid., September 23, 1963.

132. Interview with Patrick Moloney, S.J.

133. Interview with Rev. Walter Nyatsanza, Africa Synod House, Harare, May 15, 2000.

134. AAH, Box 528, File G (1962–66), McKeown to Markall, August 31, 1964, note handwritten comment in Markall's hand, "26–10–64 Bishops all gave me advice to go ahead. In [the] case of these two [it] must of course be my own decision"; Markall to McKeown, September 5, 1964. Interview with Francis McKeown, S.J.; interview with Patrick Moloney, S.J.

135. Interview with Francis McKeown, S.J.; interview with Patrick Moloney, S.J. There is extensive correspondence in JAZ, Box 117/1 from John Diamond, McKeown's successor as rector, noting that McKeown had not consulted anyone at the seminary about the decision to admit the white students. AAH, Box 528, File G (1962–66), McKeown to Markall, December 31, 1964; Markall to McKeown, January 4, 1965.

136. JAZ, Box 108, Seminary *Historia Domus*, February 9, 1965; February 19, 1965.

137. JAZ, Box 117/1, Seminary Group to His Lordship, February 1965. See also JAZ, Box 108, Seminary *Historia Domus*, February 1965.

138. JAZ, Box 117/1, Anthony Turner, Memorandum to Reverend Father Rector, March 11, 1965.

139. Interview with Rev. Christopher B. Gardiner, St. Elizabeth Ann Seton Church, Bark River, Michigan, July 8, 2000.

140. St. George's College was founded by the Jesuits in Bulawayo in 1896, moved to Salisbury in 1926, and until 1964 exclusively admitted white students. Interview with Rev. Christopher B. Gardiner.

141. Interview with Rev. Constantine Mashonganyika, IMBISA House, Harare, May 17, 2000.

142. See JAZ, Box 117/1 passim.

143. JAZ, Box 117/1, Diamond to Edward Ennis, SJ, March 29, 1965.

144. JAZ, Box 117/1, Seminary Group to His Lordship, February 1965.

145. For example, Turner wrote: "Some members of the Society [of Jesus], including Professors, are frustrated when African priests and students never seem to get even the most basic ideas into their heads, especially philosophical and economical. . . . I feel this myself and watch [it] so as not to hold fellow students in contempt for what to me is their obvious stupidity. The African is far more sensitive than the European . . . [the African] feels that he is no longer a child (though mentally he may still be one; impatient people like myself must be careful of what we say, and be ready to apologise if we hurt someone, however unwittingly."

146. Interview with Rev. Christopher B. Gardiner.

147. JAZ, Box 109, Seminary Consultors' Minutes, 1965–1966; see also Box 116/7, Diamond to Bishop Adolph Schmitt, October 29, 1965: Diamond and the seminary consultors asked Schmitt to send a letter of encouragement and appreciation to Christopher Gardiner.

148. See JAZ, Box 109, Seminary Consultors' Minutes.

149. JAZ, Box 116/5, Francis McKeown, "A Letter to Our Friends from the Seminary," December 1964.

150. JAZ, Box 116/5, McKeown to Fr. Provincial, March, 16, 1960; Francis McKeown, "Some Reflections on matters missionary after a visit to East Africa and the Congo," June, 1960; 116/7, Diamond to Edward Ennis (Superior of the Jesuit Salisbury Mission), April 19, 1966.

151. JAZ, Box 116/5, McKeown to Fr. Provincial, March 16, 1960.

152. JAZ, Box 109, Seminary House Consultors' Minutes, 1960–68, passim; interview with Patrick Moloney, S.J.; interview with Rev. Constantine Mashonganyika.

153. JAZ, Box 117/1, Diamond to Edward P. Ennis, S.J., March 29, 1965.

154. AAH, Box 528, File G (1962–66), Markall to Cardinal Sigismondi, Prefect of the Sacred Congregation for Propagating the Faith, n.d., but after May 5, 1965. Markall and the other bishops had in mind members of the staffs of the seminaries for Africans at Kachebere in Malawi and Hammanskraal in South Africa, and St. John Vianney seminary for Whites in South Africa.

155. See JAZ, Box 117/1, "Minutes of a Conversation between His Grace, the Archbishop of Salisbury and Father Diamond, Rector of the Seminary,

Friday, 7th May 1965, 5:15 p.m."; John Diamond, "Proposal of the Board of Bishops to Invite Visitors to the Seminary," May 9, 1965; "Notes of Meeting between His Grace and Father Ennis re. the Request by the SRCBC to Propaganda for Visitors to be sent to the Seminary," Monday May 10, 1965, 8:30 p.m.; Ennis to Markall, May 11, 1965; Markall to Ennis, May 12, 1965; Ennis to T. E. Corrigan [English Provincial], May 17, 1965; Markall to Ennis, May 16, 1965; Ennis to Corrigan, May 21, 1965; Ennis to Markall, May 24, 1965; Ennis to Corrigan, May 25, 1965; Ennis to Corrigan, May 28, 1965; Ennis to Corrigan, May 29, 1965; Ennis to Corrigan, June 8, 1965; Markall to Ennis, June 9, 1965; Ennis to Corrigan, June 14, 1965; AAH, Box 528, File G (1962–66), Markall to Aloysius Haene [Bishop of Gwelo—also sent to other bishops of Rhodesia], June 2, 1965; Adolph Schmitt [Bishop of Bulawayo] to Markall, June 8, 1965; Ignatius Prieto [Bishop of Wankie] to Markall, June 8, 1965; Donal Lamont [Bishop of Umtali] to Markall, June 8, 1965.

156. JAZ, Box 117/1, Minutes of Meeting with Seminary Staff, June 22, 1965.

157. Ibid.

158. JAZ, Box 108, Seminary *Historia Domus*, April 12, 1965; May 24, 1965; August 8, 15, 29, 1965; September 3, 1965.

159. Ibid., December 8, 1966. Gardiner was eventually ordained for the Diocese of Bulawayo in July 1968. See ibid., July 13–14, 1968.

160. Interview with Rev. Christopher B. Gardiner.

161. Ibid.; JAZ, Box 108, Seminary *Historia Domus*, October 1967, November 1, 1967; 1967 "Relatio Annuale to Sacra Congregatio de Propaganda Fide," in JAZ, Box 116/5 "Extracts from the Historia Domus of the Seminary [at] Chishawasha, 1937–1975" (typescript), 17.

162. JAZ, Box 116/7, Diamond to Father Superior, October 12, 1967. See also interview with Archbishop Pius Ncube; interview with Rev. Constantine Mashonganyika.

163. JAZ, Box 116/7, Diamond to the Bishops of Rhodesia, December 13, 1967.

164. JAZ, Box 116/7, "Comments on their Seminary Training by 5 African Priests (Frs. Mugadzi, Nhariwa, Chiginya, Marimazhira, Urayai)."

165. JAZ, Box 116/7, Victor Mertens, S.J., to Haene, December 22, 1967. It is unclear how Diamond was able to maintain his position as rector at the seminary.

166. JAZ, Box 116/7 Diamond to Ennis, April 19, 1966.

167. JAZ, Box 117/2, Rhodesian Catholic Bishops' Conference Minutes, October 22, 1970; Dachs and Rea, *The Catholic Church and Zimbabwe*, 223.

168. Interview with Rev. Walter Nyatsanza.

169. JAZ, Box 117/3, John Berrell, S.J., "Rector's Report: The Seminary Strike 30 September to 7 October 1974," 3–4 (Rector's report hereafter); JAZ, Box 117/4, Rhodesia Catholic Bishops' Conference, "Report of [the] Seminary Commission," December 22, 1974, 2 (Commission report hereafter). Neither report specifies what specifically Mukuwapasi had done to anger Berrell, and informants who were present as seminarians did not recall Mukuwapasi's actions either.

170. Commission report, 2–3.

171. According to Berrell, he "[offered] the deacon the opportunity of departing without embarrassment," offering to have him driven from the seminary while the other students were in classes. Rector's report, 4. Again, it is not clear what Berrell's "disturbing actions" or Mukuwapasi's reaction were.

172. Commission report, 2.

173. Rev. Ignatius Mhonda, "A Report to the Bishops concerning the October Events at the Regional Major Seminary of Ss. John Fisher and Thomas More," November 25, 1974, cited in Commission report, 2.

174. Rector's report, 6; Commission report, 4.

175. It is not clear on what day a garbage can was emptied in one of the non-striker's rooms: Commission report, 4, says it happened late Tuesday night, while Rector's report, 7, says it happened on Wednesday night.

176. Rector's report, 7–8.

177. Rector's report, 8; Commission report, 5.

178. Rector's report, 8–9; Commission report, 5–6.

179. Rector's report, 9; see also Commission report, 6–7.

180. Rector's report, 10; Commission report, 7.

181. Rector's report, 10.

182. Commission report, 10, 17.

183. AAH, Index, "Box 528/O: left after strike, 4 for guerrilla training, 22/10/74 . . . Death of Jonathan Dzumbunu and Kenneth Mzilikazi (crossfire?)." Although this file was listed in the AAH Index, access was denied. Interview with Rev. Walter Nyatsanza.

184. Interview with Rev. Walter Nyatsanza. This had been one of their demands dating to 1970, when Berrell was first appointed rector.

185. Ibid.

186. JAZ, Box 116/5, "Extracts from the Historia Domus of the Seminary [at] Chishawasha, 1937–1975," 26.
187. Interview with Francis McKeown, S.J.
188. Benedict XV, *Maximum Illud*, 5–6.
189. Pius XI, *Rerum Ecclesiae*, 287, 288.

4. A "Do-Nothing" Organization? The Catholic Association, 1934–1974

1. Leo Gallagher, *The Catholic Church in Manicaland, 1896–1996* (Harare: Kolbe Press, 1996), 37; Hugh O'Donnell, "The Catholic Association: A Short History," unpublished master's paper, May 1973, available in Archives of the Archdiocese of Harare (hereafter AAH), Box 412–1/A, 2.
2. O'Donnell, "The Catholic Association," 2.
3. A. J. Dachs and W. F. Rea, *The Catholic Church and Zimbabwe, 1879–1979* (Gwelo: Mambo Press, 1979), 193.
4. JAZ, Chishawasha *Historia Domus*, January 10, 1934: Retreat for teachers (Jeanes teachers and two Wesleyans): including Joseph Dambasa [sic], Ambrose Majombwa [sic; should be Majongwe], James Kora, Fidelis Huma, Joseph Marimo, and nine others.
5. O'Donnell, "The Catholic Association," 1–2.
6. Francis Schimlek, *Against the Stream: Life of Father Bernard Huss, C.M.M., The Social Apostle of the Bantu* (Pinetown, South Africa: Mariannhill Mission Press, n.d.), cited in O'Donnell, "The Catholic Association," 1–2.
7. O'Donnell, "The Catholic Association," 2.
8. JAZ, Box 23/1, Jerome O'Hea to Francis Johanny, January 21, 1932.
9. JAZ, Chishawasha *Historia Domus*, June 8–15, 1935.
10. JAZ, Box 23/1, Jerome O'Hea to Francis Ketterer, May 20, 1935.
11. AAH, Box 412/A, Francis Ketterer, S.J., to Congress Permanent Committee, September 11, 1935.
12. Ibid.; AAH, Box 412/A, Ambrose Majongwe to Ketterer, October 14, 1935.
13. See Terence Ranger, *The African Voice in Southern Rhodesia, 1898–1930* (London: Heinemann Education, 1970).
14. See Robin Palmer, *Land and Racial Domination in Rhodesia* (Berkeley: University of California Press, 1977).
15. AAH, Box 412/A, "Précis of Congress Committee Meeting, December 9, 1935."

16. Ibid.; JAZ, Chishawasha *Historia Domus*, "Retreat and Congress at Chishawasha," n.d.

17. "Retreat and Congress at Chishawasha."

18. JAZ, Chishawasha *Historia Domus*, June 7–22, 1936.

19. JAZ, Chishawasha *Historia Domus*, Chichester Circular Letter, June 12, 1946.

20. JAZ, Chishawasha *Historia Domus*, May 21–22, 1946.

21. AAH, Box 412/A, "Resolutions Passed at 1946 Catholic African Congress at Chishawasha." See Herbert Chimhundu, "Early Missionaries and the Ethnolinguistic Factor During the 'Invention of Tribalism' in Zimbabwe," *Journal of African History* 33, no. 1 (1992): 87–109; see also Chapter 6 on the Mwari controversy.

22. Chichester Circular Letter, June 12, 1946.

23. JAZ, Chishawasha *Historia Domus*, "The Catholic African Congress, Chishawasha May, 21–22, 1946."

24. Chichester Circular Letter, June 12, 1946.

25. Ibid. See Chapter 6 below on the Mwari controversy.

26. AAH, Box 412/A, Circular Letter of George Binns, January 17, 1947. Interestingly, Binns noted that he was writing "by order of the Bishop."

27. AAH, Box 412/A, Schedule of the Catholic African Congress at Monte Cassino, May 16–18, 1947.

28. AAH, Box 412/A, L. Boetkenhoff to Binns, January 23, 1947.

29. AAH, Box 412/A, F. C. Barr to Binns, January 31, 1947.

30. AAH, Box 412/A, Charles Ferguson to Binns, February 26, 1947.

31. AAH, Box 412/A, All Souls Mission Superior to Binns, January 22, 1947.

32. AAH, Box 412/A, J. Cogger to Binns, February 15, 1947.

33. AAH, Box 412/A, "Report from the Catholic Centres of Musami Mission," n.d.

34. AAH, Box 412/A, "Report Showing How Far the Resolutions of the African Congress 1946 Have Been Implemented at St. Barbara's Mission," n.d.

35. AAH, Box 412/A, E. Kotski to Binns, February 23, 1947.

36. AAH, Box 412/A, Fr. Reich, S.M.B. to Binns, February 10, 1947.

37. Ibid.

38. D. J. Geaney, "Catholic Action," *New Catholic Encyclopedia* (Evanston, Ill.: Gale, 1973), 262–263. For more on Catholic Action, see Theodore M. Hesburgh, *The Theology of Catholic Action* (Notre Dame, Ind.: University of Notre

Dame Press, 1946); Gianfranco Poggi, *Catholic Action in Italy: The Sociology of a Sponsored Organization* (Stanford: Stanford University Press, 1967); Jean-Guy Vaillancourt, *Papal Power: A Study in Vatican Control Over Catholic Lay Elites* (Berkeley: University of California Press, 1980); William J. Callahan, *The Catholic Church in Spain, 1875–1998* (Washington, D.C.: Catholic University of America Press, 2000).

39. Pius XI, "Discourse to Italian Catholic Young Women," March 1927, cited in Geaney, "Catholic Action." See also Pius XI, "Ubi Arcano Dei" (1922) and "Non Abbiamo Bisogno" (1931), in *The Papal Encyclicals*, ed. Claudia Carlen (Raleigh, N.C.: McGrath, 1981).

40. Geaney, "Catholic Action," 262.

41. William L. Portier, "Welcome to the 'Lay Zone,'" Comments on the panel Challenging American Catholic Laity at Mid-century, Joint Meeting of the American Catholic Historical Association and the Canadian Catholic Historical Association, University of Toronto, April 2001. I am grateful to Dr. Portier for having shared a copy of the full text of his comments.

42. Ibid.

43. JAZ, Chishawasha *Historia Domus*, Chichester Circular Letter, June 12, 1946; AAH, Box 412/A, "The Catholic African Congress. Kutama. May 11th and 12th, 1948," 2.

44. JAZ, Box 135, Kutama Diary [*Historia Domus*] 1940–1968, May 11–12, 1948.

45. AAH, Box 412/A, "The Catholic African Congress. Kutama. May 11th and 12th, 1948," 1.

46. AAH, Box 412/A, "Congress of Catholic Africans, 19th August–22nd August 1949, St. Peter's, Salisbury," 1.

47. Ibid., 5.

48. Minutes of the African Catholic Congress, Monte Cassino Mission, August 25–26, 1951, 5.

49. Ibid., 9.

50. AAH, Box 412/A, "Suggested Constitution for Monte Cassino Parish African Congress of Catholic Action."

51. Ibid.

52. AAH, Box 412/A, African Catholic Congress Central Committee minutes, December 8, 1951, and May 3, 1952.

53. AAH, Box 412/A, African Catholic Congress Central Committee minutes, April 24, 1953.

54. AAH, Box 412/A, Minutes of the meeting to draft the Constitution for a Catholic African organization for all Vicariates of Southern Rhodesia, August 17–18, 1953.

55. The territorial council of the Catholic African Association decided to use the abbreviation "CAA" so as not to confuse the organization with the Central African Airways, which used the abbreviation "C.A.A." See AAH, Box 412/A, Territorial Council Minutes, September 9, 1955.

56. AAH, Box 412/A, Minutes of the meeting to draft the Constitution for a Catholic African organization for all Vicariates of Southern Rhodesia, August 17–18, 1953. "Better homes, better hearts, better harvests" was a motto used by Bernard Huss to describe the work of the South African Catholic African Union. Majongwe adopted it to apply to the CAA.

57. AAH, Box 412/B, Territorial Council Executive Committee minutes, January 4, 1961.

58. AAH, Box 412/B, Territorial Council minutes, May 3, 1961.

59. AAH, Box 412/B, Markall to Hannan, May 25, 1961.

60. AAH, Box 412/C, Minutes of the meeting of the Committee appointed by the Hierarchy to investigate the Catholic Association and its relationship to other Catholic Associations, March 27, 1962 (Inquiry Committee hereafter), 8.

61. The question of amending the aims of the CA came up again in the wake of Vatican II, but had little bearing on the actual structure or operation of the association. All other constitutional amendments were fairly minor by comparison.

62. AAH, Box 412/C, Francis Barr, "Report on the Discussion at Bishop's House, Gwelo, 27th March, 1962"; See also Minutes of Inquiry Committee, March 27, 1962, 8, 12, 15–16.

63. AAH, Box 412–1/B, Edward N. Muchenje to Markall, May 3, 1974.

64. AAH, Box 412–1/B, Markall to Muchenje, June 11, 1974. Emphasis in the original.

65. AAH, Box 412–1/B, Muchenje to Markall, October 30, 1974.

66. AAH, Box 412–1/B, Muchenje to Mavudzi, September 24, 1974.

67. AAH, Box 412–1/B, Mavudzi to Muchenje, October 4, 1974.

68. AAH, Box 412–1/B, C. Bernard Magorimbo to Markall, April 1975; Markall to Magorimbo, April 29, 1975.

69. AAH, Box 412/B, Salisbury CAA executive committee minutes, October 1958.

70. AAH, Box 412/B, Minutes of CAA Salisbury Regional Council, December 12, 1958.

71. AAH, Box 412/C, Markall to Hannan, July 13, 1962.

72. JAZ, Box 135/4, Francis Barr, "Report of a Visit to Kutama Mission on June 27, 1960."

73. JAZ, Box 135/4, Joseph Dambaza to T.E. Corrigan, November 2, 1962. Emphasis in original.

74. JAZ, Box 100/3, 1962–1964 Annual Letters, Chishawasha Residence of St. Ignatius.

75. AAH, Box 412/C, John Dove, "A Report on Catholic Action," August 1964.

76. JAZ, Box 104/5, "Chishawasha" report.

77. Although the report provides the names of many of the people involved, in the interest of protecting those people and their relatives and/or associates, I have decided not to use their names, especially given the ongoing political violence occurring at the time of the researching and writing of this manuscript.

78. JAZ, Box 104/5, "Chishawasha" report, 1–2.

79. Ibid., 3.

80. Ibid., 8.

81. See Inquiry committee minutes.

82. O'Donnell, "The Catholic Association," 5. Emphasis in original. The *dare* was a meeting of village elders that met to resolve disputes during the precolonial era and served as a local court during the colonial period. It consisted entirely of men. See Michael F. C. Bourdillon, *The Shona Peoples* (Gweru: Mambo Press, 1987), 127.

83. AAH, Box 412/A, "The Catholic African Congress. Kutama. May 11th and 12th, 1948," 2–3.

84. Ibid., 3.

85. Ibid., 4.

86. AAH, Box 412/A, "Congress of Catholic Africans, 19th August–22nd August 1949, St. Peter's, Salisbury," 2, 4.

87. AAH, Box 412/A, "Minutes of the Fourth Meeting of the Central Committee, African Catholic Congress," December 20, 1952.

88. AAH, Box 412/A, "Minutes of the Fifth Meeting of the Central Committee, African Catholic Congress," April 24, 1953.

89. See, e.g., timetable for the 1956 Congress at St. Michael's Mission, Mhondoro in AAH, Box 412/A.

90. AAH, Box 412/A, "Congress of Catholic Africans, 19th August–22nd August 1949, St. Peter's, Salisbury," 4.

91. Ibid., 5.

92. AAH, Box 412/A, "Minutes of the Sixth Meeting of the Central Committee, Catholic African Association [CAA hereafter], Formerly called 'African Catholic Congress [sic]," December 19, 1953.

93. See, e.g., CAA Salisbury Regional Council minutes, December 12, 1958.

94. AAH, Box 412/A, CAA Report on Leadership Courses for Branch Officials, July, 1956.

95. AAH, Box 412/A, Minutes of 15th Meeting of Salisbury Regional Council CAA, May 4, 1957. This resolution was passed.

96. AAH, Box 412/A, "The Catholic African Congress. Kutama. May 11th and 12th, 1948," 4.

97. Ibid., 5.

98. Ibid.

99. AAH, Box 412/A, Minutes of the Congress at Monte Cassino Mission, August 25–26, 1951, 12.

100. AAH, Box 412/A, Hannan to Chichester, April 30, 1951.

101. AAH, Box 412/A, Catholic African Association Minutes of the Meeting to Draft the Constitution, August 17–18, 1953, Articles 46, 47, 50, 57, 58.

102. CAA Constitution, 13.

103. Ibid., 13–16.

104. AAH, Box 412/A, Report of the Training Team, Leadership Course, May 4–6, 1955.

105. AAH, Box 412/A, Minutes of the Spiritual Advisers meeting, September 6, 1955.

106. AAH, Box 412/A, Minutes of the Territorial Council, September 9, 1955.

107. AAH, Box 412/A, Minutes of the CAA Salisbury Regional Council, September 10, 1955.

108. AAH, Box 412/A, Minutes of the CAA Salisbury Regional Council, December 19, 1953.

109. AAH, Box 412/A, Minutes of the African Catholic Congress central committee, December 20, 1952.

110. AAH, Box 412/B, Minutes of the Territorial Council, May 7, 1957; Markall to Peter Simbisai, May 7, 1957.

111. AAH, Box 412/B, Minutes of the Salisbury Regional Council, October 27, 1956; AAH, Box 412-1/A, CAA Salisbury Regional Council, December 22, 1972.

112. AAH, Box 412/A, Minutes of the African Catholic Congress Central Committee, December 8, 1951.

113. AAH, Box 412/A, Minutes of the Salisbury Regional Council, September 10, 1955; D.L. Samakomva to Chichester, September 17, 1955; Chichester to Samakomva, September 26, 1955.

114. AAH, Box 412/A, Hannan to Chichester, October 13, 1955.

115. AAH, Box 412/B, Minutes of CAA Salisbury Regional Council, May 6, 1955; D. L. Samakomva to Chichester, May 20, 1955.

116. AAH, Box 412/B, Minutes of the CAA Salisbury Regional Council, April 26, 1958.

117. AAH, Box 412/B, Minutes of the CAA Salisbury Regional Council, December 12, 1958.

118. AAH, Box 412/A, Minutes of the CAA Salisbury Regional Council, December 19, 1953.

119. AAH, Box 412/B, Rev. Alois Nyanhete to Markall, November 14, 1957; Box 412-1/A, Markall's Secretary to Rev. Patrick Chakaipa, January 18, 1968; Box 412-1/B, Markall to Rev. E[mmanuel] J. Mavudzi, July 19, 1974.

120. For more on the increasingly radical African Christian perspective in *Moto* magazine, see Nicholas M. Creary, "Inculturation of the Catholic Church in Zimbabwe, 1958–1977," *The Historian* 61, no. 4 (Summer 1999): 765–781.

121. Frs. Simon Tsuro and Isidore Chikore were ordained at Chishawasha in October 1947. See Chapter 3.

122. AAH, Box 412/A, Minutes of the African Catholic Congress; CAA Salisbury Regional Council Minutes, January 10, 1955.

123. AAH, Box 412/B, Nyanhete to Markall, November 14, 1957.

124. AAH, Box 412/B, Salisbury Regional Council Minutes, April 26, 1958; Territorial Council Minutes, May 12, 1959; Box 412/C, CA Salisbury Regional Council Minutes, April 29, 1967; Box 412-1/A, Minutes of the 1968 CA congress.

125. Only a minority of Catholic parents complied with the decree of the American bishops at the third plenary council of Baltimore in 1884 that mandated that all Catholic parents send their children to Catholic schools.

126. AAH, Box 412/A, African Catholic Congress Central Committee Minutes, April 24, 1953; CAA Salisbury Regional Council Minutes, December 19, 1953.

127. AAH, Box 412/A, CAA Salisbury Regional Council Minutes, May 7, 1954. Ultimately, they did not raise the subscription fee; rather, they voted for a one shilling per capita fee from each mission.

128. AAH, Box 412/A, African Catholic Congress Central Committee Minutes, December 20, 1952.

129. AAH, Box 412/A, African Catholic Congress Central Committee Minutes, April 24, 1953.

130. AAH, Box 412/A, CAA Salisbury Regional Council Minutes, May 6, 1955; D. L. Samakomva to Chichester, May 20, 1955.

131. AAH, Box 412/A, CAA Salisbury Regional Council Minutes, September 10, 1955; D. L. Samakomva to Chichester, September 17, 1955; Chichester to Samakomva, September 26, 1955.

132. AAH, Box 412/B, CAA Territorial Council minutes, April 29, 1958.

133. AAH, Box 412/B, CAA Territorial Council minutes, May 12, 1959.

134. See, e.g., AAH, Box 412/C, CA Salisbury Regional Council Minutes April 2 and December 17, 1966.

135. AAH, Box 412/C, Territorial Council Minutes, April 25, 1962.

136. AAH, Box 412/B, Minutes of the CA Territorial Council, May 3, 1961.

137. AAH, Box 412/B, Archbishop Francis Markall to Michael Hannan, May 25, 1961.

138. AAH, Box 412-1/A, Sean Dunne, O.Carm., to The Most Reverend Ordinaries, October 12, 1970. Emphasis in original.

139. AAH, Box 412-1/A, Edward Muchenje to Markall, April 27, 1970; Sean Dunne, O.Carm. to The Most Reverend Ordinaries, October 12, 1970.

140. AAH, Box 412-1/A, Report of Ad Hoc Committee, CA territorial council, December 5, 1971; Minutes of CA territorial council, May 9, 1972; Minutes of the CA Salisbury Regional Council, December 14, 1973.

141. AAH, Box 412-1/A, Dunne to Markall, June 11, 1969.

142. AAH, Box 412-1/A, Edward Muchenje to Markall, April 27, 1970.

143. Dachs and Rea, *The Catholic Church and Zimbabwe*, 194.

144. O'Donnell, "The Catholic Association," 6–7.

145. Ibid., 8–10.

146. Conversation with John Dove, S.J., Silveira House, Chishawasha, May 22, 2000.

5. Until Death Do Us Part? African Marriage Practices and the Catholic Church, 1890–1979

1. Elizabeth Schmidt, *Peasants, Traders, and Wives: Shona Women in the History of Zimbabwe, 1870–1939* (Harare: Baobab Books, 1992); Diana Jeater,

Marriage, Perversion, and Power: The Creation of Moral Discourse in Southern Rhodesia, 1894–1930 (Oxford: Clarendon Press, 1993); Michael F. C. Bourdillon, *The Shona Peoples* (Gweru: Mambo Press, 1987), 36–49. See also Dominique Meekers, "The Noble Custom of Roora: The Marriage Practices of the Shona of Zimbabwe," *Ethnology* 32 (1993): 35–38; Jaison Andifasi, "An Analysis of Roora," in *Shona Customs: Essays by African Writers*, ed. Clive Kileff and Peggy Kileff, 28–32 (Gwelo: Mambo Press, 1970); Lydia Jahni, "Roora and Marriage," in ibid., 33–41.

2. Jeater, *Marriage, Perversion, and Power*, 98–104, 220–222.

3. Ibid., 209–210; see also Schmidt, *Peasants, Traders, and Wives*, 106–108; Martin Chanock, *Law, Custom, and Social Order: The Colonial Experience in Malawi and Zambia* (London: Cambridge University Press, 1985).

4. Cited in Schmidt, *Peasants, Traders, and Wives*, 107.

5. Jeater, *Marriage, Perversion, and Power*, 80; Schmidt, *Peasants, Traders, and Wives*, 111–112.

6. Jeater, *Marriage, Perversion, and Power*, 82–86.

7. JAZ, Box 451/2, Richard Sykes, S.J., *Native Marriages*, July 31, 1913. See also Schmidt, *Peasants, Traders, and Wives*, 115.

8. Jeater, *Marriage, Perversion, and Power*, 100.

9. Ibid., 201–204, 207, 209–212; Schmidt, *Peasants, Traders, and Wives*, 111–112.

10. Schmidt, *Peasants, Traders, and Wives*, 111.

11. See Michael Bourdillon, *The Shona Peoples*, 45 n. 48, 46 n. 51; JAZ, Box 312/2, Lachlan M. Hughes, S.J., Memorandum, "African Marriages: Comments on Report of Commission, 20th January 1968," February 2, 1968, 10, 13.

12. JAZ, Box 312/1, 1964 Marriage Act and "Notes for the Guidance of Marriage Officers."

13. JAZ, Box 312/1, Francis Markall, Ad Clerum letter, "The New Marriage Act," January, 1965.

14. 1964 Marriage Act, Sections 12–18; 1965 Marriage Regulations, No. 17.

15. See Andrew B. Meehan, "Tametsi," *The Catholic Encyclopedia*, http://www.newadvent.org/cathen/14441b.htm; W. Van Ommeren, "Tametsi," *The New Catholic Encyclopedia* (New York: Sage, 1965), 13:929, and "Ne Temere," ibid., 10:288. For the full text of the decree "Tametsi" in English translation, see http://history.hanover.edu/early/trent/ct24mar1.htm.

16. *Codex Iuris Canonici* (Rome: Vatican Press, 1918), 306; Stanislaus Woywod, O.F.M., *The New Canon Law: A Commentary and Summary of the New*

Code of Canon Law (New York: Joseph F. Wagner, 1929), 223. All subsequent references to specific canons are to the 1917 code unless noted otherwise.

17. See W. Fanning, "Mixed Marriage," *Catholic Encyclopedia*; Canons 1058–1080, especially 1060.

18. Schmidt, *Peasants, Traders, and Wives*, 95.

19. JAZ, Box 452, Emil Schmitz to J. A. Halliday, December 29, 1905. Emphasis in original. See also Halliday to Schmitz, December 28 and 30, 1905.

20. Schmidt, *Peasants, Traders, and Wives*, 11.

21. JAZ, Box 452, Edward Biehler to Charles Bert, October 23, 1906.

22. JAZ, Box 452, W. S. Taberer to Bert, November 13, 1907; NC Nesbitt to Bert, July 26, 1909.

23. Jeater, *Marriage, Perversion, and Power*, 67; Schmidt, *Peasants, Traders, and Wives*, 16–18.

24. See Council of Trent, Decree on the Sacrament of Matrimony, Canon 10; Canon 1142; William H.W. Fanning, "Widow," *Catholic Encyclopedia*.

25. JAZ, Box 452, Taberer to Bert, November 13, 1907.

26. JAZ, Box 452, Nesbitt to Bert, July 26, 1909.

27. JAZ, Fr. Richartz Letter Book, 1896–1924 (typescript), John Apel to Major Nesbitt (NC, Goromonzi), November 21, 1920.

28. JAZ, Box 452, contains copies of all marriage legislation from 1901 to 1929.

29. JAZ, Box 451/2, Richard Sykes, S.J., *Native Marriages*, July 31, 1913. Emphasis in original.

30. JAZ, Fr. Richartz Letter Book, 1896–1924 (typescript), Apel to NC Mrewa, May 25, 1920.

31. "The marriage between a person baptized in the Catholic Church, or received into the Church from heresy or schism, and a non-baptized individual is null and void." See Woywod, *The New Canon Law*, 216–217.

32. AAH, Box 670/C, Rev. S. Chifeya to Fr. McNamara, August 18, 1966.

33. Ibid.; McNamara to Chifeya, August 23, 1966.

34. AAH, Box 670/C, Chifeya to McNamara, August 18, 1966.

35. AAH, Box 670/C, McNamara to Chifeya, August 23, 1966.

36. There more than likely are records documenting a conclusion to this case, but they would be found in the marriage files, which typically are sealed for at least seventy-five years.

37. AAH, Box 670/C, Henry Swift, S.J., to Bishop Aston Chichester, October 13, 1954.

38. See Leo XIII, *Rerum Novarum*, 1891, which allowed for Catholics to join labor unions.

39. Canons 1060–1061. See Woywod, *The New Canon Law*, 214.

40. Canon 1120. See Woywod, *The New Canon Law*, 228.

41. Canon 1121. See Woywod, *The New Canon Law*, 228.

42. Canon 1138. See Woywod, *The New Canon Law*, 232.

43. JAZ, Box 312/2, S.J. Dunne, O.Carm., Circular Letter to All Priests, April 20, 1967. See also Lachlan M. Hughes, S.J., to Edward Ennis, S.J., May 31, 1968.

44. JAZ, Box 312/2, Dunne Circular Letter, April 20, 1967.

45. JAZ, Box 312/2, Noel K. Kinnane, O.F.M., Circular Letter to All Priests, February 9, 1968. See also in ibid., Lachlan Hughes Memo, "African Marriages: Comments on Report of Commission, 20th January 1968," February 2, 1968, 1; and Hughes to Ennis, May 31, 1968.

46. JAZ, Box 312/2, Hughes, "African Marriages"; Joseph Suter, "Memorandum concerning Church-Marriage versus State-Law/Natural Marriage: Another Attempt," March 31, 1968 ("Another Attempt" hereafter); Hughes, "Memorandum II: on *African Marriages*: Being a Restatement largely on the basis of Memo I and Fr. Suter's 'Another Attempt,'" May 23, 1968; Hughes, "Marriage Commission," September 29, 1968.

47. Hughes, "African Marriages," 6. The commission's preliminary report was not available in the Jesuit archives; thus, its major recommendations were gleaned from Hughes's memorandum.

48. Hughes, "African Marriages," 1–2. The text of the recommendation reads: "This commission recognises the advisability of recognising the African customary union and recommends that [a] special Commission [sic] be appointed to discuss the canonical implications of such recognition." Cited in ibid., 3.

49. Ibid., 4; see also JAZ, Box 312/2, Hughes to Ennis, May 31, 1968.

50. Conversation with Rev. John P. Beal, J.C.D., Department of Canon Law, Catholic University of America, May 30, 2001.

51. Hughes, "African Marriages," 1–4.

52. Ibid., 6.

53. Ibid., 7.

54. Ibid.

55. Ibid., 7–9.

56. JAZ, Box 312/2, Hughes to Ennis, May 31, 1968.

57. Hughes, "African Marriages," 10.
58. Ibid., 10–11.
59. Ibid., 11–13.
60. Ibid., 13–14.
61. JAZ, Box 312/2, Joseph Suter, "Memorandum Concerning Church-Marriage versus State-Law/Natural Marriage: Another Attempt," 1. "Another Attempt," hereafter.
62. Canons 1067–1079 identified the following diriment impediments: if a boy were under sixteen years of age and/or a girl were under fourteen years of age; "antecedent and perpetual impotency either on the part of the man or the woman"; if a person was "held by a previous marriage bond," with due respect to the Pauline privilege; marriage to a non-Christian; if a person were either a "cleric in major orders" or a member of a religious institute who had taken solemn vows; if a man had abducted or forcibly detained a woman and tried to marry her; if a married person committed adultery with the intent of marrying "the partner in adultery," or killed the spouse of the adulterer, or caused the death of his or her own spouse; if a person married "in the direct line of consanguinity" or within three degrees of collateral lines. See Woywod, *The New Canon Law*, 216–219.
63. Suter, "Another Attempt," 1–2.
64. Ibid., 2.
65. Ibid., 3. Canon 1094 required that a couple had to exchange consent before a priest and two witnesses for a marriage to be valid. See Woywod, *The New Canon Law*, 221.
66. Suter, "Another Attempt," 3.
67. Hughes, "African Marriages," 7; cited in Suter, "Another Attempt," 3.
68. See Canons 1138–1141 in Woywod, *The New Canon Law*, 232–233.
69. Suter, "Another Attempt," 3.
70. See Canon 1098 in Woywod, *The New Canon Law*, 223.
71. Suter, "Another Attempt," 3–4.
72. Ibid., 4.
73. Ibid. Emphasis in original.
74. Ibid.
75. Ibid., 4–5.
76. Ibid., 5.
77. Ibid.
78. Ibid., 5–6.

79. Ibid., 6–7.

80. JAZ, Box 312/2, Lachlan Hughes, "Memorandum II: On African Marriages," May 23, 1968, 1–11. "Memorandum II" hereafter.

81. Ibid., 11–13.

82. See 1964 Marriage Act, Section 10 (2).

83. "Memorandum II," 14–15. Emphasis in original.

84. Ibid., 15. Emphasis added.

85. Ibid.

86. Ibid., 16.

87. Ibid., 16–17.

88. Ibid., 15, 16.

89. Cited in JAZ, Box 312/2, Lachlan Hughes, "Marriage Commission," September 29, 1968.

90. JAZ, Box 312/2, Marriage Commission Report, April 28, 1970, 2–5. The commission defined "convalidation" as the renewal of consent in canonical form or *sanatio in radice*.

91. Ibid., 5–7; see also appendix: "Addendum to Prenuptial Statement: Customary Union."

92. Ibid., 7–8.

93. AAH, Box 670/G, Edward Ennis, S.J. to Anthony Bex, October 16, 1972.

94. Fr. Brendan Conway, AMC, "African Marriages Commission," *Pastoral Service*, December 1973, 22.

95. Ibid., 23.

96. Ibid.

97. JAZ, Box 312/1, Brendan Conway, "Some Notes on Canonical and Civil Regulations Affecting Marriage."

6. "Thou Shalt Not Take My Name in Vain": The Mwari Controversy, 1911–1961

1. Fr. Ignatius Chidavaenzi et al., "What Does the Name 'Mwari' Mean?" I am grateful to Dr. Paul Gundani of the Department of Religious Studies, Philosophy, and Classics of the University of Zimbabwe for providing a copy of this unpublished article. According to the date of an early draft of this essay, the translation project was in progress as of October 1986. As of May 2000, when I interviewed Fr. Chidavaenzi, it was still ongoing.

2. Ibid., 4. The ChiShona may be translated, Muwari "was the one who spreads out all the things that we see in the world."

3. Ibid., 6.

4. Ibid., 8.

5. Ibid., 10.

6. Ibid. Emphasis in original.

7. Ibid., 11. Emphasis in original.

8. S. I. G. Mudenge, *A Political History of Munhumutapa* (Harare: Zimbabwe Publishing House, 1988).

9. Fortune, "Who Was Mwari?" 5.

10. Ibid., 6–8.

11. See David Lan, *Guns and Rain: Spirit Mediums in Zimbabwe's Liberation War* (London: James Curry, 1985).

12. See, e.g., Francis Richartz, "Some Remarks about the Mwari Question and Other Changes in Our Original Expressions in the Catechism and Prayer Book at Chishawasha," June 1923, JAZ, Box 260/2, also in Mwari Controversy Typescript (MCT hereafter), 55–60. The original documents for MCT, pp. 1–32, are in Box 260/1; MCT, pp. 33ff, are in Box 260/2.

13. JAZ, Box 260/2, Francis Richartz, "Reasons against Mwari," n.d., c. August 1923. Emphasis in original.

14. Richartz, "Some Remarks about the Mwari Question," JAZ, MCT, 55.

15. Richartz to John Apel, S.J., June 20, 1921, JAZ, MCT, 17. Emphasis added.

16. Fortune, "Who Was Mwari?" 5–10.

17. Richartz, "Some Remarks about the Mwari Question," JAZ, MCT, 55.

18. Fortune, "Who Was Mwari?" 6–7.

19. Ibid., 7–9.

20. Terence Ranger, "Missionaries, Migrants, and the Manyika: The Invention of Ethnicity in Zimbabwe," in *The Creation of Tribalism in Southern Africa*, ed. Leroy Vail, 134–137 (London: James Currey, 1988).

21. JAZ, MCT, front page.

22. The prefect apostolic of the Zambezi Mission, Edward Parry, appointed Johanny pro-prefect prior to his (Parry's) departure from Salisbury to visit the Jesuit missions in Northern Rhodesia. Parry died in colonial Zambia on May 21, 1922, but Johanny did not receive the news until June 3. Thus he remained acting superior of the mission until the appointment and arrival of Robert Brown as prefect later in the year. See editor's note, MCT, 46.

23. JAZ, MCT, Francis Johanny to Fr. General, May 31, 1922, 33–48. Quotation at 33; emphasis in original.

24. Ibid., 34. Emphasis in original. In 1909, the Religious Missionaries of Mariannhill split from the Order of Cistercians of the Strict Observance, or Trappists.

25. JAZ, MCT, Johanny to Fr. General, May 31, 1922, 34–35.

26. Ibid., 35; cf. Richartz, "Some Remarks about the Mwari Question," JAZ, MCT, 56–57.

27. Johanny to Fr. General, May 31, 1922, 35. See Richartz, "Some Remarks about the Mwari Question," 56–57.

28. Johanny to Fr. General, May 31, 1922, 35. See also JAZ, MCT, Charles Bert to Johanny, July 15, 1922, 53.

29. Richartz, "Some Remarks about the Mwari Question," 57; Johanny to Fr. General, May 31, 1922, 35.

30. JAZ, Box 100/3, John Apel to Robert Brown, July 2, 1923.

31. JAZ, MCT, M. Ledochowski to Robert Brown, December 22, 1922.

32. JAZ, Box 13, [Robert] Brown file, Circular Letter, August 25, 1923; also in MCT, 68.

33. JAZ, MCT, 69, Brown to Johanny, September 23, 1924.

34. JAZ, MCT, 70, Fr. Ignatius Arnoz, RMM to Brown, October 12, 1924.

35. JAZ, MCT, 1, "For and Against Mwari." For Mwari: Frs. Withnell, Hornig, Gardner, Marconness, O'Neil, Burbridge, Torrend, Daignault, Apel, Bontemps, Quin. Against Mwari: Frs. Richartz, Johanny, Bert, Loubiere, Kaibach, Schmitz, Seed.

36. JAZ, MCT, 17–25, Richartz to Apel, June 20, 1921.

37. Ibid., 21. Emphasis in original.

38. Ibid., 20.

39. JAZ, MCT, 26, Richartz to Parry, June 24, 1921.

40. JAZ, MCT, 22, Richartz to Apel, June 20, 1921.

41. JAZ, MCT, 7, Anonymous, "Notes on Mwari," n.d. (attributed to Fr. William O'Neil, S.J.).

42. JAZ, MCT, 12–13, John Apel to Francis Richartz, May 19, 1921.

43. JAZ, MCT, "Notes on Mwari," 9. Emphasis in original.

44. Ibid., 7; JAZ, Box 260/1, Andrew Hartmann to Francis Richartz, July 26, 1921. I am grateful to Fr. Karl-Ferdinand Schmidt, S.J., for translating this passage from the original German.

45. JAZ, MCT, 13, Apel to Richartz, May 19, 1921.

46. For the reference to Francis Xavier, see JAZ, MCT, 8, "Notes on Mwari"; JAZ, MCT, 38, Francis Johanny to Fr. General, May 31, 1922.

47. JAZ, Box 260/1, Emil Schmitz, S.J., to Richartz, June 10, 1921.

48. JAZ, MCT, 23–24, Richartz to Apel, June 20, 1921.

49. JAZ, MCT, 43–44, Johanny to Ledochowski, May 31, 1922.

50. JAZ, MCT, 54, Fr. General Ledochowski to Brown, December 20, 1922; JAZ, MCT, 61–62, Letter of A. Delpuch, M.Afr., November 21, 1922.

51. JAZ, MCT, 5–6, 8, "Notes on Mwari."

52. JAZ, MCT, 12–13, Apel to Richartz, May 19, 1921.

53. Telephone interview with Rev. Bernard Ndlovu, Bulawayo, May 11, 2000.

54. Terence Ranger, "Missionaries, Migrants, and the Manyika," 136.

55. JAZ, MCT, 12, Apel to Richartz, May 19, 1921.

56. JAZ, MCT, 51, Remarks of F.J. Richartz redacted by Francis Johanny, May 17, 1922.

57. JAZ, MCT, 58, Francis Richartz, "Some Remarks about the Mwari Question and Others [sic] Changes in our Original Expressions in the Catechism and Prayer Book at Chishawasha," 1923.

58. JAZ, MCT, 9–10, "Notes on Mwari."

59. Interview with C. L. Muringayi, Chishawasha Mission, July 31, 2000.

60. See James C. Scott, *Domination and the Arts of Resistance: Hidden Transcripts* (New Haven: Yale University Press, 1990).

61. Conversation with Fr. Albert Plangger, SMB, Mambo House, Harare, May 16, 2000.

62. Fortune, "Who Was Mwari?" 9 n. 39.

63. Conversation with Fr. Oscar Wermter, S.J., Africa Synod House, Harare, March 6, 2000.

7. Bread and Wine, Beer and Meat: The *Kurova Guva* Controversy

1. Access to the deliberations and reports of the various committees and commissions established by the bishops as well as to the minutes of the bishops' own deliberations was severely restricted.

2. Paul Gundani, "The Roman Catholic Church and the *Kurova Guva* Ritual in Zimbabwe," *Zambezia* 21, no. 2 (1994): 123–146. Gundani evidently received access to the bishops' conference materials.

3. See, e.g., M. F. C. Bourdillon, *The Shona Peoples* (Gweru: Mambo Press, 1987), 199–223. For excellent, concise descriptions of the *kurova guva*, ceremony see Michael Gelfand, *Shona Ritual* (Cape Town: Juta Books, 1959), 184–198, and "A Description of the Ceremony of Kurova Guva: Escorting the Spirit from the Grave to the Home," *Zambezia* 2, no. 1 (December 1971): 71–74. Paul Gundani provides a brief overview of the function, theology, and different parts of the VaShona *kurova guva* ritual and the opposition of the mission churches to "traditional" African religious practices: "The Roman Catholic Church and *Kurova Guva*," 124–127.

4. Gelfand, "A Description of the Ceremony of Kurova Guva," 71, 73–74.

5. See A. J. Dachs and F. W. Rea, *The Catholic Church and Zimbabwe, 1879–1979* (Gwelo: Mambo Press, 1979), 9; Gundani, "The Roman Catholic Church and *Kurova Guva*," 123.

6. Gundani, "The Roman Catholic Church and *Kurova Guva*," 127. The first commandment states: "I, the Lord, am your God. . . . You shall not have other gods besides me. You shall not carve idols for yourselves in the shape of anything in the sky above or on the earth below or in the waters beneath the earth; you shall not bow down before them or worship them." See Exodus 20:2–6.

7. Ibid.

8. Citation taken from Rev. Raymond Kapito, "Report on *Kuchenura Munhu* Catechism," available in the ZCBC Gen/Sec File Kg 78FMM, 2. Access to the files of the Zimbabwe Catholic Bishops Conference was extremely limited in 1999–2000.

9. Gundani, "The Roman Catholic Church and *Kurova Guva*," 128–129.

10. Ibid., 129.

11. For descriptions of *bira* ceremonies, see David Lan, *Guns and Rain: Guerrillas and Spirit Mediums in Zimbabwe* (London: James Currey, 1985).

12. JAZ, Chishawasha *Historia Domus* (Typescript), April 7–8, 1902. Ellipsis in original text.

13. Ibid., September 7–9, 1930.

14. Ibid., October 6, 1902; November 30, 1902; December 2, 1944; December 25, 1931.

15. Interview with C. L. Muringayi, Chishawasha Mission, July 31, 2000.

16. JAZ, Chishawasha *Historia Domus* (Typescript), January 17, 1904, and February 7, 1904.

17. Ibid., March 6, 1926 and November 10, 1930. Emphasis in original.

18. Interview with Br. Herman Toma, S.J., Old St. Peter's Church, Mbare, Harare, May 13, 2000.

19. Interview with Sr. Bernadette Garatsa, May 23, 2000.

20. Interview with Boniface Mariwa Gumbo, Kutama Mission, July 28, 2000.

21. Interview with Teresa Joe, Kutama Mission, July 28, 2000.

22. For more on the Chinese rites controversy, see Andrew C. Ross, *A Vision Betrayed: The Jesuits in Japan and China, 1542–1742* (Edinburgh: Edinburgh University Press, 1994).

23. JAZ, Box 134/2, Francis Johanny to Edward Parry, February 15, 1920. Emphasis in original.

24. Cardinal Peter Fumasoni Biondi (Prefect of Propaganda Fide) to Augustus Gaspais (Vicar Apostolic of Kirin), May 28, 1935, in *Sylloge Praecipuorum Documentorum . . . de Propaganda Fide* (Vatican City: Polyglot Printer, 1939), 479–482. Attached to the letter were several statute norms recommended by the nascent hierarchy in China that formed the basis for Vatican approval. See also Fumasoni Biondi to Archbishop Paul Marella (Apostolic Delegate to Japan), May 26, 1936, in *Acta Apostolicae Sedis* (Vatican City: Polyglot Printer, 1936), 406–409. There may be correspondence on the part of Bishop Chichester addressing the issue, but if it does exist, it was not available in the unrestricted general correspondence in the JAZ or the AAH.

25. Fumasoni Biondi to Giovanne Delle Piane, July 14, 1938, in *Sylloge Praecipuorum Documentorum*, 576–578. I am grateful to Tommaso Astarita, Department of History, Georgetown University, for translating this letter from the original Italian.

26. JAZ, Box 357/2, "The Man Called Joseph Munyongani," English translation typescript, 3, 10. For more on Munyongani, see Nicholas M. Creary, "Spiritual Base, Material Superstructure: A Spiritual Economy of Chishawasha Mission, Southern Rhodesia, 1892–1953," *American Review of Political Economy* 5, no. 2 (December 2007): 1–30.

27. See Chapter 4. See also Gundani, "The Roman Catholic Church and *Kurova Guva*," 133–134; J. C. Kumbirai, "The Place of the Midzimu in Christian Worship," *Moto*, October, 1969, 8, and "Kurova Guva and Christianity," in *Christianity South of the Zambezi*, ed. M. F. C. Bourdillon, 2:123–130 (Gwelo: Mambo Press, 1977).

28. Gundani, "The Roman Catholic Church and *Kurova Guva*," 134, 135.

29. Ibid., 135–137.

30. Ibid., 137–138. Ellipsis in original.
31. Ibid., 137.
32. Ibid., 138.
33. Ibid.
34. Ibid., 139–140.
35. Ibid., 141–143.
36. Ibid.
37. Emmanuel Mavudzi, "*Kurova Guva, Kugadzira, Kuchenura Munhu*: A Second Look at the Rites," *Crossroads* 164 (Christmas 1998): 15.
38. Obiter dicta conversation with several Zimbabwean priests, 1999–2000. Given the sensitive nature of these ongoing discussions and the respective positions of several of these priests I have chosen not to identify the sources of these comments.
39. See, e.g., Emmanuel Mavudzi, "Communion of the Living and the Dead," *Crossroads* 161 (Pentecost 1998): 7, and "*Kurova Guva, Kugadzira, Kuchenura Munhu*," 15–16; Marko M. Mkandla, "High God and Ancestors: A Critical Analysis of the Relationship Between Ancestral Spirits (Amadlozi) and the Supreme Being in Ndebele Religion," *Crossroads* 164 (Christmas 1998): 17–18; Tadzungaira A. Dzadagu, "Inculturation and Religious Images," *Catholic Church News*, January–February 1999, 15; S. B. Muchemwa, "Ancestor-Veneration and the Value of Communalism," *Crossroads* 165 (Lent/Easter 1999): 14–15; Kyran Murphy, "Inculturation—Where Are We?" *Crossroads* 165 (Lent/Easter, 1999): 15–17; Ignatius Chidavaenzi, "Is There Anything Objectionable About *Kuchenura Munhu* or *Kurova Guva*? A Critical Look at Some Aspects of the Ritual," *Crossroads* 166 (Pentecost 1999): 16–19; Stanislaus S. P. Matindike, "*Kurova Guva, Kugadzira, Kuchenura Munhu*: A Layman's Look at the Rites," *Crossroads* 166 (Pentecost 1999): 19–20; Canisius Mwandayi, "Restless Spirits," *Crossroads* 166 (Pentecost 1999): 20; Josef Elsener, "Catholic Beliefs and Our Relations to the Living Dead," *Crossroads* 167 (August 1999): 21; Tony Bex, "Reflections by a Mere European on 'Kuchenura Munhu,'" *Crossroads* 167 (August 1999): 22; C. T. Mashonganyika, "Christ and Ancestors Play Different Roles: Response to Fr. Mavhudi's [sic] Article on 'A Theology of African Culture,'" *Crossroads* 167 (August 1999): 23–24; C. T. Mashonganyika, "Response to Fr. Mavhudzi: 'Theology of African Culture,'" *Crossroads* 168 (October 1999): 7–9; Oskar Niederberger, "Respect for the Action of the Spirit in Man: Reflections on Fr. Ignatius Chidavaenzi's Objections to the 'Kuchenura Munhu' Ritual," *Crossroads* 168 (October 1999): 9–11; [Editorial] "Comment," *Crossroads* 168 (October 1999): 12.

40. Southern African Catholic Bishops' Conference (SACBC), "Ancestor Religion and the Christian Faith," April 16, 2007.

41. Ignatius Chidavaenzi, "Is There Anything Objectionable about *Kuchenura Munhu* or *Kurova Guva*?" and "The Sacrificial Aspects of Kurova Guva (Is Kurova Guva a Sacrifice or not?)."

42. Cited in Chidavaenzi, "Is There Anything Objectionable?" 2.

43. Chidavaenzi, "The Sacrificial Aspect of Kurova Guva," 12.

44. Chidavaenzi, "Is There Anything Objectionable?" 4–6. For divinization of ancestors, see "Kurova Guva Sacrifices."

45. Chidavaenzi, "Is There Anything Objectionable?" 7–9. See also SACBC, "Ancestor Religion and the Christian Faith."

46. Chidavaenzi, "Is There Anything Objectionable?" 2, 6.

47. Ibid., 9–10.

48. Chidavaenzi, "The Sacrificial Aspect of Kurova Guva," 2.

49. Karl Herrmann, "Shona Ritual Kuchenura Munhu: An Encounter Between Shona Religion and Christian Faith—Inculturation or Conversion?" Ph.D. dissertation, Hekima College, Nairobi, 1997, Appendix, "Shona Ritual: The Rite of Installation of the Spirit of a Deceased Person," 10–11. Copy in JAZ. I am grateful to Fr. Karl-Ferdinand Schmidt, S.J., for making this dissertation available.

50. From "Novena to Our Lady of Lourdes," in Lawrence G. Lovasik, *Treasury of Novenas* (New York: Catholic Book Publishing Co., 1986), 158–159. Emphasis in original. For more on the story of the Marian apparitions to Bernadette Soubirous at Lourdes, France, see Thérèse Taylor, *Bernadette of Lourdes: Her Life, Death, and Visions* (New York: Burns & Oates, 2003).

51. From "Novena to St. Raphael," in ibid., 279–280. Emphasis in original. For more on the story of Raphael and Tobiah, see the Book of Tobit.

52. Commentary on Hebrews 10, *The New American Bible* (New York: Nelson Publishers, 1970), 1303.

53. Achille Mbembe, *On the Postcolony* (Berkeley: University of California Press, 2001).

54. SACBC, "Ancestor Religion and the Christian Faith": "All forms of divination are to be rejected: recourse to Satan or demons, conjuring up the dead or other practices falsely supposed to 'unveil' the future. Consulting horoscopes, astrology, palm reading, interpretation of omens and lots, the phenomena of clairvoyance, and recourse to mediums all conceal a desire for power over time, history and, in the last analysis, other human beings, as well as a

wish to conciliate hidden powers. They contradict the honour, respect and loving fear that we owe to God alone.... All practices of magic or sorcery, by which one attempts to tame occult powers, so as to place them at one's service and have a supernatural power over others—even if this were for the sake of restoring their health—are gravely contrary to the virtue of religion. These practices are even more to be condemned when accompanied by the intention of harming someone, or when they have recourse to the intervention of demons. Wearing charms is also reprehensible. Spiritism often implies divination or magical practices; the Church for her part warns the faithful against it. Recourse to so-called traditional cures does not justify either the invocation of evil powers, or the exploitation of another's credulity."

55. Ibid.

56. See Chidavaenzi, "Is There Anything Objectionable?" 6.

57. Paul Gundani, "Eschatology in Death Rituals Among Shona Catholics," *Studiae Historiae Ecclesiae* 21, no. 1 (1995): 35–36.

58. Adam Mkosana, "Church Must Adopt Good Customs," *Moto*, December 2, 1970, 2.

Conclusion

1. Archives of the Archdiocese of Harare (AAH hereafter), Box 412, File C (412/C hereafter), Minutes of the "Committee appointed by the Hierarchy to investigate the Catholic Association and its relationship to other Catholic Associations," March 27, 1962 (Inquiry Commission hereafter).

2. AAH, Box 412/B, Territorial Council Executive Committee minutes, January 4, 1961.

3. AAH, Box 412/B, Archbishop Francis Markall, S.J. to Rev. Michael Hannan, S.J., May 25, 1961.

4. Inquiry Commission, 8.

5. Ibid., 9–10.

6. *Catholic Directory 2000* (Gweru: Mambo Press, 2000).

7. See, e.g., Frantz Fanon, *The Wretched of the Earth* (New York: Grove Press, 1991), and Amílcar Cabral, *Unity and Struggle* (New York: Monthly Review Press, 1979), 138–154.

8. See Vincent Donovan, *Christianity Rediscovered* (Maryknoll, N.Y.: Orbis, 1982).

9. See M. F. C. Bourdillon, *Where Are the Ancestors? Changing Culture in Zimbabwe* (Harare: University of Zimbabwe Press, 1993)

10. See "Ad Gentes: Decree on the Mission Activity of the Church," http://www.vatican.va/archive/hist_councils/ii_vatican_council/documents/vat-ii_decree_19651207_ad-gentes_en.html (accessed 31 August 2009). I am grateful to Paul Kollman for suggesting this point.

11. John Ganly, "ATR [African Traditional Religion] Can Enrich Christianity," *African Ecclesial Review* 31, no. 5 (October 1989): 306–316; Salvador Ferrao, "Not Married in Church—No Sacraments," *African Ecclesial Review* 32, no. 6 (December 1990): 363–367; Tarcisius Mukuka, "Platform: Africa and the Return of Priestcraft," *African Ecclesial Review* 35, no. 6 (December 1993): 383–384; James Onyango Owino, "Towards an Analytical African Theology: The Luo Concept of God as a Case in Point," *African Ecclesial Review* 36, no. 4 (June 1994): 171–180; Aylward Shorter, "Evangelization and Culture," *African Ecclesial Review* 37, no. 2 (April 1995): 93–104; Laurenti Magesa, "Authentic African Christianity," *African Ecclesial Review* 37, no. 4 (August 1995): 209–220; Sola Ademiluka, "The Use of Therapeutic Psalms in Inculturating Christianity in Africa," *African Ecclesial Review* 37, no. 4 (August 1995): 221–227; George Kwame Kumi, "God's Image as Equivalently Father and Mother: An African Perspective," *African Ecclesial Review* 38, no. 4 (August 1996): 203–228; Mortimer F. Kane, "A Meaningful Eucharistic Celebration," *African Ecclesial Review* 38, no. 5 (October 1996): 268–273; Louis Oger, "The Pastoral Approach to Spirit Possession: A Zambian Case," *African Ecclesial Review* 38, no. 5 (October 1996): 274–290; Prisca M. Wagura, "Karl Rahner's Theology: A Basis for Searching for an African Christianity," *African Ecclesial Review* 40, no. 1 (February1998): 2–11; P. A. Kalilombe, "How Do We Share 'Third World' Christian Insights in Europe?" *African Ecclesial Review* 40, no. 1 (February 1998): 12–20; Walter Nyatsanza, "The Shona Traditional Greeting: A Value for Inculturation," *African Ecclesial Review* 40, no. 4 (August 1998): 194–202; J. O. Uburhe, "The African Concept of Sacrifice: A Starting Point for Inculturation," *African Ecclesial Review* 40, no. 4 (August 1998): 203–215; Joseph M. Lupande et al., "The Sukuma Sacrificial Goat: A Basis for Inculturation," *African Ecclesial Review* 40, no. 4 (August 1998): 244–254; Deusdedit R. K. Nkurunziza, "Ethnicity and Evangelization: An African Perspective," *African Ecclesial Review* 49, nos. 1–2 (March–June 2007): 19–36; Stan Chu Ilo, "Contemporary African Cultural Values: A Challenge to Traditional Christianity," *African Ecclesial Review* 49, nos. 3–4 (September–December 2007): 184–219; Deusdedit R. K. Nkurunziza, "Towards a New African Paradigm of Evangelization,"

African Ecclesial Review 50, nos. 1–2 (March–June 2008): 58–70; Kenneth Obiekwe, "The 2009 Synod of Bishops: Church in Africa in Service to Reconciliation, Justice, and Peace," *African Ecclesial Review* 51, nos. 1–2 (March–June 2009): 105–130.

12. Hugo Hinfelaar, "Evangelization and Inculturation," *African Ecclesial Review* 36, no. 1 (February 1994): 2–18; Aylward Shorter, "Evangelization and Culture," *African Ecclesial Review* 37, no. 2 (April 1995): 93–104.

13. Hillman, *Toward an African Christianity*, 41.

14. Compare Benedict XVI, "Faith, Reason and the University: Memories and Reflections," University of Regensburg, Tuesday, 12 September 2006, paragraphs 8–9, 14, http://www.vatican.va/holy_father/benedict_xvi/speeches/ 2006/ september/doc uments/hf_ben-xvi_spe_20060912_university-regensburg_en .html (accessed 26 August 2009):

[The] inner rapprochement between Biblical faith and Greek philosophical inquiry was an event of decisive importance not only from the standpoint of the history of religions, but also from that of world history—it is an event which concerns us even today. Given this convergence, it is not surprising that Christianity, despite its origins and some significant developments in the East, finally took on its historically decisive character in Europe. We can also express this the other way around: this convergence, with the subsequent addition of the Roman heritage, created Europe and remains the foundation of what can rightly be called Europe.

The thesis that the critically purified Greek heritage forms an integral part of Christian faith has been countered by the call for a dehellenization of Christianity—a call which has more and more dominated theological discussions since the beginning of the modern age. . . . In the light of our experience with cultural pluralism, it is often said nowadays that the synthesis with Hellenism achieved in the early Church was an initial inculturation which ought not to be binding on other cultures. The latter are said to have the right to return to the simple message of the New Testament prior to that inculturation, in order to inculturate it anew in their own particular milieux. This thesis is not simply false, but it is coarse and lacking in precision. The New Testament was written in Greek and bears the imprint of the Greek spirit, which had already come to maturity as the Old Testament developed. True, there are elements in the evolution of the early Church which do not have to be integrated into all cultures. Nonetheless, the fundamental decisions made about the relationship between faith and the use of human reason are part of the faith itself; they are developments consonant with the nature of faith itself.

with G. W. F. Hegel, *The Philosophy of History* (New York: Dover Publications, 1956), 103–10:

> The History of the World travels from East to West, for Europe is absolutely the end of History, Asia the beginning. The History of the World has an East . . . for although the Earth forms a sphere, History performs no circle around it, but has on the contrary a determinate East, viz., Asia. Here rises the outward physical Sun, and in the West it sinks down: here consentaneously rises the Sun of self-consciousness, which diffuses a nobler brilliance. The History of the World is the discipline of the uncontrolled natural will, bringing it into obedience to a Universal principle and conferring subjective freedom. The East knew and to the present day knows only that *One* is free; the Greek and Roman world, that *some* are free; the German World knows that *All* are free. The first political form therefore which we observe in History is *Despotism*, the second *Democracy* and *Aristocracy*, the third *Monarchy*. The first phase—that with which we have to begin—is the *East*. Unreflected consciousness—substantial, objective, spiritual existence—forms the basis. . . . It is the childhood of History. . . . The Greek world may then be compared with the period of adolescence, for here we have individualities forming themselves. This is the *second* main principle in human History. . . . The third phase is the realm of abstract Universality (in which the Social aim absorbs all individual aims): it is the *Roman State*, the severe labors of the *Manhood* of History. . . . The *German* world appears at this point of development—the fourth phase of World-History. This would answer in the comparison with the periods of human life to its *Old Age*. . . . This fourth phase begins with the Reconciliation presented in Christianity; but only in the germ, without national or political development. . . . This is the ultimate result which the process of History is intended to accomplish, and we have to traverse in detail the long track which has been thus cursorily traced out.

15. Aylward Shorter, *Toward a Theology of Inculturation* (London: Geoffrey Chapman, 1988), 10–12. See also Oliver Alozie Onwubiko, *Theory and Practice of Inculturation (An African Perspective)* (Enugu: SNAAP Press, 1992), 40; Xolile Keteyi, *Inculturation as a Strategy for Liberation* (Pietermaritzburg: Cluster Publications, 1998), 37; A. L. Pula, "Balimo [Ancestor] Veneration and Christianity," *African Ecclesial Review* 32, no. 6 (December 1990): 330–345; Joseph Osei-Bonsu, "Biblically/Theologically Based Inculturation," *African Ecclesial Review* 32, no. 6 (December 1990): 346–358; José Antunes da Silva, "Inculturation as Dialogue," *African Ecclesial Review* 37, no. 4 (August 1995): 198–208.

16. Paul V. Kollman, personal communication, July 2008.

17. Agatha Radoli, "Editorial," *African Ecclesial Review* 38, no. 5 (October 1996): 257; Justin S. Ukpong, "Inculturation: A Major Challenge to the Church in Africa," *African Ecclesial Review* 38, no. 5 (October 1996): 258–267; Evarist Shayo, "Mission and Inculturation," *African Ecclesial Review* 38, no. 5 (October 1996): 290–297; Joseph Kahiga Kiruki, "Polygamy: A Pastoral Challenge to the Church in Africa," *African Ecclesial Review* 49, nos. 1–2 (March–June 2007): 119–147; Jay J. Carney, "Waters of Baptism, Blood of Tribalism," *African Ecclesial Review* 50, nos. 1–2 (March–June 2008): 9–30; Joseph Bitole Kato, "Evangelization in Africa: Twelve Years After the [sic] *Ecclesia in Africa*," *African Ecclesial Review* 50, nos. 1–2 (March–June 2008): 115–131. While not specifically rooted in a presumption of African cultural difference or inferiority, the last article ultimately absolves Western missionaries for their failings to respect African cultures in the past and further makes recommendations for new models of inculturation that are not specific to African cultures, but rather are so general as to be limited in their practical applicability.

18. "The Church in Africa in Service to Reconciliation, Justice and Peace," http://www.zenit.org/article-25422?l=english (accessed 14 August 2009). *Instrumentum Laboris* hereafter.

19. Charles Coppens, "Examination of Conscience," *Catholic Encyclopedia* (New York: Robert Appleton, 1909).

20. *Instrumentum Laboris*. See also Raymond Moloney, "Lavigerie and Slave Trade Abolition: A Forgotten Century," *African Ecclesial Review* 31, no. 5 (October 1989): 272–281; Laurenti C. Magesa, "Am I Not a Human Being and a Brother/Sister? Five Hundred Years After the Atlantic Slave Trade," *African Ecclesial Review* 34, no. 2 (April 1992): 95–114.

21. Pontifical Council for Justice and Peace, "The Church and Racism: Toward a More Fraternal Society," 3 November 1988. http://www.ewtn.com/library/CURIA/pcjpraci.htm (accessed 2 September 2009).

22. See Renato Kizito Sesana, "An African Synod Without Africa?" *African Ecclesial Review* 35, no. 3 (June 1993): 134–143. See also Raymond Olusesan Aina, "The Second Synod for Africa and Its *Lineamenta*: Questions and Suggestions," *African Ecclesial Review* 49, nos. 3–4 (September–December 2007): 155–183.

23. See Onwubiko, *Theory and Practice of Inculturation*, 23–24.

Glossary

Abafundisi   preacher or clergy (IsiNdebele)
Abathakathi   witches (IsiNdebele)
Amai   mother (ChiShona)
Ambuya   grandmother (ChiShona)
Baba   father (ChiShona)
Bira   overnight outdoor ceremony to appease ancestral spirits (ChiShona)
Chimurenga   fight or struggle (ChiShona)
Chiswina/swina   VaShona people (IsiNdebele)
Hosho   musical instrument akin to maracas (ChiShona)
Imikhobo   ghost (IsiNdebele)
Induna   chief or subchief (IsiNdebele)
Ishe   chief or subchief (ChiShona)
Kuperekedzwa   to accompany the bride to new in-laws (ChiShona)
kurova guva   ceremony to settle the deceased spirit (ChiShona)
Mbira   thumb piano (ChiShona)
Mhondoro   Lion spirit (ChiShona)
Midzimu/vadzimu/mudzimu   ancestor spirits (ChiShona)
Miriwo   Leafy greens, vegetables (ChiShona)
Mukoma   older sibling of the same gender as speaker/writer (ChiShona)
Mukuwasha   groom, son-in-law (ChiShona)
Munyai   intermediary in a marriage negotiation (ChiShona)
Musha   ancestral homeland (ChiShona)
MuShona   Shona person (ChiShona and VaShona)
Musikavanhu   creator of beings (ChiShona)

Musiki   creator (ChiShona)

Mwari   God (ChiShona)

mwea wepasi   spirit of the land (ChiShona)

N'ganga   traditional healer (ChiShona)

Ngozi   evil spirit (ChiShona)

Roora   bride price (ChiShona)

Rutsambo   cash gift given to father of potential bride (ChiShona)

Sadza   cornmeal-based staple (ChiShona, IsiNdebele)

Sekuru   grandfather (ChiShona)

Shave   spirit that possesses spirit mediums (ChiShona)

Svikiro   trance state, spirit medium (ChiShona)

Tezvara/Vadzitezvara   male in-law (ChiShona)

Unhu   human qualities or cultural values, akin to *ubuntu* in IsiXhosa (ChiShona)

Usavi   relish or stew eaten with *sadza* (ChiShona, IsiNdebele)

Vafundisi   preachers or clergy (ChiShona)

Vakuru   elders (ChiShona)

Vhuramuromo   payment to initiate marriage negotiation (ChiShona)

Yave   God (ChiShona; recognized by the Catholic Church)

Bibliography

"Ad Gentes: Decree on the Mission Activity of the Church." http://www.vatican.va/archive/hist_councils/ii_vatican_council/documents/vat-ii_decree_19651207_ad-gentes_en.html.

Adamson, Walter L. *Hegemony and Revolution: A Study of Antonio Gramsci's Political and Cultural Theory.* Berkeley: University of California Press, 1983.

Ademiluka, Sola. "The Use of Therapeutic Psalms in Inculturating Christianity in Africa," *African Ecclesial Review*, 37, no. 4 (August 1995): 221–227.

Adewale, S. A. *The African Church, 1901–1986: A Synthesis of Religions and Culture.* Ibadan: Oluseyi Press, 1988.

Aina, Raymond Olusesan. "The Second Synod for Africa and Its *Lineamenta*: Questions and Suggestions." *African Ecclesial Review* 49, nos. 3–4 (September–December 2007): 155–183.

Ajayi, J. F. *Christian Missions in Nigeria, 1841–1891: The Making of a New Elite.* London: Longmans, 1965.

Anderson, Allan. *Moya: The Holy Spirit in an African Context.* Pretoria: University of South Africa Press, 1991.

Andifasi, Jaison. "An Analysis of Roora." In *Shona Customs: Essays by African Writers*, edited by Clive Kileff and Peggy Kileff, 28–32. Gwelo: Mambo Press, 1970.

Antunes da Silva, José. "Inculturation as Dialogue." *African Ecclesial Review* 37, no. 4 (August 1995): 198–208.

Arrupe, Pedro. "Men for Others: Training Agents of Change for the Promotion of Justice." In *Justice with Faith Today: An Anthology of Letters and Addresses*, edited by Jerome Aixala, 128–138. St. Louis, Mo.: Institute of Jesuit Resources, 1980.

Babalola, E. O. *Christianity in West Africa: An Historical Analysis.* Ibadan: Book Representation and Publishing, 1988.

Bane, Martin J. *The Catholic Story of Liberia.* New York: D. X. McMullen, 1950.

Bangert, William V. *A History of the Society of Jesus.* St. Louis, Mo.: Institute of Jesuit Sources, 1986.

Barber, K., and P. F. Morães Fárias, eds. *Discourse and Its Interpretation of African Oral Texts*. Birmingham: Centre of West African Studies, 1989.

Barrett, David. *Schism and Renewal in Africa: An Analysis of Six Thousand Contemporary Religious Movements*. Oxford: Oxford University Press, 1968.

Baur, John. *2000 Years of Christianity in Africa: An African History, 62–1992*. Nairobi: Paulines, 1994.

Beach, David N. "Ndebele Raiders and Shona Power." *Journal of African History* 15 (1974): 633–651.

———. *The Shona and Their Neighbours*. Oxford: Blackwell Press, 1994.

———. *A Zimbabwean Past: Shona Dynastic Histories and Oral Traditions*. Gweru: Mambo Press, 1994.

Bede the Venerable. *Ecclesiastical History of the English People*, Book I, Chapter 30.

Benedict XV. *Maximum Illud: Apostolic Letter on the Propagation of the Faith Throughout the World*. Washington, D.C.: National Catholic Welfare Conference, 1919.

Benedict XVI. "Faith, Reason and the University: Memories and Reflections." University of Regensburg, September 12, 2006. http://www.vatican.va/holy_father/benedict_xvi/speeches/2006/september/documents/hf_ben-xvi_spe_20060912_university-regensburg_en.html.

Beyerhaus, P. *The Kairos Document: Challenge or Danger to the Church? A Critical Theological Assessment of South African People's Theology*. Cape Town: Gospel Defence League, 1987.

Bhebe, Ngwabi. *Christianity and Traditional Religion in Western Zimbabwe, 1859–1923*. London: Longman, 1979.

———. "Some Aspects of Ndebele Relations with the Shona in the Nineteenth Century." *Rhodesian History* 4 (1973): 31–38.

Bhebe, Ngwabi, and Terence Ranger, eds. *Society in Zimbabwe's Liberation War*. London: J. Currey, 1996.

———. *The ZAPU and ZANU Guerrilla Warfare and the Evangelical Lutheran Church in Zimbabwe*. Gweru: Mambo Press, 1999.

Black Catholic Bishops of the United States. *What We Have Seen and Heard: A Pastoral Letter on Evangelization*. Washington, D.C.: United States Catholic Conference, 1984.

Blakely, Thomas, et al. *Religion in Africa*. Portsmouth, N.H.: Heinemann, 1994.

Boudinhon, A. "Laity." *Catholic Encyclopedia*. New York: Robert Appleton, 1910.

Bourdieu, Pierre. *The Logic of Practice*. Stanford: Stanford University Press, 1990.

———. *Outline of a Theory of Practice*. Cambridge: Cambridge University Press, 1977.
Bourdillon, M. F. C., ed. *Christianity South of the Zambezi*. Gwelo: Mambo Press, 1977.
———. *The Shona Peoples*. Gweru: Mambo Press, 1987.
———. *Where Are the Ancestors? Changing Culture in Zimbabwe*. Harare: University of Zimbabwe Press, 1993.
Brain, Joy, and Philippe Denis, eds. *The Catholic Church in Contemporary Southern Africa*. Pietermaritzburg: Cluster Publications, 1999.
Bredekamp, Henry, and Robert Ross, eds. *Missions and Christianity in South African History*. Johannesburg: Witswatersrand University Press, 1995.
Brown, William Eric. *The Catholic Church in South Africa: From Its Origins to the Present Day*. New York: P. J. Kennedy, 1960.
Bullen, Josephine. *Empandeni Interlude, 1899–1903: Journal of a Woman Missionary*. Pietermaritzburg: Cluster Publications, 2008.
Cabral, Amílcar. "National Liberation and Culture." In *Unity and Struggle*, 138–154. New York: Monthly Review Press, 1979.
Callahan, William J. *The Catholic Church in Spain, 1875–1998*. Washington, D.C.: Catholic University of America Press, 2000.
Caraman, Philip. *The Lost Empire: The Story of the Jesuits in Ethiopia, 1555–1634*. London: Sidgwick and Jackson, 1985.
———. *The Lost Paradise: An Account of the Jesuits in Paraguay, 1607–1768*. London: Sidgwick and Jackson, 1975.
Cardenal, Ernesto. *The Gospel in Solentiname*. Maryknoll, N.Y.: Orbis Books, 1976.
Carney, Jay J. "Waters of Baptism, Blood of Tribalism." *African Ecclesial Review* 50, nos. 1–2 (March–June 2008): 9–30.
Carroll, James. "Oral History: The Voice and Spirit of the Twentieth Century." Paper presented at the Spring Meeting of the American Catholic Historical Association, Villanova University, March 1999.
Catholic Institute for International Relations and Pax Christi. *War and Conscience in South Africa: The Churches and Conscientious Objection*. London: Catholic Institute for International Relations/Pax Christi, 1982.
Chamberlain, M. E. *The Scramble for Africa*. New York: Longman, 1998.
Chanock, Martin. *Law, Custom, and Social Order: The Colonial Experience in Malawi and Zambia*. London: Cambridge University Press, 1985.
Chimhundu, Herbert. "Early Missionaries and the Ethnolinguistic Factor During the 'Invention of Tribalism' in Zimbabwe." *Journal of African History* 33, no. 1 (1992): 87–109.
Chiromba, Frederick E. *Evangelization and Inculturation*. Gweru: Mambo Press, 1989.
Clarke, Peter B. *West Africa and Christianity*. London: E. Arnold, 1986.

Cobbing, Julian. "The Absent Priesthood: Another Look at the Rhodesian Risings of 1896–1897." *Journal of African History* 18, no. 1 (1977): 69–85.

Coburn, Carol K., and Martha Smith. *Spirited Lives: How Nuns Shaped Catholic Culture and American Life, 1836–1920*. Chapel Hill: University of North Carolina Press, 1999.

Cochrane, Eric. "What Is Catholic Historiography?" *Catholic Historical Review* 61, no. 2 (1975): 169–190.

Codex Iuris Canonici. Rome: Vatican Press, 1918.

Comaroff, Jean, and John Comaroff. *Modernity and Its Malcontents: Ritual and Power in Postcolonial Africa*. Chicago: University of Chicago Press, 1993.

———. *Of Revelation and Revolution*. 2 volumes. Chicago: University of Chicago Press, 1991–97.

Coppens, Charles. "Examination of Conscience." *Catholic Encyclopedia*. New York: Appleton, 1909.

Cox, James. "Characteristics of African Indigenous Religions in Contemporary Zimbabwe." In *Indigenous Religions: A Companion*, edited by Graham Harvey, 230–242. London: Cassell, 2000.

———. "Identifying African Methodologies in the Study of Religions." Paper delivered at International Association for the History of Religion Congress, Durban, South Africa, August 2000.

Crafford, D., ed. *Trail-blazers of the Gospel: Black Pioneers in the Missionary History of Southern Africa*. Pretoria: Pro Christo/Institute for Missiological Research, 1991.

Creary, Nicholas M. "African Inculturation of the Catholic Church in Zimbabwe." *Historian* 61, no. 4 (Summer 1999): 765–781.

———. "Catholic Historiographical Methodology: A Proposal." H-Catholic Discussion Logs, April 20, 2000; http://www2.h-net.msu.edu/~catholic.

———. "Spiritual Base, Material Superstructure: A Spiritual Economy of Chishawasha Mission, Southern Rhodesia, 1892–1953." *American Review of Political Economy* 5, no. 2 (December 2007): 1–30.

Cuthbertson, Greg. "'Cave of Adullam': Missionary Reactions to Ethiopianism at Lovedale, 1898–1902." *Missionalia* 19 (1991): 57–64.

———. "Missionary Imperialism and Colonial Warfare: London Missionary Society Attitudes to the South African War, 1899–1902." *South African Historical Journal* 19 (1987): 93–113.

da Silva, António. *Mentalidade ,missiológica dos Jesuitas em Moçambique antes de 1759*. Lisbon: Junta de Investigacões do Ultramar 1967.

Dachs, A. J., and W. F. Rea. *The Catholic Church and Zimbabwe, 1879–1979*. Gwelo: Mambo Press, 1979.

Daneel, Martinus L. *The God of the Matopo Hills: An Essay on the Mwari Cult in Rhodesia*. The Hague: Mouton, 1970.

———. *Quest for Belonging: Introduction to a Study of African Independent Churches.* Gweru: Mambo Press, 1987.

D'Arcy, John Michael. "Achieving the Goals of *Ex Corde Ecclesiae:* From the Heart of the Church." Diocese of Fort Wayne–South Bend, http://www.diocesefwsb.org.

Davidson, Basil. *The Black Man's Burden: Africa and the Curse of the Nation-State.* New York: Times Books, 1992.

Davidson, James West, and Mark Hamilton Lytle. *After the Fact: The Art of Historical Detection.* New York: Knopf, 1982.

Davis, Cyprian. *The History of Black Catholics in the United States.* New York: Crossroads, 1991.

de la Cruz, Sor Juana Ines. *The Answer/La Respuesta.* Translated by Electa Arenal and Amanda Powell. New York: Feminist Press, 1994.

Derrida, Jacques. *Of Grammatology.* Baltimore: Johns Hopkins University Press, 1976.

Dike, K. O. *Origins of the Niger Mission, 1841–1891.* Ibadan: Ibadan University Press, 1962.

Dolan, Jay P. "New Directions in American Catholic History." In *New Dimensions in American Religious History: Essays in Honor of Martin E. Marty,* edited by Jay P. Dolan and James P. Wind, 152–174. Grand Rapids, Mich.: William B. Eerdmans, 1993.

Donovan, Vincent. *Christianity Rediscovered.* Maryknoll, N.Y.: Orbis, 1982.

Dulles, Avery. *The Craft of Theology.* New York: Crossroads, 1995.

Durkheim, Emile. *The Elementary Forms of the Religious Life.* Translated by J. W. Swain. London: Allen & Unwin, 1964 [1915].

Ela, Jean Marc. *African Cry.* Maryknoll, N.Y.: Orbis Books, 1986.

Eldredge, Elizabeth A. "Sources of Conflict in Southern Africa c. 1800–1830: The 'Mfecane' Reconsidered." *Journal of African History* 33, no. 1 (1992): 1–35.

Etherington, Norman. *Preachers, Peasants, and Politics in Southeast Africa, 1835–1880: African Christian Communities in Natal, Pondoland, and Zululand.* London: Royal Historical Society, 1978.

———. *The Great Treks: The Transformation of Southern Africa, 1815–1854.* London: Pearson Education, 2001.

Evans-Pritchard, E. E. *Nuer Religion.* Oxford: Oxford University Press, 1956.

———. *Theories of Primitive Religion.* Oxford: Clarendon Press, 1965.

Fabian, Johannes. *Jamaa: A Charismatic Movement in Katanga.* Evanston, Ill.: Northwestern University Press, 1971.

Fanon, Frantz. *The Wretched of the Earth.* New York: Grove Press, 1991.

Femia, Joseph. *Gramsci's Political Thought: Hegemony, Consciousness, and the Revolutionary Process.* Oxford: Clarendon Press, 1981.

Ferrao, Salvador. "Not Married in Church—No Sacraments." *African Ecclesial Review* 32, no. 6 (December 1990): 363–367.

Fields, Karen. *Revival and Rebellion in Colonial Central Africa.* Princeton: Princeton University Press, 1985.

Fisher, Humphrey J. "Conversion Reconsidered: Some Historical Aspects of Religious Conversion in Black Africa." *Africa* 43, no. 1 (1973): 27–40.

Fortune, George. "Who Was Mwari?" *Rhodesian History* 4 (1973): 1–20.

Freire, Paulo. *A pedigogia dos oprimidos: Politica e educação.* São Paulo: Cortez Editora, 1993.

Gable, Eric. "The Decolonization of Consciousness: Local Skeptics and the 'Will to Be Modern' in a West African Village." *American Ethnologist* 22, no. 2 (May 1995): 242–257.

Gallagher, Leo. *The Catholic Church in Manicaland, 1896–1996.* Harare: Kolbe Press, 1996.

Ganly, John. "ATR Can Enrich Christianity." *African Ecclesial Review* 31, no. 5 (October 1989): 306–316.

Geaney, D. J. "Catholic Action." *New Catholic Encyclopedia.* Evanston, Ill.: Gale, 1973.

Gelfand, Michael. *African Background: The Traditional Culture of the Shona-Speaking People.* Wynburg: Juta & Co., 1965.

———. "A Description of the Ceremony of Kurova Guva: Escorting the Spirit from the Grave to the Home." *Zambezia* 2, no. 1 (December 1971): 71–74.

———, ed. *Gubulawayo and Beyond: Letters and Journals of the Early Jesuit Missionaries to Zambesia (1879–1887).* London: Geoffrey Chapman, 1968.

———. *Shona Ritual.* Wynburg: Juta & Co., 1959.

Gleason, Philip. *Keeping the Faith: American Catholicism, Past and Present.* Notre Dame, Ind.: University of Notre Dame Press, 1987.

Gramsci, Antonio. *Selections from the Prison Notebooks of Antonio Gramsci.* Edited by Quinton Hoare and G. N. Smith. New York: International Publishers, 1992.

Gray, Richard. *Black Christians and White Missionaries.* New Haven: Yale University Press, 1990.

———. "The Kongo Kingdom and the Papacy." *History Today* 47, no. 1 (January 1997): 44–49.

Guha, Ranajit. *Elementary Aspects of Peasant Insurgency in Colonial India.* Delhi: Oxford University Press, 1983.

Gundani, Paul. "Eschatology in Death Rituals Among Shona Catholics." *Studiae Historiae Ecclesiae* 21, no. 1 (1995): 35.

———. "The Roman Catholic Church and the *Kurova Guva* Ritual in Zimbabwe." *Zambezia* 21, no. 2 (1994): 123–146.

Hallencreutz, Carl, and Ambrose Moyo, eds. *Church and State in Zimbabwe.* Gweru: Mambo Press, 1988.

Hastings, Adrian. *African Christianity*. New York: Seabury, 1976.
———. *The Church in Africa: 1450–1950*. New York: Oxford University Press, 1994.
———. *A History of African Christianity, 1950–1975*. Cambridge: Cambridge University Press, 1979.
Hegel, G. W. F. *The Philosophy of History*. New York: Dover Publications, 1956.
Herrmann, Karl. "Shona Ritual Kuchenura Munhu: An Encounter Between Shona Religion and Christian Faith: Inculturation or Conversion?" Ph.D. dissertation, Hekima College, Nairobi, 1997.
Hesburgh, Theodore M. *The Theology of Catholic Action*. Notre Dame, Ind.: University of Notre Dame Press, 1946.
Hillman, Eugene. *Toward an African Christianity: Inculturation Applied*. New York: Paulist Press, 1993.
Hilton, Anne. *The Kingdom of Kongo*. New York: Clarendon Press, 1985.
Hinfelaar, Hugo F. *Bemba-speaking Women of Zambia in a Century of Religious Change (1892–1992)*. Leiden: E. J. Brill, 1994.
———. "Evangelization and Inculturation." *African Ecclesial Review* 36, no. 1 (February 1994): 2–18.
Hodge, Charles. *Systematic Theology*. Grand Rapids, Mich.: Eerdmans, 1982.
Hodgson, Dorothy. "Engendered Encounters: Men of the Church and the 'Church of Women' in Masaailand, Tanzania, 1950–1993." Conference paper presented at Africans Meeting Missionaries: Rethinking Colonial Encounters, University of Minnesota, May 2–3, 1997.
Hoehler-Fatton, Cynthia Heyden. *Women of Fire and Spirit: History, Faith, and Gender in Roho Religion in Western Kenya*. New York: Oxford University Press, 1996.
Hofmeyr, J. W. *A Select Bibliography of Periodical Articles on Southern African Church History*. Pretoria: University of South Africa, 1991.
Horton, Robin. "African Conversion." *Africa* 41, no. 2 (1971): 85–108.
Horton, Robin, and J. D. Y. Peel. "Conversion and Confusion: A Rejoinder on Christianity in Eastern Nigeria." *Canadian Journal of African Studies* 10, no. 3 (1976): 481–498.
Hunke, Heinz. *Church and State: The Political Context of 100 Years of Catholic Mission in Namibia*. Windhoek: John Meinert Printers, 1996.
Ignatius of Loyola. *The Constitutions of the Society of Jesus*. Translated by George E. Ganss. St. Louis, Mo.: Institute of Jesuit Sources, 1970.
Ilo, Stan Chu. "Contemporary African Cultural Values: A Challenge to Traditional Christianity." *African Ecclesial Review* 49, nos. 3–4 (September–December 2007): 184–219.
Isichei, Elizabeth. *A History of Christianity in Africa: From Antiquity to the Present*. Lawrenceville, N.J.: Africa World Press, 1995.

Jahni, Lydia. "Roora and Marriage." In *Shona Customs: Essays by African Writers*, edited by Clive Kileff and Peggy Kileff, 33–41. Gwelo: Mambo Press, 1970.

Jeater, Diana. *Marriage, Perversion, and Power: The Construction of Moral Discourse in Southern Rhodesia, 1894–1930*. Oxford: Clarendon Press, 1993.

John Paul II. *Ex Corde Ecclesiae: Apostolic Constitution on Catholic Universities*. Rome: Acta Apostolica Sedis, 1990.

Johnson, David. "Settler Farmers and Coerced African Labour in Southern Rhodesia, 1936–1946." *Journal of African History* 33, no. 1 (1992): 111–128.

Kairos Theologians. *The Kairos Document: A Theological Comment on the Political Crisis in South Africa*. London: Catholic Institute for International Relations/ British Council of Churches, 1986.

Kalilombe, P. A. "How Do We Share 'Third World' Christian Insights in Europe?" *African Ecclesial Review* 40, no. 1 (February 1998): 12–20.

Kalu, Ogbu U. *African Christianity: An African Story*. Trenton, N.J.: Africa World Press, 2007.

———. *The History of Christianity in West Africa*. London: Longman, 1980.

Kane, Mortimer F. "A Meaningful Eucharistic Celebration." *African Ecclesial Review* 38, no. 5 (October 1996): 268–273.

Kaplan, Steven. "The Africanization of Missionary Christianity: History and Typology." *Journal of Religion in Africa* 16, no. 3 (1986): 166–186.

Karefa Smart, John. *The Halting Kingdom: Christianity and the African Revolution*. New York: Friendship Press, 1959.

Karp, Ivan, and D. A. Masolo. *African Philosophy as Cultural Inquiry*. Bloomington, Indiana University Press, 2000.

Kato, Joseph Bitole. "Evangelization in Africa: Twelve Years After the *Ecclesia in Africa*." *African Ecclesial Review* 50, nos. 1–2 (March–June 2008): 115–131.

Kersten, John C. *St. Joseph's Sunday Missal*. New York: Catholic Book Publishing Co., 1986.

Keteyi, Xolile. *Inculturation as a Strategy for Liberation*. Pietermaritzburg: Cluster Publications, 1998.

Kileff, Clive, and Peggy Kileff, eds. *Shona Customs: Essays by African Writers*. Gwelo: Mambo Press, 1970.

Kiruki, Joseph Kahiga. "Polygamy: A Pastoral Challenge to the Church in Africa." *African Ecclesial Review* 49, nos. 1–2 (March–June 2007): 119–147.

Kollman, Paul V. *The Evangelization of Slaves and Catholic Origins in Eastern Africa*. Maryknoll, N.Y.: Orbis Books, 2005.

Kumbirai, Joseph. "Kurova Guva and Christianity." In *Christianity South of the Zambezi*, edited by M. F. C Bourdillon, 2:123–130. Gwelo: Mambo Press, 1977.

Kumi, George Kwame. "God's Image as Equivalently Father and Mother: An African Perspective." *African Ecclesial Review* 38, no. 4 (August 1996): 203–228.

Lamb, Christopher, and M. Darrol Bryant, eds. *Religious Conversion: Contemporary Practices and Controversies*. London: Cassell, 1999.

Lan, David. *Guns and Rains: Guerrillas and Spirit Mediums in Zimbabwe*. Berkeley: University of California Press, 1985.

Landau, Paul Stuart. "Hegemony and History in Jean and John L. Comaroff's *Of Revelation and Revolution*." *Africa* 70, no. 3 (2000): 501–519.

———. *The Realm of the Word: Language, Gender, and Christianity in a Southern African Kingdom*. Portsmouth, N.H.: Heinemann, 1995.

Larsson, Birgitta. *Conversion to Greater Freedom? Women, Church and Social Change in North-Western Tanzania under Colonial Rule*. Uppsala: Uppsala University Press, 1991.

Linden, Ian. *The Catholic Church and the Struggle for Zimbabwe*. London: Longman, 1980.

Lloyd, Moira. *Journey to Gubulawayo: Letters from Frs. H. Depelchin and C. Croonenberghs, S.J., 1879–1881*. Bulawayo: Books of Rhodesia, 1979.

Lovasik, Lawrence G. *Treasury of Novenas*. New York: Catholic Book Publishing Co., 1986.

Lumen Gentium: The Dogmatic Constitution of the Church. http://www.vatican.va/archive/hist_councils/ii_vatican_council/documents/vat-ii_const_19641121_lumen gentium_en.html.

Lupande, Joseph M., et al. "The Sukuma Sacrificial Goat: A Basis for Inculturation." *African Ecclesial Review* 40, no. 4 (August 1998): 244–254.

Luzbetak, Louis. *The Church and Cultures*. Maryknoll, N.Y.: Orbis Books, 1988.

MacGaffey, Wyatt. *Religion and Society in Central Africa: The BaKongo of Lower Zaire*. Chicago: University of Chicago Press, 1986.

Magesa, Laurenti C. "Am I Not a Human Being and a Brother/Sister? Five Hundred Years After the Atlantic Slave Trade." *African Ecclesial Review* 34, no. 2 (April 1992): 95–114.

———. "Authentic African Christianity." *African Ecclesial Review* 37, no. 4 (August 1995): 209–220.

Martin, Marie-Louise. *Kimbangu: An African Prophet and His Church*. Oxford: Basil Blackwell, 1975.

Mauss, Marcel. "A Category of the Human Mind: The Notion of Person, the Notion of Self." In *The Category of the Person*, edited by Michael Carrithers et al., 3–23. Cambridge: Cambridge University Press, 1985.

Maxwell, David. *African Gifts of the Spirit: Pentecostalism and the Rise of a Zimbabwean Transnational Religious Movement*. Athens: Ohio University Press, 2006.

———. *Christians and Chiefs in Zimbabwe: A Social History of the Hwesa People.* Westport, Conn.: Praeger, 1999.

Mbiti, John. "The Encounter of Christian Faith and African Religion." In *Third World Liberation Theologies: A Reader*, edited by Deane William Ferm, 199–204. Maryknoll, N.Y.: Orbis, 1986.

McAvoy, Timothy. "The Catholic Church in Indiana, 1789–1834." Ph.D. dissertation, Columbia University, 1940.

McGreevy, John T. *Parish Boundaries: The Catholic Encounter with Race in the Twentieth-Century Urban North.* Chicago: University of Chicago Press, 1996.

McKenna, Joseph. *Finding a Social Voice: The Church and Marxism in Africa.* New York: Fordham University Press, 1997.

McLaren, Peter, and Peter Leonard, eds. *Paulo Freire: A Critical Encounter.* New York: Routledge, 1993.

McLaughlin, Janice. *On the Frontline: Catholic Missions in Zimbabwe's Liberation War.* Harare: Baobab, 1996.

McNamara, Jo Ann, et al., eds. *Sainted Women of the Dark Ages.* Durham, N.C.: Duke University Press, 1992.

Meekers, Dominique. "The Noble Custom of Roora: The Marriage Practices of the Shona of Zimbabwe." *Ethnology* 32 (1993): 35.

Meyer, Birgit. "'If you Are a Devil, You are a Witch, and, If You Are a Witch, You Are a Devil': The Integration of 'Pagan' Ideas Into the Conceptual Universe of Ewe Christians in Southeastern Ghana." *Journal of Religion in Africa* 22, no. 2 (1992): 98–132.

Moloney, Raymond. "Lavigerie and Slave Trade Abolition: A Forgotten Century." *African Ecclesial Review* 31, no. 5 (October 1989): 272–281.

Moss, Barbara. "'And the Bones Come Together': African and Missionary Expectations." Paper presented at Africans Meeting Missionaries: Rethinking Colonial Encounters, University of Minnesota, May 2–3, 1997.

Mudenge, S. I. G. "An Identification of the Rozvi and Its Implication for the History of the Karanga." *Rhodesian History* 5 (1974): 19–31.

———. *A Political History of Munhumutapa, c. 1400–1902.* Harare: Zimbabwe Publishing House, 1988.

Mukuka, George Sombe. *The Other Side of the Story: The Silent Experience of the Black Clergy in the Catholic Church in South Africa (1898–1976).* Pietermaritzburg: Cluster Publications, 2008.

Mukuka, Tarcisius. "Platform: Africa and the Return of Priestcraft." *African Ecclesial Review* 35, no. 6 (December 1993): 383–384.

Munonguri, Masumbuko. *The Closeness of the God of our Ancestors: An African Approach to the Incarnation.* Nairobi: Pauline Publications of Africa, 1998.

Muzorewa, Gwinyai H. *An African Theology of Mission.* Lewiston, N.Y.: E. Mellen Press, 1990.
Ngada, N. H., ed. *Speaking for Ourselves: African Independent Churches.* Braamfontein: Institute for Contextual Theology, 1985.
Ngugi wa Thiong'o. *Decolonising the Mind: The Politics of Language in African Literature.* Portsmouth, N.H.: Heinemann, 1997.
Nkurunziza, Deusdedit R. K. "Ethnicity and Evangelization: An African Perspective." *African Ecclesial Review* 49, nos. 1–2 (March–June 2007): 19–36.
———. "Towards a New African Paradigm of Evangelization." *African Ecclesial Review* 50, nos. 1–2 (March–June 2008): 58–70.
Nyatsanza, Walter. "The Shona Traditional Greeting: A Value for Inculturation." *African Ecclesial Review* 40, no. 4 (August 1998): 194–202.
Obeng, J. Pashington. *Asante Catholicism: Religious and Cultural Reproduction Among the Akan of Ghana.* Leiden: E. J. Brill, 1996.
Obiekwe, Kenneth. "The 2009 Synod of Bishops: Church in Africa in Service to Reconciliation, Justice, and Peace." *African Ecclesial Review* 51, nos. 1–2 (March–June 2009): 105–130.
O'Brien, David. *The Renewal of American Catholicism.* New York: Oxford University Press, 1972.
O'Donnell, Hugh. "The Catholic Association: A Short History." Master's paper, May 1973.
Oduyoye, Mercy Amba, and Musimbi R. A. Kanyoro, eds. *The Will to Arise: Women, Tradition, and the Church in Africa.* Maryknoll, N.Y.: Orbis Books, 1992.
Oger, Louis. "The Pastoral Approach to Spirit Possession: A Zambian Case." *African Ecclesial Review* 38, no. 5 (October 1996): 274–290.
Oliver, Roland, *The Missionary Factor in East Africa.* 2nd ed. London: Longmans, 1965.
Onwubiko, Oliver Alozie. *Theory and Practice of Inculturation: An African Perspective.* Enugu: Diocese of Ahiara, 1992.
Ortner, Sherry B. *High Religion: A Cultural and Political History of Sherpa Buddhism.* Princeton: Princeton University Press, 1989.
———. "Theory in Anthropology Since the Sixties." In *Culture/Power/History: A Reader in Contemporary Social Theory,* edited by Nicholas B. Dirks, Geoff Eley, and Sherry B. Ortner, 372–411. Princeton: Princeton University Press, 1994.
Osei-Bonsu, Joseph. "Biblically/Theologically Based Inculturation." *African Ecclesial Review* 32, no. 6 (December 1990): 346–358.
Owino, James Onyango. "Towards an Analytical African Theology: The Luo Concept of God as a Case in Point." *African Ecclesial Review* 36, no. 4 (June 1994): 171–180.

Owomoyela, Oyekan. "'With Friends Like These': A Critique of Pervasive Anti-Africanisms in Current African Studies Epistemology and Methodology." *African Studies Review* 37, no. 3 (December 1994): 77–101.

Oyewumi, Oyeronke. *The Invention of Women: Making an African Sense of Gender Discourse.* Minneapolis: University of Minnesota Press, 1997.

Pakenham, Thomas. *The Scramble for Africa.* New York: Avon Books, 1992.

Palmer, Robin. *Aspects of Rhodesian Land Policy, 1890–1936.* Salisbury: Central African Historical Association, 1968.

———. *Land and Racial Domination in Rhodesia.* Berkeley: University of California Press, 1977.

———. "War and Land in Rhodesia in the 1890s." In *War and Society in Africa*, edited by Bethwell A. Ogot, 85–107. Portland, Ore.: Frank Cass, 1972.

Parratt, John. *Reinventing Christianity: African Theology Today.* Grand Rapids, Mich.: Eerdmans, 1995.

Peek, Philip M., ed. *African Divination: Ways of Knowing.* Bloomington: Indiana University Press, 1991.

Petersen, Kirsten, ed. *Religion, Development, and African Identity.* Uppsala: Scandinavian Institute of African Studies, 1987.

Pius XI. *Rerum Ecclesiae.* In *The Papal Encyclicals*, edited by Claudia Carlen, volume 3. Raleigh, N.C.: McGrath Publishing, 1981.

Poggi, Gianfranco. *Catholic Action in Italy: The Sociology of a Sponsored Organization.* Stanford: Stanford University Press, 1967.

Pontifical Council for Justice and Peace. "The Church and Racism: Toward a More Fraternal Society." November 3, 1988. http://www.ewtn.com/library/CURIA/pcjpraci.htm.

Portier, William L. "Welcome to the 'Lay Zone.'" Joint Meeting of the American Catholic Historical Association and the Canadian Catholic Historical Association, University of Toronto, April 2001.

Pula, A. L. "Balimo [Ancestor] Veneration and Christianity." *African Ecclesial Review* 32, no. 6 (December 1990): 330–345.

Radoli, Agatha. "Editorial." *African Ecclesial Review* 38, no. 5 (October 1996): 257.

Ranger, Terence. *The African Voice in Southern Rhodesia, 1898–1930.* London: Heinemann Educational, 1970.

———. *Are We Not Also Men? The Samkange Family and African Politics in Zimbabwe, 1920–1964.* Harare: Baobab, 1995.

———. "The Meaning of Mwari." *Rhodesian History* 5 (1974): 5.

———. "Missionaries, Migrants, and the Manyika: The Invention of Ethnicity in Zimbabwe." In *The Creation of Tribalism in Southern Africa*, edited by Leroy Vail, 118–150. London: James Currey, 1988.

———. *Peasant Consciousness and Guerrilla War in Zimbabwe*. Berkeley: University of California Press, 1985.

———. "Religious Movements and Politics in Sub-Saharan Africa." *African Studies Review* 29, no. 2 (June 1986): 1–69.

———. *Revolt in Southern Rhodesia, 1896–97*. Evanston, Ill.: Northwestern University Press, 1967.

Ranger, Terence, and John Weller, eds. *Themes in the Christian History of Central Africa* Berkeley: University of California Press, 1975.

Rasmussen, Ane Marie. *Modern African Spirituality: The Independent Holy Spirit Churches in East Africa, 1902–1976*. London: British Academic Press, 1996.

Ratzinger, Joseph, et al. *The Catechism of the Catholic Church*. Mahwah, N.J.: Paulist Press, 1994.

Ray, Benjamin C. *African Religions: Symbol, Ritual, and Community*. 2nd edition. New York: Prentice Hall, 1999.

Ross, Andrew C. *A Vision Betrayed: The Jesuits in Japan and China, 1542–1742*. Edinburgh: Edinburgh University Press, 1994.

Sanneh, Lamin. *Translating the Message: The Missionary Impact on Culture*. Maryknoll, N.Y.: Orbis, 1989.

———. *West African Christianity: The Religious Impact*, London: C. Hurst, 1983.

Schimlek, Francis. *Against the Stream: Life of Father Bernard Huss, C.M.M., the Social Apostle of the Bantu*. Mariannhill: Mariannhill Mission Press, n.d.

Schmidt, Elizabeth. *Peasants, Traders, and Wives: Shona Women in the History of Zimbabwe, 1870–1939*. Harare: Baobab, 1992.

Scott, James C. *Domination and the Arts of Resistance*. New Haven: Yale University Press, 1991.

Sesana, Renato Kizito. "An African Synod Without Africa?" *African Ecclesial Review* 35, no. 3 (June 1993): 134–143.

Setiloane, Gabriel. *The Image of God Among the Sotho-Tswana*. Rotterdam: A. A. Balkema, 1976.

Shayo, Evarist. "Mission and Inculturation." *African Ecclesial Review* 38, no. 5 (October 1996): 290–297.

Shembe, Londa, trans. *The Scriptures of the amaNazaretha of Ekuphakameni: Selected Writings of the Zulu Prophets Isaiah and Londa Shemba*. Calgary: University of Calgary Press, 1994.

Shorter, Aylward. *African Christian Theology: Adaptation or Incarnation?* London: G. Chapman, 1975.

———. *Christianity and the African Imagination: After the African Synod, Resources for Inculturation*. Nairobi: Pauline Publications Africa, 1996.

———. *The Church in the African City*. London: Chapman, 1991.

———. "Evangelization and Culture."*African Ecclesial Review* 37, no. 2 (April 1995): 93–104.

———. *Toward a Theology of Inculturation*. London: Geoffrey Chapman, 1988.

Simpson, Anthony. *"Half London" in Zambia: Contested Identities in a Catholic Mission School*. Edinburgh: Edinburgh University Press, 2003.

Sindima, Harvey J. *Drums of Redemption: An Introduction to African Christianity*. Westport, Conn.: Greenwood Press, 1994.

Smythe, Kathleen R. *Fipa Families: Reproduction and Catholic Evangelization in Nkansi, Ufipa, 1880–1960*. Portsmouth, N.H.: Heinemann, 2006.

Spear, Thomas. "Towards the History of African Christianity." Conference paper presented at Africans Meeting Missionaries: Rethinking Colonial Encounters, University of Minnesota, May 1997.

Steencamp, Philip. "The Churches." In *Namibia's Liberation Struggle: The Two-Edged Sword*, edited by Colin Leys and John S. Saul, 94–114. Athens: Ohio University Press, 1995.

Taryor, Nya Kwiawon. *Impact of the African Tradition on African Christianity*. Chicago: Strugglers' Community Press, 1984.

Taylor, Thérèse. *Bernadette of Lourdes: Her Life, Death, and Visions*. New York: Burns & Oates, 2003.

Thomas, Linda E. "African Indigenous Churches as a Source of Sociopolitical Transformation in South Africa." *Africa Today* 41, no. 1 (1994): 39–58.

Thomas, Richard W. *Understanding Interracial Unity: A Study of U.S. Race Relations*. Thousand Oaks, Calif.: Sage, 1996.

Thornton, John. *Africa and Africans in the Making of the Atlantic World, 1400–1800*. New York: Cambridge University Press, 1998.

———. *The Kongolese Saint Anthony: Dona Beatriz Kimpa Vita and the Antonian Movement, 1684–1706*. Cambridge: Cambridge University Press, 1998.

Turner, Victor. *The Forest of Symbols: Aspects of Ndembu Ritual*. Ithaca, N.Y.: Cornell University Press, 1967.

Uburhe, J. O. "The African Concept of Sacrifice: A Starting Point for Inculturation." *African Ecclesial Review* 40, no. 4 (August 1998): 203–215.

Udeafor, Ndubisi Innocent. *Inculturation: Path to African Christianity*. Lustenau, Austria: Privately printed, 1994.

Ukpong, Justin S. "Inculturation: A Major Challenge to the Church in Africa." *African Ecclesial Review* 38, no. 5 (October 1996): 258–267.

United States Catholic Conference. "Guidelines Concerning the Academic *Mandatum* in Catholic Universities." NCCB/USCC Web site, www.nccbuscc.org/bishops/guidelines.

Urban-Mead, Wendy. "Dynastic Daughters: Three Royal Kwena Women and E. L. Price of the London Missionary Society, 1853–1881." In *Women in*

African Colonial Histories, edited by Jean Allman et al., 48–70. Bloomington: Indiana University Press, 2002.

Vaillancourt, Jean-Guy. *Papal Power: A Study in Vatican Control Over Catholic Lay Elites*. Berkeley: University of California Press, 1980.

Vambe, Lawrence. *An Ill-Fated People: Zimbabwe Before and After Rhodes*. London: Heinemann, 1972.

Van Ackeren, G. F. "Theology." *New Catholic Encyclopedia*. 2nd ed. Washington, D.C.: Catholic University of America, 2003.

Van Onselen, Charles. *Chibaro: African Mine Labour in Southern Rhodesia, 1900–1933*. London: Pluto Press, 1976.

Vauchez, André. *The Laity in the Middle Ages: Religious Beliefs and Devotional Practices*. Notre Dame, Ind.: University of Notre Dame Press, 1993.

Villa-Vicencio, Charles. *Civil Disobedience and Beyond: Law, Resistance, and Religion in South Africa*. Grand Rapids, Mich.: Eerdmans, 1990.

Wagura, Prisca M. "Karl Rahner's Theology: A Basis for Searching for an African Christianity." *African Ecclesial Review* 40, no. 1 (February 1998): 2–11.

Walls, Andrew F. *The Missionary Movement in Christian History: Studies in the Transmission of Faith*. Maryknoll, N.Y.: Orbis Books, 1996.

Walshe, Peter. *Prophetic Christianity and the Liberation Movement in South Africa*. Pietermaritzburg: Cluster Publications, 1995.

Weber, Max. *The Sociology of Religion*. Translated by Ephraim Fischoff. Boston: Beacon Press, 1968.

Weinzierl, Ferrera. *The Dominicans, 1891–1991: A Story of Vision, Poverty and Courage, Faith and Hope, Service with Love*. Harare: Dominican Sisters, 1991.

Welbourn, F. B. *East African Rebels: A Study of Some Independent Churches*. London: SCM Press, 1961.

Welbourn, F. B., and B. A. Ogot. *A Place to Feel at Home: A Study of Two Independent Churches in Western Kenya*. London: Oxford University Press, 1966.

West, Martin Elgar. *Bishops and Prophets in a Black City: African Independent Churches in Soweto, Johannesburg*. Cape Town: D. Philip, 1975.

Wittgenstein, Ludwig. *Tractatus Logico-Philosophicus*. London: Routledge & Kegan Paul, 1978.

Woywod, Stanislaus. *The New Canon Law: A Commentary and Summary of the New Code of Canon Law*. New York: Joseph F. Wagner, 1929.

Zimbabwe Catholic Bishops' Conference. "Communion between the living and the dead: Christian Response to Spirit Possession." Pastoral Study no. 1. Harare: ZCBC Theological Commission, 1986.

Zvobgo, Chengetai J. M. *A History of Christian Missions in Zimbabwe, 1890–1939*. Gweru: Mambo Press, 1996.

Interviews

Mrs. Monica Basopo, Mbare, Harare, May 24, 2000
Br. Ignatius Bvukumbwe, Silveira House, Chishawasasha, May 22, 2000
Archbishop Patrick Chakaipa, Chancery, Archdiocese of Harare, May 5, 2000
Fr. Ignatius Chidavaenzi, Bible House, Harare, May 18, 2000
Fr. John Dove, S.J., Silveira House, Chishawasasha, May 22, 2000
Sr. Bernadette Garatsa, L.C.B.L., Chichester Residence, Chishawasha, May 16, 2000
Fr. Christopher Gardiner, St. Elizabeth Ann Seton Church, Bark River, Michigan, July 8, 2000
Sr. Hyacinth Gerbecks, O.P., Africa Synod House, Harare, May 15, 2000
Mr. Boniface Mariwa Gumbo, Kutama Mission, July 28, 2000
Mrs. Teresa Joe, Kutama Mission, July 28, 2000
Fr. Nigel Johnson, S.J., Bulawayo, May 11, 2000
Fr. Charles Mafurutu, Chancery, Archdiocese of Bulawayo, May 10, 2000
Br. Laurence Makonora, S.J., Silveira House, Chishawasasha, May 23, 2000
Fr. Constantine Mashonganyika, IMBISA House, Harare, May 17, 2000
Mr. Laurence Masundire, Archdiocesan Chancery, Harare, May 18, 2000
Sr. Catherine Mazarodze, L.C.B.L., Chichester Residence, Chishawasha, May 23, 2000
Fr. Francis McKeown, S.J., Canisius House Jesuit Residence, Harare, May 15, 2000
Fr. Patrick Moloney, S.J., Prestage House Jesuit Community, Harare, May 29, 2000
Mr. C.L. Muringayi, St. Ignatius Mission, Chishawasha, July 31, 2000
Mother Roch Mushonga, L.C.B.L., Makumbi Mission, May 28, 2000
Arcbhishop Pius Ncube, Chancery, Archdiocese of Bulawayo, May 10, 2000
Fr. Bernard Ndlovu, Chancery, Archdiocese of Bulawayo, May 10, 2000
Fr. Walter Nyatsanza, Africa Synod House, Harare May 15 and 18, 2000
Fr. Albert Plangger, S.M.B., Mambo House, Harare, May 16, 2000
Mr. Peter Gatsi Ravaya, Mbare, Harare, May 24, 2000
Br. Herman Toma, S.J., Old St. Peter's Church, Harare, May 13, 2000
Fr. Hebron Wilson, St. Patrick's Church, Bulawayo, May 11, 2000
Fr. Ignatius Zvarevashe, S.J., St. Francis Xavier Church, Braeside, Harare, May 19, 2000

Index

abafundisi, 27
acculturation, 1
African Bishops (2009), Synod of, 252, 253
African Catholic Congress. *See* Catholic Association
African Christian consciousness, 1, 2, 17, 80; and social liberation, 81
African customary law, 9, 10, 170, 172, 179, 201, 203
African customary unions, 170, 171, 174, 182, 186, 187, 201, 202
African independent/initiated Christian churches, 2, 6, 33, 250
African Marriages Act (1951), 174
African Marriages Act (1964), 174–75, 186, 200, 202
African nationalism, 123, 208, 247; and attacks on African Catholics, 132–33, 141–45, 166; at Chishawasha seminary, 80, 81, 103–4, 118; and violence at Chishawasha mission, 143–45
Africanization of the Catholic Church, 8, 244, 246, 251
Ajayi, J. F., 2
All Souls Mission, Mtoko, 128
ancestor spirits (*midzimu*), 9, 16, 222, 223, 225–26, 227, 232, 240, 246; at Chishawasha seminary, 104. See also *kurova guva*
Anglo-Boer War (1899–1902), 33
Angola, ix, xi
Apel, John, 50, 55, 83, 85, 86, 179, 181; and Mwari controversy, 204, 211, 212, 218
Arnoz, Ignatius, 213
Arrupe, Pedro, 17, 35; definition of inculturation, 17
Augustine of Canterbury, 250
Augustine of Hippo, 253

Barr, Francis, 97–98, 127, 140, 141, 151–52, 161
Beach, David, 6
Bede the Venerable, 250
Belgian Congo, 229
Benedict XV, Pope, 79, 82, 113, 118
Benedict XVI, Pope, 253, 307–9
Berhegge, Francis, 25
Berrell, John, 114, 115, 116, 117
Bert, Charles, 35, 177, 178–79
Bethlehem Fathers (Swiss Foreign Mission Society of Bethlehem), 9, 37, 103, 113, 129, 157, 158, 159, 220
Bhebe, Ngwabi, 6, 22, 31

Biehler, Edward, 86, 87, 177, 210, 213
Binns, George, 127
bonga, 49, 67
Booms, Henry, 25
Botswana, 90
Bredekamp, Henry, 2
bricolage, 15
British South African Company (BSAC), 31–32, 33, 172, 201; and first *Chimurenga*, 33; invasion of Mashonaland and Matabeleland, 31–32; policy toward VaShona culture, 172. *See also* African Marriages Act (1964); Native Marriage Ordinance (1901); Native Marriage Ordinance (1917)
Brown, Robert, 37, 44, 84, 89, 183; and Mwari controversy, 212–13; survey in response to *Rerum Ecclesiae*, 84–89, 245, 247–48
Bulawayo, 24, 25, 26, 37, 72, 212; Vicariate Apostolic/Diocese of, 96, 101, 137, 153, 158, 167
Bullock, Charles, 65, 67, 124
Burbridge, Alfred, 57, 181, 183–84

canon law, 10, 170, 175–76, 182, 186, 200
Canon Law, Code of (1917), 51, 176; canon 1098, 176, 178, 181, 196–200
Canon Law, Code of (1983), 176
Cape Colony, 23
Carmelites, Irish, 37, 103, 113, 157
Catholic Action, 120, 125, 130–32, 153, 154, 155, 157, 160–61, 166, 243, 246, 247; constraints on Catholic Association, 132; and education, 218–19; Michael Hannan's view of, 153–56

Catholic African Association. *See* Catholic Association
Catholic African Congress. *See* Catholic Association
Catholic African Union (South Africa), 121, 126, 137
Catholic Ancillary Teachers of Rural Zimbabwe (Catoruzi), ix
Catholic Association, 120–69, 246, 247; and African nationalist movements, 120, 132–33, 141–45; and bishops' inquiry commission, 139, 243–44; and clericalism, 153–61; and *kurova guva*, 164, 222, 230, 233; organization and constitutions, 132–41; and parish councils, 139–41; and racial integration, 136, 138–39; and "Reports from Mission Stations [on] Implementing [1946 Congress] Resolutions," 127–30; and social liberation of church, 120; and women, 149–53
Catholic Relief Services, ix
Catholic University of America, ix
Chakaipa, Patrick, 115, 141, 161, 232
Chichester, Aston, 37, 41, 45, 46, 47–48, 49, 50, 51, 52, 53, 55, 56, 58, 61, 62, 63, 64, 67, 68, 69, 70, 74, 75, 77, 119, 124, 126, 127, 133, 153, 245, 248; and ambivalence toward Catholic Association, 159–60, 163; and Charles Mzingeli, 184; and corporal punishment at seminary, 94; and founding of Catholic Association, 122; and founding of Chishawasha seminary, 89–91; and the LCBL Sisters, 47–53; *lobola* policy, 41, 54–55,

58, 74; and VaShona culture, 47–48
Chidavenzi, Ignatius, objections to *kuchenura munhu*, 234–37, 241; and Mwari, 204–5
Chiginya, Tobias, 117
Chikore, Isidore, 98
Chikwingwizha Minor Seminary, 103
child pledging, 172, 174
Children of the Most Holy Trinity (Trinity Sisters), 43, 44, 48, 77
Chimurenga (1896–97), 33, 171, 172; second (1965–79), xi, 8, 33, 167, 246
Chinese Rites controversy, 228–29, 234
Chishawasha Mission, x, 35, 36, 44, 45, 49, 55–58, 83, 85, 91, 122, 125, 133, 142, 152, 177, 178, 179, 230, 245; and African nationalist violence, 143–45; and Mwari controversy, 208, 209, 210, 212, 214, 215, 218, 220, 221
Chishawasha Seminary (Seminary of Sts. John Fisher and Thomas More), 79–119, 245, 247, 248; and African nationalism, 80, 81, 103–4; attrition rate, 96–98; major seminary, 93; 1967 closure, 111–14; and 1974 Seminary Commission (external inquiry), 116–17; 1974 Strike, 80, 114–17; and preparatory seminary, 90; and racial integration (1965), 80, 105–11; regional major seminary, 79, 101–10; theologate, 93
Chiwanza, Stephen, 99
Christian villages, 87

Claver, Brothers of Saint Peter, 91, 99–101; and Chichester's motives for founding, 99–100
Claver, (Saint) Peter, 45
Clement XIV, Pope, 228
Cogger, James, 128
Coghlan, Charles, 42; on female autonomy in Southern Rhodesia, 42–43, 46, 48, 55, 69
Collings, Bevis, 60, 61
Comaroff, Jean and John, xi, 2, 17, 18, 20; critique by Paul Landau, 7
Compulsory Native Labor Act (1942), 32
concubinage, 173–74
Congregation for the Evangelization of Peoples, 35, 202. *See also* Propaganda Fide
convalidation, 179–80, 185, 200
Corrigan, T. E., 105, 118
Cuthbertson, Greg, 2
Cyprian of Carthage, 253

Dachs, A. J. and W. F. Rea, 25, 30–31; 34, 36, 42–43, 44, 45, 76, 167, 222–23; and the Catholic Association, 165–66; and the dual mission to blacks and whites in colonial Zimbabwe, 34; and the failure of the Jesuit mission (1879–89), 25, 30–31; and Kutama as source of priestly vocations, 98; and the 1974 seminary strike, 81; and Robert Brown's *Rerum Ecclesiae* survey, 88–89; and the Trinity Sisters, 43–44
Daignault, Charles, 124, 219
Dambaza, Joseph, 121–22, 124, 125, 142, 150, 162, 227

Daughters of Charity of St. Vincent de Paul, 44
Daughters of St. Francis of Assisi, 41–42, 44, 45, 46, 48, 49, 77
Davidson, Basil, xi, 247
Depelchin, Henri, 24–28, 30–31, 38–40
Derrida, Jacques, 15
Diamond, John, 105, 107, 108, 110, 111, 112, 113, 118, 187
dispensation, 176, 184; from diriment impediment, 176, 200; from impedient impediment, 176, 200
Dominican Sisters, 39–40, 45, 49, 50, 52, 53, 57–58, 60, 77
Donovan, Vincent, 18–19; approach to inculturation, 18–19, 250
Dove, John, 142–43, 161, 168
Driefontein Mission, 124, 125, 133
dual mission (to blacks and whites in colonial Zimbabwe), 34
Dunbrody Estate, 29, 30

Embakwe Mission, 37
Empandeni Mission, 25, 26, 31, 37, 70, 71, 85, 219
enculturation, 1
Ennis, Edward, 110, 112, 113
Evans-Pritchard, E. E., 11–13, 16
Ex Corde Ecclesiae, 15

Federation of Rhodesia and Nyasaland, 33
Ferguson, Charles, 56–58
Fisher, Humphrey, 5–6, 15, 250
Fleischer, Adalbero, 36, 37, 43, 48–49, 77, 213

Fort Victoria (Masvingo), Prefecture Apostolic. *See* Gwelo (Gweru): Prefecture Apostolic/Diocese of
Fortune, George, 206–8, 210, 213, 220–21
Fuchs, Charles, 24

Garatsa, Sister Bernadette, 49, 50, 62, 76, 227
Gardiner, Christopher, 92, 106–7, 108, 109, 111, 248
Gardiner, Thomas, 85, 87, 89
Gartlan, Ignatius, 216
Gelfand, Michael, 25–26, 223–24; at Chishawasha seminary, 104
Georgetown University, ix
Gleason, Philip, 13
Gokomere Mission and School, 75, 125, 209
Gondo, Boniface, 99
Goodwin, Geoffrey, 105, 107
Goromonzi (district), 63; NC, 70, 71, 145, 177, 178
Grahamstown, 23
Gray, Richard, 7–8
Great Zimbabwe, 22, 206
Gregory I (the Great), Pope, 250
Gumbo, Boniface, 227, 228
Gundani, Paul, 222, 224, 230, 231, 232, 233
Gwelo (Gweru), 85, 127; Prefecture Apostolic/Diocese of, 37, 101, 103, 157, 158, 159, 167, 220, 230, 247

Haene, Aloysius, 37, 103, 113, 137, 139, 157, 220
Hannan, Michael, 125, 130, 132, 137, 162, 166, 220; and the Catholic Association constitution, 137–38;

and clericalism, 153–58, 160, 161, 163
Harare (Mbare): *see* Salisbury
Hartmann, Andrew, 25, 85, 86, 89, 204, 210, 213
Hedley, Br. Joseph, 24
Hillman, Eugene, 19–20, 247, 249
Hodson, L. M. N.; and Coghlan's opinion, 65–67, 69
Holy Ghost Fathers (Spiritans), 90
Horton, Robin, 4–5, 250
Hughes, Lachlan, 187, 201; critique of 1967 Marriage Commission, 187–91; response to Joseph Suter, 196–200
Huss, Bernard, 121

incarnation, theology of, 18, 19
inculturation, ix, xi, 1, 4, 9, 10, 18, 20, 21; in African context, x, 18; definitions, ix–x, 17–18 (Pedro Arrupe, Joseph Masson, Aylward Shorter); discourse of, 8, 244–45, 246, 248; and Ignatian Spirituality, x; and *kurova guva*, 233; and language, 281–83; and marriage, 12, 232–35; as social liberation, ix–x, xi, 17, 20; theory/theology of, 16–20; and white Rhodesian culture, 80, 118; and women in the Church, 66; and VaShona culture, 337–49
Industrial and Commercial Workers' Union (ICU), 103, 121, 123, 183
interpellation, 184–85
Islam, 4, 5, 22

Jeater, Diana, 40, 76, 173, 174, 176
Jesuits (Society of Jesus) ix, x, 8, 9, 23, 24, 25, 26, 27, 31, 32, 34, 35, 36, 37, 42, 44, 46, 50, 59, 75, 79, 83, 85, 89, 100, 101, 103, 104, 106, 108, 109, 110, 111, 113, 116, 118, 176, 179, 182; administrative structure, 28–29; and African nationalism, 141–45; British, 34, 35, 89; conflict with Mariannhill, 36–37; German, 34, 35, 89, 99, 205; and inculturation, 9–10, 20; and *Rerum Ecclesiae*, 85–89
Joe, Teresa, 227
Johanny, Francis, 42, 45, 183, 211, 212, 217, 228–29, 234
John XXIII, Pope, 139, 161, 176
John Paul II, Pope, 15, 17, 176, 253
Johnson, David, 32
Johnson, Donald, 101

Kapito, Raymond, 100
Karanga (Chi-) dialect, 206, 207, 209, 218, 220
Ketterer, Francis, 91, 122, 125
Kinnane, Kevin, 79, 115–16
Kotski, Ernest, 125, 129, 150, 162
kuchenura munhu, 222, 233, 234–39, 241–42, 246, 247, 251
Kumbirai, Joseph, 230
Kupara, Katarina, 181
kuperekedzwa, 171, 187, 200
kurova guva, 9, 222–42, 245, 246, 247, 248, 250; definition, 10; 306–13, 321–332; prayers during, 226–28
Kutama Mission, 45, 55, 67, 87, 89, 90, 121, 125, 129, 133, 142, 150, 153, 163, 227
Kutama Teacher Training School, 89, 90, 95, 102, 123; agreement between Chichester and Marist

334 | INDEX

Brothers, 100; and seminary attrition rate, 97–98
kutiza, 171, 174, 176–77, 200

Lamont, Donal, 37, 163
Lan, David, 208
Land Apportionment Act (1931), 32, 123
Land Tenure Act (1968), 32, 164
Landau, Paul, 2, 6–7, 17, 18; and African religion, 18; critique of Comaroffs and Lamin Sanneh, 7
Law, Augustus, 24, 34–35
League of Nations, 52
Ledochowski, Wlodimir, 212, 217
Lewanika, 24, 25, 30
Linden, Ian, 8
Little Children of Our Blessed Lady (LCBL Sisters), 39, 45, 46–54, 72, 75, 95, 99–100, 245; autonomy, 102; and Chichester's *lobola* policy, 54–55, 58; Coloured Sisters, 53–54; constitution, 51, 77; governance, 50–51; indigenization of leadership, 39–40, 51, 74; vows 50, 53
Livingstone, David, 23
Lobengula, 23, 24, 26–28; and Jesuit mission, 1879–89, 26–28
lobola, 41, 42, 46, 54–55, 56, 67, 76, 162, 171, 172, 173, 174, 178, 179, 181, 186, 187, 200, 201, 246
Loreto Mission, Que Que (Kwekwe), 127
Loubière, Jean-Baptiste, 85, 86, 87, 89, 227

Mabvuku, 140–41
Magwaza, Peter, 151, 152
Majongwe, Ambrose, 120–21, 125, 133, 134, 149, 152; and founding of Catholic Association, 121; vision for Catholic Association, 122–23
Makaka, Patrick, 101
Makumbi Mission, 49, 50, 55, 60, 62, 67, 68, 75, 127, 141, 152, 161, 245
Makumbi Tax, 52
Malabar Rites controversy, 228, 229
Malawi. *See* Nyasaland
Manyika, 35, 49, 89; ChiManyika dialect, 126, 127, 210, 218, 221; ChiManyika-speakers, 35
Marandellas (Marondera), 152, 165
Marege, Goto, 226, 245
Margwisa, Clara, 63–74, 77, 78
Mariannhill (Congregation of Mariannhill Missions), 29, 35, 36–37, 40, 41–42, 43, 44, 45, 48, 83, 85, 89, 158, 207; conflict with Jesuits, 36–37; and Mwari controversy, 210, 211, 213, 215, 218, 221; responses to Robert Brown's *Rerum Ecclesiae* survey, 85–89
de Marillac, (Saint) Louise, 44
Marist Brothers (Little Brothers of Mary), 98; agreement with Chichester to administer Kutama Teacher Training School, 100
Markall, Francis, 35, 39, 64, 65, 70, 73–74, 101, 110, 115, 116, 157, 175, 182, 186; and the Catholic Association, 140–41; and clericalism, 153, 158–60
marriage, 9, 10, 16, 162, 170–203, 244, 246; African 170, 172, 177, 179–80; banns, 175, 179; and

Chichester's *lobola* policy, 54–55, 72; consent, 172, 174, 175, 187–200, 246; elopement, see *kutiza*; forced, 172, 174; polygamous, 173, 179–80; service, 171; Western Christian, 170, 173, 177, 179–80, 184

Marriage Commission (1967), 186–87, 202; critique by Lachlan Hughes, 187–91; final report (1970), 200–2. *See also* Hughes, Lachlan; Suter, Joseph

Marriage Commission (1972), 202

Marumbeni, Theresa, 55, 58

Mashonganyika, Constantine, 97, 107, 111, 112, 113

Masson, Joseph, definition of inculturation, 17

Mavudzi, Emmanuel, 141, 161; and *kurova guva*, 231, 234

Maximum Illud, 79, 82, 83, 89, 93, 248; and Brothers of Saint Peter Claver, 100

Maxwell, David, 8, 10

Mazorodze, Sister Catherine, 53, 58–63, 75, 78

Mbembe, Achille, 240

Mbiti, John, 240

McKeown, Francis, 101, 104, 105, 106, 109, 118

McLaughlin, Janice, 8

McNamara, Patrick, 115

Melsetter (Chimanimani) Minor Seminary, 103

Membere, Britto, 122, 124, 125

Mhonda, Ignatius, 116

Mhondoro cult, 206, 208

midzimu. *See* ancestor spirits

mission farms: and ancestor ceremonies, 306–16; drinking, 308–12

Modikayi, Gilbert, 100

Moloney, Patrick, 93, 105, 108

Monte Cassino Constitution (1948), 134–37, 157; and Ambrose Majongwe, 136; and Michael Hannan, 137–38

Monte Cassino Mission, 36, 42, 45, 63, 64, 70, 73–74, 75, 127, 134, 135, 152, 156, 213

Morosi, Francis, 63–74, 78

Morris, S. E., 61, 62

Mosi wa Tunya (Victoria Falls), 24, 26

Moss, Barbara, 8

Moto magazine, 162

Mount St. Mary's Mission, Hwedza, 39, 75

Mozambique, x, xi

Muchenje, Edward, 140–41, 167

Mudenge, S. I. G., 206, 208

Mugabe, Robert, ix

Mugadzi, Francis, 117

Mukoma, Maria, 55–58, 78

Mukuwapasi, Ernest, 79, 114, 115, 117

mukuwasha, 171, 187, 200

munyai, 171

Munyongani, Joseph, 230, 234

Muringayi, C. L., 226

Mushonga, Mother Rocha, 39, 55, 74–76, 77

Muvirimi, Joseph, 181

Muzira, Emilio, 125

Mwari, 9, 16, 204–21, 244, 245, 246, 247

Mwari controversy, 89, 206, 207, 208–21, 229, 230

Mwari cult, 23, 203–6, 208
Mwemba, 24, 25, 27–28
Myerscough, Cedric, 143
Mzilikazi, 22–23
Mzingeli, Charles, 183–85

National Democratic Party, 103
Native Marriage Ordinance (1901), 172–73, 174
Native Marriage Ordinance (1905), 173
Native Marriage Ordinance (1912), 173, 179–80
Native Marriage Ordinance (1917), 173–74
Native Marriage Ordinance (1929), 65, 174
Ndlovu, Bernard, 91–92, 231–32, 234
"Ne Temere," 176
Newbury, David, 8, 247
n'ganga, 223, 226, 232, 235, 243, 244
Nigg, Brother, 24, 25
Northern Rhodesia, 33, 34, 96, 159
Nyanhete, Alois, 161, 162
Nyasaland, 33, 85, 217
Nyatsanza, Walter, 114, 117

O'Donnell, Hugh, 121, 165, 167
O'Hea, Jerome, 54–55, 89, 121–22, 227
Oliver, Roland, 2, 3
O'Neill, James, 83
Order in Council (1898), 172, 179

Pacelli, Eugenio, 51. *See also* Pius XII, Pope
Palmer, Robin, 32
Pandamatenga, 24, 25, 26, 28
Parkhurst, D. C. H., 55–58, 78
Parry, Edward, 212, 228, 234

Pashane, Andrew, 99
de Paul, (Saint) Vincent, 44
Paul of Tarsus (Saint), 19
Pauline Privilege, 184–85
Pearce Commission, 164
Pfanner, Franz, 35, 36
Pius IX, Pope, 237
Pius X, Pope, 131, 176
Pius XI, Pope, 51, 53, 83, 100, 118–19, 131, 132
Pius XII, Pope, 51. *See also* Pacelli, Eugenio
Portier, William, 131–32
Precious Blood Sisters, 36, 41–42, 44, 45, 53, 58–62, 75, 77
Prestage, Peter, 24, 25, 26, 31
Propaganda Fide, 35, 37, 48–49, 51, 101, 110, 212, 229, 248. *See also* Congregation for the Evangelization of Peoples

Quin, Henry, 85, 87

racial integration: and Catholic Association, 136, 138–39, 164; at Chishawasha seminary, 105–11
Ranger, Terence, 8, 40, 42, 76, 88, 173, 206, 208, 210, 218, 220
Raposo, Dominico, 85
Rea, Maurice, 68
Rea, W. F., 44, 96; and 1974 seminary strike, 117–18. *See also* Dachs, A. J.
Reckter, Helmut, 35
reducciones (Paraguayan), 30
Rerum Ecclesiae, 53, 83–84, 88, 93, 248; and Brothers of Saint Peter Claver, 100; Zambezi Mission survey in response to, 84–89

revelation and religious knowledge, 16, 20–21, 251
Rhodes, Cecil, 25, 31–32
Rhodesian Catholic Bishops Conference, 79
Rhodesian Front, 33
Rhodesian Native Labour Supply Commission, 32
Rhodesian Unilateral Declaration of Independence (UDI), 32, 164
Ricards, Bishop James, 23, 35
Ricci, Matteo, 31, 228, 250
Richartz, Francis, 35, 36, 85, 86, 89; and Mwari controversy, 204, 208–10, 211–12, 213–15, 217, 218, 219, 221, 225
Roma (St. Augustine's Seminary, Lesotho), 90
Ross, Robert, 2
Rozvi state, 22, 23
Rudd Concession, 25
rutsambo, 172
Ruzive, Raphael, 150, 151

Sacred Heart, Cathedral of (Salisbury), 49
Sacred Heart, Confraternity of the, 90–91
de Sadeleer, Brother, 24
sadza and *usavi*, 92, 106
St. Barbara's Mission, 36, 49, 128–29
St. Benedict's Mission, 36, 46, 57
St. George's College, 107
St. John Vianney Seminary (Pretoria), 105, 107, 111, 248
St. Joseph's Mission, Gwelo (Gweru), 129
St. Michael's Mission, Mhondoro, 59–60, 128, 153

St. Paul's Mission, Musami, 59, 63, 102, 128
St. Peter's Parish, Harare (Mbare), x, 83, 99, 134, 150, 156, 161, 162, 181, 182–85
St. Theresa, Sisters of (Hermanas Teresianas), ix
Salisbury (Harare), 34, 37, 45, 49, 57, 60, 61, 63, 100; Vicariate Apostolic/Archdiocese of, 37, 48–49, 52, 77, 100–1, 134, 137, 142, 153, 157, 163, 165, 167, 202, 222
Samakande, Kilian, 89, 126, 245
sanatio in radice, 185
Sanneh, Lamin, 3–4, 250; critique by Paul Landau, 7; critique by Thomas Spear, 16
Saunders, Peter, 105, 107
Sawada, Lorenzo, 219
Schmidt, Elizabeth, 40, 76, 174, 176, 177
Schmitt, Adolph, 106
Schmitz, Emil, 45, 85, 86, 88, 89, 91, 177, 226
Schomberg Kerr, Henry, 35
Scott, James C., 2, 249
Second Vatican Council, 17, 20, 21, 23, 25, 161, 165, 176, 220, 233
Seed, Henry, 87–88, 226
Selous, Frederick Courtney, 24
Seminary Board of Bishops; request for external investigation of seminary (1965), 110
Seminary Group, letter to Southern Rhodesian Bishops, 106, 107–8, 110
Senegal, 90
Setiloane, Gabriel, 6

Shorter, Aylward, definition of inculturation, 18
Silveira, Gonçalo da, 22, 23
Sinoia (Chinoyi), 34, 46, 129; Prefecture Apostolic of, 35
Smith, Ian, 33
South Africa, 33, 34, 36, 41, 42, 43, 48, 49, 81, 83, 89, 90, 213
Spanish Missionary Institute, 9
Spear, Thomas, 13–15
Suter, Joseph, 187, 201; response to Lachlan Hughes, 191–96
Sykes, Richard, 82, 89, 179–80, 211, 212, 216, 225

Taberer, W. S., 178, 179
"Tametsi," 176
Tanganyika, 90
Taoneyi, Simon, 122, 124, 125, 226
Tarasinja, Geronimo, 125
Tati, 24, 26
Teroerde, Anthony, 24
tete, 171
tezvara, 171, 173, 187, 200, 246
theological analysis, 15
Thornton, John, 16, 20–21, 251
translatability of Christianity (Sanneh), 3–4
Trappists. *See* Mariannhill
Triashill Mission, 35, 36, 40, 43, 75, 83, 122, 125, 127, 151, 213, 215, 218
Tsuro, Simon, 98
Turner, Anthony, 106, 107; letter to Francis Markall, 106, 108, 110

Uganda, 90
Umtali (Mutare), 35; Prefecture Apostolic/Diocese of, 37, 101, 103, 137, 157, 163, 167

van Onselen, Charles, 32
van Rossum, Willem, 49
VaShona culture, 223; ChiShona language, 158, 204–6, 207, 208, 220–21; and marriage, 12, 162, 177, 178, 181, 202; origins in Zimbabwe, 32–33; and women 40, 42, 58, 73, 76, 162; women in the church, 56–57, 72
vernacular African religion, 1, 4, 5, 6, 8, 16
vhuramuromo, 171

Wankie (Hwange), Vicariate Apostolic/Diocese of, 101, 157, 167
Wehl, Charles, 23
Weld, Alfred, 23, 25, 27–30, 34
Wermter, Oscar, 220
White Fathers (Missionaries of Africa), 85, 217
women: and the Catholic Association, 149–53; marriage, 149–51; parental consent for becoming nuns, 58, 68–73; social mobility and the church, 40–41, 76, 245; widows, 178–79

Xavier (Saint) Francis, 31, 45, 216–17, 218

Yardley, A. G., 64

Zambezi Mission, 9, 26, 28–30, 34, 35, 36, 37, 43, 44, 87, 89, 90, 103, 179–80, 183, 206, 210–11, 213, 228, 234, 240, 244, 245
Zambia. *See* Northern Rhodesia
Zawaira, Tom, 159, 164

Zezuru (Chi-) dialect, 207, 208, 210, 221
Zimbabwe African National Union (ZANU), 34, 117; guerrillas/freedom fighters, 75, 76, 117
Zimbabwe African Peoples Union (ZAPU), 117
Zulu state, 22–23
Zvarevashe, Ignatius, 101